JOHN DEE'S NATURAL PHILOSOPHY

John Dee has fascinated successive generations. Mathematician, scientist, astrologer and magus at the court of Elizabeth I, he still provokes controversy today. To some he is the genius whose contributions to navigation made possible the feats of Elizabethan explorers and colonists, to others an alchemist and charlatan.

This is the definitive study of John Dee, the fruit of Nicholas Clulee's twenty-year quest to arrive at a satisfactory understanding of Dee's intellectual career. Clulee's interpretation of John Dee is far more detailed than any that have gone before and will establish this book as the standard authority for many years to come.

Clulee's book is the result of intensive study of Dee's writings, the available biographical material, and careful consideration of his sources as reflected in his extensive library and, more importantly, numerous surviving annotated volumes from it. Nicholas Clulee is the first writer thoroughly to examine Dee's natural philosophy, and in so doing provides a new and balanced evaluation of his place, and the role of the occult, in sixteenth-century intellectual history.

John Dee's Natural Philosophy will appeal to anyone interested in the history, literature and scientific developments of the Renaissance, and to students of the occult.

Frontispiece Portrait of John Dee (Courtesy of the Ashmolean Museum
Oxford)

JOHN DEE'S NATURAL PHILOSOPHY

Between Science and Religion

NICHOLAS H. CLULEE

ROUTLEDGE
London and New York

To my parents
and
Carol, Crystal, and Nicole

First published in 1988 by
Routledge
11 New Fetter Lane, London EC4P 4EE
29 West 35th Street, New York NY 10001

Phototypeset by Input Typesetting Ltd, London

Printed in Great Britain by T. J. Press (Padstow) Ltd,
Padstow, Cornwall

British Library Cataloguing in Publication Data
Clulee, Nicholas H.
John Dee's natural philosophy: between
science and religion.
1. Science. Dee, John, 1527–1608 –
Biographies
I. Title II. Series
509′.2′4

Library of Congress Cataloguing in Publication Data
Clulee, Nicholas H.
John Dee's natural philosophy: between science and religion/
Nicholas H. Clulee.
p. cm.
Bibliography: p.
Includes index.
1. Dee, John, 1527–1608. 2. Hermetism – England – History – 16th
century. 3. Occultism – England – History – 16th century. I. Title.
BF1598.D5C58 1988
133′.092′4—dc19

ISBN 0 415 00625 2 (hb)
0 415 03122 2 (pb)

Well, well, It is time for some to lay hold on wisdome, and to Iudge truly of thinges: and not so to expound the Holy word, all by Allegories: as to Neglect the wisdome, power and Goodness of God, in, and by his Creatures, and Creation to be seen and learned. . . . The whole Frame of Gods Creatures, (which is the whole world,) is to vs, a bright glasse: from which, by reflexion, reboundeth to our knowledge and perceiuerance, Beames, and Radiations: representing the Image of his Infinite goodness, Omnipotency, and wisdome.

John Dee, *Mathematicall Praeface*

Until then I had thought each book spoke of the things, human or divine, that lie outside books. Now I realized that not infrequently books speak of books: it is as if they spoke among themselves. In the light of this reflection, the library seemed all the more disturbing to me. It was then the place of a long, centuries-old murmuring, an imperceptible dialogue between one parchment and another, a living thing, a receptacle of powers not to be ruled by a human mind, a treasure of secrets emanated by many minds, surviving the death of those who had produced them or had been their conveyors.

Umberto Eco, *The Name of the Rose*

CONTENTS

List of Illustrations   ix

Preface   xi

Abbreviations   xiv

I JOHN DEE AND RENAISSANCE
  INTELLECTUAL HISTORY   1

  PART ONE: THE *PROPAEDEUMATA
                 APHORISTICA*, 1558   19

II 'OUTLANDISH AND HOMISH STUDIES AND
   EXERCISES PHILOSOPHICALL'   21
   Cambridge and Louvain   22
   Patronage and Private Study   29

III THE OUTSTANDING VIRTUES OF NATURE   39
    Astrology   39
    Astrological Physics and Optics   42
    Optics, Mathematics, and Nature   52
    Optics, Magic, and Empirical Research   64
    Conclusion   70

  PART TWO: THE *MONAS HIEROGLYPHICA*, 1564   75

IV THE HIEROGLYPHICS OF NATURE   77
   The *Arbor Raritatis* and Hieroglyphical Writing   81
   The Alphabet of Nature   86
   The Discourse of Alchemy   96
   The Writing of Things   105

CONTENTS

V THE GREAT METAPHYSICAL REVOLUTION 116
Aphorisms and Theorems 116
The Office of the Adept 121
The Unity of Knowledge and the Ancient Theology 125
Magia 135

PART THREE: THE *MATHEMATICALL PRAEFACE*, 1570 143

VI *VIA MATHEMATICA* 145
'*Thynges Mathematicall*' 149
Philosophy, Mathematics, and Technology 154
Philosophy, Mathematics, and Science 162
Philosophy, Mathematics, and Magic 166
Archemastrie 170

VII THE VAGARIES OF PATRONAGE, 1565–1583 177
Exploration and Imperial Ideology 180
Aristotle in Search of Alexander 189

PART FOUR: THE *LIBRI MYSTERIORUM*, 1583–1589 201

VIII THE MYSTICAL AND SUPERMETAPHYSICAL PHILOSOPHY 203
Dee, Kelley, and the Spirits 204
The Books of Enoch 208
The Prophets of Prague 220

IX CONCLUSION 231
John Dee 231
Magic and the Occult in the Renaissance 239

Notes 242

Bibliography 302

Index 337

ILLUSTRATIONS

Frontispiece: Portrait of John Dee

between pages 178 and 179

2.1 Title page, *Propaedeumata aphoristica*, 1558
4.1 Monas hieroglyphica, Dee, *Monas hieroglyphica*
4.2 Title page, *Monas hieroglyphica*, 1564
4.3 'Arbor raritatis', Dee, *Monas hieroglyphica*
4.4 'Y' moralised, Tory, *Champ fleury*
4.5 Point, line, circle, Dee, *Monas hieroglyphica*
4.6 Monas and cosmos, Dee, *Monas hieroglyphica*
4.7 Construction of 'I', Tory, *Champ fleury*
4.8 'I' and the Golden Chain, Tory, *Champ fleury*
4.9 'I' and the Muses, Tory, *Champ fleury*
4.10 'O' and the Liberal Arts, Tory, *Champ fleury*
4.11 Signs of the planets generated from Monas, Dee, *Monas hieroglyphica*
4.12 Alchemical vessels generated from Monas, Dee, *Monas hieroglyphica*
4.13 The 'exaltation of the moon and the sun by the science of the elements', Dee, *Monas hieroglyphica*
4.14 Numbers, weights, measures, Dee, *Monas hieroglyphica*
4.15 Title page, Joannes Pantheus, *Voarchadumia*, 1559
4.16 Dee's notes, Pantheus, *Voarchadumia*
4.17 The genesis of lunar mercury, Dee, *Monas hieroglyphica*
4.18 The seven stages, Dee, *Monas hieroglyphica*
4.19 The celestial egg, Dee, *Monas hieroglyphica*
4.20 The seven celestial revolutions, Dee, *Monas hieroglyphica*

4.21 Geometrical construction of the Monas, Dee, *Monas hieroglyphica*
4.22 Finished Monas, Dee, *Monas hieroglyphica*
4.23 Cosmic correspondences, Dee, *Monas hieroglyphica*
5.1 Colophon, Dee, *Monas hieroglyphica*
5.2 Title page, Dee, *Propaedeumata aphoristica*, 1568
6.1 The 'crosse of graduation', Dee, *Mathematicall Praeface*
6.2 'Ars sintrillia', *Artetii ac Mininii apologia in artem magicam*
7.1 Title page, Dee, *General and Rare Memorials*
7.2 Title page, Dee, *A Letter . . . Apologeticall*, 1599
7.3 Title page, Dee, *Parallaticae commentationis praxeosque*, 1573
8.1 Dee's obsidian speculum
8.2 Dee's 'crystal ball'
8.3 Table from the 'Book of Enoch', Dee, *True and Faithful Relation*
8.4 Table of spirits, Dee, *Liber Scientiae, Auxilij,* & *Victoriae Terrestris*
8.5 King Naspol, Dee, *De heptarchia mystica*
8.6 The Holy Table or Table of Practice, Dee, *True and Faithful Relation*
8.7 Dee's Wax Disk
8.8 Twenty four seniors, Dee, *De heptarchia mystica*

PREFACE

In 1968, as part of a seminar on Renaissance natural philosophy, Allen G. Debus sent me to read John Dee's *Monas hieroglyphica*. Without knowing it at the time I was hooked, and with some hiatus I have ever since been trying to arrive at a satisfactory understanding of the intellectual career of John Dee (1527–1608), Elizabethan mathematician, scientist, and magician. This study is also an inquiry into the character of natural philosophy and the occult sciences in the intellectual history of the Renaissance. To state this second subject may seem obvious. Any study in intellectual biography of necessity requires attention to the 'context' in which the subject was situated. In the case of Dee, however, there is no readily accessible context to which his intellectual activities may be related. To be more exact, in the course of taking a fresh look at Dee's intellectual career I have found it necessary to examine anew the interpretation of Renaissance occultism that has usually been taken as the context in which to situate Dee's activities. For quite some time now, scholars have been discovering and exploring the myriad ways astrology, magic, kabbalah, alchemy, and other 'occult' arts, sciences, and philosophies manifested themselves in the culture of Renaissance and early modern Europe. In a number of books, beginning in 1964 with *Giordano Bruno and the Hermetic Tradition*, Frances A. Yates attempted to draw these discoveries together into a synthetic interpretation of Renaissance occultism. It has been against the background of this interpretation that she and others have attempted to interpret John Dee.

The results of this approach to Dee are no longer satisfactory for two reasons. First, continuing scholarship, while building upon and extending Yates's work, has increasingly dissolved her synthetic interpretation of Renaissance occultism and raised new issues. Second, careful examination of Dee's intellectual career has revealed facets that ill fit with this interpretation. The justification for yet another book on Dee is that this study presents a consideration of Dee considerably more detailed and nuanced than any currently available. I have also attempted to relate Dee's intellectual work to its social context in Dee's efforts to define and secure for himself what he considered a satisfactory status and role. From this has emerged a more satisfactory understanding of Dee which also has a good deal to say about Renaissance intellectual history. Dee was in many ways a unique individual, who was not only in touch with many of the well-known strands of Renaissance thought but who also drew on intellectual traditions and texts whose importance in the sixteenth century have been little recognized. Dee therefore allows us to see features of Renaissance thought that would otherwise be difficult to discern.

In the course of my inquiries I have accumulated considerable debts to individuals and institutions whose encouragement, assistance, and aid have in ways both tangible and intangible contributed to my ability to complete this study. While not adequate to the debt, I offer the following acknowledgments as an expression of my deep gratitude, and I am chagrined that I have completed my work too late for my expressions to reach all who deserve them.

Although at times I take issue with the work of Frances A. Yates, my study of Dee is ultimately an outgrowth of my encounter with her presentations of the occult philosophies of the Renaissance. It was her book on Giordano Bruno which opened for me an entirely new dimension of Renaissance intellectual culture, and a long, pleasant, and rewarding conversation with her in the early stages of my work was both encouraging and helpful. Allen G. Debus and Hanna H. Grey guided my studies in Renaissance thought and natural philosophy at the University of Chicago. In all of my studies I have continually had occasion to appreciate the superb education offered at Hobart College and my enduring intellectual debt to Francis J. M. O'Laughlin, Nancy Struever, and Katherine Cook. For many years I have enjoyed the support and encouragement of Robert S. Westman, Charles B. Schmitt, David C. Lindberg, and Bert Hansen, who have shared their knowledge and have raised questions and issues which shaped in crucial ways the directions of my research. Julian Roberts and Andrew Watson have generously shared with me information about books and manuscripts in Dee's library. Specific indications in the notes will testify how indispensable this information has been. Owen Hannaway and Mordechai Feingold as well as Robert Westman and David Lindberg have read all or substantial parts of this manuscript and contributed numerous refinements. For what faults remain, I bear sole responsibility.

A significant portion of the research for this study was carried out in the summer of 1982 with the support of a grant from the Johnson Fund of the American Philosophical Society and a Summer Stipend from the National Endowment for the Humanities. A College Teachers Fellowship, also from the National Endowment for the Humanities, provided me with a leave from my academic duties for 1984–5 during which I was able to complete the manuscript. Without the aid of this modern form of patronage, this project might never have been completed. I have also enjoyed hospitality and assistance from the staffs of the Bodleian Library, the British Library, the Royal College of Physicians, the Warburg Institute, the Wellcome Institute for the History of Medicine, and the Library of Congress. The reference staff of Frostburg State University Library have been of help on numerous occasions, and Patricia Ward, Interlibrary Loan Librarian, has done wonders obtaining some rather odd materials. I have particularly warm regards for the Folger Shakespeare Library, its staff, and community of scholars which made my stay in 1984–5 as pleasant as it was productive.

Less direct but no less important has been the support of my family; for them the warmth and depth of my gratitude and affection defy words. To my mother and father, who nourished me in the development of my vocation, and to my wife and daughters, who have had to share my attentions with John Dee, I dedicate this book.

ABBREVIATIONS

CR   *The Compendious Rehearsall of John Dee . . . anno 1592; Autobiographical Tracts* edition.

LA   *A Letter Containing a most briefe Discourse Apologeticall; Autobiographical Tracts* edition.

MH   *Monas hieroglyphica*; Josten edition. Citations are either to paired page numbers of text and facing translation, or to Roman numerals of indicate individual 'Theorems'.

MP   *Mathematicall Praeface*, to Euclid's *Elements*. Citations are to signatures.

NA   *A Necessary Advertisement*, by an Unknown Friend . . ., from John Dee, *General and Rare Memorials*; *Autobiographical Tracts* edition.

PA   *Propaedeumata aphoristica*. Citations are to the text and translation in *John Dee on Astronomy*. Citations are either paired page numbers of the text and facing translation, or to the Roman numerals of the individual aphorisms. All citations are to the readings of the 1558 edition, unless otherwise noted with the date 1568.

T&FR   *A True & Faithful Relation of what passed for many Yeers Between Dr. John Dee . . . and Some Spirits.*

JOHN DEE AND RENAISSANCE INTELLECTUAL HISTORY

John Dee has had the mixed fortune to have lived a notably interesting life. His fortune has been good largely because certain facets of his career contain much of popular and even sensational interest, assuring that his life exerted considerable fascination ever since his death in 1608.[1] His fortune has been ill because these very same features have presented great obstacles to any satisfactory understanding of his career. His contemporary reputation for arcane learning, his practice of astrology and alchemy, and most spectacularly his long association with Edward Kelley, as the spiritual medium for his conversations with spirits and their exploits in the domains of Emperor Rudolf II, have provided matter for moralizing and romance. His relationship with the Earl of Leicester, Sir Philip Sidney, Lord Burghley, and Francis Walsingham among others at court, and not least with Queen Elizabeth herself has made him party to perennial interest evoked by the Elizabethan Court; and the hints that he was consulted on arcane and mysterious matters is scantily enough documented to allow ample room for imaginative and often titillating speculations. Until the present century, much of the biographical literature on Dee has been concerned with him as a personality and with the drama of his life; it has devoted little attention to the study of his writings, and has been less than scholarly.[2] The romantic, adventurous, and conspiratorial possibilities of his biography exercise a continuing attraction, from which even the scholarly literature has not been immune.[3]

Most literature which took notice of Dee recognized that he was not only a devotee of the occult but also accomplished in fields considered more legitimate by modern standards, particularly in mathematics, navigation, and astronomy. His substantive writings in any field, however, are slight, difficult to understand, and of little obvious long-range significance in mathematics, science, or philosophy. Scholars who have attempted to take account of Dee's substantive work have had, therefore, both to counteract those features of Dee's biography that had popular appeal but that served to detract from any claim to serious intellectual consideration, and to establish in what ways his career was of any serious historical consequence. Initially, the approach adopted typically ignored the more questionable dimensions of Dee's biography and focused upon his position within the evolution of some narrowly scientific development that aimed to indicate the importance of his role in that evolution. E. G. R. Taylor took the lead in rehabilitating Dee's reputation, emphasizing his work and his role as a teacher of practitioners in mathematics and navigation. Much of her account of the history of English navigation from 1547 to 1583 in *Tudor Geography, 1485–1583* is actually told in the context of a biography of Dee that avoids his less 'legitimate' activities.[4] Likewise, Frances R. Johnson considered Dee largely in terms of his accomplishments as an astronomer, his attitude toward Copernicus, and his formulation of an idea of experimental scientific method.[5]

This approach, while not entirely claiming for Dee a position of the first rank, did serve to earn for him some right to consideration in sixteenth-century intellectual history, but at the expense of divorcing aspects of Dee's activity from the rest of his work and biography. Since 1950 a succession of scholars have attempted to integrate the seemingly disparate aspects of Dee's career and to render him 'whole', maintaining his claim to importance in sixteenth-century intellectual developments and the evolution of a more modern science while at the same time acknowledging and accommodating to this his apparently less 'modern' occultist interests, ideas, and activities. The view that has emerged may well be called the Warburg interpretation because each of these scholars has had either a direct or an indirect connection with the Warburg Institute, and their works reflect a certain characteristic and shared approach. I. R. F. Calder, whose dissertation 'John Dee Studied as an English Neoplatonist' is the earliest reflection of this view, was a student of Frances A. Yates at the Warburg.[6] Dame Yates herself contributed significantly to this view in a series of writings in which Dee assumed an increasingly central place. Peter J. French, whose *John Dee. The World of an Elizabethan Magus* is the best currently available book-length study of Dee, although not formally a student of Dame Yates or of the Warburg, drew the foundation of his interpretation from her works and acknowledges her guidance.[7] A recent dissertation by Graham Yewbrey also takes the framework developed by Yates and French as the starting point for interpreting Dee's ideas.[8] Despite variations in specific interpretation, what is common to these works is that all approach Dee as a problem of finding the correct intellectual tradition into which he appears to fit, both as a way of making sense of his disparate and often difficult to understand works and activities and as a way of establishing his importance by associating him with an intellectual context of recognized importance for sixteenth-century and later intellectual developments. Paradoxically, despite the extent that Dee has been studied since Calder, he remains little studied in his own right and is more often considered only as an embodiment of some pre-existent intellectual tradition. This historiography of Dee bears some exam- ination, for it is largely problems and issues associated with it that have motivated my research on Dee and the study that follows.

Although it has remained unpublished because of its unwieldy size, Calder's dissertation has remained the touchstone for all subsequent work on Dee because it contains an exhaustive investi- gation of the biographical record, a close reading and analysis of all of Dee's extant writings, and attempts to trace many of the sources of Dee's ideas. Calder presents these materials within the framework of a number of interpretive strategies designed to show how Dee's works coherently relate to each other and to a single author and to establish Dee's historical importance. Calder accomplishes this by relating all of Dee's work and activities to a central philosophical position which he believes aligns Dee with the progressive movement of science in the sixteenth century.

For Calder the central philosophical position that reveals the unity in Dee's highly diversified endeavors is a scientifically oriented form of Renaissance Neoplatonism, which also laid the foundations for the methods of modern physical science because this Neo- platonism provided the atmosphere in which a mathematical approach to nature could develop.[9] Calder examines Dee's works in the light of Edwin Burtt's thesis that the mathematical aspects of seventeenth-century science were an outgrowth of the conception of mathematics implicit in the Platonism that was revived and developed in the Renaissance. This Neoplatonism, in which Pythagoreanism was an important element, conceived of the universe as made of numbers, or constructed according to mathematical ideas, so that mathematics became the pathway to the study of the fundamental aspects of the natural world. In contrast to Aristotelian science, in which mathematics plays an indifferent role, Burtt argued that the Renaissance Neoplatonic conception of mathematics was a significant factor in the formulation of a mathematical science by Copernicus, Kepler, Galileo, and Descartes.[10] Dee's advocacy of Renaissance Neoplatonism, according to Calder, puts him in line with Kepler and Galileo as a proponent of the extension of methods of quantitative analysis to natural questions in place of the qualitative approach of Aristotelian science.[11]

Following Robert Lenoble, Calder sees in the emergence of a mechanistic view of the universe, in which all causality involved observable and calculable physical forces in place of the occult qualities of Aristotelian science, another essential change contributing to seventeenth-century science in addition to a new appreciation of mathematics. Again, Calder claims that such a mechanistic causality was implied by the systems of the mathematical Neoplatonists of the sixteenth century, including Dee. To emphasize Dee's modernity, Calder does all he can to associate Dee with the intellectual background of seventeenth-century Cambridge Platonism, which he considered favorable to the mechanistic science of the seventeenth century, and to disassociate Dee from Renaissance magical and naturalistic traditions.[12]

Alternately, Frances A. Yates has suggested that the apparently contradictory activities and ideas of Dee can more effectively be understood as all belonging within the outlook of a *magus* inspired by the revived Hermetism of the Renaissance, rather than merely through the philosophy of Renaissance Neoplatonism.[13] Yates turned to Dee as much for what he offered in the way of support for her claims about the role of Hermetism in Renaissance culture as for what Hermetism contributed to understanding Dee; so before looking at how she treats Dee, it is worth sketching the historiographic context into which she introduces him.

Hermetism in its Renaissance guise was a product of the recovery and translation in the fifteenth century of the full body of Greek philosophical and religious texts attributed to Hermes Trismegistus. Until their correct dating in the seventeenth century showed them to be third-century products of gnostic Neoplatonism, these texts were thought to contain a pristine divine revelation of great antiquity because Hermes, as the Egyptian Thoth, was considered a near contemporary of Moses.[14] These texts aroused considerable interest because they presented a particularly exalted conception of man as a semi-divine intermediary between the divine and the terrestrial and as capable of creating his own nature, the key to which was the practice of magic for both power over the created world and the attainment of spiritual communion.[15] Hermetism and magic are thus considered to go hand-in-hand, the revival of Hermetism entailing a revaluation of magic. Belief in magic was widespread in the Middle Ages and the Renaissance, but it was almost always condemned by ecclesiastical authorities, theologians, and philosophers as a practice inherently involving demonology and, therefore, a threat to the stability of the universal order and contrary to religion.[16] Hermes himself had been associated with magical practices in the Middle Ages, and these techniques continued into the Renaissance, but the Renaissance added something more with the revival of the full body of Hermetic religious and philosophical texts. It was these texts, it is argued, with their mixture of magic, philosophy, and religion, that dignified and theologically legitimated magic as part of an ancient, divinely inspired, and proto-Christian religious wisdom.[17] No longer a despised conjurer of devils, the magician was now seen as a pious religious philosopher with insights into the secrets of the divine and natural order.[18]

Although Yates's work builds upon a considerable amount of previous scholarship, she became one of the major exponents of this view. Much of her influence in this regard is the result of her *Giordano Bruno and the Hermetic Tradition* (1967) in which she formulated an imposing historical synthesis of Renaissance intellectual history centered on the theme of magic as promoted by the Hermetica.[19] Here the influence of the Hermetica in the Renaissance is not just one element within the culture but becomes a distinct and major intellectual tradition. Deriving from Ficino's revival of Hermes Trismegistus and his blending of Hermetic magic with Neoplatonism and Orphism, this tradition evolved through Pico della Mirandola's addition of kabbalah and kabbalistic magic and the Christianization of this magic and the *magus* through the influence of Pseudo-Dionysius, culminated in Agrippa's synthesis of Renaissance magic and kabbalah, and reverberated through sixteenth-century developments in art, philosophy, science, politics, and religious reform, only terminating in the early seventeenth century when the exact dating of the Hermetic texts deprived Hermes of his antiquity and status as an embodiment of a pristine divine revelation.

One element of this new approach to magic in the Renaissance that has generated considerable controversy has been the suggestion that ennoblement of magic and the occult sciences contributed to the development of important aspects of what became the new science of the seventeenth century. Central to the new Renaissance idea of magic was the notion that the magus as operator could draw power from the divine and natural order. This new magical idea of knowledge as power provided a new attitude toward the cosmos conducive to the rise of science because it broke with the static medieval idea of reality and the medieval attitude of contemplative resignation toward the material world.[20] Again, the idea of a connection between magic and science is not original to Yates, nor has it been the central concern in her works, in which symbolic, religious, political, and artistic issues are of equal if not greater importance than science.[21] She has, however, popularized and elaborated this idea in ways that have attracted the attention of historians of science to the extent that the entire recent historiography of Renaissance magic and Hermetism has been referred to as the 'Yates thesis'.[22]

Yates suggested two specific ways the valuation of operational power inherent in Hermetic magic was conducive to science. First, the adoption of Copernican cosmology by Hermetic magi such as Giordano Bruno as a magical symbol promoted the wider adoption of Copernican astronomy and also supplied a foundation for a heliocentric dynamics.[23] Second, she suggested that it was the union of Hermetic magic with the Neoplatonic-Pythagorean view of number as the key to the secrets of nature that promoted an interest in the mathematical study of nature and the application of mathematics to the control of nature through the mechanical arts and physics. It was as support for this element of her synthesis that Yates first turned to Dee, for which he was eminently suited. Unlike most of the writers who figure in her account of magic, Dee was not only a philosopher but a competent mathematician and astronomer who actually practised angel magic and many of the mechanical arts.[24]

Dee is significant to Dame Yates because in his *Mathematicall*

Praeface to the English translation of Euclid's *Elements* of 1570 he strongly advocated the study of the mathematical and mechanical sciences that were to triumph in the seventeenth century.[25] The source, she would suggest, of not only Dee's advocacy but also of his actual practical scientific work and of the central place of mathematics in the expressions of his natural philosophy in the *Propaedeumata aphoristica* and the *Monas hieroglyphica*, was union within the Renaissance Hermetic tradition of magic with Pythagorean speculative mathematics as an embodiment of the ancient esoteric wisdom also found in the Hermetica.[26] According to Yates, therefore, Dee is a

> clear example of how the will to operate, stimulated by Renaissance magic, could pass into, and stimulate, the will to operate in genuine applied science. Or of how operating with number in the higher sphere of religious magic could belong with, and stimulate, operating with number in the lower sphere of 'real artificial magic'.[27]

Yates's association of Dee with Hermetic magic preserves Calder's theme that Neoplatonic mathematicism was preparatory to the development of early modern science. What is new is the role of magic. Calder was not unaware of the Hermetica and of some elements of magic in Dee's thinking, but he does little with them because associating Dee with Lenoble's formulation of a mechanistic view of causality antithetical to the qualitative causality of Renaissance naturalism bears the burden of aligning Dee with seventeenth-century science.[28] In place of Calder's emphasis on Dee and mechanism, Yates substitutes the idea of operational power inherent in Hermetic magic as the key both to understand how Dee's angelic conversations and his practical scientific activities and interest in mechanics flow from a single source but also to explain why the view of mathematics inherent in Neoplatonism came to be actively applied to the study of nature.

In her later works Dee becomes even more of a central concern. As she admits, the Elizabethan Renaissance and its continental connections had been an early and persistent concern, and Dee increasingly became the medium through which she extended the influence of the 'hermetic-cabalist tradition' into even wider areas of sixteenth-century culture than she had in her work on Bruno.[29] Yates eventually came to distinguish two phases within the

Hermetic tradition: an early Renaissance phase and a later Rosicrucian phase. While earlier Renaissance magic, such as Ficino's, aimed at psychological effects and was associated with artistic expression in music, poetry, and art, the Rosicrucian type of magic, so-called because of its role in the later Rosicrucian manifestoes, evolved in the later sixteenth century and aimed at more direct operation in the external world and contributed most directly to science of all the threads of the Hermetic tradition.[30]

Yates traces the formation of this Rosicrucian type of Hermetism to John Dee who combined magic, kabbalah, and alchemy in such works as the *Monas hieroglyphica* and the spiritual exercises he carried on with angels. In 1583 Dee carried his brand of Hermetism to eastern Europe and became the leader of a religious movement centered on a kabbalist and alchemical philosophy that became the root of the later Rosicrucian movement.[31] Because of Dee's promotion of mathematics and mechanics under the influence of Hermetic magic and because of his position as the catalyst behind the formation of the Rosicrucian movement within the Hermetic tradition, which channelled Hermetic influences in the direction of science, Dee therefore becomes a 'towering figure' in the history of European thought.[32] The culmination of Yates's progressive unravelling of the English Renaissance is *The Occult Philosophy in the Elizabethan Age*. Here she finds the key component of Elizabethan culture to be a kabbalistic variety of the Hermetic occult philosophy built from Lull, Ficino, Pico, Agrippa, and Francesco Giorgi, given a particularly English and Rosicrucian expression by Dee with his addition of alchemy. In the context of this philosophy, she interprets English literature as a battle ground between competing ideologies, with Sidney, Spenser, Shakespeare, and Chapman defending the occult philosophy of Dee, and Marlow, the proponent of reaction, attacking the occult philosophy and Dee.[33]

The interpretation that emerges from Yates's works is in the end quite similar to Calder's in its strategy of fitting Dee within an acknowledged intellectual tradition and building claims to his historical importance on the propagandization of mathematics and mathematical mechanics entailed by his espousal of that tradition. Her identification of that tradition with the Renaissance influence of the Hermetica proves hermeneutically more powerful than Calder's Neoplatonism in one respect, and that is in accomodating the strain of religious reform and prophecy that emerges in Dee's angelic conversations and his activities in eastern Europe in the 1580s. Her elevation of Dee to a position of cultural leadership in the Elizabethan Renaissance and the Rosicrucian movement on the basis of the evidence of his associations with Elizabeth, her court, Rudolf II, and the intellectual milieu of late sixteenth-century Bohemia also goes well beyond Calder. In this she pursued a course already set by Peter French's study of Dee.

French's *John Dee* appeared when Yates's interpretation of Dee was still a group of scattered suggestions.[34] French elaborated these suggestions into a comprehensive interpretation of Dee as a Hermetic magus encompassing not only Dee's works but arguing Dee's importance in English culture through his work in navigation, the influence of his *Mathematicall Praeface* on English mechanicians, and the influence of his philosophy in literature through his association with the 'Sidney circle' and patrons at court.[35] Dee's intellectual relations with patrons and the English court are even more central in Graham Yewbrey's dissertation on 'John Dee and the "Sidney Group"'. Yewbrey argues that much of Dee's work on navigation and his espousal of British Imperialism reflected a political philosophy that he urged upon the 'Sidney group' of 'Protestant activists' in the 1570s. This philosophy of 'Cosmopolitics', involving a theocratic state and magical government that would realize the redemption of the human race, translated into a political program the magical philosophy of Hermetism that Dee held.[36]

In the course of attempting to define Dee's place in sixteenth-century intellectual history and the history of science, each of these interpretations has highlighted and illuminated important features of Dee's career. Nonetheless, they also involve methodological difficulties which in fact obstruct our understanding of Dee himself and render dubious the larger historiographic framework that has been educed from this faulty understanding. Concerning Dee himself, the difficulty in each case is that the unifying philosophy thought to inform Dee's writings is derived either in an abstract and *a priori* fashion and then applied to Dee's particular works, or from some of Dee's later writings and then applied retrospectively to earlier material on the assumption that his basic ideas were already well formed by the time he completed his formal studies in 1548 and did not change thereafter. Thus, because Neoplatonic numerology, Hermetic religion and magic, kabbalah, alchemy, and astrology all turn up in Dee writings in the course of his career, it is assumed that he had steeped himself in all these things by 1548.[37] This 'myth of coherence', as Quentin Skinner has referred to the pursuit of an author's central thought and the presumption that it received systematic exposition, combined with the desire to place Dee within some progressive movement, has led to a distorted picture of Dee because his writings are frequently interpreted without careful attention to what he did or could have intended or how he intended his meaning to be taken by his audience.[38]

Central to these previous studies of Dee is his natural philosophy, which will be the primary focus of this study. My aim is to delineate the main elements of his natural philosophy, the basic motives behind his study of nature, and his intentions in the works that he wrote, determining the sources of his ideas and how he used them, and the relation of his natural philosophy to other Renaissance intellectual currents. I have chosen to pursue this study by closely examining selected texts that explicitly or implicitly represent significant statements of a theoretical nature regarding the natural world, its constitution and behaviour, and the epistemology and methodology of the study of nature. Dee did not leave a large body of writings on natural philosophy. The writings that he published that have philosophical import are three: the *Propaedeumata aphoristica* of 1558, the *Monas hieroglyphica* of 1564, and the *Mathematicall Praeface* of 1570. Widely spaced and hastily composed in response to immediate circumstances, these deal with matters of natural philosophy from widely differing perspectives. Although considerable manuscript material survives, it is frequently fragmentary and serves more to indicate the variety of Dee's interests than to bridge the gaps in Dee's intellectual career that separate one published work from the next. Other published and manuscript writings deal with mathematics, astronomy, navigation, and exploration. Some of these have received and others may merit scholarly attention. I have used these in so far as they pertain to issues raised by the major texts, but I have not attempted to treat each of Dee's writings in its own right.

Even though rather isolated and disparate, the *Propaedeumata*, the *Monas*, and the *Praeface* must bear the burden in any study of Dee's thought, and the organization of this study reflects this. It has been divided into sections, almost as individual studies, centered on the individual texts, their interpretation, and their situation within

Dee's intellectual career at that point. In addition to the three published texts, I have devoted a section to the group of manuscript material, which I refer to as the *Libri mysteriorum* following Dee's usage, that grew out of his angelic communications in association with Edward Kelley.[39] While not a work of natural philosophy in itself, these materials nonetheless do reveal features of Dee's thinking about nature at an important point in his career and are also significant as one of the few records of a Renaissance intellectual involved in the actual practice of religious ceremonial magic.

Intimately related to the analysis of these texts will be a consideration of the social dimension of Dee's intellectual career. Very early in his career he chose to work outside the institutional framework of the university, seeking to pursue a career as an independent scientific intellectual, and this meant the pursuit of aristocratic or royal patronage. I have included a considerable amount of biographical material on certain episodes of Dee's life for the purpose both of situating his writings on natural philosophy within the context of the intellectual activities and issues from which they arose and of exploring the relationships between his natural philosophy and his efforts to define and secure what he considered his proper intellectual role within society. My intent, however, has not been to do either biography or even intellectual biography. Although I believe that I have been able to clarify important aspects of Dee's biography and to contribute significantly to understanding his intellectual career, this study pretends neither to cover the entire biographical record and present the person whole, nor to interpret all of Dee's writings and activities in a biographical context. Although Dee lived from 1527 until 1608 or possibly 1609, the chronological scope of this study begins with Dee's university studies in 1542 and effectively ends with 1589 after his association with Kelley ended. Prior to 1542 we have little evidence; for his years after 1589 there is substantial material of a biographical nature, but he produced nothing that would add materially to an understanding of his natural philosophy.

Materials related to Dee's biography are not rich. His surviving correspondence is sparse and scattered. He did keep diaries in the form of notes in the margins of various ephemerides but only two of these survive.[40] Except for some brief notes Elias Ashmole made from an earlier ephemerides, the record from these diaries is rich beginning only in 1577. The entries themselves are of limited value.

Dee records comings, goings, and visitors but only occasionally the purpose and results of his business. Other notes record weather observations, birth dates for nativities, and domestic affairs. Although limited to bare facts and not always as revealing as we might wish, this material is generally trustworthy, objective, and often quite intimate. Similar material is found in annotations in surviving copies of some of the books Dee owned. Dee's *Compendious Rehearsall* and several passages in other works are autobiographical in character.[41] Where this material can be checked with other sources, Dee reports factual detail with great care. The autobiographical sources, however, all had a polemical purpose that variously colours his presentation of details. This is particularly true of his rendition of his contemporary reputation and of his relations with Elizabeth and the court.

A considerable portion of this study is devoted to delineating with some care the sources that contributed to the formation and the expression of the ideas in the texts under discussion. This has assumed such importance as much because uncovering Dee's sources contributes so much to understanding precisely what he intended in his various writings as because the issue of Dee's filiations with particular intellectual sources such as Neoplatonism, kabbalah, or Hermetism, has constituted a central element in previous interpretations of his thought. The catalogue that Dee prepared of his library in 1583 is an incomparable resource for this purpose but it must be used with considerable caution.[42]

Dee's library was clearly one of the most remarkable for his time, containing more than 2000 printed books and 198 manuscript codices. It was very clearly a working library and the survival of its catalogue presents a valuable guide to the resources Dee had available and the things that may have influenced his thinking. Andrew Watson and Julian Roberts are currently preparing a scholarly edition of Dee's library catalogues, a resource which, although regrettably not available in time to aid this study, should put any future study of Dee's sources on a secure footing. Listing books and having read them are clearly very different things, and listing something in 1583 does not tell us how much earlier than that it was read if at all. For instance, the catalogue contains a considerable number of Paracelsian works, the earliest of which was acquired in 1562.[43] However, none of Dee's works from this point show any extensive Paracelsian influence, so it is difficult to conclude anything about the extent to which Dee assimilated Paracelsian ideas. His library may be evidence of some of the most extensive early penetration of Paracelsian literature into England, but it is essentially a lost chapter. Since Dee's catalogue represents the state of his library some years after all his major writings except for the *Libri mysteriorum* were completed, it gives us little direct indication of the intellectual influences at work earlier in his career.[44] Some guidance is offered by earlier book lists, one of manuscripts he owned, borrowed, and bought in 1556, and another of books and manuscripts owned sometime between 1557 and 1559.[45] Here again these lists are not unfailing indications of influence without knowing what he read at what time and how he used the material he read.

An indication of how treacherous using the library lists by themselves can be is offered by Dee's copy of the 1516 Aldus edition containing Marsilio Ficino's *De triplici vita*, and Ficino's translations of the Hermetica and miscellaneous Neoplatonic texts on magic and the occult.[46] Dee's copy is signed but not dated. We might assume that he was studying Renaissance occult Neoplatonism and Hermetism quite early, since this appears in his list from 1557/59.[47] From internal evidence, however, the annotations in this all appear to date from the late 1560s, indicating that he read and absorbed this material a decade after acquiring the book.[48] I have, therefore, been very circumspect in drawing conclusions directly from Dee's library lists. If his own writings suggest a source through some similarity of idea, problem, or wording, I have used these lists to confirm that he had ready access to the source. Otherwise, I have preferred to work from dated surviving copies of works Dee owned because these give the greatest assurance of what he was using and, most important, how he was using them. The number of surviving books and manuscripts from Dee's library with annotations is quite rich, and, while significant material has undoubtedly been lost or escaped my attention, what remains presents a view of a mind at work digesting and remaking available intellectual resources. In considering Dee's place within sixteenth-century intellectual currents, my approach, therefore, has been to consider Dee as the focal point on which converged various elements of the intellectual heritage available in sixteenth-century Europe.

Complementary to this decision to approach Dee in terms of his reception and use of previous materials has been a decision not to consider Dee's influence either on contemporaries or on future developments in natural philosophy, science, or general intellectual culture. This has been dictated not only by the purely practical limitations of time, resources, and space, but also by the realization that just as the contribution of Dee's sources to his thought depended so much on the individual way that he understood and combined them, so the 'influence' or significance of Dee on future developments depends on how his thought was assimilated by others. From our perspective, we may see elements in his work that point toward future developments, but an assessment of their significance in historic terms will depend on the investigation of the extent and to what effect his ideas and works were used by others. Thus, while one of the historiographic issues that has prompted this study is the question of the role of Renaissance magic and occultism in the development of science, I have confined my concern to Dee's science and natural philosophy, leaving to others the matter of the 'modern' science of the 'scientific revolution' of the seventeenth century.

By this sleight of hand I side-step the thorny issue of the demarcation between the 'new science' of the scientific revolution and pre-modern science, pseudo-science, and non-science. Modern distinctions between science and non-science are fraught with anachronism, retrospectively applying reified notions of science to earlier situations. One feature of the process through which proponents of the new science of the seventeenth-century eventually carried the intellectual field against their competitors was the polemical definition of competing natural philosophies as non-science.[49] Such definitions may well not be entirely appropriate for seventeenth-century conditions. They are even less so earlier before the domains of science, magic, and religion had been marked out and distinguished in any standard way.[50] Distinctions were at times made, the most common segregating magic from both religion and science, not because it was different but because it was considered an illegitimate version of one or the other. Yet the situation was extremely fluid, in which competing conceptions of science and of magic were as prevalent as the competing religions of the time. As in the case of Dee's central philosophical commitment, it seems safer to discover what science, magic, and religion amounted to for Dee as these emerge from his works than to approach him with definitions that are necessarily artificial and will invariably falsify his intellectual world.

What will emerge is that the expressions of Dee's intellectual life assumed considerable variation. If Dee had a coherent natural philosophy that persisted throughout his career, he never developed a systematic exposition of it, and the texts that remain are just so many fragments. A close analysis of the *Monas hieroglyphica* in juxtaposition to the *Propaedeumata aphoristica* suggests a radical disjuncture in his thinking between 1558 and 1564 encompassing the content and aims of the natural philosophy of each, the sources upon which each drew, and social and intellectual function each was intended to fill at that point in Dee's career. The *Mathematicall Praeface* does suggest a philosophy within which Dee came to see the *Propaedeumata* and the *Monas* as complementary. The prefatory function of this piece, however, did not allow ample exposition of this philosophy, leaving the connections with his earlier writings and many facets of his thought veiled. The *Libri mysteriorum* pick up themes that emerge in the *Monas*, but the single-minded pursuit in the 1580s of the activities they reflect marks another decisive shift, rejecting as they do important possibilities within his thought in favour of others.

This is not to say that there are no elements of continuity in Dee's intellectual career. What threads do serve to tie the various manifestations of his natural philosophy together, however, consist not so much of philosophical content and principles but of intellectual intent and method, and of intellectual ambition. Dee was fond of referring to nature as a 'bright glasse' in which the divine creator was reflected in creation. Natural philosophy was to him a religious quest for an understanding of divinity. His objective was to discover divinity as revealed in the hidden springs of nature and the ultimate reasons behind the processes and the very existence of the cosmos, guided by the conviction that mathematical principles and procedures offered important aid in understanding creation. Throughout this quest Dee also sought to define for himself an intellectual role that would sanction efforts in natural philosophy that had little recognition in academic natural philosophy and support his claims to aristocratic and royal patronage.

The various expressions of Dee's natural philosophy, however disparate, may be seen as various attempts to realize these objectives. Yet the objectives themselves did not emerge fully developed or remain static. In the course of his career, Dee's intent became clearer and assumed added dimensions; concomitantly, as his natural philosophy shifted direction, he enhanced and expanded his conception of his social role. The interaction of the themes of Dee's articulated natural philosophy, his intellectual objectives, and his social ambitions was not simple. These themes worked themselves out rather differently at different times in response to changes in the issues of active concern to Dee, his reaction to and assimilation of different readings, the purpose and audience of each work he wrote, and the relation of the text to his current social position and ambitions. In his earliest work Dee's thinking was less Renaissance and Neoplatonic than medieval and Aristotelian. In the course of time his thinking became more explicitly Neoplatonic and absorbed more from Renaissance works of occultism and magic. His concerns in natural philosophy became at the same time more religious, and a religious magic aimed at establishing direct communication with angelic ministers of God replaced other approaches to knowledge of the natural world. As his conception of natural philosophy changed so did his conception of his appropriate social role, leading him to more grandiose ambitions that accorded ill with English expectations of the scientist's role. The disappointment of his aspirations at Elizabeth's court induced him to pursue them with Albrecht Laski in Poland and at the court of Rudolf II, and may also have contributed to his increasing turn to angelic magic.

The way Dee interacted with his sources was also an important factor in this process and will be an additional theme of this study. Dee's thought does not represent purely a reflection or instance of contemporary ideas. Rather, his intellectual life was a dialogue with received positions on various issues, a dialogue largely carried out with and through the books he read. At various points in his intellectual career, Dee encountered and to varying degrees absorbed a somewhat different mix of materials and wove them together in rather different ways. The texts that Dee used were often not part of the canon of philosophical and scientific texts of the time, allowing him considerable intellectual latitude. In addition, how he read his sources and selectively absorbed and transformed them often depended on his previous thinking as well as the immediate issues with which he was concerned, his social ambitions, and the reinforcement of other readings.

Throughout this study there will be a certain tension between these elements of continuity and discontinuity within Dee's career. The sense of fragmentation is stronger in the earlier chapters where analysis of Dee's writings predominates and there is less supplementary documentation. In the later parts of his career more elements of continuity appear as it is possible to see him picking up and elaborating earlier strands. Yet even here there is no strong impression that Dee had settled into a well-thought-out and stable position. Despite Dee's faith that he would find divinity reflected in the glass of creation, his works present us with a broken mirror reflecting in different ways different fragments of creation, behind which we hear the continuous murmur of the voices in his library.

Aside from the intrinsic interest inherent in achieving some more adequate understanding of Dee, the role Dee has been assigned in the historiography of Renaissance Hermetism also gives further study of Dee a wider significance. The whole issue of Renaissance Hermetism has generated considerable controversy and is currently in a state of flux.[51] It is not my intention to consider all the issues raised by the historiography of Hermetism, but Dee is relevant to two of the central issues: the relation of Renaissance Hermetism to the nature and status of magic, and the relation of magic to science. Dee is well suited as a test case for evaluating these claims because he was one of the few individuals of the fifteenth, sixteenth, and seventeenth centuries who was a genuine mathematician, knowledgeable and practised in astronomy, optics, navigation, and mechanics, an avid student of astrology and the most esoteric alchemy, and finally an unabashed practitioner of kabbalistic angel magic. The suggestion that hermetic magic was a direct and positive influence in the creation of the new science that emerged in the 'scientific revolution' of the seventeenth century has generated perhaps the most controversy but is not a particularly useful statement of the problem in this context. Dee still practised the 'normal' non-revolutionary science and natural philosophy of the sixteenth century. What he does suggest are the ways in which magical interests and the motives behind those interests contributed to the reworking of received science and natural philosophy, and were instrumental in suggesting a novel understanding of the aims and function of natural philosophy and the social role of the natural philosopher.

Critical attention has less often been devoted to the basic claim that Renaissance Hermetism was the key to a new understanding of the nature, status, and function of magic and the occult sciences in the Renaissance. Dee's idiosyncratic and eclectic blend of various sources, both medieval and Renaissance, highlights dimensions of occultism and magic in the Renaissance that have received less than adequate attention because of the predominance attributed to the occultism and magic associated with Florentine Neoplatonism and Hermetism originating with Ficino. Renaissance magic was not in all cases significantly different from that of the Middle Ages, nor was all Renaissance occultism based on a single 'occult philosophy'. Both natural magic as a technology and spiritual-demonic magic as a means of spiritual enlightenment were inspired as often by medieval sources as by the Neoplatonic and Hermetic sources recovered in the fifteenth century. Dee's case suggests that his interest in applied science, mechanics, and an activist approach to nature was modelled on Roger Bacon's idea of a natural magic, that this appreciation for mathematics and understanding of the application of mathematics to the study of nature was inspired by the example of Bacon and by Proclus's philosophy of mathematics, not magic, and that only his spiritual magic owed anything to Renaissance Hermetic or Neoplatonic influences.

Part One

THE *PROPAEDEUMATA APHORISTICA*, 1558

II

'OUTLANDISH AND HOMISH STUDIES AND EXERCISES PHILOSOPHICALL'

The first work of any significance in natural philosophy that Dee published was the *Propaedeumata aphoristica* that appeared in 1558.[1] Dee's 120 aphorisms make a very slim volume, although the claims Dee makes for the content are not unpretentious. The subtitle indicates that the treatise concerns 'certain preeminent virtues of nature', and the title-page engraving shows the qualities of heat and humidity and the elements earth and water joined to the sun and the moon under the starry vault of the heavens through a symbol that will become Dee's famous 'hieroglyphic monad' (figure 2.1). While the nearest subject matter of the *Propaedeumata* is astrology, the term 'astrology' did not have a simple, unambiguous meaning in the sixteenth century, or earlier for that matter. It could mean, as it does presently, judicial astrology – that is, predicting the influence of heavenly bodies on human affairs, an aspect of the subject that Dee also practised – but it could also mean mathematical astronomy, or simply mathematics.[2] The *Propaedeumata* is concerned less with the issues of astrological practice than with the cosmology, the natural philosophy, and the scientific method of astrology. I will argue that in the *Propaedeumata* Dee was addressing himself to astrology primarily as the theoretical and mathematical study of the influences operating on all things in the natural world in the spirit of his later definition of astrology as 'an Arte Mathematicall, which reasonably demonstrateth the operations and effects, of the natural beames, of light, and secret influence: of the Sterres and Planets: in every element and elementall body . . .' (*MP*, b.iij). He represented the ideas that comprised the *Propaedeumata* as 'hypotheses for the confirmation of astrology', indicating that they were nothing less than a contribution to establishing the foundations and certitude of astrological theories (*NA*, 58–9).

Despite all this, the interpretation of the *Propaedeumata* is not an easy task. Besides the non-systematic format, Dee admits that poor health prevented him from preparing a full exposition of his ideas (*PA*, 112/3). Not all of the aphorisms are lucid in themselves, many being brief and cryptic, and the aphoristic nature of the entire work often obscures the general connections between particular aphorisms and the meaning of the entire work. Dee rarely, if ever, cites authorities or sources for his ideas, thereby offering very little help in filling out his thoughts or penetrating his intentions.

Dee does, however, indicate that the *Propaedeumata* drew upon a considerable period of his intellectual development when he spoke of those aphorisms as the 'chief Crop and Roote, of Ten yeres his first Outlandish & Homish studies and Exercises Philosophicall' (*NA*, 56). Although there is very little substantial material dealing with Dee's career before 1558, what does exist does contribute to clarifying what interests and ideas contributed to the making of the *Propaedeumata*. This evidence indicates that astrology was one if not the major focus of Dee's natural philosophy from as early as 1548 and that Dee's aphorisms involve a convergence of previous intellectual interests focussed upon the problems of astrology. Before actually examining the *Propaedeumata*, therefore, I propose to examine what is known of Dee's intellectual career to that point by reviewing his education and social situation as well as his studies and ideas in natural philosophy and astrology prior to 1558.

CAMBRIDGE AND LOUVAIN

Dee himself leaves us in some uncertainty about when the 'Outlandish & Homish studies' that led to the *Propaedeumata* actually began. His comment that these studies began ten years before the *Propaedeumata* would exclude his studies at Cambridge, but in the *Monas hieroglyphica* he implies that he had begun the studies leading to that work as early as 1542, the year he entered Cambridge (*MH*, 7ᵛ). Despite the possibility that Dee was not very precise in his references or that he traced different aspects of his work to different influences, this last comment has led most scholars to attribute all of Dee's ideas and interests, including Neoplatonism, Hermetism, and the kabbalah, to his university days.[3] Dee's opinion of the

English universities is also not clear, discussing them warmly in some contexts and highlighting their failings in others.[4] Some discussion of the role of his university studies in his intellectual formation may, therefore, be of some value.

After instruction in Latin, first in London and then at Chelmsford, Dee went up to Cambridge in November 1542 where he entered St John's College. Whatever he later thought of his education there, he claims to have pursued his education so enthusiastically that he studied eighteen hours a day. This claim, however, may have been designed more to impress an audience in 1592 with his extraordinary learning than to reflect his former experience (*CR*,5). There is little direct evidence of what Dee might have studied at Cambridge, either for the BA he received in 1546 or for the MA which he received in 1548 (*CR*,5–6). Not only does Dee not tell us much about his studies, but there is considerable uncertainty in modern scholarship regarding the curriculum and intellectual milieu at Cambridge while Dee was there in the 1540s, coming as it did during the English Reformation, the growing influence of humanism in education, and the transformation of the social role of the universities in England.[5] Without pretending to make a significant contribution to the study of university education in the period before 1560, I would nonetheless like to venture some suggestions regarding what the curriculum was in its formal outlines and what was available to Dee as a student. I say available to Dee, because without direct evidence from his own perspective or contemporary lecture notes it is impossible to determine the actual content of his studies.

All indications suggest that the study of logic and Aristotle's philosophy remained the core of instruction in the arts curriculum while Dee was at Cambridge. Dee himself says that he went there 'to begin logic and so to proceede in the learning of good arts and sciences', and on another occasion associates the universities with the study of 'Academicall, or Peripateticall' philosophy (*CR*,5; *MP*,A.iiij).[6] The Cambridge statutes nearest in time to when Dee was there specified two years study of Terence, one year of logic, and one year in either natural philosophy or metaphysics.[7] The substitution of Terence for Priscian and the allotment of two years to its study reflect the encroachment of humanism into the traditional scholastic curriculum that accompanied the establishment of salaried university lectures in classics, logic, and philosophy in the late fifteenth century.[8] Otherwise, the curriculum seems quite traditional. Where specific texts are indicated in logic and philosophy, these are still Aristotle. For logic we find the mention of the *De sophisticis elenchis*, *Topica*, *Analytica Priora*, and *Analytica Posteriora* encompassing both the old and the new logics. For natural philosophy the texts mentioned are the *Physica*, *De anima*, and *De generatione*. The *Metaphysica* had become an optional alternative to Aristotle's natural philosophy.[9]

How seriously the growth of humanism affected the curriculum is less than clear. The study of languages certainly prospered, with the establishment during the early decades of the century of a public university lecture in either Greek or Hebrew and the requirement that the colleges have lecturers in both Greek and Latin.[10] Humanism also led to the replacement of the medieval scholastic approach to dialectic, focussed on syllogistic and the analysis of terms and propositions as they applied to formal disputation, with humanist dialectic, emphasizing the rules of natural language more appropriate to the analysis of texts, spoken discourse, and persuasive argumentation.[11] This shift seems to have been in progress between 1530 and 1550, so that some teaching of medieval dialectic most likely persisted while Dee was at Cambridge.[12] 'The Art of Logicke' and 'The 13 Sophisticall Fallacias' that Dee claims to have written in 1547 and 1548 were undoubtedly related to Dee's studies at Cambridge, but whether they were medieval or humanistic in approach is uncertain (*LA*,74). Dee may well have been exposed to both the late medieval scholastic approach to dialectic and humanist dialectic.

The fate of scientific teaching during this period was also quite mixed. While there may have been some erosion of the natural scientific core of Aristotelian teaching for undergraduates, it did not disappear and was considerably supplemented by instruction in the mathematical sciences.[13] From the early sixteenth century there was a provision for a mathematical lecturer at Cambridge who was to cover in successive years arithmetic and music, geometry and perspective, and astronomy. These lectures were to be attended by both undergraduates and students for the MA.[14] Although the early English humanists may not have made original contributions in the sciences, they did contribute to making Greek scientific works available in new Latin translations and were solicitous about improving the quality of scientific and mathematical teaching.[15]

24

Important with regard to Dee's education was John Fisher, Bishop of Rochester, who was a patron of Erasmus, Chancellor of the University of Cambridge from 1503 to 1535, and instrumental in completing the foundation of St John's College.[16] The St John's statutes in effect during Dee's studies, those drawn up by Fisher in 1530, provide for college lecturers in Greek and Hebrew, and four mathematical lecturers, one each in arithmetic, geometry, perspective, and cosmography.[17] The statutes specify that all fellows and scholars are to attend both college and university lectures. Not only were there fines for non-attendance at these lectures, but St John's appointed four examiners, one each in classics, logic, mathematics, and philosophy, who were to examine pupils daily on the public lectures and on days when there were no lectures the examiners set exercises for the students. Combined with the provision that students devote their first seven months of study to arithmetic and geometry, these provisions seem to assure a respectable exposure of undergraduates and masters to instruction in the mathematical sciences, including astronomy.[18] In 1545 St John's received a new set of statutes from Henry VIII that were drawn up by John Cheke, a fellow of St John's with whom Dee was closely associated as a student and the first holder of the Regius Professorship in Greek established in 1540.[19] What is noteworthy is that these new statutes differ hardly at all from Fisher's 1530 statutes, the main changes in the curriculum being the elimination of *quaestiones* drawn from Duns Scotus. The place of Aristotle in the curriculum and the emphasis on languages and mathematics remain almost identical to the previous statutes.[20] Since one of the most progressive and humanistic minded members of the University and of St John's saw fit to tamper very little with Fisher's work, we can have some confidence that while Dee was studying at St John's these provisions represent the curriculum he was expected and encouraged to fulfil.

The education available to Dee was therefore highly eclectic. As an undergraduate, he certainly studied Aristotelian logic and natural philosophy and possibly the new humanistic approach to dialectic. He studied Greek, and through that may have been introduced to Plato and other ancient platonic works as well as Aristotle's works in the Greek. He would also have been required to do some elementary work in arithmetic and geometry and expected to follow the university and college lectures in arithmetic, geometry, perspective, music, cosmography, and astronomy. Dee also took an MA at

Cambridge in 1548, and this curriculum would have reinforced the predominant Aristotelian influence in his education, requiring further study of the *Analytica Posteriora* and considerable additional work in the natural scientific works, the ethics, and the metaphysics, as well as additional studies in mathematics, including Euclid, and astronomy.[21]

In addition to the formal curriculum there was private instruction carried on with individual tutors.[22] It is in this context that Dee may have been introduced to some of the 'occult' sciences through his association with Cheke and Smith. Both men had more than a casual interest in astrology, Cheke having Prince Edward write a Latin exercise in praise of astrology and perhaps even arranging for Girolamo Cardano to cast Edward's nativity, and Smith is recorded as having instructed Gabriel Harvey in alchemy.[23] Mordechai Feingold has clearly shown both that there was no official prohibition of private study of the occult sciences in the universities as long as illicit and unlawful practices were avoided and that 'numerous university men studied and practiced various components of the occult tradition.'[24] Dee's claim that he had been working in the 'hermetic science' since 1542 most likely refers to some informal studies at Cambridge. What cannot be determined, however, is the philosophical content of these studies. The 'hermetic science' was a generic term for alchemy in the sixteenth century and should not lead us to conclude that he had been introduced to the 'Hermetism' that Yates associates with Ficino and Pico or any fully developed 'Hermetic tradition'. Nothing of what is known of Cambridge in the 1540s and of Cheke and Smith indicate that Dee had been introduced as a student to any *specifically* Renaissance variety of Neoplatonism or Hermetism or as yet to the kabbalah. Roger Ascham, who was a student of Cheke's at St John's from 1530 and remained at Cambridge until 1542, when Dee was there, reports in his *Toxophilus* (1545) that the texts Cheke read privately with students were Homer, Sophocles, Euripides, Herodotus, Thucydides, Xenophon, Isocrates, and Plato.[25] Whatever the extent of his exposure to alchemy and astrology, it was most likely in the form that these traditionally had in the Middle Ages and continued to have throughout the sixteenth century.

Dee leaves no uncertainty about the importance of his foreign studies in contributing to the formation of the *Propaedeumata*. In the prefatory letter to the *Propaedeumata*, addressed to Gerard Mercator,

Dee offers the work to Mercator as 'the first fruits of my labors while abroad', where 'from your discussions with me my whole system of philosophizing in the foreign manner laid down its first and deepest roots' (*PA*,110/11; cf. *MP*,b.iij^v–b.iiij). Dee actually made two trips abroad in the late 1540s. The first began in May 1547 and lasted only a few months between terms at Cambridge. He went to consult with continental scholars and his interest in mathematics and science is already clearly apparent because he primarily sought out mathematicians, of whom he mentions Gemma Frisius, Gerard Mercator, Gaspar à Mirica, and Antonio Gogava. He returned home with two of Mercator's globes and two astronomical instruments designed by Gemma Frisius – an astronomer's ring and an astronomer's staff (*CR*,5). One of the fruits of Dee's contact with the continent was the popularization of the astronomer's staff in England and its later development by Thomas Digges into an accurate astronomical instrument through Dee's influence.[26] His second trip to the continent was longer, lasting from June 1548 until sometime in 1551.[27] Again he spent most of the time in Louvain where he says he became a student and 'for recreation' studied civil law, although there is no indication that he followed a formal course of study or received any degree (*CR*,6–7). Foreign study in civil law as a preparation for government service was not an uncommon finishing touch for English gentlemen after their university education, so Dee's foreign studies were not unusual. Such study was often supported by the patronage of individuals already in government service, and Dee may have been at least partially supported at this time by William Pickering whom he tutored in 'logick, rhetorick, arithmetick, in the use of the astronomer's staff, the use of the astronomer's ring, the astrolabe, in the use of both Globes, &c' (*CR*,7).[28] Pickering, serving as English ambassador to the court of Emperor Charles V in Brussels, had studied with Cheke at Cambridge and was one of a number of Cambridge men who had assumed government positions with the accession of Edward VI, including Cheke and William Cecil who later secured patronage for Dee.[29]

It is clear, however, that Dee's real interest at Louvain was in mathematics and science and continuing his studies with Gemma Frisius, Mercator, Gogava, and the Spanish geographer, Pedro Nuñez (*PA*,110–15). Louvain seems to have been recognized as a center for mathematics, including astronomy and geography, since the early sixteenth century, and at the time Dee was there Gemma Frisius was known for his interest in arithmetic and astronomy and seems to have given the first public lectures in mathematics in 1543.[30] Since Dee attributes the basic idea of the *Propaedeumata* to discussions and debates among himself, Mercator, Gogava, and Gemma Frisius, astrology must have been a major focus of Dee's mathematical and scientific studies at this time (*PA*,112–3; *MP*,b.i–ij^v–b.iiij). Amongst these scholars astrology was not taken as unquestioned doctrine but engaged them as a problem for study. While Mercator was quite critical of contemporary astrological practice and theory, he did not reject it outright but contemplated writing a treatise of reform.[31] If astrology was subject to criticism in the group, apparently none of them rejected the idea that astral influences played some causal role in the natural world, for Mercator related the force of the sun and the stars to the growth of sublunar bodies, and Gemma Frisius, as a physician, considered astrology important in medical practice.[32] In both cases, the problem of astrology related not to prognostication but to an astrological physics, which is the main focus of Dee's theory in the *Propaedeumata*, and both were also interested in more precise determination of the sizes and distances of the planets, which are the most important parameters in Dee's astrology.[33] Further, concurrently with Dee's arrival in Louvain in 1548, Gogava was working on a translation of Ptolemy's *Tetrabiblos*, which was published that year with a preface by Gemma Frisius recommending this fundamental work for the study of astrology. Significant perhaps for the role optics and the optical ideas of Roger Bacon were to play in the formation of Dee's mature astrology, Gogava appended to his translation two medieval treatises dealing with burning mirrors, one of which was mistakenly attributed to Roger Bacon.[34]

Besides participating in discussions on astrology, there are signs that Dee was carrying out his own work in this area while at Louvain. In 1547 he 'began to make observations (very many to the houre and minute) of the heavenly influences and operations actuall in this elementall portion of the world', which he was to continue making throughout his life (*CR*,5). In 1548 he acquired and annotated two books on astrology in which he recorded similar observations.[35] Among the works that Dee claims to have written but which were not published and no longer survive, is a *Mercurius Caelestis*, written at Louvain in 1549 or 1550, which apparently deals with some astronomical or astrological subject (*CR*,24; *LA*,74).[36] Working among men who were all actively involved in geography and navigation, it is reasonable to assume that Dee's later interests in these subjects were also stimulated at this time and it may be that a work Dee calls *De nova navigationum ratione* also dates from this period (*PA*,116–17). In the summer of 1550 Dee made a trip to Paris where, in addition to meeting the prominent mathematicians there, he lectured publicly on the first two books of Euclid's *Elements* (*CR*,7–8).[37] Considerable attention has been given to Dee's characterization of these lectures as '*Mathematicè, Physicè, et Pythagoricè*' as evidence of a fully developed Platonic/Pythagorean philosophy replete with all the related Renaissance hermetic ramifications at this point in his career.[38] Without the actual text, it is risky to draw any conclusions about a work on the basis of a cryptic description of it by the author more than forty years after the fact in a passage marked by hyperbole.[39] It is more reasonable to think of what Dee did as similar to the traditional threefold approach to geometrical figures, considering them mathematically in their pure geometrical properties, physically in their practical applications, and pythagorically or speculatively in their philosophical import. It was also quite common to support the recommendation of the study of geometry with references to Pythagoras.[40]

PATRONAGE AND PRIVATE STUDY

Dee's performance in Paris was impressive enough to have elicited the offer of a stipend of 200 crowns a year as 'one of the French kinge's mathematicall readers', as well as the attempt of several French nobleman to outbid one another for his services, all of which offers he declined (*CR*,8). It may very well be that Dee was expecting and confident of attaining a court position in England when he returned. Dee describes a work *De Caelestis Globi amplissimis commoditatibus* written in 1550, presumably while still at Louvain, and another *De Planetarum, Inerrantium stellarum, Nubiumque a centro terrae distantiis: & stellarum omnium veris inveniendis magnitudinibus* written in 1551 as both dedicated to King Edward VI (*PA*,116–17; *CR*,26; *LA*,75).[41] The first was most likely similar to other introductions to the use of the celestial globe but the second, dealing with the sizes and distances of heavenly bodies, bears on questions of concern to Mercator and Gemma Frisius and is related to Dee's astrological studies at Louvain and in the *Propaedeumata*. In late 1551, probably soon after his return to England, his expectations were fulfilled when he was introduced to William Cecil, then a junior Secretary of State, and to Edward VI. This resulted in the grant of a yearly pension of 100 crowns which was later exchanged for the income from the rectory of Upton upon Severn in March of 1553. Later the same year Long Leadenham was added, giving him a total revenue of £80 (*CR*,9–10).[42]

The foundations for Dee's preferment at court involved both family connections at court and his connections with St John's. Dee's father, Rowland, is described as a mercer and 'the King's servant' to Henry VIII, although it is not clear exactly what trade he carried on in London or how he may have served the king. An indication that he was held in some favour at court is a grant to him from Henry VIII in 1544 of the position to supervise in both London and its suburbs the packaging of all merchandise for export. This position was instituted to reduce the loss of customs duties by the crown, and Rowland was to split with his counterpart appointed by the Mayor of London all the fees charged for this service. There is also indication that Rowland had come into possession of some monastic lands from Henry's dissolution of the monasteries.[43] If Rowland sent Dee to Cambridge as a route to professional and social advancement into the ranks of gentleman, a function the universities increasingly played in the sixteenth century, Dee could not have succeeded better.[44] By 1551 key people with whom Dee had ties at Cambridge and particularly St John's had moved into positions of great influence at court and were in a position to promote his fortunes.

The migration of Cambridge men to the royal court began following Henry's marriage to Catherine Parr in 1544. Thomas Smith became a clerk to Catherine's council and John Cheke, among others from St John's, entered the Royal nursery, newly reorganized by Catherine, as a tutor to Prince Edward.[45] It was largely through their efforts that the threat of confiscation of college lands was averted and the new foundation of Trinity College was initiated.[46] It was also through their efforts that Dee was appointed a foundation fellow and under-reader in Greek in Trinity in 1548.[47] Following Henry's death, the position of the Cambridge group became even stronger. Cheke, as tutor to the young king, was in an important strategic position; Roger Ascham became a tutor to the Princess Elizabeth; and William Cecil, who had studied at St John's with Cheke in the 1530's and had married Cheke's sister, joined the household of the Duke of Somerset.[48] Both the Duke of Somerset and John Dudley, Earl of Warwick, were patrons of the Cambridge group, and when Dudley replaced Somerset at the centre of the government, Cheke and Cecil assumed more influence, both receiving honors at the same time that Dudley was elevated to Duke of Northumberland in 1551.[49] Cecil was described by the Imperial ambassador as 'the Duke of Northumberland's man', and was responsible for preparing much of the business for the Privy Council and for overall financial planning.[50] As Edward began to take a more active role in the government in 1551 and 1552, Cheke's relation to the King as a tutor gave him an influential position and Cecil was given the role of intermediary between the Council and the King to keep him informed politically.[51] Cheke and especially Cecil were therefore in a central position to provide introductions not only to Edward but also to other prominent figures at court. Cecil began to receive numerous dedications of humanistic works at this time but he also was an important supporter of the sciences throughout his career.[52]

Dee's introduction to Edward through Cheke and Cecil was, in effect, an introduction to Northumberland who would have had authority over grants made in the King's name given Edward's youth. Therefore, in addition to the grant from the King, Dee had opportunities for patronage from other members of the government. He tells us that he entered the service of the Earl of Pembroke in 1552, but there is little indication of the extent or type of service he rendered.[53] Dee's major services were to Northumberland and his family. Dee describes two works he wrote in 1553 at the request of Jane, the Duchess of Northumberland, one on 'The true cause, and account (not vulgar) of Fluds and Ebbs' and the other on the origins, the configurations, and the names of the signs of the zodiac (*LA*,75).[54] Since these were written in English, they were probably for the instruction of the Duchess or her children, and Dee's account of John, Earl of Warwick and son of Northumberland, as a student of the arts who learned the value of mathematics in military affairs indicates that Dee may have served as tutor to the Northumberland children (*MP*,*.iiij^v–a.j).

The connection with Northumberland was also the vehicle for Dee's involvement in the first important English voyage of discovery, the voyage of Richard Chancellor and Hugh Willoughby in 1553 to find a northeast passage to the Indies, or Cathay as it was called then. This voyage grew out of efforts of the Merchant Adventurers, who were experiencing a significant decline in their traditional Antwerp cloth trade, to find new markets. Significantly, they enlisted the aid of Northumberland's government in pursuing an aggressive policy of acquiring new markets, first by having the trading privileges of the Hansa in England revoked when the Hansa refused to grant reciprocal privileges to English merchants, and second by obtaining a crown monopoly for a company to engage in exploration and trade with the Indies by way of a northeast or northwest passage.[55] Since Spain and Portugal already monopolized trade via the south Atlantic, the objective was to find an 'English' route to the north of either the North American or Eurasian continents. Not only did the government grant the monopoly, but members of the government, including privy councillors and Cecil, invested in the company, and the technical expertise was supplied by Northumberland and his associates. The chief pilot for the voyage, Richard Chancellor, was maintained by Henry Sidney, who was Northumberland's son-in-law, and Dee, whose studies with Mercator, Gemma Frisius, and Pedro Nuñez constituted excellent credentials, provided geographical guidance to the company and navigational training to Chancellor.[56] It seems to have been at Dee's suggestion, which was not unreasonable given the vagueness of contemporary geographical knowledge of the northern regions, that the company chose to pursue the northeast route. He also worked with Chancellor to collect new astronomical data and instructed Chancellor in the techniques of calculating ephemerides for use in navigation (*CR*,28).[57] The voyage did not succeed in finding a passage to Cathay, but Chancellor did reach Russia, or Muscovy, and returned with trade agreements from the Tsar that fulfilled some of the merchant's expectations and led to the formation of the Muscovy Company in 1555.[58]

What Dee's patrons expected of Dee was that he make his learning available to them and that he use his expertise in the service of their projects. Thus he taught, because he was MA, and he consulted on geography and navigation, because he was more than commonly trained in mathematics, astronomy, and geography. On the other hand, Dee does not mention in the prefatory letter to the *Propaedemata* anyone in England who had encouraged him in the philosophizing that was the foundation of that work. It is doubtful that his patrons considered the support of theoretical research one of their responsibilities, and at this time Dee does not seem to have begrudged the work of the mathematical practitioner. Even after most of his patrons passed from the scene with the accession of Mary in 1553, he continued this type of activity. He continued to serve as consultant to the Muscovy Company, developing new techniques for navigating in the high latitudes of the North and, after Chancellor died in 1556, providing navigational instruction for their new pilots.[59] He also wrote several other works in 1557 and 1558 that seem to be of a practical or popularizing nature, even though he had at that time no obvious patron.[60]

There is no evidence that Dee lost the two livings he had received from Edward when Mary came to the throne in July of 1553, but he did lose his major patrons because most of them had supported the claims of Jane Grey. The Duke of Northumberland was executed in August 1553 and the family fortunes were dispersed. In addition, John, the Earl of Warwick, died in 1554, and Jane Dudley died early in 1555.[61] John Cheke was also arrested as a traitor and, though he was pardoned, he went into exile and was dead by 1557.[62] William Cecil managed to disassociate himself enough from the attempt to exclude Mary to survive but he was no longer in a position of influence.[63] In 1554 Dee was offered a yearly stipend to 'read the mathematicall sciences' at Oxford University, which would have provided him with some support and the opportunity to pursue his studies (*CR*,10). Either the position did not materialize or Dee did not accept the offer but what happened is not exactly clear from the evidence.[64] The fact that Dee entered the service of Queen Elizabeth in the first months of her reign on the introduction of the Earl of Pembroke and Robert Dudley indicates that he continued to maintain contacts with and may even have received some support from his original patrons (*CR*,11–12). In fact, Dee claims to have done some service on behalf of Elizabeth at the request of some of her servants and supporters during Mary's reign but he quickly learned that this could be dangerous, for in May of 1555 the government arrested him.[65]

Dee claims that he was arrested because of his service to Elizabeth on the charge that he 'endeavored by enchantmentes to destroy Queene Mary', which is substantially correct. Arrested at the same time were Christopher Carye, who seems to have been an associate and student of Dee's, and Thomas Benger, who was the servant of Elizabeth for whom Dee worked.[66] The original charge was that they had calculated the nativities of King Philip, Queen Mary, and the Princess Elizabeth, which may have been what Dee calls the 'travailes for her Majesties behalfe, to the comfort of her Majesties favourers . . .' (*CR*,20). The records speak of 'calculating', 'conjuring', and 'witchcraft', which may only refer to calculating nativities, since astrology was often considered a variety of conjuration, but whatever Dee's actual activity, the incident cast a sinister pall over Dee's reputation that he was never entirely able to live down. The government's informer, George Ferrers, also accused Dee and his associates of having a 'familiar spirit', and implied that following his original accusation they had caused his children to be stricken, one dead and the other blind.[67] Dee was imprisoned, his papers searched, and his London dwelling sealed. After responding to a number of articles in writing to the Privy Council, he was sent to the Court of Common Pleas and then to the Star Chamber. He was acquitted of charges of treason but sent for examination on religious matters to Bishop Bonner of London, in whose custody he remained for some time until the Privy Council ordered his release.[68]

Examination by Bonner was potentially more threatening than by the Privy Council or Star Chamber. Bonner was a very conservative Henrician who was humiliated and imprisoned under Edward VI for opposition to the more Protestant course of the regime. When restored to his see by Mary, he remarked of the reformers that 'their sweet shall not be without sour sauce'.[69] Not only did he become a persecutor of Protestants, he was very unsympathetic to any form of magic and not likely to look kindly on those associated with the governments of Somerset and Northumberland.[70] Yet Dee does not seem to have had a hard time of it. In Foxe's *Acts and Monuments* he is the bedfellow of Bartlet Green, as Dee claims he was, but more as Green's keeper than as his fellow prisoner, and Dee appears a number of times in interrogations on the Bishop's side of the table supporting papal supremacy and transubstantiation.[71] Either Dee was a very good dissembler capable of playing a very convincing role over the course of several months or he may in fact have had nothing to worry about.

Prior to this episode, there is no evidence whatsoever on Dee's religious stance. He may very well have been a closet Catholic or have had personal convictions that allowed him to flow with the current. The fact that he was associated with Northumberland, Pembroke, and others who pursued a strongly Protestant policy in Edward's reign says nothing of his religious convictions, since he was not patronized as a religious advisor or propagandist and Northumberland himself remained a Catholic and pursued the Protestant policy from expedience.[72] This experience nevertheless left hard feelings and was the most important basis for Dee's reputation as a conjurer that was to follow him the rest of his life. Foxe's *Acts and Monuments* did a great deal to publicize the incident and promote this reputation which the removal of explicit references to Dee in the 1576 and later editions was unable to correct.[73]

The incident may also have some bearing on the *Propaedeumata* because the letter to Mercator makes vague reference to the many inconveniences that have hindered his studies. The concluding passage of the letter, where Dee speaks of sending forth the *Propaedeumata* as a scout to elicit the judgments of learned men so that Dee might consider 'whether I should now extend my forces, such as they are, immediately into foreign fields or should train them still more diligently in military discipline at home', sounds as if Dee was impatient with his situation at home and was considering the pursuit of patrons abroad (*PA*,114/15, 116/17–118/19). Connected with this may be the actual format in which Dee published the *Propaedeumata*. It originally appeared with its own title page in a volume following a treatise on nativities by Cyprian Leowitz prefaced with a defence of astrology by Jerome Wolf, both extracted from a larger work published the previous year by Leowitz.[74] Leowitz, with whom Dee was acquainted, was mathematician to the Elector Palatine Otto Henry and had connections with the Austrian Habsburgs.[75] Since Dee substituted a 'Regula' of his own at the end of Leowitz's treatise it is likely that Dee was responsible for the whole volume and used the work of an established mathematician as the springboard for his own first publication and a bid for patrons in 'foreign fields'.[76]

Despite his occupation with practical activities and the inconveniences that Dee speaks of, he was not idle but continued his 'studies and Exercises Philosophicall' between 1551 and 1558. Dee continued making astronomical observations, 'made by very grave & apt instruments carefully and circumspectly used, An° 1553, An° 1554, Anno 1555 in ye presence & with ye judgement of Expert and famous Mathematicians, Mechanicians, and others.

. . .'[77] This may refer to his work with Richard Chancellor, to whom Dee refers as a 'mechanician', but Dee had also been working at this time with Joannes Franciscus Offusius on observations of the stars (*NA*,58–9). Offusius later published a work on astrology that Dee claimed was a plagiarism of his *Propaedeumata*, and in correspondence wih Dee in the fall of 1553 Offusius pressed Dee to share with him his 'hypotheses for the confirmation of astrology', concerning the 'causes of atmospheric changes' (*NA*,58–9).[78] These hypotheses most likely refer to the 'Aphorismi Astrologici 300' that Dee claims to have written in 1553 – very likely an early version of the *Propaedeumata* (*CR*,26; *LA*,75).[79]

The books and manuscripts that Dee acquired between 1547 and 1556 also indicate that mathematics and astrology represented the strongest interests in Dee's personal studies during this same period. Although a wide variety of different subjects are represented among this material, astrology, astronomy, and mathematics far outweigh any other category. It is also worth noting that Aristotelian works make up the largest amount of the philosophical material, while there are no works reflecting Renaissance Neoplatonic or Hermetic influence. Owning books and having read them are not necessarily the same thing, but a number of these books are annotated, showing careful reading, of which the largest number are astrological works.[80]

Indications of Dee's reading interests in natural philosophy become more extensive for 1556 because Dee compiled a list of the manuscripts that he owned at that time and recorded numerous other manuscripts that he consulted, borrowed, and perused in that year.[81] It is doubtful that Dee actually read all of these at that time, for according to my count there are at least 249 separate titles, although some were acquired before 1556 and some were not returned until two years later, giving him ample time to study them.[82] Nevertheless, these lists indicate that Dee had a fairly sizeable manuscript collection in 1556 and that in May and July of that year he examined manuscripts in several different collections. The materials that turn up in these lists are therefore a fairly good indication of the subjects that attracted Dee's attention and interest at this point. Here again, astronomy, astrology, and mathematics remain as predominant interests. In addition, two other categories assume pre-eminence in 1556: optics, which appears for the first time, and alchemy, which was only slightly represented earlier.

Again, there are no Hermetic books and although some Platonic
material appears at this point, it is still far outnumbered by works
in the Aristotelian tradition.

Most of the previous evidence concerns manuscripts. The 1557/
1559 list shows a considerable collection of printed books, but this
evidence is less decisive. Whether all this material was acquired
before the *Propaedeumata* depends on the date of the list. With few
exceptions, the manuscripts on this list are the same as on the 1556
lists. Likewise, even if the list is as late as 1559, many of the
books were undoubtedly acquired early enough to influence the
Propaedeumata, but unless a book survives with a date, we have no
assurance which these might have been. Much of the printed
material reflects the pattern we have already observed. Mathematics, astronomy and astrology, perspective (optics), navigation,
and geography are very strongly represented in classical, medieval,
and some Renaissance texts. The philosophical literature is still
predominantly Aristotelian. There do occur here, however, the earliest appearance of distinctly Renaissance Neoplatonic and magical
texts. These are the Ficino edition of the Hermetica and Neoplatonic
magical writings mentioned in the Introduction, Pico's *Conclusiones*,
Francesco Giorgi's *De harmonia mundi*, Reuchlin's *De verbo mirifico*,
and Agrippa's *De occulta philosophia*.[83] These make a fine library of
Renaissance magic, but without a clear indication that he actually
read them at this time, of which there is none, it would be a mistake
to give these six books undue importance out of a library that
numbered at least 316 printed books and in which they are far
outweighed by Aristotelian philosophy and other types of scientific
literature.[84]

Somewhere in the mid-1550s and continuing to 1558, therefore,
the scope of Dee's interests appears to have expanded. From Dee's
own works dating from 1557 and 1558 it is clear that the interests
which were most strongly translated into active consideration on
his part were astrology and optics. In these years he wrote three
works on various subjects related to optics, one on astronomy,
and the *Propaedeumata aphoristica* (*PA*,116/17; *CR*,25–6; *LA*,75).[85] In
addition, he also claims to have written a work on Roger Bacon in
1557 in which he defended Bacon against charges that he
accomplished great things with the aid of demons rather than
naturally (*PA*,116/17).[86] In fact, Dee seems to have discovered
Bacon in the mid-1550s, a discovery that elicited a lively interest

on Dee's part. Bacon's works comprise or are present in nine of the manuscripts in the 1556 lists, and Dee acquired an additional Bacon manuscript in 1558.[87] While Bacon's works are few in Dee's holdings prior to 1556, by 1558 Dee possessed or had consulted all of Bacon's major works.

While alchemical titles constitute a sizeable proportion of the works in the 1556 lists, alchemy does not appear to have had a significant impact on Dee's own work in natural philosophy in 1557 or 1558.[88] Dee makes a brief reference in the *Propaedeumata* to alchemy as analogous to astrology, and alchemy does seem to have been an early interest of his, but not one that was under active consideration in this early period (*PA*,LII; *MH*,136/7).

It seems safe to conclude that the astrology of the *Propaedeumata* is the culmination of Dee's earliest interest in natural philosophy, as indicated both by his readings and his own early writings on that subject. Further, Dee's long-standing interest in mathematics and the attention he focused on optics and Roger Bacon from the mid-1550s through 1558 provide the most concrete foundations for an understanding of the substance of the *Propaedeumata aphoristica*. The emergence of new interests in Dee's readings in 1556 indicates that this first period of Dee's intellectual development comprised two phases. The following chapter will examine the indications of Dee's ideas on astrology and natural philosophy prior to the emergence of his interest in optics and then follow their development through his growing interest in optics.

III

THE OUTSTANDING VIRTUES
OF NATURE

ASTROLOGY

The 'observations (very many to the houre and minute) of the heavenly influences and operations actuall in this elementall portion of the world', which Dee began to make while at Louvain in 1547, undoubtedly refer in part to some brief manuscript notes found in one of the first astrological works he acquired.[1] These notes include a chart of planetary positions that, when corrected for time and place, would give the positions of the planets at Louvain at noon on the first of November 1548, from which the horoscope for that month could be cast. The horoscope for the first day of a year, a quarter, or a month was also the horoscope for the entire period beginning with that day and provided a basis from which weather predictions for those periods could be derived. Further, these notes include a list of weather observations that note the temperature, the direction and force of the wind, and various atmospheric conditions, such as the type and extent of cloud cover and precipitation, along with the time when changes in these conditions occurred at Louvain for each day of August 1548. Although the weather observations and the table for planetary positions do not coincide chronologically, they serve as examples of Dee's programme to observe the influences and operations of the heavens in the elemental sphere by relating concrete meteorological events to the changing dispositions of the heavens. Dee continued to make similar observations throughout the rest of his life, recording the place, time, and characteristics of meteorological phenomena alongside the planetary configurations given in the *ephemerides* that he used as a diary.[2]

Other early notes on astrology give us a glimpse of Dee's views on the subject prior to the *Propaedeumata*, and these indicate that Dee thought of astrology primarily as a physics by which the phenomena of the terrestrial sphere are explained by reference to the influence of the celestial bodies. He accepted what was in its basic outlines a qualitative physics, according to which the generation, alteration, and corruption that take place in the sublunar sphere of the elements (earth, air, fire, and water) are the result of changes in the secondary qualities of things, which in turn are generated from the primary qualities (heat, cold, humidity, and dryness).[3] The agent of these qualitative changes is the heavens because the primary qualities are generated in the inferior world by the hidden virtues of the celestial bodies, which are conveyed through motion and light.[4] The different climates and physical environments of various regions derive from these influences, and the environment, along with particular configurations of the heavens, produces various mixtures of qualities from which is generated the great diversity of mortal creatures. Dee seems to accept an entirely naturalistic conception of man at this early stage, considering him to be an integral part of his environment and affected in both body and soul by his physical surroundings and the celestial influences operating at his birth.[5]

In their physics, Dee's early notes are quite traditional, emphasizing the Aristotelian physics of four primary qualities that was the basis of most traditional astrology. While there is a division in the Aristotelian scheme between the incorruptible heavens and the corruptible sublunar sphere of the four elements, Aristotle nevertheless acknowledged a certain continuity between the two realms by which the order and alterations in the terrestrial world are derived from the motions of the eternally moving celestial bodies.[6] The ultimate causes of the changes that occur in the mutable elemental sphere are the heavenly bodies which generate heat through the influence of their rays and their motion.[7] While Aristotle was certainly no theorist of astrology, which was not developed in its classic Western form until the Hellenistic period, his physics did provide later astrologers with the theoretical basis for describing and accounting for celestial influences. In the *Mathematicall Praeface* for instance, Dee cites a collection of Aristotelian texts in defense of astrology (*MP*,b.iij).

An echo of this physics is found at the very beginning of Ptolemy's

Tetrabiblos in conjunction with his appeal to the obvious connection of the sun with variations in climate and weather in defence of astrology. The most basic changes on earth, those things which most directly affect life, seem to be directly related to variations in the degrees of heat, cold, humidity, and dryness, and by implication, to the influence of the sun. Ptolemy then generalizes this observation to include all of the planets and stars among those celestial bodies affecting the earth.[8] Continuing a passage that surely inspired Dee's notes on man's relation to his environment and to the heavens, Ptolemy claims that the germination and fruition of the seed of plants and animals are moulded by celestial influences to the same extent as are meteorological phenomena.[9]

The association of astrology with Aristotelian physics was reinforced by Arabic texts which transmitted much astrological thought to the Latin West. The astrological work of Abū Ma'shar (787–836; first Latin translation ca. 1120), with which Dee was familiar, presented astrology as a valid natural science in the Aristotelian sense.[10] Abū Ma'shar's ideas in turn reflect the teachings of the Harranians or 'Sabaeans' in which astrology was developed within the context of Aristotle's physical works (the *Physica*, *De caelo*, *De generatione et corruptione*, and *De meterologia*).[11]

Another group of Dee's manuscript jottings, recording ideas from his readings and his own thoughts on the soul, belong to this context of an early phase of an Aristotelian physics and a naturalistic interpretation of man's place in the order of nature.[12] Most of the notes seem to be based upon various works of Aristotle, who with one exception is the only author cited, and the emphasis throughout is on aspects of Aristotle's philosophy relevant to the nature of the soul.[13] The most outstanding feature of the notes is their critical and even negative character regarding the accepted views of Christian theology on the immortality and spirituality of the human soul. The general tenor of the Aristotelian propositions noted by Dee emphasizes the unitary nature of man that results from the natural generation of his body and soul, rather than a dualistic nature composed of matter and spirit.[14]

Dee questions the idea that the soul is eternal or that it is an incorporeal form joined to a material body contrary to its own nature; instead, he thinks that it is a quality or form of that body.[15] Because the soul is present in the seed and has need of the body for its operations according to Aristotle, Dee concludes that it cannot be something eternal added to the mortal body from without.[16] The unity of the soul and the body, and the dependence of the soul on the body are further indicated by the nature of the intellect. Although reason has been considered an indication of the immortality and spirituality of the soul because it is the distinguishing characteristic that differentiates man from the other animals, reason is in fact nothing other than the power of leaping from one imagination or cognition to another.[17] The intellect, furthermore, is dependent upon the senses and the sensible conditions of things for its operation, which indicates that the intellect is a functional part of the body and, therefore, mortal along with the body.[18] Dee's notes on the soul, with their supposition of a naturalistic interpretation of the soul as a material form of the body, seem to deny any dualistic division of the cosmos into separate realms of nature and spirit subject to different laws and to make the soul a natural inhabitant of the physical universe and subject to the laws of that universe.[19] As such, these notes suggest that Dee had read extensively in Aristotelian natural philosophy by the early 1550s and strengthen the indications that the orientation of his early natural philosophy and astrology was fundamentally Aristotelian in their physics and anthropology.

ASTROLOGICAL PHYSICS AND OPTICS

According to Dee's early astrological physics, to summarize the very scant evidence, the heavens cause and order all change in the elemental world, the impression of rays of celestial virtue through motion and light generating primary qualities. These basic ideas are continued in the *Propaedeumata aphoristica*. Whatever moves in the world is maintained in motion by the species of motion, and since motion is most proper to the celestial bodies, all motion in the terrestrial world is caused and ordered by the heavens.[20] In the same way, it is the light of the celestial bodies that excites the action of all qualities, the most important of which is the heat of the sun that causes the changes of the seasons (*PA*, XVIIII, XXII, CII, CVII).[21] Finally, the development of the seed of living things is conditioned by their natural habitat and the forces emanating from the heavens (*PA*, XXI). In an even more general sense the *Propaedeumata* continues Dee's early concern with astrological physics. In the *Propaedeumata* Dee does not deal with techniques of judicial astrology but elaborates his early views on astrological physics into a conception of nature that will provide a theoretical foundation for astrology.

This elaboration of Dee's theory of astrology involves two basic components: a naturalistic causality that is constant and uniform, and a mathematical method for studying the operation of this causality. These two components are intimately related, for the method depends upon the nature of the causality that Dee proposes and, as I shall argue, this in turn derives from certain cosmological assumptions about the fundamental causes and processes of the universe. Both of these components derive from Dee's adoption of certain medieval optical theories. The development of Dee's mature astrology in the *Propaedeumata* is directly related to the emergence of an interest in optics and Roger Bacon in his readings in the mid-1550s, which will be examined following a discussion of the *Propaedeumata*.

Nature, according to Dee, began with the creation, and the distinctive features of the universe are the result of the character of that creation. The creation of the world from nothing took place contrary to the laws of reason and of nature, so that created things can never be reduced to nothing unless it is through the power of God again working in exception to the laws of nature and reason (*PA*, I). Dee implicitly assumes here that the operation of the universe is rational and governed by an inviolable natural law. Any normal changes that occur in the universe can only be accomplished through the agency of natural processes and causes (*PA*, II). Dee still regarded the first aphorism on the creation as the most important when, in 1574, he explained that it was the firm foundation and the origin of all the others, which together served to develop the implications of that basic proposition.[22] In its normal course of operation, therefore, nature is entirely regular and predictable; for unless the power of God intervenes, all phenomena are subject to the laws of reason and nature. This regularity is best exemplified in the heavens, where the eternal immutability of the fixed stars and the constant and uniform motion of the seven planets describe a marvellous harmony (*PA*, LXXV).[23] This leads Dee to liken the universe to a lyre, whose harmonious relation of notes and chords best exemplifies the way in which the infinite variety of the parts of the universe are interrelated among themselves in an accord and unity, so that occurrences in one part influence all other parts through sympathy, or consonance, and antipathy, or dissonance (*PA*, XI, XII).

These interrelationships extend throughout nature, and while some are apparent there are many that are latent or hidden (*PA*, III). As an example of the hidden mechanism of nature, God has provided man with the magnet which can act and influence things at a distance and can even project its rays through solid bodies (*PA*, XXIIII). This projection of rays of active power is a property of all things, for

> whatever exists in actuality spherically projects into each part of the world rays, which fill up the universe to its limit. Whence every locality in the world contains rays of all things existing in it in actuality. (*PA*, IIII)

Although both substance and accident emit such rays of virtue, substantial species are much more excellent than accidental species; and the species of incorporeal substances are far more effective than those of corporeal things (*PA*, V). Emitted rays differ in their effective virtues according to the different nature of the things from which they emanate, but the effects of similar rays will also differ according to differences in the material upon which they act (*PA*, VI, VII). The influences of the species of bodies are thus not absolute but depend upon the relation of the nature of the species to the context in which they act; the nature of those species can, therefore, only be determined from their effects. For an effect to take place there must be some similarity between the nature of the agent and that of the patient, but if they are both exactly alike no change can or will occur (*PA*, VIII).

The natures of the stars and planets also emit species, whose characteristics, like seals, are imprinted on matter by virtues similar to the unseen virtues of the magnet (*PA*, XXVI). Thus, occult rays of virtue emitted by the stars spread throughout the universe and penetrate everything, regardless of whether it is solid or diaphanous (*PA*, XXV, XXVII).[24] Whatever moves in the world is moved by the species or virtue of motion, which most properly pertains to the eternal, uniform motion of the celestial bodies; consequently, the heavens excite and order all inferior motions (*PA*, XVI, XVII). Since the virtues projected by the celestial bodies are the cause of all that happens in the universe, all things that exist in the elemental world are the effects of the total harmony of the heavens (*PA*,

CXIIII). Differences in the nature of the sublunar material, however, combine with the astral virtues to modify the absolute nature of celestial influences, so that the diversity of effects in the elemental sphere is the result of the interaction of the passive inclinations of 'the diversity of material things and the differing operation of stellar rays' (*PA*, CXIII). All entities and events, while deriving from common causes and influences, will nonetheless have an absolute individuality because

> there is such a conjunction of rays from all the fixed stars and planets upon every point of the whole universe at any moment of time that another conjunction which is in every way like it can exist naturally at no other point and at no other time.
> (*PA*, LI)

Because the parts of man's body and his humours and spirit are formed of a certain proportion of the elements, the influence of astrological forces on the elements will influence individual men. While the potentialities of any individual are derived from the parents and are present in the seed from which he grows, the development of these characters is induced and conditioned by sidereal influences (*PA*, XX, XXI). The senses are the witnesses of the sensible rays flowing from things, but all other species also affect us and 'show themselves to us principally in our imaginative spirit, just as they coalesce in a mirror, and act in us wondrously' (*PA*, XIII, XIIII). Dee concludes that these elemental and celestial sympathies establish and maintain the orderly continuity of natural occurrences throughout the universe and are the foundation of man's knowledge of nature (*PA*, CXIX, CXX). While Dee quotes Hermes Trismegistus at this point, the quotation is from the *Iatromathematica*, a collection of precepts of astrological medicine that circulated widely well before the Renaissance. This is one among the 'popular hermetica' containing antique occult lore but devoid of the religious and philosophic content of the *Corpus hermeticum* upon which Renaissance Hermetism was based.[25]

These radiations of virtues or species thus provide Dee with a fundamental mechanism of causality that is entirely natural and predictable.[26] Terrestrial events are not subject to the will or whim of planetary demons or governors but determined by the regular and predictable virtues constantly emanating from celestial objects. His general conception of the cosmos is one in which all things are related to each other by a structure of relationships and sympathies resulting from the emanation of species (*PA*, IX, X). Dee uses species, virtues, and rays almost interchangeably, and they are closely connected. Species are the forms and configurations of the essences or qualities of things, while virtue refers to the active quality or efficacy which enables these species to impress themselves upon and change things. It must be emphasized that these influences are of no one specific kind. They emanate from all aspects of all things, and range from the sensible to the completely occult. It is clear that the most important and potent species are also the most recondite (*PA*, CX). These are the foundation and, in a sense, the soul of the world; for 'the insensible or intelligible rays of the planets are to the sensible rays as is the soul of something to its body' (*PA*, CXI). Not that Dee's universe is animistic in the spiritual sense; just as the human soul, though non-spiritual and mortal but also unseen, orders and motivates the behavior of the body, so these occult species order and excite the phenomena of nature.

The entirely natural, regular, and predictable character of astrological causality is emphasized by Dee's conviction that, although astral virtues are occult, there is nothing mysterious about their operation. While the magnet indicates that unseen powers emanate from bodies and act at a distance, light provides an illustration of the manner in which all species are propagated. Just as in the celestial world 'it is the prerogative of the first motion that without it all other motions should become quiescent, so it is the faculty of the first and chief sensory form, namely, light, that without it all other forms could do nothing' (*PA*, XXII). This aphorism is crucial because its implications provide the foundation for the mathematical method that Dee will develop for treating astrological causality.

The activity of all qualities is derived from and dependent upon light, just as the prototype and cause of all motions is the motion of the *primum mobile*. The species and virtues of all qualities are thus assumed to propagate themselves in the same way as light is propagated. Light is a visible model that serves to represent the emanation of all virtues and species, including astrological influences. Traditional optical theory, with which Dee was familiar, supposed that light propagated itself in all directions from its source by a process of self-reproduction through which the species produces a likeness of itself in the surrounding medium, a process that is then multiplied throughout the entire medium. The assumption that this diffusion could be represented as occurring in straight lines, or rays, was the basis for the mathematical study of light according to the rules of geometrical optics or perspective.[27] Dee's description of the diffusion of species as rays indicates that he considered that their behaviour was also subject to the rules of optics (*PA*, IIII). As Dee later emphasized, perspective concerns not only light but 'all Creatures, all Actions, and passions, by Emanation of beames perfourmed. Beames, or naturall lines, [here] I mean, not light onely . . . but also other *Formes*, both *Substantiall*, and *Accidentall*, the certaine and determined active Radiall emanations' (*MP*,b.j). The propagation of the species of any celestial body will follow exactly the propagation of the light from that same body, so that the behaviour of light is a visible model of the behaviour of the rays that propagate astral virtues, and optics thereby becomes a general science for the study of astrological influences. What began in the early 1550s as a vague idea that the agents of astrological influences were some kind of rays has now been developed, under the influence of concepts derived from Dee's study of optics in the mid-1550s, into the very precise idea of astrological causality that appears in the *Propaedeumata*.

A basic cosmological assumption provides Dee with the principle that allows him to consider the diffusion and behaviour of species and that of light as identical, and thus allows him to extend optical principles to the study of all influences. This assumption is that light was the first form whose diffusion generated body or corporeity by drawing dimensionless first matter into three dimensions.[28] This radiation of light gives the universe a fundamental unity and is the foundation of a physics of light according to which 'radiation is the universal instrument of natural causation' such that all other forms or species behave in the same way that light does.[29] Dee speaks several times of light as the earliest, noblest, and principal quality of the universe, which strongly indicates that he presupposed this cosmology as the basis for the causal mechanism he develops in the *Propaedeumata* (*PA*, XXII, XV). In the *Mathematicall Praeface* he also emphasizes the importance of perspective or optics 'bycause of the prerogative of *Light*, beyng the first of Gods Creatures . . .' (*MP*,b.j). This should not imply, however, that all species are conveyed by light or that there is no emanation of influences in the absence of visible light. 'The rays of all stars are double: some are sensible or luminous, others are of more secret influence,' and in a number of places Dee is careful to distinguish occult rays from specifically sensible rays such that they are not to be equated or considered to depend upon the presence of visible light (*PA*, XXV, XIIII, XLIX, XCIIII).

There may be some question whether Dee actually follows through on the optical analogy, for he does not consider how the rays are received. In the medieval optical tradition upon which he drew, a lens or, in the case of sight, some organ of vision was necessary to translate the rays into an image.[30] However, Dee speaks of both optics and catoptrics, the latter referring specifically to the science of mirrors (*PA*, XLVIII, LII). When he speaks of optics, he refers merely to the general geometric study of rays, rather than specifically to sight. The specific analogy he has in mind is that of focusing mirrors, by which the rays of the sun can be focused in a cone, so that at the vertex the convergence of the rays concentrates their energy to produce heat and even combustion. By analogy he could conceive of the rays of astral influences converging in cones, so that their form, whether it is heat or some other species, is impressed upon the matter at the vertex.

Dee's study of optics was not only the basis for the precise idea of astrological causality developed in the *Propaedeumata* but also, because optics was the mathematical study of rays, provided the basis for a mathematical method of astrology. After relating stellar virtues to light rays and discussing the nature and operation of these rays of influence, Dee goes on to set forth the place of mathematics in the study of astrology.[31] Dee appeals for more and increasingly accurate astronomical observations to be made in the interests of astrology. It is necessary for the astrologer to know the true size not only of the earth but also of the planets and all the fixed stars (*PA*, XXX). Dee claims that the rays emanating from any planet or star to any external point will take the form of a right circular cone, with the vertex at the external point, the base formed by the luminous portion of the surface of the star, and the axis passing from the vertex through the centre of the star (*PA*, XXXIII).[32] Dee implies that this configuration can be used to determine the sizes of celestial bodies (*PA*, XL). He must establish the true distances of the planets and fixed stars at all times from the centre of the earth, as well as the altitude of clouds and other atmospheric phenomena that impede or alter the passage of rays (*PA*, XXXI).[33] It is also particularly necessary to know the angles of incidence made by the rays of any fixed star or planet with all other places on earth at the same moment that these celestial bodies are perpendicularly above the observer (*PA*, XXXII). All these measurements are important because they determine the size of the base and the length of the axis of the cone of rays influencing the earth (*PA*, XXXIX). While Dee claimed that in the *Propaedeumata* he had 'Mathematically furnished up the whole Method . . .' of astrology, his remarks are not very specific (*MP*,b.iij^v). He had, however, already worked on the problem of making these measurements and did later publish the method he had developed as early as 1551.[34] In the *Propaedeumata* his intention seems to have been to provide only an outline of the principles and method of astrology.

The most important implication for the study of astrology drawn by Dee from the mathematical treatment of celestial influences is that, knowing the sizes and relative distances of the celestial bodies from the earth, it is possible to determine the differing strengths of the influences of astral virtues. In particular, the dimensions of the cone of rays, the length of its axis and the size of its base, determine the amount and strength of the influence acting on particular points on earth. Rays along the axis of the cone of rays from a star or planet to the point on earth are strongest, and the other rays in the cone will be stronger with respect to the depth of the portion of the star from which those rays emanate (*PA*, XXXIIII).[35] With regard to stars both smaller or greater than the earth, rays of all types impress themselves more strongly on the earth as the star is closer to the earth than when the distance between the source and the object is greater (*PA*, XXXVII, XXXVIII).

Although it seems quite clear that the influence of the rays from a nearer source would be stronger than those from a more distant source, this last rule is not unequivocal, for it is theoretically conceivable that a longer cone could contain more forceful rays. As Dee says,

The longer luminous right cones of a star are, for certain
reasons, stronger than the shorter ones; but for other reasons
they are far weaker. They can be recognized as stronger,
indeed, from the fact that luminous bases are greater and again
from the fact that their angles with the vertical are less. From
these two causes together, the following principle arises: that in

longer cones more abundant rays, not only incident but also reflected, are more concentrated; hence a greater force is exerted about such a vertex. But naturally and simply, the nearness of the agent to that upon which it acts makes the shorter cones stronger. (*PA*, XLIII, cf. LXXXVIII[1])

Dee's position is clear but he seems to present both possibilities because they were both stated in his sources.[36]

For practical purposes Dee accepts a basic rule that posits some sort of relation of direct proportion between the size and proximity of the source of a celestial influence in relation to the object and the strength of that influence, which is as close as he comes to developing a concrete mathematical expression for the determination of the strengths of astrological influences. Dee further states that influences that strike perpendicularly will be stronger than oblique rays, and rays from a slower moving source will be focused longer and make a stronger impression (*PA*, LIIII, LV). From the different combinations of these three things – that is, distance, angle of incidence, and velocity – arise a multitude of ways in which the forces of the stars and planets are exercised so that they all have a variety of potency and significance, which, by implication, can be calculated (*PA*, LVI, XC).

As an example of how his method should be applied, Dee discusses the heat produced by the celestial bodies. All stars that give off light are also causes of heat, and the sun, because it is the major source of light, is the 'chief producer of sensible and vital heat' (*PA*, XCIIII, XCV). Dee suggests that the value of one hundred be assigned to the most intense heat produced by the rays of the sun when it is closest to the earth and when the axis of the cone of its rays is perpendicular to a given point on earth (*PA*, XCVI). From this base figure, it is then possible to determine the degree of heat produced by the sun at other points on earth at the same time or when the sun is in different positions (*PA*, XCVII, XCVIII). By this same procedure, the degree to which the heating power of the other planets and stars is less than that of the sun can also be determined through a comparison of the dimensions of the visual cones of the planets and stars with the dimensions of the sun's visual cone. In this way, the precise force exerted by celestial bodies at any time and at any place on earth can be calculated (*PA*, C). Again, Dee implies a relation of direct proportion between

the dimensions of the cone of rays and the intensity of the astrological virtues. Thus, the varying strength of not just heat but
of all celestial influences can be determined with mathematical
precision.

The moon has an important place in astrology along with the
sun, for

> as LIGHT and MOTION are the most distinctive properties
> of heavenly bodies, so, among the planets, the Sun surpasses
> all others in its proper LIGHT, and the MOON is superior to
> all the rest in the briskness of its proper MOTION. Therefore
> these two are rightly judged to be the most excellent of all the
> planets. (*PA*, CII)

The moon is also associated with humidity as the governor of the
effects of humidity, so that, as heat accompanies the light of the
sun, 'so, by a wonderful analogy, an effective and governing force
of moisture is joined with the moon's motion' (*PA*, CIII, CIIII).
As with heat, Dee implies that the effects of humidity can be calculated and are stronger in relation to the greater proximity of the
moon and the velocity of its motion (*PA*. CV).[37] Similar methods
should also be applied to determining the specific influences and
their magnitudes for all other celestial bodies (*PA*, CXV, CXVIII).

According to Dee's theory, therefore, differences in astrological
effects are the result not only of the different natures of the species
and virtues emitted by the various celestial bodies but also of the
varying strengths with which these influences are impressed upon
matter. If more than one planet operates at any one time, the
astrological effect will depend upon a combination of influences.
Dee indicates that the nature of the combination can be determined
by the art of graduation, which refers to Roger Bacon's *De graduationibus rerum compositionum*, a copy of which Dee had in 1556 and
which is the basis for his own treatment of the same subject in the
Mathematicall Praeface (*PA*, XIX, XC).[38] According to the rules of
Bacon, which Dee clearly adopts, like qualities combine in mixtures
producing an additive strengthening of the quality, while in a
mixture of opposite qualities (e.g., hot–cold or wet–dry) the weaker
negates an equal degree of the stronger leaving a single quality
diminished in degree by the degree of the weaker quality.[39] Thus,
knowing the strengths of particular celestial qualities, the astrologer
can calculate the nature and strength of the quality resulting from

the combined influence of two planets. If more than two planets are involved, the same rules can be applied to successive pairings until a single resultant quality is determined. It might seem that this would involve impossibly complex and extensive calculations if all or even a group of planets act together with each varying in strength, but Dee shows that the possible permutations and combinations are strictly finite, although they do run to five figures (*PA*, CXVI, CXVII).[40] In the ideal realization of Dee's programme the calculations would in fact be close to infinite, because not only the planets but all the stars need to be considered at each moment and for all locations (*PA*, LI, CXVII).

What has emerged in the *Propaedeumata* is an astrological physics in which Dee has developed and elaborated his earlier ideas with much greater detail and precision concerning the mechanism of astrological influence and has also developed a method for quantifying the strength of astral virtues and mathematically determining the nature and strength of astrological effects, thereby fusing his interest in astrology with his early interest in mathematics. Much of Dee's general theory can be traced to standard works on astrology and to Renaissance formulations of astrological theory, despite the fact that Dee rejects or minimizes the usual components of astrological prediction: the constellations, the aspects, the houses, ascendants, and so forth. These sources could have provided Dee with a vague notion of rays of force analogous to light as the mechanism of astrological influence, which is present in Dee's astrological notes from the very beginning. These works do not, however, account for all the details of Dee's theory. Most important, they do not apply the mathematical treatment, which is characteristic of Dee's mature astrology, to the diffusion of virtues. It is in this regard that Dee's study of optics in the mid-1550s provides the essential foundation for the astrology of the *Propaedeumata* and the development of Dee's early natural philosophy in general.

OPTICS, MATHEMATICS, AND NATURE

The optical works that Dee began to collect and study in the mid-1550s are almost entirely medieval Latin or Latin translations of Arabic treatises, and in many cases they are by authors, such as al-Kindī, Robert Grosseteste, and Roger Bacon, for whom optics was not just the science of ray geometry but also an integral part of a natural philosophy.[41] There was a long tradition of speculation in theology, metaphysics, and epistemology in which light served metaphorical and symbolic functions, deriving ultimately from Platonic and Neoplatonic sources and often referred to as light metaphysics. In the texts that Dee used, however, light is not a metaphor or a symbol but a visible manifestation of the radiation of natural powers.[42] For these authors optics was clearly associated with astrology because optical phenomena were considered the model or prototype of physical causality. These ideas supplied Dee both with a concrete mechanism of astrological influence and with a rationale for applying mathematics to the study of physics, enabling him to place astrology on what he considered was a scientific basis and to establish his credentials as a natural philosopher.

The medieval tradition of optically based natural philosophy began with al-Kindī (d. ca. 873), who continued the Neoplatonic view of being as a hierarchy of perfection produced by emanation from the One analogous to the radiation of light, but, unlike Neoplatonic light metaphysics, he considered radiating light as corporeal.[43] On this foundation al-Kindī's *De radiis*, or *Theorica artium magicarum*, presents a natural philosophy in which astrological and magical effects are explained through the action of astral and other forces propagated as rays.[44] Dee's dependence on the *De radiis* was very close, including the borrowing of specific language.[45] According to al-Kindī, the proper natures and conditions of the stars are projected by rays emitted by the stars, the rays of each star differing from those of other stars in their nature and effects as the natures of the stars differ from one another. All terrestrial events derive from the total harmony of the heavens, since the rays of all stars fill the universe and fall ubiquitously upon the earth. All local events have their own individuality, however, because the totality of celestial influences will differ in particular instances according to the changing aspects of the heavens and the differing passive tendencies of the material affected.[46] Differences in the strength of different rays were recognized by al-Kindī, hence rays that fall directly from the center of a star to the center of the earth are stronger than those that fall obliquely, as are those from a source closer to the object affected.[47] These differences in the force of various rays are a common sense assumption for al-Kindī, however, and are neither based upon a mathematical theory nor subject to mathematical treatment.[48] Dee's conception of the nature and operation of astral influences as stellar rays were quite dependent upon some of the formulations that he found in al-Kindī's treatise, but these were only contributory elements to his theory of astrology. In Dee's theory, stellar rays are subject to geometric treatment because they are an aspect of a general cosmology in which an essential light is the formative and structural principle of the universe – a cosmology most explicitly developed by Robert Grosseteste.

John Dee's knowledge of Robert Grosseteste (1168/70–1253) was limited to what he was able to find in a few of the short works that Grosseteste devoted to a natural philosophy based upon optical principles.[49] From the ideas presented in the *Propaedeumata*, what Dee seems to have found in those works was the idea of a physics, in which light is the fundamental causal principle, that provided him with the key for the development of an astrological physics.[50] According to Grosseteste, the universe was the result of the union of a formless prime matter and light, which were the first things created by God. Although only a simple form, this essential light, of which visible light is only an aspect, had by its nature the function of diffusing and multiplying itself and other agents associated with it in every direction instantaneously, so that a point of light could produce a sphere of any size.[51] The essential function of light was to be the basis of spatial dimension and physical extension, and to be the original physical cause of all natural movement and change.[52] Through its self-diffusion light produced the physical universe and generated all the forms of that universe. The universe is a unified structure because all forms and all causal agents are related to and ultimately derived from the first essential light, and it is through light, and influences that behave as light does, that the more perfect celestial bodies act upon the earth.[53]

Mathematics had a great appeal for Grosseteste because the clarity and self-evidence of its premises gave assurance of the certainty of its demonstrations and conclusions.[54] This certainty is also conveyed to optics, the laws of which are derived *a priori* from the principles of geometry.[55] Despite the abstract nature of pure mathematics, it could be applied to the study of the world of experience because Grosseteste's cosmology implied that mathematical relations actually existed as quantitative aspects of physical things.[56] In Grosseteste's universe, light was the principle and model of all natural operations, including the emanation of the species and virtues of things; hence all causes of natural effects operate as light does by lines, angles, and figures. The qualitative differences in effects are, therefore, the result of quantitative differences in the multiplication of virtues and species that are subject to geometric study according to the laws of optics, or perspective.[57]

Geometric optics thereby becomes the basis and key for a mathematical philosophy of nature, which includes and has implications for astrology.[58] Not only do the heavens influence terrestrial things, it is also that this influence is propagated by the multiplication of species and is, consequently, subject to mathematical study.[59] Besides the varying configurations of the heavens, the differing strengths of celestial influence are a factor in the differences in the effects caused by the stars. A virtue will act more strongly if it is concentrated rather than diffused through refraction or reflection, or if it strikes perpendicularly rather than obliquely. The rays of influence converging from the visible portion of a celestial body to a point on earth form a cone, whose dimensions will vary with respect to the distance between the star and the earth. Although Grosseteste clearly thought that the influence and effects of celestial rays are stronger as the source is nearer to the earth and, consequently, as the cone is shorter, he also considered that it could rationally be argued that the rays of a longer, narrower cone were more concentrated and nearer to the perpendicular and, therefore, of greater influence and stronger effect than those in a short, wide cone.[60] This and similar considerations in Roger Bacon are the source of Dee's ambiguity regarding the relative strengths of the influence acting through a short or a long cone.

Robert Grosseteste thus presents the exact configuration of elements – a physics of light, astral influences as rays that behave as light, and a mathematical interpretation of nature according to geometric optics based upon the behavior of light as the model for all natural operations – that was crucial to Dee's theory of astrology. For the elaboration of these ideas, and those he took from al-Kindī, Dee relied most heavily upon Roger Bacon (ca. 1214/20–ca. 1292). In Bacon's hands Grosseteste's physics of light is divorced from its metaphysical and cosmological context and is systematically developed 'into a comprehensive doctrine of physical causation.'[61] More expansively than Grosseteste, Bacon continually emphasized the importance of mathematics as the most certain means of demonstrating the connections between events when applied to the evidence of experience.[62] From Grosseteste's cosmology, Bacon derived his notion that the efficient causes of every action in nature are virtues or species propagated by the qualities of substances.[63] Nature has an essentially mathematical structure because the effects of a quality are propagated by a multiplication of the species of that quality with respect to lines, angles, and figures through any medium, whether it is translucent or opaque.[64] From a spherical body such a multiplication takes the form of a cone of rays converging from the surface of the agent to a vertex on the affected object.[65] Throughout nature there is a reciprocal influence of forces from various agents and particularly from the celestial bodies to events and effects in the elemental sphere. Mathematics is thus necessary not only for a knowledge of the positions and movements of the planets and stars but also for the study of astrological effects.[66] This mathematical study of celestial influences involves the determination of the relative strengths of various influences by the laws of optics. Grosseteste's formulae for the determination of such strengths are repeated by Bacon, with the exception that he clearly maintains, despite his presentation of arguments to the contrary, that a shorter cone will have a greater effect than a longer cone.[67]

The idea that light was a model or an agent of natural causation continued to be employed in texts on optics, natural philosophy, and philosophy after Bacon's time, but it is unlikely that any other sources could independently have offered enough for the development of the ideas in the *Propaedeumata*. Dee was familiar with the work of Ibn al-Haytham, which was the major source of geometrical optics in the Middle Ages, and with the *Perspectiva* of Witelo (b. ca. 1230) and the *Perspectiva communis* of John Pecham (d. 1292), which were the major Latin text books of mathematical optics that continued to be influential into the early seventeenth century.[68] Both Witelo and Pecham reflect the influence of Grosseteste and Bacon, particularly in the understanding of light or species as corporeal, which remained the predominant view of European writers on optics.[69] Yet these works restrict their concern to geometrical optics rather than an optically based natural philosophy and offer no explicit suggestion that optics provides a key to physics, let alone any application to astrology. Likewise, Dee could have found some, but not all or even the most characteristic, of the elements that he developed in the *Propaedeumata* in the more fully Neoplatonic light metaphysics given currency in the Renaissance by Marsilio Ficino (1433–99) concomitant to his revival of Neo-platonism. Although Ficino suggests that astrological influences are conveyed by the radiation of light and other forces, the possibility that light serves as a model of physical causation is not pursued to the mathematical study and manipulation of celestial rays by optics.[70] Even if Dee had studied Ficino and other Renaissance Neoplatonists at this point in his career, there is no evidence that he gave to any the attention he devoted to medieval optical works. Ficino's astrological practice in which music, chants, and images capture not a corporeal radiation but the immaterial spirit of celestial beings is of quite a different character than the astral physics of the *Propaedeumata*.[71]

The theory of astrology in the *Propaedeumata* thus reflects an effort of intellectual archaeology through which Dee recovered a tradition of optically based natural philosophy that had continued in only attenuated form after its culmination in Roger Bacon. In combi-nation, al-Kindī, Grosseteste, and Bacon provided the foundations on which Dee was able to build the theory of astrology that he developed in the *Propaedeumata*. Yet al-Kindī did not suggest that the mathematical definition and study of radiation was relevant in an astrological context, and although Grosseteste and Bacon implied that astrological influences were subject to study by the philosophy of the multiplication of species, they never systematically developed the full implications of their ideas for astrology. It was left to Dee, who in his early years was most intensively interested in both mathematics and a causal mechanism for astrological physics, to take these ideas out of the contexts in which he found them and weld them into a theory specifically focused on the problem of astrology.

Other than as the serendipitous result of Dee's interest in old manuscripts leading him to fall upon the ideas of al-Kindī, Grosse-teste, and Bacon and to see their relation to his concerns in astrology, we may well wonder why Dee pursued this intellectual pilgrimage. One very revealing possibility is that the remnants of these ideas that he found in association with what was perhaps the most formidable intellectual challenge to astrology – that of Nicole Oresme (ca. 1320–1382) – suggested to him how the physics of light might serve to counter Oresme's own challenge. An out-spoken critic of astrology in his own day, Oresme's most novel argument against astrological predictions was that the probable incommensurability of the motions of the heavenly bodies rendered impossible the precise prediction of conjunctions, oppositions, quadratures, the entry of planets into different signs of the zodiac, and similar celestial events upon which astrologers were accustomed to base their predictions. In fact, he considered it likely that no two celestial configurations could ever be identical, thereby removing the possibility that astrology could base predictions upon the empirical evidence of the effects of similar configurations in the past.[72]

Despite his opposition to judicial astrology, Oresme did not entirely reject celestial influences which are propagated spherically and act upon a point through a cone whose strength varies with its length and angle of incidence.[73] Oresme clearly drew upon Ibn al-Haytham and Witelo and was familiar with al-Kindī's *De radiis*, of whose determinism and reduction of all causes to the action of rays he was critical.[74] In the *Questio contra divinatores* this optical conception of the propagation of influence is used not as the theoretical foundation for the study of astrological influences but as part of a sustained critique of astrology in the context of a broader critique of all 'occult' causality. Oresme is willing to admit some celestial influence but he limits this to the only sensible features of the heavens, motion and light propagated as rays which also produce heat, and excludes all hidden virtues or influences as assumed by Bacon and Dee. Further, the most he is willing to allow to celestial motion and light is some remote and universal causality, arguing that particular terrestrial effects are sufficiently explained by the more immediate causes of the various configurations of the elements and the character of the material affected. To appeal to unknown and hidden virtues that are more remote and that cannot be linked unequivocally to particular effects is to Oresme to violate the principles of sound natural philosophy.[75]

Dee had access to Oresme's *De proportionibus proportionum* and *Questio contra divinatores* in 1556, but it is not clear whether he studied them with care, the manuscript containing the *Questio* now being lost and the *De proportionibus* bearing no significant annotations.[76] Dee's statement in the *Propaedeumata* that 'There is such a conjunction of rays from all the fixed stars and planets upon every point of the whole universe at any moment of time that another conjunction which is in every way like it can exist naturally at no other point and at no other time' (*PA*, LI), may reflect his acknowledgement of Oresme's ideas on incommensurability.[77] If so, his substitution of calculations of the unique influences of the heavens at each moment by combining the individual strengths of all planetary and stellar influences for the traditional recurrent astrological configurations may be an attempt to develop a theory of astrology that circumvented the problems raised by Oresme. Given the immensity of the number of calculations required by Dee's method, however, Dee's theory does little in practice to challenge Oresme's claim that precise astrological prediction is an impossibility.

The *Propaedeumata*, however, so inadequately deals with the heart of Oresme's critique in other ways that it is unlikely that Dee was directly responding to the *Questio contra divinatores*. Although Dee emphasizes the preeminence of motion and light, he clearly admits a host of 'occult' influences in addition. This failure to confront directly Oresme's critique of 'occult' causality suggests that Dee may not have had a thorough and direct knowledge of Oresme's views, but he may well have received a somewhat different exposure to Oresme's views through a small work, *De his quae mundo mirabiliter eveniunt* by Claudio Celestino, published in 1542 under the auspices of Oronce Finé, who has even been suggested as the actual author.[78] This is an abbreviated but faithful account of Oresme's arguments in the *Quodlibeta* (*De causis miribilium*) that all kinds of extraordinary events commonly attributed to demons or God can be explained by purely natural causes.[79] What is of interest is that Celestino includes a chapter 'De influentiis caelorum' defending astrology against Oresme's attack. Using many of the same Aristotelian texts as Oresme does against astrology, Celestino argues that there are 'occult' influences from the heavens in addition to light and motion affecting all qualities in the elemental world, that influences vary in strength and consequently in their effects, and, citing al-Kindī, that the heavens are the source of all causation.[80] Equally important, Celestino's summary of Oresme's objections is quite inadequate, giving little indication of the depth of Oresme's critique of astrological causality and of the existence of occult virtues.[81]

Several things suggest that this work may have served as one stimulus for Dee's engagement with the issue of astrological causality in the 1550s. Dee met Finé in 1550 and he quotes Celestino in the *Mathematicall Praeface* on the power of perspective to provide the cause for marvels in the context of discussing a 'self-moving' wonder he had seen in Finé's company at St Denis.[82] Even in the likely case that Finé was not the author, the circumstances of Dee's acquaintance with him were an ideal opportunity for him to discuss Celestino's ideas with Dee, which he seems to have accepted. A textual resonance also suggests that Dee knew of Celestino when he was at work on the *Propaedeumata*. Among the propositions condemned as errors in 1277 was one to the effect that fire would not burn if the heavens stood still, implying the dependence of all action in the elemental world on the motion of the heavens. Oresme cites this condemnation in support of his denial of astrological determinism, but Celestino agrees with the proposition and elaborates it to the effect that all motion and the action of all other causes are caused and conserved by the motion of the heavens. Dee very clearly echoes this idea as a key point in supporting the dependence of terrestrial effects on celestial causation.[83] In Dee's rendition there is a noteworthy departure from Celestino. Where Celestino has all terrestrial activity depend on the motion of the heavens, Dee has only terrestrial motion depend on celestial motion and ties the activity of terrestrial qualities to the action of celestial light. This gives an independent role to celestial light in astrological causality and is the foundation for the role perspective plays in his theory. Other than an occasional reference to perspective in providing a natural explanation for apparent marvels, Celestino does not rely much at all on arguments from perspective in his defence of astrology. Finé, however, was interested in optics, publishing a treatise on burning mirrors in 1551, and including with his edition of Celestino's work what may be the earliest printed edition of Roger Bacon's *Epistola de secretis operibus artis et naturae*, in which optical devices are given prominence in the production of natural marvels, on the grounds that it was particularly concordant with Celestino's ideas.[84]

Finé, and through him Celestino, most likely contributed to Dee's concern with astrology and occult causality that had begun in his discussions with Mercator and may also have suggested the relevance of Roger Bacon and perspective theory in general to these issues. By 1555 and 1556 Dee was quite intensively studying Roger Bacon and other authors in which perspective played a significant role, and there is very concrete evidence that the application of optics to physical phenomena that he found well developed only in these authors provided him with the crucial breakthrough he needed to place astrology on what he considered to be a scientific basis. Dee's stated objective in the *Propaedeumata* was to establish 'by rational processes' 'the true virtues of nature' (*PA*,112/13). Although he says that his health has prevented him from providing a true demonstration, he believes that what he provided offered the 'main principles of the science' and the means of 'proceeding demonstratively in the art', which cannot be understood by observation alone (*PA*,112/13). What Dee meant by demonstration is more precisely indicated by the passage on astrology in the *Mathematicall Praeface* where Dee says that astrology is founded 'not onely (by Apotelesmes) τὸ ὅτι, but by Naturall and Mathematicall demonstration τὸ διότι', which he claims he provided in the *Propaedeumata* where he 'Mathematically furnished up the whole method' (*MP*,b.iijᵛ–b.iiij).

Now the distinction between knowledge τὸ ὅτι from effects (Apotelesmes) and demonstrative knowledge τὸ διότι refers to the distinction in Aristotle's *Analytica posteriora* between knowledge of facts and demonstrative science, which is knowledge of the cause or reason for the fact, a distinction traditionally rendered in the Latin West as 'science *quia*' and 'science *propter quid*'.[85] Dee would have been aware of this from his university studies, but a more concrete idea of Dee's thinking on the matter in the 1550s is found in Dee's copy of the *Mathemalogium* by Andreas Alexander, which is heavily annotated and bears a note that Dee read it in 1555 while in Bishop Bonner's house.[86] The *Mathemalogium* is a commentary on mathematics and its treatment and role in the context of Aristotle's logical works. While not very novel, either in its treatment of mathematics or of Aristotle's logic, and following Aristotle's texts very closely, it is interesting in focusing on the importance of mathematics for understanding Aristotle.[87]

Alexander points out that while science *quia* considers effects, science *propter quid* involves the demonstration of necessary conclusions from the causes of things, mathematics being the preeminent example of *propter quid* demonstration because of its certainty.[88] Alexander also considers whether mathematical demonstrations can apply to physical things and to natural philosophy. In the case of some natural phenomena facts and effects can be explained by causal principles drawn from the mathematical disciplines. Optics, or perspective, uses the conclusions of geometry to discover the causes of the facts of vision and of the propagation of light. In a further step, perspective can provide the principles for a knowledge of the causes (*propter quid*) of a phenomenon such as the rainbow, of which the meteorologist has only a knowledge of the facts (*quia*). This process of subordination, by which the conclusions of one of the strictly mathematical sciences become the principles by which another science provides causal knowledge of physical phenomena, creates a linkage between the normally distinct realms of physics and mathematics. Likewise, music is subordinate to arithmetic and astronomy is subordinate to geometry.[89]

Alexander, however, follows the strict Aristotelian position on the limits of mathematical demonstration regarding physical things. Aristotle had placed rather narrow limits on the latitude in which *metabasis*, the transference of principles from one discipline or science to another, was legitimate. True demonstrative knowledge required that the principles upon which the demonstrations are based must be essential attributes of the subject of the science and not imported from some other science. This insistence imposed sharp boundaries between the various sciences, in particular between mathematics and physics. The subordinate mathematical sciences, even though they provide some causal knowledge of natural phenomena, do not provide an exhaustive knowledge of physics because they consider their subjects abstracted from matter and thus take no account of the peculiarities of the sensible physical world.[90] Thus, for Alexander, astronomy is a demonstrative science subordinate to geometry because it considers the planetary bodies only in their dimensions and motions, astrology is neither demonstrative nor mathematical because it concerns the experiential effects of the material of the heavens.[91]

This in itself might seem to be a disappointing conclusion for Dee. However, the physics of light at the foundation of the natural philosophy of Grosseteste and Bacon puts the matter in a different light by subsuming in the domain of natural phenomena subject to treatment by perspective all of the qualitative change and material effects resulting from the multiplication of species. Both Grosseteste and Bacon accept the Aristotelian distinction between knowledge *quia* and knowledge *propter quid*, both maintain a distinction between physics and mathematics without reducing physics to mathematics, but both enlarge the place of mathematics in natural philosophy beyond that implied in Aristotle.[92] One of the central problems with astrology was that other than light, heat, and motion, the celestial influences were occult and insensible. Strictly interpreted, Aristotle's epistemology that all knowledge originated in sense experience was often taken to imply that occult qualities did not exist or, if their existence was admitted on the basis of phenomena such as magnetism, that they could not be studied scientifically. That is, experience of their effects might produce knowledge *quia*, but the occult influences themselves could not be studied as causes to yield knowledge *propter quid*.[93] On the assumption that light was the first corporeal form of the created universe from which all other forms are derived, all natural causation, including occult, takes on the characteristics of light and legitimately, in Aristotelian terms, becomes subject to demonstrative knowledge through the principles of perspective. Yet for both there remained areas of natural philosophy in which empirical knowledge from effects, or demonstration *quia*, provides legitimate knowledge.[94] Likewise Dee maintains that the nature of celestial influences can only be established on the basis of empirical observations of their effects. What perspective provides are the principles for establishing a demonstrative science of how and to what varying degrees celestial influences, once their natures are established, produce the observed effects and from which predictions of future effects can be calculated. In the mid-1550s, then, as Dee was wrestling with the problem of developing a demonstrative science of astrology he read Alexander, where perspective has a prominent place as a bridge to extending mathematical science to natural phenomena, suggesting to him that, if anywhere, it was in works of perspective, which he began collecting and consulting avidly at just this time, that he might find the materials on which to build such a science.[95]

The ability of perspective, through a physics of light, to provide a bridge between the disciplines of mathematics and physics also suggests another reason why Dee turned to this medieval tradition of an optically based natural philosophy. If the *Propaedeumata* was an attempt to elicit better patronage abroad, as the letter to Mercator suggests, one of Dee's concerns may well have been to establish his claims to status as a philosopher, not just as a mathematical teacher and practitioner as he seems to have been considered in England. As Robert Westman has shown, the social and intellectual status of mathematicians was relatively low in the sixteenth century because mathematics, which included astronomy and astrology, had little disciplinary autonomy within the universities and was granted largely a service role in relation to other disciplines. In particular, academic philosophers did not regard mathematicians as competent to speak on physics or other matters of natural philosophy.[96] Court patronage often allowed greater opportunities for intellectuals to cross disciplinary boundaries and forge new intellectual constellations, giving more intellectual scope to mathematicians, but this was not Dee's experience at Edward's court.[97] In the *Propaedeumata* Dee very much assumes the status of natural philosopher and the physics of light provided an ideal foundation from which a mathematician could assert a legitimate claim to speak on the 'true virtues of nature', that is physics, as a natural philosopher (*PA*, 114/115).

OPTICS, MAGIC, AND EMPIRICAL RESEARCH

Of the writers with whom Dee was familiar and from whom he drew specific inspiration, Roger Bacon was preeminent. Bacon's works far outnumber those of al-Kindī or Grosseteste in Dee's collection and contributed not only to Dee's ideas on astrology but served as a powerful source of inspiration for all aspects of his natural philosophy. Unlike al-Kindī and Grosseteste, whom Dee never mentions, Dee acknowledges Bacon and seems to have taken a personal interest in reviving Bacon's reputation and in promoting his ideas. Dee first enunciated his return to Roger Bacon in the prefatory letter to the *Propaedeumata*, where he lists among the works he had previously written a *Speculum unitatis: sive apologia pro fratre Rogerio Bachone anglo* written in 1557 to defend Bacon against the reputation that his science involved the practice of magic and other demonic arts.[98] Dee's concern was not misplaced. A. G. Molland has called attention to the considerable legendary material about Bacon as a magician that circulated in the sixteenth century.[99] Not only did a host of alchemical works circulate under Bacon's name, but his name was also associated in a number of manuscripts with magical works that are plainly demonic.[100] Although some of the legends about Bacon and magic may have had some basis in fact, as Molland shows, Bacon's reputation was distorted by a considerable amount of misinformation. Not only did John Bale describe Bacon in 1548 as a 'juggler and necromantic mage' who consorted with evil demons and performed great marvels 'not by the power of God but by the operation of evil spirits', Bale's list of Bacon's works bears little resemblance to a modern bibliography, giving only twenty-three titles of which a quarter are occult and magical works no longer attributed to Bacon.[101] By 1557 Bale had changed his opinion, Bacon now being a most acute philosopher who 'was possessed of incredible skill in mathematics and devoid of necromancy, although many have slandered him with it', and his list of Bacon's works, comprising eighty-one titles, many of them recognizable, contains none of the magical titles from 1548.[102] Dee's defence that Bacon 'did nothing with the aid of demons but was a great philosopher and accomplished great works naturally and by ways permitted to a Christian man which the unlearned crowd usually ascribe to the wickedness of demons' thus speaks to a very real situation. Whether there was any relation between Bale and Dee in their thinking on Bacon is difficult to determine, but it is clear that in his assimilation of Roger Bacon Dee confronted the issue of the nature of magic and its legitimacy.[103]

What Dee found in Bacon was a distinction between magic as such, which involves the aid of demons and was condemned by Bacon, and the legitimate performance of marvellous feats by human artifice using the secrets of nature as instruments. Others of Bacon's time also attempted to disassociate the practical application of knowledge of the natural but hidden powers of nature, which William of Auvergne referred to as natural magic, from illicit magic employing incantations and ceremonies, and directed at spirits and demons. Bacon avoided any connection of legitimate practices with the term magic, using instead 'wonders' or 'admirable works of art and nature' for those practices which, for convenience, following the common usage of Bacon's time and later, I will call natural magic.[104] The best statement of Bacon's idea of natural magic is the *Epistola de secretis operibus artis & naturae, & de nullitate magiae*, which Dee annotated and intended to have published.[105] An example of the cooperation of artifice and nature with respect to celestial influences, which Bacon was fond of emphasizing, was the use of lenses and mirrors that gathered and concentrated the rays of the sun so as to produce heat and even combustion.[106] In fact, Bacon was fascinated with the variety of effects, ranging from multiplying images, magnification, and the projection of images, in addition to igniting fires, that could be produced with mirrors and lenses.[107] Although many of these effects were not new, being found in reports in antiquity and as part of the conjuring tricks of medieval jugglers, Bacon was interested in them not merely as tricks but as examples of how theoretical knowledge of nature involving the principle of the multiplication of species could be turned to practical ends.[108] In the *De speculis comburentibus* Bacon analysed the propagation of light to determine the physically correct mode of propagation and applied his findings to a discussion of both spherical and parabolic burning mirrors.[109] Bacon did not limit the production of marvellous effects only to mechanical devices. While he condemned incantations, images, and all the rituals of ceremonial magic directed toward demons, he allowed that words can have potent effect when they convey the power of the soul and that characters can be effective if made when celestial dispositions are appropriate. He considered these effects natural because they resulted from the propagation of rays of force and influence by the multiplication of species. Although Bacon was clearly intrigued by the literature of ceremonial magic circulating at his time, he also seems to have sought a naturalistic explanation for magical effects, which he patterned very much on al-Kindī's *De radiis*, in which the effective mechanism in all magic is the action of rays.[110]

The basic astrological premise that the sublunar world is subject to the influences of celestial virtues had practical implications for Dee's natural philosophy in the form of astral magic, and it is not surprising to find a magical element in the *Propaedeumata aphoristica* and that this magic closely resembles Bacon's idea of natural magic.[111] Since the parts of the universe are mutually harmonious, things that are separated can be joined together and things that exist only potentially can be brought into actuality in wondrous ways that nonetheless are natural, and neither violate faith in God, nor detract from Christian piety (*PA*, X). Dee therefore claims that 'wonderful changes may be produced by us in natural things if we force nature artfully . . .' (*PA*, II). With an understanding of the structure and causal mechanism of the cosmos, which is provided in the *Propaedeumata*, and with a knowledge of the correspondence of celestial influences and their effects in the world, man can by his own industry and artifice control these natural forces and manipulate them to produce desired effects (*PA*, XXVI, LXXIII, XCIX). Dee was quite circumspect in anything with overtones of magic; he only hints at talismans and mentions nothing having to do with the power of words.

As with Bacon, optics plays a crucial role in Dee's magic as well as in his astrology because of the conformity of natural causes to the laws of optics (*PA*, XLV). Dee points out that, 'if you were experienced in catoptrics, you would be able, by art, to imprint the rays of any star much more strongly upon any matter subjected to it than nature itself does', which practice is the greatest part of natural magic (*PA*, LII). Through the use of optical devices, particularly mirrors which are the subject of catoptrics, whose effects on celestial rays are determined by the geometric laws of optics, the influences and virtues of the heavens can be modified and manipulated in order to produce predetermined effects (*PA*, XCIX). This magic, since it does not call upon spiritual or demonic powers, is enirely natural and, since it relies for its operation upon optics and Dee's mathematical astrology, is entirely mathematical.[112]

As noted earlier, the knowledge of effects (science *quia*), according to Aristotle, depends on the peculiarities of matter and cannot be entirely accounted for by a mathematical model of causality (science *propter quid*). Bacon accepted the Aristotelian position, and his 'scientia experimentalis', in which experience investigates the conclusions reached by reasoning in other sciences and discovers truths that cannot be reached by reasoning alone, presented his conception of a science of effects.[113] Not only did Dee accept Bacon's idea of 'experimental science' in the *Mathematicall Praeface* and indicate there that the astrologer needs to study celestial influences '(by *Apotelesmes* [effects]) τὸ ὅτι [*quia*]', but in the *Propaedeumata* indicated a number of times the necessity of empirical observations relating elemental effects to celestial dispositions because the exact nature of celestial influences can only be determined by experience and because celestial influences differ in their effects through the different dispositions of matter.[114] The other aspect of Dee's programme to improve astrology was, therefore, the collection of empirical observations of terrestrial events and their relation to particular dispositions of the heavens (*PA*, CXVIII). This is undoubtedly the import of the weather observations that Dee began to make at Louvain and continued to make throughout the rest of his life. These serve as an example of Dee's programme to observe the influences and operations of the heavens in the elemental sphere by relating concrete empirical events to the changing dispositions of the heavens and deriving the nature of the various astral influences from the correlation of these factors. This programme remained largely unfulfilled, for there is no evidence that Dee ever organized the observations that he collected or tried to derive from the correlation of his observations and celestial dispositions any general relationships between changes in the heavens and changes in the weather based upon his astrological theory.

Optical devices play a role in the empirical as well as in the magical aspect of Dee's astrology. In the *Mathematicall Praeface* he says that without perspective astrology cannot be 'naturally Verified', and in the *Propaedeumata* he suggests that catoptrics can be used to investigate the effects of the moon and other planets and stars whose effects, unlike the heat of the sun, are normally too weak for our senses to notice (*PA*, LIII, C). But it is far from clear in the *Propaedeumata* exactly what Dee had in mind both in this regard and in the use of catoptrics to manipulate celestial influences for magical purposes. Dee devoted considerable attention to the study of optics in the late 1550s. He claims to have written 'De tertia & praecipua Perspectivae parte, quae de radiorum fractione tractat' dealing with refraction, which is now lost but may have touched on lenses in addition to the rainbow which was a classic issue in the discussion of refraction (*PA*,116/17).[115] In the same year that he published the *Propaedeumata*, Dee also wrote the *De speculis comburentibus libri 5* of which a fragment survives.[116] The discussion of burning mirrors is another topic with a long history in optical literature, of which Dee collected a great deal.[117] Dee does not demonstrate but rather assumes that a parabolic mirror was the surface necessary to focus the parallel rays coming from the sun to a single point since this was well established in most treatments of burning mirrors. He does claim to give a comprehensive exposition of the subject of parabolic mirrors, and what remains consists of numerous definitions relating to cones, conic sections, and parabolas, and numerous propositions dealing with the relationship of various measures of parabolas, so that given one measure it is possible to derive another dimension or the point of combustion.[118] Parabolic mirrors would seem to be the ideal device for focusing celestial rays at a point both to study them and to impress them more strongly than nature does unassisted.

Like Bacon, Dee was fascinated by all kinds of optical devices and tricks both because they were marvellous but also because they might be profitable (*MP*,b.j^v). At the end of the manuscript on burning mirrors there are also some diagrams pertaining to image formation in concave and convex spherical mirrors and a drawing of a device for measuring and showing the equality of the angles of incidence and of reflection in mirrors.[119] The section of the *Mathemat-*

icall Praeface on perspective discusses many of the optical illusions mentioned in Bacon's *Epistola de secretis operibus* and in addition describes a mirror that Dee acquired from William Pickering that formed an image in front of itself as if it were hanging in the air.[120] Further, William Bourne refers to Dee in conjunction with a discussion of using lenses in combination with a mirror for magnifying images.[121] It appears, therefore, that Dee's astrological theory, based as it was on optics and implying the use of optical devices for both magical and experiential purposes, served as a stimulus to mathematical study, mathematical work in its own right, and the exploration of the practical uses of lenses and mirrors.

Bacon's *Epistola* also mentions alchemy, which he seems to have considered a part of natural magic. In his notes to the *Epistola*, Dee drew upon Bacon's other works to illustrate Bacon's idea of alchemy.[122] According to Bacon, theoretical alchemy is the basis for natural philosophy and both theoretical and practical medicine because it teaches the principles of the generation of all living things from the four elements.[123] To Dee, this undoubtedly struck a responsive chord in terms of the naturalistic tendencies of his early natural philosophy. Practical alchemy, on the other hand, uses these principles to teach how to make higher metals, medicines, and other chemical changes by an art that works better and more copiously than nature does alone, which conforms exactly to Bacon's definition of natural magic.[124] Although Dee does not treat alchemy specifically in the *Propaedeumata*, he hints that there is some relation between his astral magic and 'Astronomia Inferior', a phrase often used in reference to alchemy (*PA*, LII). Dee says that the symbols of this lower astronomy accompany the treatise enclosed in a 'certain Monad', referring to the symbol of Dee's Monad figured on the title page. In the *Monas hieroglyphica*, Dee shows that this symbol contains within it the symbols of all the planets and metals.[125] The title-page of the *Propaedeumata* also indicates that the Monad contains all of the planets and all that wise men seek and seems to refer to the harmonious connections existing between all things in the universe and the ability of the astrologer to join together things which normally exist separately. This interest in finding the unifying principles in nature provides the common theme that relates the *Propaedeumata* and the *Monas hieroglyphica*. From the extensive alchemical entries in the 1556 manuscript lists, the appearance of an alchemical interest in the *Propaedeumata* is not surprising and seems to be related to Dee's study of Bacon, who indicated the connection of alchemy with astrology, natural magic, and mathematics, as suggested by the *Speculum unitatis* in the title of his defence of Bacon.

CONCLUSION

The *Propaedeumata*, despite its brevity and signs of hasty composition, reflects and touches upon a wide variety of issues and subjects. Not only was it the culmination of an interest in astrology that dated from Dee's studies in Louvain; it was also the product of a continuing dialogue of assimilation, adaptation, and debate that Dee carried on with his acquaintances and his books. Dee's early natural philosophy was founded upon a naturalistic conception of the world and of man in which there was little dualism between the natural and the supernatural, and all phenomena were considered natural and self-sufficiently explainable without appeal to the intervention of extra-natural demons, spirits, or intelligences. With respect to astrology, Dee was concerned to find a physics that would provide a mechanism for astrological influence and would place the study of celestial influences on a firm scientific basis. As his thinking developed, the study of medieval optics and his perception of an 'optical physics' in al-Kindī, Grosseteste, and Bacon provided him with a precise mechanism in the form of the emanation of rays of virtue. This optical physics of the emanation of rays provided the key for the development of a mathematical theory of astrology that conformed to the criteria of a demonstrative science and the foundation for a mathematical astral magic. Magic, however, is not the central subject of the *Propaedeumata*. Dee may have been interested in natural explanations and mechanisms for the production of wondrous effects, but in the *Propaedeumata* magic, as an implication of the physics, is tangential to his main concern. While the *Propaedeumata* is predominantly theoretical, Dee's programme for the reform of astrology also implied a significant empirical element where the emanation of rays, again, makes optical devices important instruments for the investigation of the nature of astral influences. Optics thus appears to be the nexus through which Dee's interests in mathematics, astral physics, and natural magic were articulated and elaborated into a coherent natural philosophy.

Dee's natural philosophy and astrology was an eclectic individual creation that does not have very much specifically in common with any distinctly Renaissance philosophy whether Aristotelian, Neoplatonic, or Hermetic. Where we have texts that Dee read during this period, they are texts in which Aristotle is cited as the predominant authority on matters of natural philosophy. It is in this respect that Dee's natural philosophy was basically Aristotelian at this point. Dee showed little concern to approach the Aristotelian texts in terms of their historical context or their linguistic purity, nor did he range over the whole corpus of Aristotelian texts as an authority, so his approach was neither that of the humanist nor that of the professional or scholastic Aristotelian. Instead, he was Aristotelian, as were many others in Charles Schmitt's characterization, in looking to Aristotle either to understand some features of reality or to legitimate his own views.[126] This way of using Aristotle resulted in varied understandings of the world and was often quite eclectic in absorbing other philosophical and scientific ideas.

This feature of Aristotelianism is as apparent in works on astrology as anywhere else. Neoplatonism and Hermetism did not have a privileged claim to support astrology, magic, or a view of nature encompassing occult influences. In the Middle Ages and the Renaissance astrology was accepted by philosophers of many different persuasions and, as a result, was developed upon the basis of different philosophies of nature. Some of the earliest indications of Aristotle's natural philosophy accessible in the Latin West before Latin translations of Aristotle's actual works became available were found in Arabic texts in which astrology was presented in conjunction with an apparently Aristotelian natural philosophy.[127] It is now clear in retrospect that the philosophy of universal emanation that served to relate the celestial and sublunar worlds in some Arabic natural philosophies was not strictly Aristotelian, blurring as it did the clear distinction between the ethereal and the elemental spheres. The emanationism which makes for the similarities among Neoplatonism, the Hermetica, and Arabic Aristotelianism was ultimately Neoplatonic and was absorbed by the Arabs because they were heirs to the Alexandrian tradition of a Neoplatonic interpretation of Aristotle.[128] Unaware of these Neoplatonic contaminations, the Arabs nonetheless considered themselves Aristotelians. Since the understanding of Aristotle in the Latin West was formed as much through the Arab commentators as through Aristotle's texts, Latin Aristotelianism was likewise eclectic and neoplatonizing.[129] The Aristotelian tradition was therefore an important vehicle

through which elements of whatever ultimate philosphical provenance important for a natural philosophy based on a theory of
occult action were made available independently of many of the
other philosophical and religious elements of Neoplatonism and
Hermetism. The Aristotelian context in which these elements were
embedded also meant that they were handled in rather different
ways than when they were found directly in a Neoplatonic or
Hermetic context, and it has become clear that key features of the
Propaedeumaa indicate that Dee was working very explicitly within
the context of an Aristotelian model of natural philosophy and
science.

The fact that Dee's idea of natural magic was derived in close
association with his study of Roger Bacon also should warn us
that an interest in magic is not a specific indicator of a particular
philosophic position in the Renaissance. While magic is associated
with Renaissance Neoplatonic and Hermetic philosophies, Pomponazzi also discusses magic in terms that differ very little in some
respects from Giovanni Pico della Mirandola's discussion of natural
magic.[130] Renaissance occultism was not a monolithic tradition but
had a variety of sources and manifestations.[131] Dee may have found
in the writings of Roger Bacon a philosophical justification for magic
that others in the Renaissance found in the writings of Hermes
Trismegistus and the late antique Neoplatonists.

It would be vain to argue that Dee's work on astrology represents
any contribution to the progressive development of science. His
most fundamental insights were adaptations of medieval ideas
whose only novelty was their resurrection after centuries of obscurity
and relative neglect. His concept of science is Aristotelian, his
natural philosophy is still limited to a qualitative view of nature,
and his ideas on method and 'experimental science' come from
Aristotle with the admixture of Bacon. The significance of Dee's
astrology lies more in its attempt to deal with contemporary criticisms and doubts concerning the validity and precision of astrology
than with its role in any long-term revolution in natural science. In
these terms Dee's astrology was a significant and novel attempt to
develop a physical theory and mathematical method for astrology.
The *Propaedeumata* was a notable exception to the low level of astrological knowledge and the absence of original work and efforts
to reform astrology that characterized England compared to the
continent in the early sixteenth century.[132] In its ingenuity, Dee's

theory compares well with Kepler's proposals for a reformed astrology, and, in its linking empirical observation with a coherent theory and mathematics, it has a good deal more to recommend it than Cardano's collection of particular precepts derived from the analysis of numerous horoscopes.[133]

Part Two

THE *MONAS HIEROGLYPHICA*, 1564

IV

THE HIEROGLYPHICS OF
NATURE

The *Monas hieroglyphica*, published at Antwerp in 1564, is a curious text. The device of the monad (figure 4.1) that appeared on the title-page of the *Propaedeumata* here becomes the central matter, with the text, as Dee puts it, explicating that hieroglyph 'mathematically, magically, cabalistically, and anagogically' (*MH*,113/14).[1] In twenty-four quasi-Euclidean 'theorems' this device of the Monas is geometrically constructed, and then its disassembled parts, both singly and as variously recombined, are shown to have cosmological, astronomical, numerological, alchemical, magical, and mystically spiritual meanings. As a single symbol, the Monas represented to Dee a powerful hieroglyph revealing the unity of created nature and embodying the unity of knowledge about the unity of creation.

Such manipulation and interpretation of symbols became a popular intellectual sport in the sixteenth century. Except for one digression, which Dee characterizes as 'play', indicating an awareness, as did Kepler, that some symbolization is an arbitrary game, Dee attributed great significance to what he was doing in the *Monas*.[2] In the letter of dedication to Maximilian of Habsburg, Dee claims that the *Monas*, despite its slight size, was a work of 'great rarity and remarkable quality', and that philosophers will frequently wish to expend 'intense studies and work, examining its depths' to discover the 'great secret' and the 'philosophical treasures of our monad' (*MH*,114/15, 120/21, 150/51, 186/7). What these secret treasures might be; that is, what specific content and message Dee intended philosophers to extract from his text, is far from clear however. The *Monas* as a text is exceptionally opaque and has remained largely unintelligible to modern commentators who consider it a professional responsibility to grant that it must mean something yet may be inclined to sympathize with Meric Casaubon's confession that 'I can extract no sense nor reason (sound or solid) out of it; neither yet doth it seem to me very dark or mystical'.[3]

It has become customary to consider the alchemical quest for the philosopher's stone the main subject of the *Monas* and to look to alchemy for the elucidation of the text. Dee himself indicated that his Monas pertained to *astronomia inferior*, a very old synonym for alchemy, in both the *Propaedeumata* and the *Monas* (*PA*,LII; *MH*,164).[4] Very shortly after 1600, Thomas Tymme prepared 'A Light in Darkness' and some explanatory notes to serve as an introduction to accompany an English translation of the *Monas* that never materialized, in which the *Monas* is interpreted in alchemical terms.[5] Although Tymme's discussion does provide some assistance, it does not entirely banish the night. This alchemical association was solidified by the adoption of the *Monas* and its symbol almost exclusively by alchemical writers in the later sixteenth and seventeenth centuries.[6]

That the *Monas* is predominantly alchemical has also been the starting point for most modern interpretations of the text, although some broader perspectives have also been suggested.[7] Frances Yates has suggested that within the context of Renaissance Hermetism Dee's *Monas* formulated a kabbalist mathematical alchemy in which the Monas was the magical amulet whose 'unified arrangement of significant signs' 'infused with astral power' would have a 'unifying affect on the psyche' and facilitate a gnostic ascent through the scale of being.[8] Developing another suggestion of Yates, van Dorsten and Yewbrey have argued that the *Monas*, with its dedication to Maximilian Habsburg, may be Dee's proposal for a cosmopolitan, non-sectarian, tolerant religion based on Hermetic occultism or even part of a system of magical government designed to prepare mankind for salvation.[9] Closer to the issue of interpreting the text, Michael T. Walton has suggested the importance of Dee's use of kabbalah in addition to alchemy, and suggests that the Monas was a type of alphabet of nature.[10] While alchemy may be an important component in any understanding of the *Monas*, the fact that it does not exhaust the text indicates that a careful reexamination of the *Monas* may yield further 'rare mysteries'.

Another problem presented by the *Monas* is its relation to Dee's previous thinking. All of the most obvious indications suggest a very strong continuity between the *Propaedeumata aphoristica* and the

Monas hieroglyphica. The title-pages of the two books are almost identical, the symbol of the Monas prominently displayed on each (figures 2.1, 4.2). Besides the association of the Monas with *astronomia inferior* indicated in the *Propaedeumata* (*PA*,LII), which is echoed in the *Monas* (*MH*,164), Dee states in the letter of dedication that he had devoted twenty years' hard work to the 'hermetic' science and that his mind had been 'pregnant' with the *Monas* for seven years (*MH*,136, 146). These indications have generally been taken to indicate that Dee had studied the kinds of things prominent in the *Monas* – kabbalah, alchemy, numerology, Hermetic magic – from 1542, the year he entered Cambridge, and that a fully formulated conception of the *Monas* dates from 1557 or 1558 making the *Propaedeumata* and the *Monas* complementary works within a unified philosophy.[11] Yet the two works are remarkably different in a number of important respects and the lack of any solid evidence that kabbalah, alchemy, or numerology contributed in any significant way to Dee's thinking in the *Propaedeumata* raises the question of identifying what is new in the *Monas* and what circumstances may have elicited this different articulation of ideas.[12]

The *Monas* thus presents several problems in relation to understanding Dee's natural philosophy. The most fundamental is the interpretation and understanding of the text, which will be the focus of the following chapter. With some understanding of the text, we will then proceed to consider the wider significance of the *Monas*, both in terms of its relation to the *Propaedeumata* and the subsequent development of his natural philosophy, and in terms of its implications for any politico-religious programme and Dee's conception of the role of the natural philosopher.

The problems posed by the *Monas* as a text are significantly greater than those of the *Propaedeumata*. With few exceptions, Dee's aphorisms are not difficult to understand in themselves. What was not clear were the problems they were meant to address and how they all fit together. Recovering Dee's sources of inspiration allowed us to reconstruct the larger context of ideas and problems of astrology to which the aphorisms pointed and to visualize how the aphorisms, in a sketchy fashion, reflected a coherent and systematic theory of astral physics and its practical applications. The *Monas*, however, is much more opaque to modern readers because even the individual statements are puzzling, particularly if we accept, as Dee wants us to, that they apply to the physical world. The *Monas* shares many of the characteristics common to occult writing in its division of its potential audience into the vulgar, from whom the secrets of the text must be protected, and the wise and virtuous, to whom the text pretends to disclose great mysteries presented, however, in a tantalizingly obscure and mystifying way to prevent disclosure to the unworthy.[13] The rhetoric of occult writing puts its readers under the burden of agreeing that they understand the text lest they be numbered among the vulgar and creates the paradoxical situation that the text is revealing, through a discourse intelligible only to initiates, mysteries and secrets the initiates already possess.

It is not necessary to assume, however, that Dee's specific message is inaccessible to us because it reflects the secrets of initiates and a lost oral tradition of alchemy to rescue the *Monas* from Casaubon's verdict that it contains 'no sense nor reason'.[14] Dee was very much a bookish intellectual whose thinking was a rich digest of things he read. Regarding alchemy in particular, there is no indication that he actually practised the art before he established residence at Mortlake, where he eventually built elaborate laboratories, sometime after returning to England from Europe in June 1564.[15] As with the *Propaedeumata*, the sources Dee drew upon should go a long way to helping us decode the *Monas*. This reconstruction will perhaps be less complete and satisfying than that accomplished for the *Propaedeumata* for two reasons. First, there does not seem to be as compact and coherent a source of inspiration for the *Monas* as al-Kindī, Grosseteste, and Bacon were for the *Propaedeumata*, which makes it difficult to be sure we have found all the relevant texts that might illuminate the *Monas*. Second, numerology, alchemy, and mysticism – the most troubling aspects of the *Monas* – have a perennial vagueness about them, so that however successful we may be in identifying Dee's sources, a penumbra of indistinctness will always surround the concrete contents of the *Monas*. Beyond specific content, what Dee was trying to do with the content and to accomplish through the *Monas* is primarily a matter of analysing the text itself and attending to what Dee himself says he is doing in the text, of which he gives perhaps more indications than he did for the *Propaedeumata*.

THE *ARBOR RARITATIS* AND HIEROGLYPHICAL WRITING

In the letter of dedication to Maximilian which prefaces the *Monas*, Dee gives his reasons for offering so small a work to the king which go a long way toward revealing Dee's conception of the *Monas*. The first reason is Dee's good will toward Maximilian, whom Dee had seen crowned King of Hungary in Pressburg the preceding September, where he witnessed Maximilian's 'admirable virtues' (*MH*,114/15).[16] The second reason is the 'great rarity and remarkable quality of the gift itself' (*MH*,114/15). Dee attempts to convey the dimensions of this rarity by means of a diagram of the 'arbor raritatis' (figure 4.3). Here Dee combines the Pythagorean 'Y' or crossroads found in Renaissance moral tracts and images designating the choice between a life of virtue or of vice confronting individuals at the beginning of adulthood (figure 4.4) with Roger Bacon's use of a progression of powers of ten to exemplify levels of truth and the 'rarity' of those perfect in wisdom, truth, and science.[17] In Dee's image the choice is between a life devoted to pleasure and profit or a life devoted to philosophy. The earthly path leading to the *abyssus* (hell) has three levels of rarity – *sollicitudo* (cares and anxieties), *fraus* (deceit), and *vis* (violence) – the number of those reaching each level standing in ratio of 1:10 to the preceding level and presided over by *tyrannus* (tyranny or despotism). The path of philosophy, presided over by *pneumaticus* (the spiritual), likewise with three levels, leads from the *philosophos* corresponding to the element water and having a 'taste of the fundamental truths of natural science', through the *sophos* corresponding to air and having explored 'celestial influences' and 'the reasons for the rise, condition, and the decline of other things', to the *Adeptiuus* corresponding to fire who aspires to the 'exploration and understanding of the supercelestial virtues and metaphysical influences', each level again bearing a ratio of 1:10 to the preceding level. For each one thousand who choose the earthly life only one chooses philosophy. Thus, for each 1,000,000,000 at the level of *sollicitudo*, there are 1,000,000 at the level of *fraus* and of *philosophos*, 1,000 at the level of *vis* and *sophos*, and only one at the level of *adeptiuus*. Dee leaves it an open question where such a 'unique and most fortunate specimen' and 'magnanimous' and 'singular hero' can be found, suggesting with apparent modesty that the *Monas* should be placed at the lowest degree of philosophizing (*MH*,114–21).

Yet, as Dee continues, it becomes clear that Dee places the *Monas* and, by implication himself, much higher on the scale of philosophical rarity, at the level of *adeptiuus* in fact. Dee enumerates eight progressively greater ways in which the *Monas* is a 'rare thing', which are noticeably numbered in the margin of the text. Even though Dee speaks of a three-tiered division of philosophical rarity, a second look at his diagram will indicate that there are also eight divisions on the 'Y' from *infantia* to *adeptiuus*. What these eight measures of rarity amount to is that the *Monas* involves a hieroglyphic manner of writing that has never before been used and that brings to its subject a mathematical clarity. Through this new writing astronomy will be rebuilt and restored because

> the common astronomical symbols of the planets (instead of being dead, dumb, or, up to the present hour at least, quasi-barbaric signs) should have become characters imbued with immortal life and should now be able to express their especial meanings most eloquently in any tongue and to any nation. (*MH*,120/21)

Furthermore, these planetary symbols and also those of the signs of the zodiac have been restored to their true proportions and symmetry. Mercury, or rather Dee's symbol of the Monas in which the astronomical symbol of Mercury predominates, is thus the restorer of all astronomy and was sent to Dee by God 'so that we might either establish this sacred art of writing as the first founders of a new discipline, or by his counsel renew one that was entirely extinct and had been wholly wiped out from the memory of men' (*MH*,122/23).

What is fundamental to Dee's conception of the 'rarity', the novelty and unique contribution of the *Monas*, is that it is concerned with a new and sacred art or manner of writing. It is revealing that when describing his attempt to explain the *Monas* to Queen Elizabeth, Dee refers to the 'strange and vndue speeches deuised of that hieroglyphical writing', as the apparently most noteworthy feature of the book.[18] With this new hieroglyphic and mathematical writing Dee becomes the divinely inspired founder of a new discipline through which *all* astronomy, both superior and inferior, will be restored. If this is the case, the *Monas* is not about astronomy or alchemy, but about a new form of writing and how this new writing will restore astronomy and alchemy. Dee then goes on to indicate what this new discipline implies in terms of fourteen disciplines, again carefully numbered in the margin of the text, encompassing grammar, arithmetic, geometry, music, astronomy, optics, the science of weights, the science of space (*pleno & vacuo*), kabbalah, magic, medicine, scrying, 'voarchadumia', and adeptship (*MH*, 122/23–138/39).[19] While some of these are recognizable as parts of the traditional syllabus, others – kabbalah, magic, scrying, 'voarchadumia', and adeptship – fall outside the traditional disciplines and are in some cases quite odd. Of those that may require some explanation, scrying is a practice of divination using transparent and reflective surfaces; voarchadumia is a reference to a book by that title dealing with alchemy; magic, as Dee describes it, also carries alchemical connotations; and, although not very enlightening, adeptship is the highest level of philosophizing which Dee says he had already written about in 1562 (*MH*, 134/35–136/37).[20]

The only work that Dee claims to have written in 1562 is a *Cabbalae Hebraicae compendiosa tabella*, which no longer exists.[21] Dee says that this work on adeptship addressed to the Parisians contained all he had learned in his twenty years' work in the hermetic science, 'hermetic science' usually referring to alchemy. In two other places he also refers to the ideas as contained in this work to the Parisians: in the alchemical passage on magic and in his discussion of kabbalah when he distinguishes between Hebraic kabbalah which concerns what is said and Dee's own 'real' kabbalah which concerns what exists (*MH*,134/35). Adeptship thus seems to involve a combination of 'real' kabbalah, magic, and alchemy. Since Dee says that the *Monas* contains all that he had written in the earlier work on adeptship, we may anticipate that the *Monas* will reveal something about adeptship and that it in some way involves a similar combination of these three disciplines (*MH*,136/37).

The distinction between the Hebraic kabbalah of what is said and the 'real' kabbalah also points to a division within Dee's list of disciplines. One group – grammar, arithmetic, geometry, music, astronomy, optics, statics, the science of space, and Hebraic kabbalah – are considered inadequate but improved through Dee's new discipline; the other group – 'real' kabbalah, magic, medicine, scrying, voarchadumia, and adeptship – are not considered defective but are embodied in Dee's new discipline. An even more revealing division hinges on the disciplines dealing with writing – grammar, Hebraic kabbalah, and 'real' kabbalah – to which Dee devotes the most space. Ordinary grammar and Hebraic kabbalah, according to Dee, both deal with the same thing: the well-known letters that can be written by man and the grammar of what is said. Dee dismisses the ordinary 'philosophers of letters and of language' because the 'vulgar' grammarians and the 'vulgar' kabbalah do not concern themselves with the divine language of things inscribed on the world at creation (*MH*,122–9, 132–5). These two disciplines call for complete transformation through Dee's new art of writing and the discipline of 'real' kabbalah, which 'invents new arts and explains the most abstruse arts very faithfully' (*MH*,134/35). This new discipline will include the traditional 'exoteric' disciplines and improve them by transcending their limitations. Thus Dee does not call for a thorough transformation of the mathematical and physical sciences in his list but indicates that this new discipline will discover things unheard of or normally considered impossible, such as squaring the circle in geometry or earth floating on water in statics (*MH*,128–33). The non-traditional 'esoteric' disciplines, while not requiring improvement are subsumed within and illuminated by this new discipline. Medicine may seem an odd member of this group of non-traditional 'esoteric' disciplines, but what Dee indicates is that his new discipline will reveal the 'mystical intention' of Hippocrates that is ignored in 'exoteric' medicine. Thus the *Monas* is not a complete exposition of alchemy, or magic, or astronomy, or even of this new discipline, but provides examples of how the new art of hieroglyphic writing illuminates the mysteries of these arts and the sayings of the most ancient philosophers (*MH*,124/25, 126/27, 134/35, 138–41, 192–5). Dee's reformation of the disciplines, therefore, might be diagrammed as in Table 4.1.

This view of the *Monas* as a work reforming disciplinary constellations through a novel kind of writing and grammar will provide the starting point for understanding the text. It can also provide a framework for understanding how Dee saw the *Monas* in relation to his previous work. In his discussion of grammar in the dedication, Dee refers to his apology in 1557 in defence of Roger Bacon and says that at that time he had argued that the rarest person in the world would be whoever could demonstrate that the grammar of all languages was one science capable of being taught by one man (*MH*,124–7).[22] From the way he phrases this, it seems clear that

Table 4.1   Dee's Reformation of the Disciplines

Vulgar Linguistic Disciplines: Grammar & Hebraic Kabbalah

Transformed and Superseded
by Dee's
Real Kabbalah or Hieroglyphic Writing

Improves and Transcends	*Subsumes and Elucidates*
'exoteric' disciplines	'esoteric' disciplines
Arithmetic	Magic (alchemical)
Geometry	Medicine (its mysteries)
Music	Scrying (divination)
Astronomy	*Voarchadumia* (alchemy)
Optics	Adeptship (Hermetic
Statics	science, alchemy)
Pleno & Vacuo	

neither he nor anyone else to his knowledge had accomplished this as of 1557. Since Dee's symbol of the Monas dates from 1558, or perhaps was even associated with some concept of unity related to the *Speculum unitatis* of his defence of Bacon, he apparently had not yet associated the Monas with a new discipline of grammar. By the time of the *Monas*, or even by the *Cabbalae Hebraicae* of 1562 if that work ever existed, Dee had become just that rarest of grammarians through the development of the 'real' kabbalah, which he had also associated with his Monas and with adeptship and magic/alchemy.

If we look at Dee's writings and studies between 1558 and 1564, a revealing pattern emerges. Dee claims to have written four works in that period, of which only the *Monas* was ever published, the others not even surviving in manuscript. In addition to the *Monas* and the *Cabbalae Hebraicae*, these are a *De itinere subterraneo* (1560) and a *De triangulorum areis libri demonstrati 3* (1560).[23] The two works from 1560 are clearly not preparatory to the works of 1562–1564 and are more likely a continuation of the practical interests of the mid and late 1550s. At the same time Dee was involved in a re-edition of Robert Recorde's *The Grounde of Artes* that appeared in 1561. This also appears to have been the product of Dee's earlier practical interests and involvement in mathematical teaching. Dee's substantive additions to Recorde's text were in any case rather slight.[24] The dated book acquisitions from this same period also indicate a similar pattern. Not only do the works on Hebrew, which included rudimentary discussions of kabbalah, and those on magic, the occult, and alchemy combined constitute more than a majority of the total for this period, the greater part of these, comprising largely Hebrew and magical works and only one alchemical title, cluster in the years after 1560, whereas the works on mathematics and physics cluster between 1558 and 1561.[25] Again, as in the case of Dee's reading in the 1550s, the amount of material is scant, but what is there indicates a shift of interest away from mathematics and physics toward an active study of Hebrew, magic, and occult works in the early 1560s. What seems to have occurred is that Dee, who had not studied Hebrew or kabbalah earlier, developed an intense interest in these things in the early 1560s, associated them in some way with an intensified study of magic at the same time, and grafted both kabbalah and magic on to his previous interests in astrology and alchemy.

What we have found thus far is that the *Monas* sets forth a radical reform of the disciplines. The traditional, institutionally sanctioned 'exoteric' sciences are considered in need of improvement and to be brought to fulfilment not from within on the basis of their own principles, but from outside through the new 'sacred art' of Dee's hieroglyphic writing. Even more of a challenge involves the 'esoteric' arts of magic and alchemy, traditionally outside the established syllabus and on the fringes of intellectual respectability, which are to be disclosed and elevated to a status equal or superior to the other disciplines through this new art. Central to this reform is Dee's conception of language and the new discipline or art of writing.

THE ALPHABET OF NATURE

What distinguishes Dee's 'holy language' of the 'real' kabbalah from that of the Hebrews is that Dee's is a kabbalah of 'that which is' while Hebraic kabbalah is merely a grammar of 'that which is said' and 'rests on well-known letters that can be written by man' (*MH*,134/35). Dee's new language is an alphabet of nature and a 'writing of things' because it corresponds to the 'written memorial . . . which from the Creation has been inscribed by God's own fingers on all Creatures' and speaks of 'all things visible and invisible, manifest and most occult, emanating by nature or art from

God himself' (*MH*,124/25). God has revealed his goodness, wisdom, and power through creation and the book of nature as much as he has in scripture.

The hieroglyphic manner of writing embodied in Dee's Monas is a predecessor of the frequent seventeenth-century attempts to devise a 'natural' language and a 'real' character and parallels a popular Renaissance conviction that there was an original divine language of creation in which words were not mere human conventions but precisely embodied the essence of things. Associated also with the idea of a language of Adam, through which Adam gave names to all things in creation based upon his knowledge of their inner natures, the idea of a 'natural' language had the great appeal that it offered direct access to a knowledge of nature, an intimate knowledge of and communication with God, and the prospect of universal religious peace and harmony by revealing the common core among Jews, Moslems, and Christians, both Protestant and Catholic. As Dee says to the Hebrew kabbalist, his art will show 'that, without regard to person, the same most benevolent God is not only the God of the Jews, but of all peoples, nations, and languages' (*MH*,132/33).[26]

Just where this divine language was to be found was a significant question. While the philological approach to language of the humanists, particularly of Lorenzo Valla, suggested that all language was based on convention and historical usage, thereby severing the magical ontological connection of words and things in favour of the cultural connection of language and its referents, there was a strong commitment among writers of Neoplatonic inspiration that words had an essential relation to the things that they signified and that all languages as well as images and symbols had great power not only in human communication but over the material and spiritual worlds as well.[27] In fact, the realist conception of language and the issue of the power of languages seems to hav been most closely associated with those writers, namely Ficino, Pico, Reuchlin, Agrippa, who are also closely connected with the legitimation of magic in this period.[28] While all languages, in this view, have some remnant of divine power because all ultimately derive from the same source, most have lost much of their original power because of remoteness from the original source and human ignorance of the correct rules or grammar for manipulating them.[29] This seems to be one of the reasons Dee finds fault with grammarians and Hebraic kabbalists: they do not give the reasons for 'the shapes of the letters, for their positions, for their place in the order of the alphabet, for their various ways of joining, for their numerical value'; they do not know the real origins of the signs and characters; and they have not discovered the universal grammar and language that stands behind the three holy languages of Hebrew, Greek, and Latin (*MH*,122/23, 126/27, 132/33).

As the oldest of the languages, and that of God's earliest verbal revelation to mankind, Hebrew was the prime candidate for the divine language of creation, a privilege reinforced or stimulated by its association with kabbalah, in which Hebrew was the vehicle of cosmological truths, magical powers, and gnostic and mystical communion with God.[30] There were competitors to Hebrew, however. Egyptian could claim to be older, and the association of the Hermetic texts with Egypt endowed hieroglyphic writing with the aura of embodying a wisdom and a revelation even older and purer than that of Hebrew.[31] Dee's materials on Hebrew and ancient languages give some indications of the views on language that Dee had encountered.[32] A theme shared by some of these works is the idea that all languages have a common foundation and source and can therefore be harmonized with one another. They all promote the view that these ancient languages are imbued with magical power or the keys to religious mysteries which can be revealed through appropriate esoteric exegetical techniques, such as kabbalah. While Hebrew is privileged among living languages, Jean Cheradame noted that all languages are uncertain and ambiguous because they have fallen away from divine inspiration, and Guillaume Postel indicated that there were languages earlier than historical Hebrew, such as those of Enoch and Abraham, that were closer to the original language of Adam who had the names of all things infused from God. Dee also notes 'hieroglyphica litterae' among the ancient languages that Postel discusses, and Jacques Gohory associated hieroglyphic characters with magical powers.[33] What Dee seems to think he has done, I believe, is to reconstruct the original divine language of creation that stands behind all human languages.

In the letter of dedication Dee says that

the first and mystical letters of the Hebrews, the Greeks, and the Latins, issued from God alone and were given to mortals.

The shapes of all those letters were produced from points,
straight lines, and the circumferences of circles, disposed by a
wonderful and most wise artifice. (*MH*,126/27)

Likewise, Dee's Monas is generated from a point, lines, a circle, and
semi-circles (figures 4.5 and 4.6). The construction of the Monas has
a clearly cosmographic character. The point represents the earth and
the circle represents both the sun but also the entire frame of the
heavens surrounding the earth. The semi-circle represents the moon
and the double semi-circle at the base represents the zodiacal sign
of Aries, which is the first sign of the zodiac, the sign under which
creaion took place, and can be taken as an analogue of the entire
zodiac and the fixed stars. While the circular components of the
Monas relate to the heavens, Dee relates the cross, composed of
straight lines, to the sublunar realm of the elements (*MH*,154–61).

The structure of the Monas not only epitomizes the structure of
the cosmos; it also embodies a cosmogony in so far as the genesis
of the symbol mirrors the mathematical genesis of the universe. The
straight line and the circle represent nature because 'the first and
most simple manifestation' of things happened by means of the
straight line and the circle, but, since the line is generated by the
point and the circle by a line rotated around a point, 'things first
began to be by way of a point and a monad (*MH*,I, II). While the
geometric progression from point to line to circle culminates in
the heavenly spheres, the elemental realm does not progress in a
geometric sequence beyond the straight line. This elemental realm,
however, is the domain of a pattern of numerical relations familiar
as the 'Pythagorean' tetractys and frequently associated with a
numerological portrayal of cosmogony in the Renaissance.[34] Just as
rectilinear motion is proper to sublunar bodies, so the lines of the
elements (figure 4.6) are produced by the 'flowing of a point' and
arranged as a cross corresponding to the pattern of the four elements
(earth, air, fire, and water) and four qualities (cold, hot, dry, and
moist). With four arms and four right angles, the cross embodies
the number four, or the quaternary, which in Pythagorean
cosmology was the source of hosts of patterns of fours.[35] Besides the
number four, the cross also embodies the preceding numbers. The
point is a monad and corresponds to One, the flowing point is a
line which, as bounded by two points and capable of division, is a
dyad and corresponds to Two, and the two segments of the line,

when crossed, have one point in common and so correspond to the ternary or Three. The cross of the elements thus corresponds to the sequence from One to Four, the sum of which is the denary or Ten (*MH*,15–9, 180–7).

As an embodiment of the Pythagorean tetractys ($1+2+3+4=10$), Dee's cross of the elements resonates with a host of meanings that were associated with this. The monad, as the primeval unit which is the source of all number but not a number itself, and the analogous point, which is a dimensionless unit with position, were associated with God. The number two, which is even and divisible, corresponds to unlimited, formless original matter and to the single dimension of the line. Three points define a triangle and the first surface, and the number four, besides corresponding to numerous quaternaries, defines the first solid body through the four points that mark out a solid angle. The progression from One through Four thus corresponds to the generation of the physical world and also sets the limit to that creation because through addition this series produces Ten, through which the progression returns to unity, perfection, and ultimate stability ($10=1+0=1$). As transmitted through later literature, these Pythagorean associations were amalgamated with a conception of the created world as the product and manifestation of the ideas in the mind of the divine creator. The universe was actually created by numbers, which are the intelligible principles underlying the flux and imperfections of the sensible world, and it was through the progression of the tetractys that the actual unfolding of creation took place. The tetractys, therefore, is not merely a symbol; in a very real way it *is* the universe and understanding it provides access to the actual thoughts of God.[36]

The *Monas* indicates that Dee was familiar with this Pythagorean conception of the power of numbers and the tetractys as the pattern of creation, ideas which he had encountered in his readings.[37] What is interesting about the *Monas*, however, is the very individual treatment that these ideas receive from Dee. In most Renaissance texts the tetractys and its association with the progression from point through line and surface to solid usually exhausts the idea that creation was mathematical and took place through number. Dee confines these ideas to his discussion of the cross of the elements, implying that this Pythagorean notion pertains only to the sublunar, 'rectilinear' realm of the elements where qualitative alterability is the rule. To the heavens, Dee applies a different progression, from

point to line to circle, the clearest source for which was not Pythagorean materials, where it is rarely if ever found to my knowledge,
but Proclus, in his *Commentary on the First Book of Euclid's 'Elements'*,
which Dee had read before 1563.[38]

Proclus posits the line and the circle as the basic principles of all
figures, much as Dee does in Theorem I, and then identifies the
point as the ultimate principle of both the line and the circle. He
gives the Pythagorean association of the monad with the point
which, as a limit, has great power in the cosmos and a resemblance
to the first cause.[39] The line, defined as the flowing of a point just
as we find it in Dee, corresponds to the dyad, the unlimited, and
the world of generation, while the circle pertains to the cosmic and
the supercosmic worlds and is close to divine because it is the first,
simplest, and most perfect figure.[40] Taking its origin from a point
and enclosed within a single line, the circle is akin to the monad and
unity. It epitomizes and serves to constitute cosmic order because
between the limits of the centre and the circumference the indefinite
extendedness of the lines issuing from the centre is bounded and
gathered back into the centre.[41] Proclus associates the circle with the
'triadic god' – Mercury or Hermes Trismegistus – who was the inventor of writing and all the arts and sciences dependent on writing,
including mathematics.[42] It is not implausible that this is one of
the number associations intended by Dee's reference to his Monas
as his 'seal of Hermes' containing the symbol of Mercury who is
the 'rebuilder of all astronomy' and the 'astronomical messenger'
send by God to 'establish this sacred art of writing' (*MH*,122/23).

In combining well-known Pythagorean elements with ideas on
the circle from the lesser-known Proclus, Dee's Monas was a very
clever cosmological symbol. It represents the cosmos as a monadic
unit both in the genesis of all things from the point or monad and
in its representation of all things in a single symbol. Yet, while all
parts of the Monas derive from the point and the line just as all
things in the cosmos have a common origin, the symbol also reflects
the qualitative division of the universe between the celestial and the
elemental realms. Genesis in the terrestrial realm progressed only
so far as the line which as the analogue to the dyad pertains to
imperfection and change, while the celestial realm progressed
beyond the line to the circle which is monadic and therefore perfect.

These considerations indicate something of the symbolic content
of the Monas that gave it such significance in Dee's eyes, but they

do not indicate why Dee felt justified in claiming that his Monas represented a new art of writing. The first clue to this is Dee's claim that the mystical letters that issued from God were 'derived from points, straight lines, and the circumferences of circles' (*MH*,126/ 27). This refers, I believe, to the geometrical construction of alphabets by ruler and compass from points, lines, and circles that was in great vogue in the Renaissance.[43] A curious example of this, both because it is particularly rich in developing symbolic associations and because Dee may have used it, is Geoffrey Tory's *Champ fleury ou l'art et science de la proportion des lettres* of 1529.[44] Tory believes that letters were invented by divine inspiration and his aim is to construct letters in their true proportions.[45] All letters, according to Tory, are constructed from straight lines and circles, both of which depend on the point, and he begins his work with an elementary geometrical discussion of the point, the line, and the circle drawn from Euclid and Charles de Bouelles. Rather than proceeding directly through the alphabet, he first constructs the letters 'I' and 'O', which correspond to the line and the circle and are the models from which all other letters are derived (figure 4.7).[46] The proportions of all letters is controlled by each being constructed within a Ten by Ten grid because the decade is the perfection and consummation of number, containing within itself both equal and unequal and through which the progression beginning with unity reverts to unity.[47] Tory goes on to construct the entire Latin alphabet according to these principles, and suggests that Hebrew and Greek, the other 'holy languages', are constructed in the same way. Dee undoubtedly found suggestive Tory's constant emphasis on the cosmic and intellectual associations of properly proportioned letters, such as the reflection of the 'Homeric Golden Chain' linking heaven and earth and Apollo and the nine muses in the ten divisions of the 'I', and Apollo and the seven liberal arts in the 'O' (figures 4.8, 4.9, 4.10). Constructed from points, lines, and circles, and proportioned according to the Pythagorean decade, Dee's Monas is thus founded on the same basis as other divinely ordained forms of writing.

The second clue to how the Monas can be considered a form of writing is suggested when Dee says that he shows how *gematria*, *notarikon*, and *tsiruf*, which he calls the principal keys of kabbalah, are used outside the confines of the holy language of Hebrew in his real kabbalah.[48] *Gematria*, *notarikon*, and *tsiruf* were Hebrew exegetical techniques which, although not the exclusive prerogative of kabbalah, were used extensively in kabbalah to derive hidden, mystical, and at times magical significance from the Old Testament.[49] Dee, in applying them to the symbol of his Monas, implies that the Monas is like other alphabets not only in its geometrical construction but in its ability to yield a variety of meanings beyond its literal sense.

Notarikon, a form of shorthand in which letters, dots, and dashes are used to represent whole words or concepts, is the most basic 'kabbalistic' technique Dee applies to his Monas. An outstanding example of this in Hebrew is the use of abbreviations for the name of God, the tetragrammaton (*yod, he, vau, he*), in which the first letter, the *yod*, represents the entire name.[50] Often the abbreviation was taken to stand for not only the word it abbreviated but hosts of other things as well. We find Dee doing this when he speaks of 'the trinity of consubstantial monads as appearing in the unity of the iod itself, while the oneness of a chirek remains immobile at the top' (*MH*,126/27). He thereby derives a trinitarian and Christian interpretation from one substitute for the tetragrammaton in which the *yod* was signified by three *yods* with a dot (the *sureq* or dot vowel point) above them.[51] That the *yod* could be considered a line and the *sureq* was a point, two of the geometrical constituents of all writing, made this representation of God all the more significant to Dee.

In the case of the Monas, *notarikon* involves taking geometrical components of the total symbol as abbreviations. As we have seen in the construction of the Monas, the point represents the earth, the circle with the point at the centre represents both the sun and the geocentric universe, the upper semi-circle represents the moon, the cross represents the elements, and the double semi-circle represents Aries. In addition to being abbreviations of astronomical things, these same components also had alchemical significance. Thus, in alchemical discourse the sun was commonly the symbol for gold and the moon represented silver. Because Aries is also the first sign in the triad of constellations corresponding to the element fire, the double semi-circle also represents fire (*MH*,160/61).

While *notarikon* considers parts of words, or in Dee's case parts of the Monas, as abbreviations, through *tsiruf* the individual letters of words are rearranged to discover other words. With the Monas, Dee shows how the individual parts can be recombined in various ways to yield still more symbols and meanings. The upper part of the Monas, combining the sun and the moon, represents the evening and morning of the day of genesis on which the 'light of the philosophers was made' (*MH*,156/57). Dee considers the same part of the Monas to represent the sign of Taurus and the exaltation of the moon (*MH*,166/67). Through various other recombinations of components of the Monas, Dee is able to construct not only the signs for all the planets in addition to the sun and moon, but also symbols for several alchemical vessels, including a retort and a mortar and pestle (figures 4.11, 4.12, 4.13) (*MH*,160–5, 194–7).

The final kabbalistic technique, *gematria*, which was the use of the numerical equivalents of letters to reveal hidden meanings, is used extensively by Dee. Numbers associated with individual letters not only had mystical significance, but if the sum of the numerical values of the letters of two words was the same, the two words could be considered identical in meaning. In the *Monas*, numerical interpretation is applied largely to the cross of the elements. We have already noticed how the cross represents various numbers, but through these numbers, according to Dee, the cross also reveals the rationale behind certain alphabetic facts. In representing the denary, the cross reveals why the Latin 'X' (which is merely a cross tilted over) is used to signify the number ten. Not only this, but the cross, by including the ternary and the septenary, which when multiplied give twenty-one, establishes why 'X' is the twenty-first letter of the alphabet (*MH*,158/59). Likewise, the cross can be taken apart into two right angles, which, depending on how the results are tilted, give the Latin 'V', the number five. Since the cross yields two of these, their sum is ten but even more significant their product is twenty-five, which places 'V' as the twentieth letter and the fifth vowel. In another position the divided cross yields two letters 'L', which individually signify the number fifty and the product of ten and five, and together produce the sum 100 and the product 2500. As a product of ten, 'L' is situated mid-way between the ten letters beginning with 'A' and the ten letters ending in 'X', or ten. Dividing the square of fifty by the square of five yields 100 which is also the sum of two fifties. This points to the progression of one, ten, one hundred as being of particular significance (*MH*, 168–73). Through a further consideration of the numerical equivalents of the cross, Dee finds that they can also be combined to yield the number 252 (*MH*,172–5). These numerical sleights of hand culminate in a table (figure 4.14) which shows 'that certain useful offices in Nature were assigned by God to the numbers' Dee has derived from the Monas 'when elements are to be weighed, when measures of time are to be determined, and finally when the power and virtue of things have to be expressed in certain degrees' (*MH*, 208–13). Thus, by *gematria* the numerical equivalents of the Monas and their permutations yield numbers corresponding to natural processes and reveal hidden explanations of nature's mysteries.

Dee's geometrical construction of the Monas and the derivation of meanings from the placement, arrangement, and rearrangement of its parts and their numerical equivalents fulfil his charge to grammarians that 'reasons must be given for the shapes of the letters, for their position, for their place in the order of the alphabet, for their various ways of joining, for their numerical value, and for most other things . . .', and thereby establish the Monas as a kind of writing (*MH*,122/23). Since the construction of the Monas mirrors divine creation and the components and the meanings derived from the Monas correspond to the constituents and the processes of the natural world, this new form of writing is a kabbalah of that which exists. It is also clear that Dee considered this new art of writing to be prior to all verbal languages and therefore a more suitable candidate for the alphabet of nature. The verbal alphabets of Hebrew, Greek, and Latin are derivative not only because they are based on the points, lines, and circles of the Monas, but also because the Monas contains and explains elements of all three. The Monas contains the alpha and the omega of Greek, it contains Latin letters and explains both their numerical value and their position in the alphabet, and it indicates why the *yod* and the *sureq* are so significant in Hebrew.[52]

What Dee seems to have found in his study of Hebrew and kabbalah in the 1560s was a concept of language as a vast symbolic system and the exegetical techniques with which to generate meanings from the manipulation of symbols. He applied these to his symbol of the Monas, which he had already developed and associated with the symbols of alchemy or inferior astronomy by 1558. We have already noticed that alchemy is the common element in the 'esoteric' disciplines that Dee sets out to illuminate through his new art of writing. What I believe helps to make sense of the *Monas* is to think of this new art of writing as a discourse that Dee thought would encompass and illuminate what he had encountered in his studies in alchemy. Alchemical texts are notoriously opaque, heavily employing the rhetorical devices common to occult writing intended to reveal only what was already known to the adepts and obscuring their secrets for the uninitiated. Through extensive use of specialized terminology, jargon, analogy, and metaphor, alchemical writing made access difficult, dispersed its message, and invited commentary.[53] In Maurice Crosland's apt characterization, 'alchemical literature was a conspiracy between successive generations of writers to use a maximum number of words to give a minimum of information'.[54] Confronted with a vast literature in which each author was supposedly writing about the same thing but saying it in many different ways, it is not unreasonable to suppose that Dee was befuddled, just as Libavius would be later.[55] Unlike the disciplines taught in the universities and even astrology, there was in alchemy no fixed discourse and vocabulary and no primers providing a ready introduction to the art. Despite the extensive reading Dee seems to have done in alchemy there is no evidence that he actually practised alchemy before moving to Mortlake; Dee's knowledge of alchemy was therefore largely the knowledge of a body of discourse. The *Monas*, in its treatment of alchemy, is an attempt to illuminate received alchemical discourse by translating it into the universal and standard discourse of Dee's new hieroglyphic writing. Before looking at how Dee thought the *Monas* accomplished this, it will be useful to review the basic alchemical materials that Dee had at his disposal.

THE DISCOURSE OF ALCHEMY

It is not possible, as was the case with the *Propaedeumata*, to pinpoint a specific author or school of thought within the alchemical literature from which to reconstruct an idea of what Dee had experienced in his alchemical readings through the early 1560s. The list of fifty-six alchemical works Dee read in July 1556 that marks the beginning of his serious interest in the subject is an imposing body of material from which it is difficult to identify individual works of singular importance for understanding the *Monas*.[56] The lists of things he owned, however, are not rich in alchemical literature, and there survive few alchemical books and manuscripts with inscriptions dated before 1564.[57] He acquired the *Opera* of Arnold of

Villanova in 1557, in which the alchemical works are well annotated, and a manuscript alchemical collection also in 1557, which
is also annotated with cross-references to other alchemical works
and the notation of alchemical symbols and vocabulary.[58] In 1559
he acquired the *Voarchadumia* of Joannes Pantheus, and acquisitions
in alchemy continued into the early 1560s, although the bulk of the
alchemical collection in his 1583 catalogue post-dates the *Monas*.[59]

Dee was clearly studying the subject with interest, and the
surviving acquisitions indicate what he attended to, but only the
annotations in the *Voarchadumia* look forward to the *Monas*. The
following summarizes what seems to be the core of ideas that stands
behind much of the alchemical literature that Dee could have read,
guided by parallels with the *Monas* and, where available, by annotations. I will then turn to two authors who were of clear importance
in how Dee came to handle alchemical matters in the *Monas*.

The preeminent concern of alchemy was the transmutation of the
lower metals into silver and gold. Although there was a considerable
body of alchemical knowledge that concerned various chemical
processes, the analysis of mineral waters, and the preparation of
pharmaceuticals and other substances without reference to transmutation, prior to the eighteenth century the alchemical quest for
transmutation cannot be segregated as a pseudo-scientific delusion
in opposition to a legitimate chemistry. The possibility of the transmutation of metals was a legitimate scientific hypothesis resting on
the respectable foundation of Aristotle's theory of the elements and
the generation of metals, and the alchemical literature dealing with
transmutation employed common chemical substances, apparatus,
and processes.[60]

As in the case of astrology, Aristotle provided a legitimate theoretical framework upon which alchemical writers could draw even
though Aristotle himself predates the actual development of western
alchemy. Transmutation was possible on Aristotelian foundations
because all substances were composed of some combination of the
four elements (earth, air, fire, water) in various proportions, so that
altering the proportion of elements within a substance would change
the substance. Even the elements themselves were interconvertible
because they were not truly primary. Rather, each element was the
product of prime matter informed with a pair of the primary qualities, such that earth was cold and dry, air was hot and wet,
fire was hot and dry, and water was cold and wet. Changing the

component qualities would result in a transformation of an element, which in turn would transform the substance of which that element was a part.[61] The application of this theory to the transformation of metals is also based on a hint in Aristotle that minerals and metals are the product of the exhalation of an 'earthy smoke' and a 'watery vapour' from inside the earth. The earthy smoke was small particles of earth on the way to becoming fire and the watery vapour was water in the process of becoming air. When these became imprisoned within the earth and combined, they formed various metals according to the different proportions of smoke and vapour.[62]

These ideas were elaborated by Arabic alchemists of the eighth and ninth centuries into what became known as the mercury-sulphur theory of the metals. According to this theory, Aristotle's earthy smoke and watery vapour were first transformed into sulphur and mercury, respectively, which then combined in the earth under the influence of the planets to form metals. This mercury and this sulphur were not the ordinary substances of those names, but hypothetical intermediary substances, often called philosophical or sophic mercury and sulphur, whose purity and nature are only approximated by ordinary mercury and sulphur. Different metals result from the combination of mercury and sulphur depending on their relative purity and differences in the proportion of the two principles in the combination. If perfectly pure and combined in perfect equilibrium, they produce gold, otherwise one of the inferior metals results. Yet, since all metals have the same constituents as gold, purification and readjustment of the proportion of the constituents by means of suitable elixirs should transform the inferior metals into gold.[63]

This theory was the basis for almost all Islamic alchemy, receiving its most important expression in the body of writings that circulated under the name Jābir ibn Ḥayyān as well as in writings by Ibn Sīnā and al-Rāzī.[64] Latin alchemy in turn was largely founded on the translations of these writings that were made beginning in the twelfth century. There is no evidence that Dee directly used any of these writings, but he was familiar with texts in which the mercury-sulphur theory is fundamental, including Roger Bacon, Arnold of Villanova, Paul of Taranto, the Latin pseudo-Geber, and Petrus Bonus.[65] According to this theory gold developed quite naturally in the bowels of the earth as a result of the long action of heat on mercury and sulphur.[66] The problem of the alchemist, then, was how to speed up nature and to imitate the natural process. In most views this involved not the generation of gold directly from its primitive constituents but the creation of an elixir or the 'philosophers' stone' which had the power to rapidly transform large quantities of imperfect metals by rectifying their imperfect composition.[67]

Where things become difficult is in determining exactly what the philosophers' stone is and how it is produced because alchemical authors are generally reticent about the exact ingredients and the process is so variously and vaguely described. Basically, the philosophers' stone is presented sometimes as a blend of philosophical mercury and philosophical sulphur and at others as philosophical mercury containing an inner and non-volatile or non-flammable sulphur. In either case, philosophical mercury is a mercury from which fluidity and humidity have been removed. The philosophical or inner sulphur likewise has had its flammability and earthiness removed.[68] The actual process involves taking some substance, which in many interpretations could be any common substance, breaking it down into its constituent qualities, and subjecting these qualities to a series of operations through which accidental imperfections are purged and the remaining purified substances are combined and unified, first into philosophical sulphur and mercury and then into the stone. As [pseudo]-Geber expresses it, 'imperfect bodies have superfluous humidities and combustible sulfurity, with blackness corrupting them, an unclean, feculent, combustible and very gross earthiness', but the 'spoilation' of these accidental parts of bodies through the use of fire will yield a substance in which only mercury and sulphur remain.[69]

The process by which the stone is produced seems to vary from one author to the next, usually involving some sequence of standard chemical operations, including such things as calcination, solution, sublimation, distillation, fermentation, and others not found in modern chemical vocabulary but corresponding to recognized procedures at the time.[70] While it is never very clear exactly what was taking place through these operations, other than references to a variety of colour changes usually beginning with black and culminating in red that correspond to various stages in the work, the important thing seems to be that the operations followed some kind of cycle that often corresponded to some natural pattern. A common example is a series of twelve operations matched to the signs of the zodiac.[71] Arnold of Villanova gives a four-stage process corresponding to a cyclic conversion of the four elements from fire through air, water, and earth back to fire.[72] The most interesting example in its relevance to the *Monas* is Thomas Norton's presentation of the process in *The Ordinall of Alchemy*.[73] Norton's process begins with breaking down the beginning matter into the four elements, whose qualities are then recombined

> . . . by ponders right,
> With Number and Measure wisely sought,
> In which three resteth all that *God* wrought:
> For *God* made all things, and set it sure,
> In Number Ponder and in Measure,
> Which numbers if you do chaunge and breake,
> Upon *Nature* you must doe wreake.[74]

The process by which this recomposition occurs involves seven circulations of the elements presided over by the astrological influences of the planets. The seven circulations are divided into two sequences. The first sequence begins with (1) fire acting on (2) earth producing (3) pure water then leading to (4) air. The second sequence begins with (5) air and leads through (6) clean earth to return to (7) fire.[75] The theme of the dependence of the natural growth of metals and the process of the alchemical work on planetary and astrological influences is common to alchemical writings and may be the basis not only for the designation of alchemy as 'astronomia inferior' but also for the practice of designating the metals with the symbols of the planets.[76]

Returning to the elixir, which would seem to be gold itself because it is composed of pure philosophical mercury and sulphur in perfect proportion, it is nonetheless something much more than gold because of its power to convert larger quantities of impure metals to its own perfection when 'projected' upon them. At times the texts speak of two varieties of the elixir, one white, which converts metals to silver, and the other red, which produces gold.[77] Because of this mysterious power, the stone or elixir is usually spoken of with almost religious awe as something almost spiritual that encompasses and unifies all things in creation.[78] Some texts emphasize that full knowledge of the art cannot be taught or acquired through experience but is a gift of God through revelation and that the 'great work' is possible only with divine aid.[79] Indeed, at times the spiritual language is so strong as to invite the interpretation of the alchemical quest to resurrect the pure and spiritual nature hidden in all matter as merely a metaphor for the alchemist's quest for spiritual salvation.[80]

Two authors, Joannes Pantheus and Johannes Trithemius, exercised an identifiable and particularly significant role in how Dee came to present his understanding of alchemy in the *Monas*. Pantheus has already been noticed as the author of a book Dee acquired in 1559 and annotated extensively.[81] An indication of the importance this had for Dee is his mention of it in the letter of dedication, where he says that his doctrine of the Monas will be pleasing to a *Voarchadumicus*, and the fact that it is one of the few annotated works in which he uses his symbol of the Monas.[82] Not only does he equate the Monas with Pantheus's references to the philosophers' stone, but on the title page wrote 'Pan=' 'theus' on either side of a drawing of the symbol (figure 4.15). It would certainly not be incongruous with the *Monas* if this was intended to indicate that the Monas was the god of or within all things.

The *Voarchadumia* is a very curious text which presents alchemy in unique ways, some of which have obvious parallels to what Dee sets out to do in the *Monas*. First, voarchadumia, as a method of purifying gold, by which Pantheus means not extracting gold from its ore but bringing to purity the gold in lesser metals, is presented as a new art distinguished from vulgar alchemy. In fact, Pantheus distinguishes four ways of transmuting metals. Alchemy he equates with the most vulgar form of transmutation which feigns silver and gold through tinctures but does not change the substance. Archimia is the search for an elixir which will transmute things into pure silver or a yellow metal that appears to be gold. This he equates with the traditional body of alchemical works which are filled with enigmas and metaphors but which cannot truly teach how to produce the elixir.[83] Voarchadumia is the third method, and the fourth is sophia which seems to be an extension of voarchadumia because it multiplies or increases the pure gold and silver produced by voarchadumia.[84] Not unlike the claims Dee makes for his Monas, Pantheus, while rejecting the received tradition of alchemy which had always been excluded from the circle of legitimate arts and sciences, claims that voarchadumia is a liberal art endowed with virtue and occult wisdom that will aid in the discovery of the most secret mysteries of nature.[85]

Secondly, what makes voarchadumia a novel science with the dignity of a liberal art is that it is, like the *Monas*, an art of signification established by God that Pantheus calls the kabbalah of metals which harkens back to the most primitive characters of Enoch's time.[86] Throughout the text Pantheus uses letters to refer to ingredients and stages in the alchemical process and employs *gematria* extensively to find equivalences among combinations of these letters and the equation of the alchemical process with 'NVTV DEI', the creative command of God.[87] These *gematria* are some of the areas of the text most heavily annotated by Dee. Pantheus explicitly presents God's creation of the universe as an alchemical process and the work of the alchemist as a recapitulation of genesis.[88] The secret regimen of this art beings to light the 'son of truth' by revealing through the arcana of the four elements the unity of the cosmos and demonstrating the hidden natural bonds between the celestial and the terrestrial, the divine and the human, body and soul, form and matter, and a host of other similar dichotomies.[89]

In the *Voarchadumia* Dee relates his symbol of the Monas to Pantheus's version of the philosophers' stone called 'aqua duris' (figure 4.16).[90] This mercury of the philosophers, or first matter of the art, is the body, soul, and spirit of metals and contains within itself the mercury and sulphur of metals. Pantheus actually speaks of three mercuries: the ordinary mercury, a purified mercury with which Dee equates the ordinary planetary sign of mercury, and the mercury of the philosophers. This last is the product of a progressive compounding of heat from red gold, cold from ordinary mercury purified by fire into the principle mercury, humidity from purified silver, and dryness from a compound of animal, vegetable, and mineral salts.[91] By the action of fire and the command of God, this compounding yields the new Adam (mercury of the philosophers or red sulphur) after seven reiterations of a four-stage process.[92] Through corruption the original material is broken down so that the primary qualities are disposed to mix; through generation a new form, which is the principle mercury, is produced; through augmentation this new form becomes lunar as white silver; and finally through alteration and fixation the new form becomes solar as cold and humid give way to the hot and dry of red gold.[93] The corruption and generation stages of this process are equated by

Pantheus with Aristotle's theory of the elements and true mixtures in which the component elements are unified into a new unitary form through their alteration.[94] Pantheus associates specific values with the duration and power of the stages of this process, which not surprisingly, correspond to the numbers Dee gives in the *Monas* as significant in the 'measures of times' and the 'powers and virtues of things'. The four stages of the process correspond to twenty-four hours, and all together require thirty-six days. The seven reiterations thus require 252 days and each reiteration increases the power or virtue of the product ten-fold.[95] Dee derives the number 252 from his kabbalistic interpretation of the cross of elements and clearly relates it to the philosophers' stone, makes frequent use of progressive multiples of ten, which are related to the virtues of things, and associates the number twenty-four not only with the hours of the day but also with other 'most secret proportions' (*MH*, 116–19, 160/61, 170-5, 208–17).

Johannes Trithemius became important to Dee in a number of ways, some of which will be deferred until the next chapter. In terms of the *Monas*, Dee found in Trithemius the conception of alchemy as a type of magic and the idea that Pythagorean numerology was the key to both alchemy and magic. Dee records his encounter with Trithemius's writings in a letter he wrote to William Cecil from Antwerp in 1563 in which he requests permission to extend his stay abroad and appeals for funds to aid in his studies.[96] What has attracted the most attention in this letter is Dee's report of finding and making a copy of a manuscript of Trithemius's *Steganographia*. In the present context, however, what is most significant is the context in which Dee mentions this. He begins by saying that, despite the presence in the English universities of men learned in many kinds of learning,

> yet forasmuche as the wisdome infinite of our Creator is
> braunched into manifold mo sortes of wonderfull sciences,
> greatly ayding our dymme sightes to the better vew of his powre
> and goodnes, wherin our cuntry hath no man (that I ever yet
> could herre of) hable to set furth his fote, or shew his hand: as
> in the Science *De numeris formalibus*, the Science *De Ponderibus
> mysticis*, and the Science *De mensuris divinis*: by which three the
> huge frame of this world is fashioned, compact, rered, stablished,
> and preserved) and in other sciences, eyther with these

collaterall, or from them derived, or to themwards greatly us
fordering.[97]

He claims that he had gone to Antwerp to arrange the printing of
some of his writings pertaining to these sciences and that he had
also found books and men more helpful in those sciences than he
had ever hoped to find. It is as an example of this kind of book
that Dee mentions not only the *Steganographia* but also Trithemius's
Polygraphia and his letters.

Both the *Polygraphia* and the *Steganographia* deal with cryptography
and esoteric alphabets and characters, which would have fit with
Dee's interest at the same time in oriental languages, kabbalah, and
hieroglyphic writing, but it is Trithemius's letters that most clearly
relate to the sciences 'de numeris formalibus, de ponderibus
mysticis, and de mensuris divinis', which echo the 'Number,
Ponder, and Measure' of Norton's *Ordinall*.[98] Trithemius develops
the idea of a connection of numerology with magic and alchemy in
several letters in which he defends himself against the reputation
he had gained as a devotee of demonic magic, arguing that his
magic was natural and the foundation of a mystical theology.[99]

Trithemius does not deny his interest in magic but attempts to
dignify his magic as a spiritual quest of the soul that is religiously
legitimate.[100] Thus his major theme is that the key to all magic is
an understanding of the process by which diversity, embodied in
the binary, is restored to unity through the ternary, which clearly
echoes trinitarian associations. All things proceed from an original
creative monad, which is the source of all number but not a number
itself, and the order, number, and measure that establish the
harmony of the universe are governed by the Pythagorean tetractys
through which the diversity that is generated from unity nonetheless
returns to unity in the decade through the ternary and the quaternary. It is through the understanding of these numbers that the
soul can ascend to mystical insights, gain insight into occult
mysteries, and achieve the power to perform miraculous feats.[101]

Alchemy is an aspect of this magic because it is only through an
understanding of the restoration of the ternary and the quaternary
to unity that the reduction of composites of the four elements to
purity, simplicity, and unity by fire can be understood and
accomplished.[102] In Dee's annotations to Trithemius's phrase, 'a
ternario in vnitatem per binarium divisum', he associates the

symbols for mercury, salt, and sulphur with the ternary, compounds of mercury-salt and sulphur-salt with the two units of the binary, and his Monas symbol with the unity that results from the union of these.[103] Trithemius's letter to Germanus de Ganay is of particular interest because it presents this defence of magic through numerology in the context of explicit quotations from and commentary on the Emerald Tablet (*Tabula Smaragdina*) of Hermes Trismegistus, which was one of the most influential of alchemical texts. The Emerald Tablet, although containing only thirteen brief and cryptic precepts, nonetheless conveys two themes of importance. The first is the monadic character of the philosopers' stone (the *una res*) from which all things are produced by adaptation similar to the creation of the universe from the unitary word of God. This *una res* is capable of penetrating all solids and conquering every subtle thing and is the source of perfection throughout the world. The second theme is the interdependence of the terrestrial and the celestial. The *una res* can accomplish miracles because 'what is below is like that which is above, and what is above is like that which is below'; therefore it is necessary 'to ascend with greatest sagacity from the earth to heaven, and then again descend to the earth, and unite together the powers of things superior and things inferior'.[104] In Trithemius's magical interpretation the Emerald Tablet is understood as presenting not merely an enigmatic alchemical recipe but rather a cosmology that is modelled on the alchemical process, which is the role assumed by alchemy in Dee's *Monas*.[105]

THE WRITING OF THINGS

We have seen how the *Monas* is a commentary on the Monas as a new form of writing that is meant to mirror nature because it reflects the geometrical and numerological principles inherent in creation. In discussing the Monas as an alphabet of nature, we focused attention on the Monas and its parts as an alphabet and a lexicon and on the kabbalistic 'grammar' of *notarikon*, *tsiruf*, and *gematria* by which these elements are manipulated. Following the preceding review of alchemical writings, we can now look at the *Monas* as a commentary on how the alphabet, lexicon, and grammar of the Monas serve to constitute a discourse or text that reveals and illuminates the alchemical nature of the universe.[106] I refer to the *Monas* as a commentary because, while Dee may have had a coherent idea of alchemy, what he gives in the *Monas* is essentially a series of examples of how his hieroglyphic writing embodies alchemical principles and disclaims giving a complete elaboration of his new discipline or of alchemy (*MH*,206/207).[107] This new discipline incorporates three themes that emerged in the review of alchemical writings: the alchemical process as mirror of genesis and as subject to astronomical influences, alchemy as a magic of the elements governed by the tetractys, and alchemy as a mystical natural theology of ascent to God.

Inferior-Superior Astronomy

The dominant theme of the *Monas* as a contribution to the literature of alchemy is its development of the idea of a relationship between astronomy, or rather astrology, and alchemy. Dee says that 'celestial astronomy is like a parent and teacher to inferior astronomy', and his Monas, as the 'rebuilder and restorer of all astronomy', not only develops more explicitly the dependence of alchemy on the heavens, which is only a cliché in most alchemical texts, but also reveals the true natures and interrelations of the planets in the light of their correspondence to alchemical processes (*MH*,174/75, 122/23).

As a mirror of the cosmos the very arrangement of the components of the Monas was significant. The earth, at the centre, is encircled by the sun and the orbits of all the planets on whose influences it is dependent. The moon is represented as a semi-circle because it emulates and is dependent on the sun (*MH*,156–9). Of all the planets these two are explicitly represented because 'Sun and Moon infuse their corporeal virtues into all inferior bodies that consist of elements in far stronger manner than do all the other planets' (*MH*,180/81). This strongly echoes a similar aphorism in the *Propaedeumata*, but here the corporeal virtues of the sun and the moon are not merely the vivifying heat and moisture of the earlier work (*PA*, CVI). In the *Monas* the 'aqueous moisture of the Moon' and the 'fiery liquid of the Sun' are revealed through the analysis of corporeal things by fire, symbolized by the sign of Aries (*MH*,180/81, 160/61). This separation of the sun and the moon by the 'magic' of the four elements of the cross adds an alchemical dimension to the Monas. Sun and moon are not only symbols of those planets but are also alchemical symbols both for gold and silver and, as a 'fiery liquid' and an 'aqueous moisture', the sulphur and mercury that are the principles of gold and silver and of the philosophers' stone.[108] Dee quotes the Emerald Tablet that the father and the mother of the *una res* are the sun and the moon, and his title-page evokes the four elements and depicts drops of liquid descending from the sun and the moon (figure 4.2) (*MH*,164–7).[109] The quotation from Genesis 27 at the foot of the title-page referring to the 'dew of heaven' and 'the fat of the earth', which are alchemical references to mercury and sulphur respectively, completes the alchemical motif.[110] Dee does not intend his Monas merely as a concatenation of symbols, however, because he indicates that through the first ten theorems the hieroglyphic writing of the Monas yields the message that 'the sun and the moon of this monad desire their elements, in which the denarian proportion will be strong, to be separated, and that this be done with the aid of fire' (*MH*,160/61).

The technique of *tsiruf*, by which the symbols for all the planets are constructed from components of the Monas, takes on alchemical significance in revealing by analysis both the astral and the elemental components of the philosophers' stone and astronomical significance in revealing the character and interrelationships of the planets. Dee divides the planets into a lunar group and a solar group based on the presence of the symbol of the moon or of the sun in their symbols. The lunar group, displaying the cross of the elements and a semi-circle, comprise the sequence of Saturn, Jupiter, Moon, and Mercury, represented by the unconventional symbol of a semi-circle on top of a cross (figure 4.17). As the diagram indicates, each successive symbol in the series is related to the one before it by a simple rotation of the symbol, or addition or subtraction of parts, implying, according to Dee, that these four lunar planets constitute a hierarchy in which the shared lunar quality is progressively enhanced. Reference to this sequence as the result of four revolutions of the lunar nature around the earth, in which the work of 'albification' (whitening) is carried out by applying the moon to the elements, invokes the alchemical dimension. The moon has already been identified with mercury, and what seems to be at work here is the separation and purification (albification) of the mercurial or lunar principle from the elements to yield lunar mercury, represented by the cross topped by the lunar crescent (*MH*,160–3).[111]

Mars and Venus, along with the Sun, are solar planets interrelated by a shared characteristic and their sequence, from Mars through Venus, involves a similar progressive enhancement of the solar principle, or sulphur, inherent in the elements. These three solar revolutions of the elements, when joined to the previous lunar revolutions, unites lunar mercury with solar sulphur to yield the conventional symbol for mercury, containing both the lunar semi-circle and the full solar circle (figure 4.18). It is this composite mercury that Dee call the Mercury of the philosophers (*MH*,162–5). This total process and the full integration of alchemy and astronomy is illustrated by Dee in two diagrams (figures 4.19 and 4.20). Through the egg-shaped figure Dee evokes both a common alchemical image and the notion found in some sixteenth-century astronomical texts that Mercury's deferent was oval shaped (*MH*,176/77).[112] Within the egg the seven planets are in their Ptolemaic order and follow geocentric paths, but in addition the Sun and the solar planets Mars and Venus are shown within the yolk while the Moon, lunar Mercury, Jupiter, and Saturn are shown within the white. In Dee's suggested interpretation the shell, which commonly represented earth, is dissolved by heat, compounded with the lunar mercury of the white, and then that mixture is saturated with the solar sulphur of the yolk by repeated rotation (*MH*,176–9).[113] These rotations, echoing the seven revolutions previously discussed, are represented in another figure (figure 4.20) as a spiral through which the 'terrestrial centre' of the Monas ascends through seven stages corresponding to the planets. Thus, in representing the planets, the metals, and embodying the essence of the alchemical work the egg is an analogue of the Monas, which itself is a hieroglyph of the cosmos and the alchemical work rather than a component of either.[114]

The murkiest astronomical/alchemical interpretation of the Monas comes when Dee inverts the symbol. Again he is able to derive the signs of the planets from parts of the symbol, but in this case they emerge in the order Saturn, Jupiter, Mars, Venus, Mercury, Sun, and Moon, which he says is the order Plato ascribes to them (*MH*,186/87). While conforming to the order of the planets accepted by Plato, Aristotle, and others earlier than the second century BC, it is difficult to know what Dee intends since he defers treating the astronomical issue to another place. He does say that this inverted arrangement is meaningful.[115] It puts the Sun and Moon, which both astrologically and alchemically as sulphur and mercury are the most powerful influences, closest to the earth and the other planets further away in decreasing order of importance. He also shows how, in addition to those of Jupiter and Saturn, the sign for Venus can be made from the inverted cross by closing the semi-circles of Aries at its top. Since this circle is smaller than that of the Sun, however, this appears to imply that Venus by itself cannot yield true gold (Sun) (*MH*,188–93). The enigmas of the inverted *Monas* are not yet exhausted, for they reappear in the context of the mystical dimension of the *Monas*.

The *Monas* also contains the sign for Aries, which is the house of Mars (strength) and the exaltation of the Sun, and the sign of Taurus, which is the house of Venus (love) and the exaltation of the Moon (figure 4.13). Thus, after telling us to separate the elements of the sun and the moon by means of fire, the *Monas* summarizes the remainder of the alchemical process as the 'exaltations of the Moon and the Sun by means of the science of the elements' (*MH*,168/69). This idea of the *Monas* as a hieroglyphic writing containing a discourse on alchemy and its celestial correspondences also emerges in the 'magic parable' of the dedication. Here Dee says that the *Monas* 'teaches without words' how the terrestrial body at its centre is to be actuated by a divine force and united with the generative lunar and solar influences that have been separated both in the heavens and on earth (*MH*,134/35). In a very thorough way, therefore, Dee's *Monas* exemplifies the precept of the *Emerald Tablet* that 'what is below is like that which is above, and what is above is like that which is below' and takes seriously the injunction to ascend 'from the earth to heaven, and then again descend to the earth, and unite together the powers of things superior and things inferior'.[116]

Serving as an 'astronomical messenger' of a new art of writing, the *Monas* therefore rebuilds and restores *all* astronomy, both inferior and superior, by making explicit the intimate similitude and correspondence between celestial astronomy and elemental alchemy (*MH*,122/23). With these correspondences revealed, the 'common astronomical symbols of the planets (instead of being dead, dumb, or, up to the present hour at least, quasi-barbaric signs)' assume the status of 'characters imbued with immortal life and should now be able to express their properties most eloquently in any tongue and to any nation' (*MH*,120/21). Since the *Monas* itself not only incorporates all of these symbols but also reveals the order of their geocentric orbits, the astronomer can now dispense with his instruments and avoid the discomforts of vigils in the cold air under the open sky and study his subject without observations, a rather surprising turn given the emphasis on observation in the *Propaedeumata* (*MH*,130/31).

Alchemical Magic

Dee refers to this alchemical process as the 'magic' of the elements which in conjunction with the numerology of the cross of the elements echoes Trithemius's presentation of alchemy as a magic governed by the tetractys and Norton's view of the alchemical work as the recombination of the elements by 'Number, Ponder, and Measure'. The ternary of the cross evokes the unified trinity of body, spirit, and soul (*MH*,156/57). While the elements do not exist in equal proportions in any created thing, they can be brought to that equality by art (*MH*,200/201). The Monas shows how the elements of the earth, through the separation and exaltation of the sun and the moon and the elimination of impurities, are restored through the binary and the ternary to a purified unity in the decade produced by the quaternary (*MH*,184–7).

This view of alchemy as a kind of magic not only explains Dee's reference in the dedication to the alchemical process embodied in the Monas as a 'magic parable' but also helps understand the rather bizarre ways advanced there that the teachings of the Monas will supersede the conventional sciences. To the arithmetician, who considers numbers as things abstracted from matter pertaining to the realm of the Platonic *dianoea* or understanding which treats concepts devoid of matter, the Monas shows numbers as 'concrete and corporeal' whose 'souls and formal lives' can be put to use. The geometer will find the square quaternary of the elements reduced to a circle, and the musician will perceive in the tetractys 'celestial harmonies without any movement or sound' (*MH*,128–31).[117] Alchemical heat can reduce any material to its constituents more readily than the burning mirrors of the optician, and the alchemical elevation of the element earth above water and air into the region of fire will confound the sciences of statics and *de pleno et vacuo* (*MH*,130–3). Through the Monas the scryer will be able to see into all sublunary things, and in teaching the true proportions of perfection, the Monas will teach the physician the 'mystical' intention of Hippocrates when he says that medicine is subtraction and addition (*MH*,136/37).[118] The claims in the dedication have the strongly rhetorical quality of inflating the importance of his rather meagre gift, but if we take them seriously one dimension of Dee's reform of the disciplines seems to be that the new writing of the Monas reveals powers of nature that allow the limitations of the conventional sciences to be transcended. The very exacting directions Dee gives for the rendering of an image of the Monas through the geometrical construction of the figure in its true proportions seems to indicate that the Monas not only revealed magical knowledge but could possibly be used as an amulet as well (figures 4.21 and 4.22) (*MH*,200–7).

Adeptship

The third dimension of the *Monas* as a new discipline superior to the traditional sciences is that it reflects a knowledge, which Dee in his letter to Cecil claims to have obtained, of the 'wonderfull sciences, greatly ayding our dymme sightes to the better vew of his [God's] power and goodness'. At times Dee can barely contain his astonishment at the wonders and mysteries that emerge from the analysis of his Monas and bursts forth in praise of the wisdom of the 'Almighty and Divine Majesty' (*MH*,182/83). In the *Monas* the knowledge of nature is not something circumscribed by the limits of the physical world and pursued for its own sake but always points beyond itself as a revelation of the creator (*MH*,124/25). Because 'the logos of the created universe works by rules so that man, godly-minded and born of God, may learn by straightforward work and by theological and mystical language', even without the written record of God's revelation in scripture mankind would still have a knowledge of God (*MH*,200/201, 124/25). This knowledge, however, is not only a rational natural theology but also a mystical doctrine with the soteriological function of effecting 'a healing of the soul and a deliverance from all distress' (*MH*,198/99). The sin of Adam may be repaired by way of the Monas because knowledge will clothe 'the nakedness brought down on us by Adam' and protect against the 'raw colds of ignorance' (*MH*,138/39).

The emphasis on the necessity of piety and faith and of the aid of divine illumination or revelation in the success of the alchemical work has already been noticed in our discussion of alchemical litera-ture. This is, in fact, a very old dimension of alchemical literature which may have been a part of the craft of the early metallurgists but clearly emerges in Hellenistic times when alchemy was amalgamated with a host of intellectual and spiritual traditions spanning Greek philosophy, Neoplatonism, Egyptian magic, astrology, Gnosticism, and Christianity. From this point at least, the alchemical work as a path to a mystical knowledge of God and a metaphor for the salvation of the soul through its liberation from the impurities of matter and ascent to heaven became a significant theme of much, albeit not all, alchemical writing.[119] The readings Dee was doing in the 1560s point more concretely to the content of Dee's religious views in the *Monas*. Trithemius's defences of magic and alchemy through numerology are actually statements of a mystical theology. Trithemius, who says that his philosophy is celestial, not earthly, very clearly intends his discussion of alchemy as an analogy for the inner transformation of the soul and its assent to communion with the divine. Ascent to the supercelestial realm, with which the human mind has a natural affinity, begins with study and knowledge but requires divine illumination to understand the mysteries of magic and alchemy necessary for the complete ascent of the soul, and it is only through the complete ascent of the soul to the supercelestial that endows the *magus* with full knowledge of all sciences and the power to perform miraculous works.[120] Along with Trithemius, a commentary on the magical sections of Pliny's *Natural History*, which Dee annotated, provides a guide to what Dee meant by adeptship (adeptivus). Here again is the idea of a threefold world, divided between terrestrial, celestial, and supercelestial, and it is through magic that the soul ascends to the supercelestial. Significantly, Dee has written the word *adeptiva* in the margin next to the passage describing the soul as carried off and drawn by God into himself after it has ascended to the stage of divine illumination.[121]

It would appear, therefore, that for Dee the adept was one who through 'an exploration and understanding of the supercelestial virtues and metaphysical influences' had risen to the supercelestial realm and been absorbed by divine illumination. Dee emphasizes that only the 'godly-minded' of 'heavenly origin' can grasp all the divine mysteries of the Monas, which he considers a gift from God, referring at one point to the spirit of Jesus Christ writing through his pen (*MH*,122/23, 198–201, 218/19).

With due allowance for the inherently ineffable character of the mystical experience we should not be surprised if even the 'almost mathematical clarity and strength' of the Monas becomes inadequate in its expression of spiritual mysteries. It is in regard to the mystical message of the Monas that the *Monas* exhibits the strongest tension between the promise of revelation and the reluctance to reveal. Dee admits that there are some conclusions that exceed what 'it is proper to express in clear words' (*MH*,214/15). Nonetheless, he presents a diagram (figure 4.23) which seems to present the mystical ascent to the supercelestial realm as an integral part of the astro-alchemical and magical dimensions of the Monas. If what this means is not entirely clear, it is at least consistent with the rest of the *Monas*.

This scheme derives from different aspects of the quaternary, on which number the Monas rests and which is the ultimate power in art and nature. Various parts of the scheme are disposed according to the ternary, the septenary, the octonary, and the denary, which Dee had earlier derived from the quaternary of the cross of elements. The ternary governs the division of the universe into terrestrial, celestial, and supercelestial realms, and the division of being into body, spirit, and soul, spirit being the bridge between the terrestrial body and the celestial soul. The quaternary is related to the four elements, the septenary to the revolutions producing philosophical mercury, and the denary to the multiplication by ten of virtue in the alchemical work. The association of the colour changes involved in the alchemical work and the numbers twenty-four and twenty-five, which are related to the purity of the highest quality of gold, with the progression from body to soul draws a parallel between the ascent of the soul on the right side and ascent of the elemental on the left. All of this is confined to the temporal world below the 'horizon temporis'. In the supercelestial level there is a continuation of the quaternary of the elements into the octonary, which echoes the eight divisions of the *arbor raritatis* leading to adeptship, and a new quaternary, both of which lead from the temporal to the eternal. Here we find what seems to be a graphic representation of a metamorphosis leaping from the temporal to the eternal, where we again confront the puzzling inverted Monas. Dee describes this metamorphosis as occurring when the Monas, after being 'correctly, wholly, and physically restored to itself' in perfect unity, undergoes four 'supercelestial revolutions', which bring forth the inverted form absolutely endowed with all the powers of the elemental, celestial, and the supercelestial worlds (*MH*,214–17). What the four super-

celestial revolutions are is not explained. Appropriately, the final
theorem, which immediately follows this schema, evokes the vision
of God depicted in Revelation 4:1–11, after John passes through the
open door to heaven (*MH*,216–19).

Since the progression from body to soul is related in this scheme
to the alchemical process, it is likely that the mystical ascent of the
soul is intended as an analogue to alchemical transformation. It is
even suggested that the alchemical process is in some way the
medium through which the ascent of the soul is accomplished.
When discussing the Monas as a magical parable in which a terrestrial body is united with solar and lunar influence, Dee says that
once this '*Gammaaea*' (magical talisman) has been completed and
following 'the fourth, great and truly metaphysical, revolution', 'he
who fed the Monas will first himself go away into a metamorphosis'
(*MH*,134–7). This revolution is explained no more clearly than
the four supercelestial revolutions. This metamorphosis from the
'horizon temporis' to the 'horizon aeternitatis' and the supercelestial, however, evokes associations of spiritual religious magic
more than of alchemy. This is suggested not only by Dee's reading
in Trithemius and Pliny. The likely source for Dee's idea of a
horizon between the temporal and the eternal was Pico della Mirandola's magical conclusions, where Pico uses almost identical terms
to differentiate the realms of magic and kabbalah, magic pertaining
to the celestial realm above the temporal and kabbalah pertaining
to the supercelestial realm above the horizon of eternity.[122] In the
context of this and of Trithemius's rendition of the ascent of the
soul, the completion of this talisman, the restoration of the Monas
to itself after it has been dissected, is intended to be the attainment
of the integrated knowledge of the cosmos that is preliminary to
divine rapture rather than any actual alchemical experiment in the
laboratory. Rather than being about alchemy, or astronomy, or
magic, the *Monas* is a gnostic work in which mystical ascent to and
knowledge of God is an integral part of and the culmination of the
attainment of an integral knowledge of the cosmos.[123]

After all of this it is difficult to assess the *Monas* as natural philosophy. It does not make any new contribution to the sciences, as
Dee attempted to do in the *Propaedeumata*, and it seems to be merely
a very clever blend of kabbalah, numerology, astronomy, alchemy,
and gnostic magic. The alchemy and the magic are ordinary and

what happens to astronomy and mathematics is far from an advance. Yet Dee was convinced that he was doing something new, profoundly revolutionary, and of great significance. What does make all the ordinary and even banal scientific content of the *Monas* new is the idea of the Monas as writing, a writing that reduces astronomy, alchemy, magic, and mysticism to the same discourse and in one breath speaks a knowledge of each. The Monas was for Dee a powerful symbol of cosmic unity and of the unity of natural and divine knowledge. This unification of these sciences also had the implication of challenging the exclusion of alchemy and magic from the institutionally sanctioned constellation of disciplines. In relation to the *Propaedeumata* and the intellectual development of Dee's natural philosophy, the *Monas* also raises a multitude of issues. The next chapter will turn from this look at the *Monas* from the inside to attempt to situate it both in the context of Dee's study, development, and activities since 1558, and as an indication of his future developments.

V

THE GREAT METAPHYSICAL REVOLUTION

This chapter considers some of the broader questions related to the *Monas* that extend beyond the confines of the text itself. The juxtaposition of the *Propaedeumata* and the *Monas* will highlight the extent of any continuity between the two works and will provide a foundation for filling in the picture of Dee's intellectual development between 1558 and 1564 and considering the issue of the possible political and religious significance of the dedication of the work to Maximilian. It will be my contention that in this period Dee passed through a significant shift in his thinking. I call this shift Dee's 'great metaphysical revolution', echoing his own phrase in the *Monas*, not only because it marked a profound change but also because the mystical communion with God through nature that marks the formation of the adept through that revolution seems to be the fundamental preoccupation behind Dee's intellectual change at this time. Involved in this change was a significant expansion of his conception of magic to include the spiritual and demonic religious magic associated with the Renaissance vogue of the 'ancient theology', and a notable enhancement of his conception of his social role.

APHORISMS AND THEOREMS

The immediate impression given by the comparison of the *Propaedeumata* and the *Monas* is one of vast dissimilarity. In contrast to the insistence on accurate observations in the *Propaedeumata*, the *Monas* implies that understanding the language of the symbol of the Monas makes observation unnecessary. The *Propaedeumata* concerns the physical mechanism of the relationship between celestial bodies and terrestrial events, and analogies are used merely to illustrate some physical fact or process, as when the familiar influence of the magnet is invoked to illustrate the invisible rays of the stars. The *Monas*, on the other hand, is built entirely upon analogies and metaphors taken as substantial identities, a linguistic characteristic that was particularly prominent in alchemical literature.[1] The Monas and its component parts are taken to be signs that correspond directly to the things they signify and to have the power of those things.[2] Thus, it is assumed that nature conforms to any of the relationships and processes that are derived from the various manipulations of the symbol of the Monas. In the *Propaedeumata* mathematics serves to express the pattern of the propagation of force and the relations among quantitative measurements. In the *Monas* the geometric figures and the numbers derived from the quaternary are hieroglyphic diagrams and formal numbers that are considered to have a 'concrete and corporeal' status, not as measurements of things but as things in themselves that constitute the inner essence of the cosmos. The *Monas* is so difficult to interpret because the predominance of analogy and metaphor make its discourse polysemous, continually opening out to yield additional correspondences and meanings.

Despite these differences, Dee asserted the continuity of the two works in a variety of ways. Most explicitly, the dedication to the *Monas* states that his 'mind had been pregnant' with the *Monas* for the seven years since the *Propaedeumata* (*MH*,146/7). This and other continuities between the two texts have led most commentators to consider them as complementary expressions of a stable philosophical position that has justified reading the ideas of the *Monas* back into the earlier period.[3] Clearly, the relation of the two texts is problematic and merits some consideration because there are some themes that do unite the works and looking directly at the issue will more clearly define some dimensions of Dee's development in the interim.

Obvious signs of continuity are the presence of the Monas symbol on the title-page of the *Propaedeumata* (figure 2.1), with the inscription that it is the image of all the planets and contains all that wise men seek, and the reference in aphorism LII to the Monas as containing the symbols of inferior astronomy as derived from the theories of the *Propaedeumata*. In theorem XIX of the *Monas* Dee quotes aphorism CVI of the *Propaedeumata* to the effect that the humidity of the moon and the heat of the sun sustain all terrestrial things, and throughout the *Monas* the alchemical analogies of sun–sulphur–fire and moon–mercury–humidity are a consistent analogue of the astrological role of the sun and moon in the *Propaedeumata*. Both works begin with a reference to creation and in both natural philosophy serves as a commentary on nature as the expression of divine creation. The fact that Dee reissued the *Propaedeumata* in 1568 also indicates that he considered the two works to be complementary.

Other than indicating that Dee still considered the *Propaedeumata* valid and complementary to his thought in the *Monas* and after, these similarities do not support any assumption that the characteristic features of the *Monas* were fully developed in the earlier period. All that can be said on the basis of the *Propaedeumata* is that Dee had already conceived of the Monas as a symbol of the unity of nature that united the signs of all the planets and the symbols of alchemy. It is only on the title-page and again on the end-page of the *Monas* that the Monas appears associated with the tetragrammaton of kabbalah, the numbers of the tetractys, and inscriptions of alchemical import (figures 4.2 and 5.1). Significantly, the 1568 edition of the *Propaedeumata* shows revisions that reflect the newer ideas of the *Monas*. The title-page and the end-page of this edition are now reproductions of the device from the end-page of the *Monas* (figure 5.2). The new letter to the reader cautions against revealing this knowledge to the unworthy, a warning Dee thought unnecessary to include in the 1558 edition, and speaks of the addition of second thoughts. These amendments to the text in several cases make the connection with the *Monas* more explicit by introducing microcosmic analogies and alchemical, magical, and kabbalist references from the *Monas*.[4] These emendations mirror what Dee's new reading interests between 1558 and 1564 indicate: his understanding of the Monas symbol was broadened and enriched in that period by his study of kabbalah, magic, and numerology.

The *Propaedeumata* and the *Monas* are also similar and yet different in their character as intellectual performance. Both texts fall outside the standard repertoire of genres of academic writing in the sciences, neither appeals to any authority other than that of Dee himself, who presents himself as conveying a new knowledge superior to that previously available. In both cases this new knowledge is the product of integrating normally distinct disciplines, the *Propae-*

deumata joining mathematics, astronomy, optics, and physics, and the *Monas* even more radically joining grammar, mathematics, astronomy, alchemy, magic, and theology and at the same time criticizing the inadequacy of most of the traditional disciplines. Being outside the disciplinary limitations of a university position, which he intentionally shunned, gave Dee the freedom to engage in such forays across disciplinary boundaries but as a consequence both texts raise the issue of how Dee legitimates and authenticates his unconventional approaches and claims to speak with authority without the sanction of a university position.[5] We have seen how the *Propaedeumata* attempts to do this. Addressed to scholars of the 'republic of letters' and dedicated to Mercator, with whose status as renowned mathematician *and* philosopher Dee associates himself and his work, Dee mitigates any novelty of the work by presenting it as the product of his university training in the liberal arts and as conforming to the Aristotelian ideal of a demonstrative science.

The *Monas*, however, presents much greater problems. Unlike astrology, which had a recognized place in the arts curriculum as a branch of astronomy and as subordinate to the authority of philosophy, alchemy had practically no recognized disciplinary status. Indicative of the problem is Libavius's characterization of alchemists as a counter-culture sworn to silence similar to that of rogues and vagabonds and alchemy as not taught in the universities because it was not thought worthy of being a part of philosophy or liberal studies.[6] If Dee's claim in the *Monas* to raise alchemy to the same status as astronomy and to pronounce on natural philosophy through the mathematically constructed astronomical/alchemical symbols of his new art of writing were not audacious enough, the *Monas* also claims to speak authoritatively on natural theology independent of both scripture and the sanction of any licence in theology. The fact that Dee claimed an extraordinarily wide intellectual authority beyond that normally conceded to a mathematician and a master of arts was apparent to at least one acquaintance, Johan Radermacher, who in reference to the *Monas* speaks of Dee as a 'celebrated philosopher', and 'a truly great mathematician wise in all the sciences, all philosophy, and even theology'.[7] Not only does Dee transgress normal disciplinary boundaries, but the constellation of disciplines he creates shatters even the most flexible Aristotelian classification of the sciences and the most liberal interpretation of Aristotle's prohibition of *metabasis*.[8]

In the *Monas* Dee therefore adopts rather different strategies to legitimate what he does in the text. What serves to unify his treatment of alchemy, astronomy, and theology is the common discourse of hieroglyphic writing based on geometry. In the texts Dee read in the early 1560s he encountered an alternative to the Aristotelian classification of the sciences in Proclus and Neoplatonic and Pythagorean ideas according to which mathematics was an intermediary that served as a bridge between physical, theoretical, and divine knowledge because mathematical things had a three-fold existence as the underlying principles of physical bodies, as concepts in the understanding, and as the exemplars in the divine mind.[9] His hieroglyphic writing can therefore range across alchemy, astronomy, and theology because it is based on the geometrical principles of divine creation that span the terrestrial, celestial, and supercelestial realms. To further sanction the novelty of the *Monas* Dee claims the authority of divine inspiration and rejects all human authority. His audience is now not the republic of letters but only the truly wise. Yet because there are those who will betray their 'childishness, malice, and arrogance' as well as their ignorance by condemning his work, Dee appeals to Maximilian to approve, ratify, and defend the *Monas*.

Dee was not wrong in anticipating the need for a prestigious protector and in believing a monarch would provide a less critical if not sympathetic audience for the book. The *Monas* arrived in England before Dee returned and Elizabeth was 'gracious' enough to defend Dee's credit if not the book itself against 'such University-Graduates of high degree, and other gentlemen, who therefore dispraised it, because they understood it not' (*CR*,10). Clearly a courtly and royal patron would be less likely to judge Dee's work in terms of the standards of traditional academic disciplines, and by accepting the work would not only be honoured by the great value of the rare present but also enhance his glory by proving himself to be as wise and virtuous as Dee claims he is (*MH*,138–47). In the following section we will look more closely at the dedication of the *Monas* to Maximilian for what it reveals about Dee's conception of the role of philosophy and his presentation of his role as a philosopher.

Underlying these many differences between the *Propaedeumata* and the *Monas* there are nonetheless some common themes that mark the real continuity in Dee's intellectual life. Both attempt to integrate normally independent disciplines in a natural philosophy that embodies the unity of creation through occult influences and correspondences. Both begin with statements about the nature of divine creation linking natural philosophy with a natural theology. And in both mathematics is the key element in achieving this vision of unity. Although achieving a very different articulation by 1564, these basic intellectual commitments as well as the intention to integrate alchemy and astrology were present at the time of the *Propaedeumata* and the first appearance of the symbol of the Monas. As in the very specific characteristics of the *Propaedeumata*, I believe that it is from Roger Bacon that Dee derived the basic inspiration to seek an integral knowledge of nature. After looking at the dedication to Maximilian, we shall return to the issue of how Dee developed Bacon's idea of the unity of science in the *Monas*, which constituted a significant part of the rationale for the role of the adept that Dee claimed for himself.

THE OFFICE OF THE ADEPT

The dedication of the *Monas* to Maximilian II Habsburg is problematic in terms of motivation, an issue relevant to the question both of the intent of the text and of the function of natural philosophy in Dee's conception of his intellectual role. Normally such dedications are a bid for patronage and the status conferred through recognition by someone as prestigious as the immanent heir to the imperial crown. The appeal to Maximilian to sanction a work whose novelty and authorship by someone without the authority conferred by academic status has already been noted. The bid to Maximilian, however, is curious in terms of Dee's previous history of declining foreign in preference for English patronage (*CR*,8–9). While the *Propaedeumata* may have been a bid for foreign patronage, the accession of Elizabeth supposedly returned him to secure position, relieving him of any awkwardness entailed by his difficulties under Mary and dependence on the good will of Bishop Bonner.[10] There are indications, however, that Dee's expectations of Elizabeth were disappointed in the first years of her reign, making alternative patronage attractive.

The accession of Elizabeth would seem to have been full of promise for Dee. The Cambridge educated group, who had been important in Edward's government and with whom Dee had contacts from St John's, returned to prominence in Elizabeth's government. Of these the most important was William Cecil, now Elizabeth's principal secretary, who had facilitated Dee's introduction to court.[11] Pembroke and the Dudleys, now as Robert, the Earl of Leicester, with whom Dee was closely associated in Edward's reign, were again in a position to advance his career, which they did even before Elizabeth's coronation (*CR*,11–12). It was at Leicester's suggestion, and apparently with the approval of Elizabeth and Cecil, that Dee advised the new queen on the astrologically most propitious day for her coronation, which may also have reminded Elizabeth that Dee's troubles during the previous reign had been supposedly related to his astrological services on her behalf.[12]

Although Dee reports that Elizabeth expressed her regard for him and said that 'where my brother hath given him a crowne, I will give him a noble', there is no evidence that he received any tangible rewards early in the reign (*CR*,12). In addition to the two livings he had received from Edward, Elizabeth was willing that he receive the mastership of the hospital of St Catherine's by the Tower, but Dee's nomination was 'politickly prevented' by a Dr Willson.[13] This was to become a frequent pattern. Dee was subsequently proposed for other livings but always passed over in favour of other candidates (*CR*, 12–13). There is little clear evidence for the reasons behind these decisions, but Dee implies that the other candidates were either of more political importance or more favoured by the ecclesiastical authorities. Dee clearly was not an indispensable political asset to Elizabeth, and there were a number of factors that contributed to the reluctance of ecclesiastical authorities to sanction Dee's appointment to church positions. Not only did he lack clerical training, which limited him to appointments without cure of souls, but his recent and friendly association with Bishop Bonner was bitterly remembered by Protestants and undoubtedly tainted Dee with suspicions of being either a Nicodemite or a crypto-Catholic.[14] Clerical opinion was also clearly unfavourable to astrology, of which he was a known practitioner, and inclined to suspect all mathematics of being tainted with magic, for which he also had a reputation both from the charges against him in Mary's reign and the astounding feat of mechanics he devised for a theatrical production while at St John's. The official religious and political atmosphere was less than hospitable to the overly public employment of someone like Dee and perhaps contributed to his apprehension of hostility from among his countrymen.[15] Elizabeth's reluctance or inability to secure a church position for Dee is therefore not difficult to understand.

While the proceeds from Dee's two rectories supplemented by fees for astrological consultations and private teaching probably offered him an income similar to that he enjoyed under Edward, Dee seems to have developed a grander notion of his vocation by Elizabeth's time which demanded a larger and more secure income and more freedom for private study. Dee's letter to Cecil from Antwerp in 1562, in which he reports his success in gaining knowledge of the 'manifold mo sortes of wonderfull sciences' aiding an understanding of God and his creation and his acquisition of Trithemius's *Steganographia*, is both a request for permission to prolong his stay abroad and an appeal that Cecil procure for him 'that sweet leisure' with which to pursue his studies.[16] Dee's scholarly activities and travels were certainly extensive and costly. He left England for the continent in late 1561. Although he seems to have stayed in Antwerp most of the time, he visited Louvain and possibly Paris in 1562, and in the spring of 1563 began a journey that took him to Zürich in April where he discussed Paracelsus with Conrad Gesner, to Venice in June, and to Urbino by mid-summer, where he met and gave to Federico Commandino the manuscript of Machometus Bagdadinus's *De superficierum divisionibus* that Commandino later published. In September he was in Pressburg for Maximilian's coronation and then went to Venice in November and Padua in December before returning to Antwerp by January 1564 where he wrote the *Monas*.[17]

Throughout his travels Dee was purchasing books and having manuscripts copied which exhausted the £20 that he took with him, forcing him to borrow additional funds and to offer private instruction in return for help in copying the *Steganographia*.[18] While Dee tells Cecil that his zeal for learning was so great that 'my flesh, blud, and bones shuld make the marchandyse, yf the case so requyred', he appeals to Cecil's justice, wisdom, and 'zeale toward the avauncement of good letters and wonderfull divine and secret sciences' 'in procuringe leave, ye and ayde to my small habilitye to abyde the better by the achieving so great a feate, as (by the enjoying of these men and bokes) by Godes leave I entend to assaye'. Not only will such support rebound to Cecil's honour in England and the entire republic of letters, but will contribute to the 'honor and weale publik' of England which has been brought to prosper under Cecil's guidance. Support for Dee and his philosophical activities is thus presented as a kind of public obligation, in return for which he offers to present Cecil with the *Steganographia*, something he claims will be most useful to a prince.[19] Dee appears to aspire to the role of royal intellectual with the financial security and complete freedom to pursue and enrich England with the secret and divine sciences that are overlooked by the universities. Cecil did indicate his approval of Dee's activities, although his reply does not survive, so it is not clear that he provided Dee with any material support, but it is clear that no permanent preferment ensued (*CR*,10).

In the *Monas*, Dee offers to Maximilian the same secrets of divine science that he had offered to Cecil. Without a strong commitment from Cecil and with fresh memories of Maximilian and the cosmopolitan Habsburg court, Dee very likely dashed off the *Monas* as soon as he returned to Antwerp and dedicated it to Maximilian for no other reason than the hope of obtaining the sinecure he had hoped for from Cecil. Maximilian had received the dedication of other 'occultist' works, and Dee was acquainted with Bartholomeus de Rekingen, the imperial physician, with whom Dee discussed medical, occult, and alchemical matters. The Habsburg court provided recognition and untroubled working conditions, and Maximilian's apparent sympathy for a variety of intellectual pursuits, including the occult, may have encouraged Dee in believing Maximilian would be receptive to the *Monas* and a bid for preferment.[20]

Jan van Dorsten and Graham Yewbrey go beyond this limited conclusion and suggest that the *Monas* was the instrument of a political and religious programme of toleration and reunion within an ecumenical empire guided by the divine wisdom revealed in the *Monas*, an interpretation that needs more substantial evidence to be plausible.[21] While the imperial ideology that Dee was to champion later (see ch.VII) may have begun to take form at this time, contemporary evidence does not reveal much about it.[22] The *Monas* itself does not contain any outspoken or even implicit call for a religious or political programme, and the fact that it was composed hastily also suggests that it was not part of a concerted prgramme directed toward Maximilian.[23]

Irrespective of any religious and political programme and

message, Dee was clearly using natural philosophy to define an intellectual role and domain for himself as a philosopher of esoteric and spiritual wisdom that would elevate him above the narrower and strictly instrumental role that had previously been allocated to him as a mathematician providing instruction in mathematics, navigation, and consultation in practical astrology. A key ingredient in the assumption of this more elevated status as an adept was the evolution of his natural philosophy to include a more Neoplatonic philosophy of nature and a more spiritual concept of magic that allowed him to tender to Cecil and Maximilian the power of the 'divine and secret sciences' in exchange for 'sweet leisure' to pursue his studies. This new conception of his role came through working out another element of his inspiration from Roger Bacon: the ideal of the unity of knowledge.

THE UNITY OF KNOWLEDGE AND THE ANCIENT THEOLOGY

One of the most distinctive features of Bacon's philosophical endeavour was his conviction of the unity of all knowledge and his pursuit of a universal science.[24] Not only did he believe that true philosophy required an integrated knowledge of all sciences but that the attainment of this *integritas sapientiae* had the moral and religious purpose of improving human life in this world through the practical utility of the sciences and of leading to salvation through a knowledge of God.[25] The achievement of this unitary knowledge involved a vast interdisciplinary programme spanning languages, the natural sciences, ethics, and theology. While in particular instances, such as his work in optics, Bacon could justify the application of one science (mathematics) to the domain of another (physics) in terms of the Aristotelian division of the sciences, his larger enterprise involved the wholesale reduction of the boundaries separating disciplines.[26] One key to Bacon's unification of the natural sciences was an idea of the legitimate role of mathematics that went far beyond Aristotle to encompass practical as well as theoretical sciences and extending into the domain of physical sciences beyond the study of perspective, acoustics, and physical astronomy that were strictly subordinate to theoretical mathematics.[27] The other key was Bacon's concept of 'scientia experimentalis' that not only produces practical applications of the sciences but also stands above and moves between other sciences to enhance and perfect them by discovering principles and demonstrations beyond those they are capable of themselves.[28] Since 'scientia experimentalis' includes inner spiritual experience and divine illumination in addition to physical sense experience, it also constitutes a bridge between the natural and human sciences and theology.[29] Dee was certainly sufficiently familiar with and indebted to Bacon to be aware of Bacon's programme which is quite similar to Dee's own conception of natural philosophy. Without the actual text of Dee's lost *Speculum unitatis* of 1557 in defence of Bacon it is impossible to argue with assurance, but it seems reasonable that the 'mirror of unity' reflects Dee's awareness of Bacon's programme and was an inspiration for Dee's own programme in natural philosophy symbolized by the Monas devised only shortly after that.

Significantly, it was Bacon's encounter with the occultist pseudo-Aristotle *Secretum secretorum* that prompted his vision of the unity of science and conditioned the character of his programme.[30] What Bacon found in the *Secretum secretorum* was the vision of a unified knowledge that reflected the unity of the created world.[31] The occult sciences of astrology, alchemy, and magic are integral to this knowledge because the terrestrial world is governed by the celestial and the supercelestial worlds, and it is through these that this knowledge can be beneficial to mankind.[32] In Aristotle's revelation of the secrets of this knowledge to Alexander, Bacon found a role for the philosopher as an advisor to rulers and benefactor of mankind, a role with which he came to identify himself.[33] Bacon associates Aristotle with a tradition of ancient theology revealed by God to Enoch, whom Bacon identifies with the Egyptian Hermes, and passed to Aristotle from the Hebrews through the Egyptians and the Chaldeans.[34] This not only legitimated this knowledge but very likely served as a warrant for Bacon as a philosopher to speak on theological matters for which he had no institutional credentials, a point that may not have been lost on Dee.[35] Although this unity was subsequently lost, it can be recovered, Bacon thought, by those worthy of it by their virtue and moral character through study supplemented by divine illumination. Bacon's insistence on the importance of learning languages, particularly Hebrew and Greek in addition to Latin, which he considers interrelated, is that understanding the true grammatical reasons behind these languages is important for the recovery of the single perfect wisdom that was given to man by God.[36]

It is this importance of grammar for Bacon's programme that is reflected in Dee's reference in the *Monas* to his claim in the *Speculum unitatis* that the rarest person in the world would be whoever could demonstrate that the grammar of all languages was one science (*MH*,124–7). We have noted that he implies that he had only accomplished this by 1562 at the earliest through his 'real' kabbalah. In this light it is possible to reconstruct the main outlines of the development of Dee's thought from 1558 to 1564. In 1558 the Monas was associated with the signs of the planets and the metals, and perhaps with the unity of knowledge, but not with grammar or a kind of writing. In Pantheus's *Voarchadumia* Dee first encountered kabbalah as the 'kabbalah of metals' through which alchemy is part of a pristine wisdom revealed by God to the earliest men, remnants of which is expressed in all languages. This was followed by Dee's more active study of oriental languages and kabbalah and the 'manifold mo sortes of wonderfull sciences, greatly ayding our dymme sightes to the better view' of God that he speaks of in his letter to Cecil.[37] In contrast to the heavily medieval reading of the mid-1550s, this took Dee to sources that increasingly date from the Renaissance and reflect the occultist current of late antique and Renaissance Neoplatonism.

One of the striking differences between the *Monas* and the *Propaedeumata* is the nature and function of the magic associated with each. In the *Propaedeumata* the magic is natural in the strictest sense, being dependent upon the physical theory of astral influences as a technique for the practical application of that theory by which the strength and effect of rays of virtue can be enhanced and redirected. In the *Monas*, by contrast, magic refers to not only the 'magical' transformation of the elements in alchemy that confounds the limits of conventional physical theory but most importantly it also now includes the spiritual transformation of the soul and its mystical ascent from the material to the supercelestial realm. This magic implies a physics and a metaphysics very different from that of the *Propaedeumata* and assumes a preeminently religious function. Of considerable importance in this shift was Dee's conception of the religious function of natural philosophy as leading to God, which is significant in Trithemius and other Renaissance texts where it is associated with a more spiritual magic. The *Monas* marks Dee's assimilation of a new conception of magic far less natural than that he had encountered in Roger Bacon.

The heritage of magic available to someone like Dee in the mid-sixteenth century was exceedingly various and any discussion of the subject that attempts to distinguish the different types and sources of magical thought presents considerable problems of terminology. The discussion of magic in the Renaissance has been dominated since 1958 by D. P. Walker, who traces to Marsilio Ficino a uniquely Renaissance notion of magic based on his particular variety of Neoplatonism. This Neoplatonism derived from Ficino's reading of the late antique Neoplatonists – Plotinus, Porphyry, Jamblichus, Proclus, and others – for whom Plato was primarily a religious thinker, and his assimilation of a group of mis-dated texts – the *Corpus hermeticum*, the supposedly Pythagorean *Carmina aurea*, the *Orphica*, the *Oracula chaldaica*, and the *Oracula sibyllina* – that presumably embodied the 'ancient theology' of a mosaic or pre-mosaic revelation from God. The traces of Christian belief found in both the ancient theologians and the Platonic and Neoplatonic texts served to facilitate the assimilation of both into Christianity by Ficino and other Renaissance thinkers. And both, reflecting the popularity of religion, particularly the mysteries, astrology, and magic during the third, fourth, and fifth centuries when they were actually written, carried a good deal of occultism with them. The Neoplatonism of the Renaissance was, therefore, more a theology than a secular natural philosophy, and it reflected the religiously oriented interest in magic, astrology, and theurgic ceremonies of its sources.[38]

From Ficino's formulation, according to Walker, magic developed in two directions: either the natural spiritual magic that Ficino himself attempted to maintain, or a supernatural demonic magic that was more religiously suspect. Ficino's magic was spiritual in that it operated through spirit as a fine corporeal substance that served as intermediary between body and soul in man and between the material world and the world soul in the cosmos at large. This magic was natural because it relied upon the universal impersonal and corporeal spirit and not the individual souls and intelligences of demons and angels, and it was religiously safe because it only indirectly affected the human soul and was not used for transitive effects on other individuals.[39] While Ficino struggled to maintain the spiritual limitations of his magic, his theory clearly implied the possibility of a demonic magic operating with individual elemental, planetary, and angelic souls, which was developed by Ficino's less cautious followers, such as Trithemius and Cornelius Agrippa, who combined his theory with medieval sources of planetary demonic magic.[40]

Frances Yates, emphasizing the Hermetic texts as critical to the genesis of Ficino's magic, subsumed Walker's rendition within a broader intellectual phenomenon she called the 'Hermetic tradition' that incorporated Giovanni Pico della Mirandola's Christian kabbalah, which legitimated a magic directed at celestial demons and supercelestial angels, and thenceforth became the well-spring of most if not all Renaissance magic and occultism in general.[41] In this view there was a coherent Renaissance 'occult philosophy' based on Hermetic-kabbalist magic that was fundamentally religious in its concern with magic as a discipline of personal spiritual perfection and as a path to salvation through the ascent of the soul to communion with God through the celestial hierarchies.[41] This new occult philosophy gave magic a religious legitimacy and a philosophical dignity not associated with magic in the Middle Ages, and through it magic also encouraged science by directing attention to nature as a source of knowledge and encouraging an operative approach to the natural world.[43]

Recent studies indicate a considerably richer picture of magic in the Renaissance. To the typology of magic as a dichotomy of either a natural spiritual or a demonic magic must be added other types of magic of which there are important historical examples in the Renaissance. While Ficino's spiritual magic may indeed be called natural, Ioan Petru Culianu notes that the term natural magic also applies to magics, such as della Porta's, that are not spiritual in that they do not depend on a theory of the human or world spirit. Likewise, demonic magic can be an aspect of Ficino's spiritual magic, but there are also examples, Johannes Trithemius for instance, where demonic magic is not based on a theory of the spirit, the demons and angels being appealed to directly as separate intelligences or souls that act directly in the world and in man without the medium of the spirit.[44] Thus, not all natural or demonic magics are spiritual magics and are not historically derived from Ficino's spiritual magic.

Furthermore, a more nuanced understanding of the role of the Hermetica in Ficino's magic and subsequent magical philosophies of the Renaissance is emerging in conjunction with a more subtle appreciation of the variety of magical sources in play at the time. Brian P. Copenhaver has argued that the Hermetica exercised a rather insignificant role in the formulation of the novel elements of Ficino's magical theory which he traces primarily to Ficino's use of the late Neoplatonists. According to Copenhaver, the Hermetica were popular in the Renaissance because of their religious character, providing an optimistic cosmology, theology, anthropology, psychology, ethics, soteriology, and escatology. While the Hermetica also make reference to magic, particularly the celebrated passage in the *Asclepius*, they do not supply the philosophical framework that justifies a belief in magic. These Ficino developed from traditional Arabic and medieval medicine, matter theory, physics, and metaphysics elaborated through his reading of the Neoplatonists even before he confronted the Hermetica.[45] Extending Walker's discussion of the sources of Ficino's magic, Copenhaver has emphasized the importance of Proclus and the idea that the world is constituted of a hierarchical structure of orders emanating from the divine, natural magic using the divine qualities in lower things to elevate the soul toward immortalization and union with God, and Culianu has emphasized the importance of the Stoic theory, derived most probably from Synesius, of the pneumatic continuity and sympathy throughout the universe and between man and the world as providing the theoretical foundation for the mechanism of magical action developed by Ficino.[46] In this view, the Renaissance magic deriving from Ficino was predominantly Neoplatonic, the Hermetica being assimilated to it because they contained hints of magic and served the rhetorical purpose of lending to that magic the historical and religious dignity of a genealogical association with what purported to be a very ancient theology.[47]

Copenhaver also suggests that the occult or 'popular hermetica' of late antiquity were the richest source for the actual magical data found in Renaissance magical literature. These materials were transmitted through the Middle Ages in a rich manuscript literature and embodied in compendia such as the *Picatrix* and the writings of medieval authors.[48] As in so much else, Arabic sources were a particularly significant vehicle through which ancient magic was not only transmitted to the West but also often reformulated and philosophized. The *Picatrix* is a particularly significant instance of this medieval literature derived from the Arabic because it is a rich compendium of wide variety of magical beliefs and practices and, despite its somewhat confusing organization, this magic is presented as a science based upon a Neoplatonic cosmology.[49] Garin has argued that the Neoplatonic cosmology of the *Picatrix* was one channel by which Neoplatonism entered Renaissance thought and was a significant source for the magic of Ficino, Pico, and Agrippa. The idea of the cosmos as unified by a world spirit and the correspondences and sympathies among the hierarchies of creation and populated with spirits and souls through which man as the microcosm can dominate and thereby transform nature through his science and magic is well developed in the *Picatrix*.[50] Given the importance of ceremonial demonic magic in the *Picatrix*, Ficino's difficulties and Agrippa's failure to exclude the demonic from their magics is not difficult to understand.

David Pingree's investigation of the sources of the magic of *Picatrix* also indicates another importance of this text: it brought together under one umbrella of a Neoplatonic philosophy a variety of magics that were philosophically and historically distinct, and sorting them out provides a more historical and genealogical typology of magic than does Walker's more conceptual typology. In Pingree's typology, the *Picatrix* reflects three types of magic: a celestial angelic type based on and concordant with a Neoplatonic cosmology and psychology, a more primitive demonic type, and a sympathetic type, the latter two being historically earlier and less philosophically sophisticated.[51] Derived from the Neoplatonic theory of hypostases, in which the hierarchies of being in the universe are emanations from the One which is the Good, all magical power derived from God and employed the power of God acting through the angels and spirits of the celestial spheres without the taint of using satanic forces. This celestial magic sought to elicit the services of planetary deities either through talismans into which the celestial spirits were drawn or ceremonially by inducing the deities to do the bidding of the magician. Although originally developed by late antique Neoplatonists such as Proclus to explain the power of oracles and to facilitate communication between the human and the divine by assisting the ascent of the soul to cognition of the One, this theory was perverted into a magic concerned with the terrestrial pursuit of health and power. The earlier demonic type of magic also employed liturgical rituals, incantations, and talismans to compel the aid or good favour of demons, but in this variety the demons are either

131

unreleased souls of the dead or the agents of a Manichaean, Jewish, or Christian devil who populate the sublunar world as spirits of the elements or of the seasons, hours, or days. Sympathetic magic relied on the association of certain stones, plants, and animals with the planets and zodiacal signs. The sympathetic relationship of these things and of images and amulets with planetary lords or decanic demons gave them innate powers useful for magical purposes.

The amalgamation of these different types of magic with a Neoplatonic philosophy in *Picatrix* rendered the distinctions between them meaningless, so that they were often taken over as whole cloth. Elements of these different types of magic were also present, either singly or in various amalgamations, in other medieval manuscripts. A variety of pseudonymous texts attributed to Hermes, Ptolemy, and others, as well as the Hermetic *Cyranides* transmitted lore on the astrological powers of natural substances and amulets. Some treatises on planetary images, such as the *De imaginibus* of Thābit ibn Qurra, reflect the talismanic variety of Neoplatonic celestial magic, while al-Kindī's *De radiis* presents both the talismanic and the liturgical varieties of this magic in the context of a philosophy of causation based on the emanation of rays.[52] The lore of demonic magic was transmitted through a varied literature often associated with King Solomon and deriving from the fourth-century *Testament of Solomon*. Reflecting Jewish and Christian popular culture of the time, the *Testament* is an eclectic mixture of popular Hellenistic magic, including astrological and sympathetic magic, but overwhelmingly concerned with a ritual magic of prayers and conjurations toward a variety of demons to gain their secrets and to control their powers or toward angels to counteract the works of demons.[53] The *Testament* presents neither a systematic demonology or angelology, nor a theory of magical operations, but it does present Solomon as magician with power over demons as an integral feature of Solomon the favourite of God. Magic is therefore part of the divine wisdom bestowed on Solomon in response to his prayers.[54] This image of Solomon and the magus pervades the medieval literature of ritual magic, such as the *Clavicula Solomonis*, the *Sefer Razi'el*, the *Ars notoria*, and others, cataloguing demons and angels, their powers, and their invocations.[55]

How these various strands of magic were received in the Latin West varied considerably. Although it has become a convention of Renaissance scholarship that magic assumed a considerably enhanced intellectual status in the fifteenth and sixteenth centuries, the process of assimilating and accommodating the magical heritage of late antiquity began in the Middle Ages. Early Christian writers tended to condemn all types of magic as inherently dependent on demonic power and, therefore, as idolatrous and a derogation from proper reliance upon God.[56] Beyond any evil (*maleficium*) done by occult means, demonic magic clearly posed a threat to Christian orthodoxy, both in threatening the subversion of the precarious order of nature by diabolic agents and as a rival to official liturgy, as Peter of Abano's equation of magical incantations with the Mass and the recorded prosecutions of ritual magic indicate.[57] Yet any marvellous effect, if it fell outside what was considered the normal course of nature and did not have a readily apparent cause, could be considered magical, and cautious opinion, such as that of Thomas Aquinas, saw the threat of demonic agency implicit in even non-demonic types of magic.[58]

Not all thought such caution necessary. Many of the Arabic texts that accompanied or were vehicles for the assimilation of Aristotelian natural philosophy in the West were favourable to magic and other occult sciences as applied science. This suggested that some features of what had been uniformly condemned as magic were legitimate, and the natural philosophy of Aristotle and the Arabs provided a framework in which William of Auvergne, Albertus Magnus, Roger Bacon, and others could interpret a variety of magical effects as the result of natural causes and, therefore, neither unnatural, not demonic, nor dangerous.[59] Bacon, for instance, argued that many useful sciences had been needlessly condemned and still suffered the stigma of illegitimacy because of the confusion of philosophy with magic made by early Christian theologians.[60] Few medieval philosophers denied the existence of demons or the possibility of demonic ritual magic, being quite familiar with the Solomonic literature, but whether as William of Auvergne's 'natural magic' or as Bacon's 'magnificent sciences' or 'marvellous works of art and nature', there was an interest in distinguishing from this and saving those aspects of magic that were a technology that merely used the principles of other sciences and the hidden or unfamiliar powers of nature to produce new effects.[61] Bacon's curiosity may have taken him quite close to practices of dubious legitimacy, but he, and others before the fourteenth century, resolutely rejected magic as a religious rite and offered with the aid of al-Kindī's theory of rays naturalistic explanations of the power of words, chants, and incantations.[62]

Natural magic as the operative or practical part of natural philosophy, a definition common in the Renaissance, was thus not new to the Renaissance, and although it was used by Ficino, Pico, and Agrippa, it was independent of the new theories of magic developed during the Renaissance.[63] What the revival of Neoplatonic and Hermetic materials did for magic in the Renaissance was to legitimate magic as a religious rite amalgamating the traditions of ritual demonic magic with Neoplatonic celestial/angelic magic, the central focus of the Renaissance interest in magic being its religious rather than its scientific function.[64] Despite Ficino's theory of the spirit, it is clear that his magic was ultimately aimed at good planetary demons or angels.[65] This was even more the case when kabbalah became associated with magic in Pico, Reuchlin, and Agrippa. Not only a technique for extracting esoteric interpretations from scripture, kabbalah was also a mysticism that in some authors took the form of a gnostic magic for aiding the ascent of the soul to God by subduing hostile planetary demons and invoking the aid of angels.[66] Moshe Idel has shown that it was contemporary Christian interest in magic that prompted fifteenth-century Italian Jewish kabbalists to become interested in magic, absorbing material from *Picatrix* and the *Sefer Razi'el*; so kabbalah as Pico and as Reuchlin and Agrippa who followed him understood it was intimately bound up with magic as a religious rite.[67]

All of this should indicate that the magical heritage of the Renaissance was exceedingly complex and that the distinctions between various types of magic had become blurred through frequent intermingling. While there may have been a coherent magical philosophy within the intellectual community of Ficino and those who were associated with him, such as Pico, Francesco Cattani da Diacceto, Lodovico Lazarelli, and extending to those who visited Italy and established contacts with Ficino, such as Reuchlin and Agrippa, Ficino's magic was not the only variety available. In addition there were the medieval natural magic tradition, varieties of ancient sympathetic magic, and demonic and angelic ritual magics, all continuing independently of the theoretical framework of the Florentine tradition. By the mid-sixteenth century those whose curiosity inclined them to study magic had a wide variety of sources to which they could turn, and the evidence of English sources points to a wide and indiscriminate syncretism in the assimilation of magic. A sixteenth-century catalogue of magical manuscripts lists works reflecting a variety of types of magic, and a notebook of John Caius, founder of Caius College, contains excerpts from Peter of Abano, the spurious fourth book of Agrippa's *De occulta philosophia*, which is actually derived from manuals of demonic conjurations, and copies of conjurations.[68] The number of sixteenth-century manuscript copies of magical works of Solomon and others on conjuring spirits, books of planetary images, and various forms of divination, at times interspersed with excerpts from Renaissance authors such as Agrippa, Trithemius, and Ficino, indicates how catholic were the tastes of those interested in magic.[69] Headings by those making the copies and extracts often indicate the object of the copyist's interest, which is most often the promise of secret wisdom, knowledge of the future, and the religiously motivated desire to communicate with God through divine spirits, giving the overwhelming impression that the theurgic invocation of spirits was what was most sought after.[70] There are even examples of the composition of original treatises of magic, the recopying of old works giving way to the amalgamation of these diverse previous materials into contemporary compilations and imitations.[71]

MAGIA

The magical materials that Dee had available by 1564 reflect the same variety. The lists of manuscripts that he owned or borrowed in 1556 list several works on chiromancy (palm reading), extracts from Peter of Abano, an *Ars notoria*, an *Ars sintrillia* probably dealing with divination, a *Libellus Ptolomaei de lapidibus et sigillis eorundem*, and a *De herbis 12 signorum et 7 planetarum*, besides al-Kindī's *De radiis*.[72] This selection represents popular fortune telling, hermetic sympathetic magic, demonic magic, and Neoplatonic celestial magic. His book list from 1557/59 shows that he had acquired the 'classics' of Renaissance Neoplatonic magic. In addition to the *Iatromathematica Mercurij Trismegisti*, which was one of the popular occult hermetica, he had Reuchlin's *De verbo mirifico*, Pico's *Conclusiones*, Agrippa's *De occulta philosophia*, and Ficino's compendium of the Hermetica and Neoplatonic texts on magic, which included works by Jamblichus, Proclus, Porphyry, Psellus, Synesius, the *Corpus hermeticum* and *Asclepius*, and Ficino's *De triplici vita*. He also had Trithemius's *De septem secundadeis*, which is not explicitly magical but treats the idea of spiritual planetary governors that play a role in some magics, and Francesco Giorgi's *De harmonia mundi totius*, also not explicitly magical but containing a summa of the Neoplatonic and kabbalistic ideas on which the magic deriving from Ficino was based.[73] There followed in the early 1560s Dee's acquisition of Trithemius's *Steganographia* containing a type of demonic magic, Jacques Gohory's *De vsu & mysteriis notarum liber* dealing with the magical properties of characters, and the sections from Pliny's *Natural history* on magic reflecting ancient popular divination and demonology with a commentary in terms of Renaissance Neoplatonic magic theory.[74]

Dee's copies of very little of this material survive, making it difficult to know at what time and to what degree he read them and incorporated their ideas into his thinking. The bulk of Renaissance classics might indicate that this exercised a preponderant influence, but this is the material that has not survived. We have argued earlier that there is little evidence of this material in the *Propaedeumata* which was written by the summer of 1558. He echoes Pico's *Conclusiones* in the *Monas* and quotes Agrippa's *De occulta philosophia* in the *Mathematicall Praeface* of 1570 but not before (*MP*,*.jᵛ, c.iiij). Without surviving copies of this material to indicate when Dee read it and what he attended to in it, it is risky to claim any determinant influence for it. The only classic of Renaissance Neoplatonic magic of which Dee's copy survives is Ficino's compendium, and although he had this between 1557 and 1559 it is not dated and the annotations, which are not heavy, indicate that it was annotated if not read only after the *Monas* and possibly as late as 1567.[75] The most certain sources providing some understanding of the magic Dee studied in the 1560s therefore are Trithemius, whom he tells us he avidly studied, and the Renaissance commentary on the magical chapters of Pliny, which is heavily and enthusiastically annotated.

In approaching Dee's encounter with this kind of magic priority must be given in the first instance to Trithemius because of the importance Dee attributes to him in his discovery of the 'wonderfull divine and secret sciences', referring to the *Steganographia* as 'the most precyous juell that I have yet of other mens travailes recovered'.[76] Although ostensibly a method of cryptography and the communication of messages by occult means, the *Steganographia* is the reason for Trithemius's notoriety as an exponent of forbidden demonic magic. Written in 1499 but left unfinished and unpublished because of the reaction it provoked in those Trithemius allowed to see the manuscript, it was only printed in the seventeenth century but had a certain underground circulation in the sixteenth century.[77] Unlike his *Polygraphia*, which is unmistakably cryptography, the *Steganographia* concerns both cryptography and the transmission of messages by occult means which have much to do with spirits, and their images, invocations, and conjurations. While the magic of the first two books can successfully be interpreted as disguising methods of encipherment, an approach taken by some defenders of Trithemius, the third book is completely resistant to such rationalization and all of the magical material is so clearly modelled on the extensive manuscript literature of demonic magic that it is difficult to conclude that the *Steganographia* is not a work of demonic magic.[78] Even if the *Steganographia* is cryptography disguised by magic, what is important in the present context is that almost all sixteenth-century readers of that text took the magic seriously as the fundamental feature of the work. While the cryptographic features of the work may have been the reason Dee recommended it to Cecil as useful to a prince, it was the magical content that made it so valuable an aid in Dee's search of divine sciences.[79]

The three books deal with the names, sigils, prayers, and invocations of progressively more powerful spirits. In each case there are a host of subordinate minions for each of the primary spirits. Book one treats of spirits of the air, which are very difficult and dangerous to deal with because of their arrogance and rebelliousness. These must be bound and compelled through conjurations.[80] The second book treats of the spirits of each hour of the day and night, and book three, which is incomplete, deals with operations with the angels and spirits of the seven planets.[81] In book three there is no possibility that the magic is a cover for cryptography, there being no examples of encipherment, which is unnecessary since the message is transmitted directly by the spirit to the recipient. These spirits are invoked through the pronouncement of prayers and incantations over an image of the spirit at the astrologically appropriate time. The third book is based on the idea that God, the first intellect, delegated the governance of the lower world to seven secondary intelligences corresponding to the seven planets, each of whom ruled for a fixed period governing the course of human history in which major political and religious changes corresponded to a change in planetary governor.[82] Each planetary angel governed through subordinate spirits, each of whom could be called upon for particular purposes, and because the planetary angels were next below God and supervised all that happened on earth throughout history, this sort of magic was also the source of knowledge.

Trithemius devotes so much space to the details of these spirits' names, characteristics, domains, images, and invocations that it is difficult to think that all of this was just window dressing. Even if they were such for Trithemius, he has faithfully reproduced for less discriminating readers important materials from the body of magical literature concerning the invocation of spirits that was universally condemned because of the presumption in Christian society that any spirit answering a human summons was necessarily diabolic.[83] Trithemius's sources were almost entirely medieval works of the *notory art*, such as the *Clavicula Solomonis*, the *Ars notoria*, the *Liber Raziels* (*Sefer Razi'el*), and others that catalogue various orders of spirits and demons along with the sigils, prayers, and incantations necessary to summon them, usually for the purpose of attaining knowledge, but which contain very little theoretical material.[84] Another of Trithemius's sources, the Latin *Picatrix*, does present elements of the Neoplatonic theory of celestial magic, but the *Steganographia* reflects none of this. Trithemius's magic involved the manipulation of supernatural spirits and angels and does not alter the substance of his medieval sources as Ficino and Pico attempted to do.[85]

Trithemius's writings present not so much a philosophical theory of magic as a theological and religious justification of magical operations with spirits, demons, and angels. Any justification of magic in the face of traditional cultural disapprobation as well as particular attacks by contemporaries is necessarily polemical special pleading, but his justifications reflect an important dimension of the vogue of magic in the sixteenth century. Trithemius claimed that his magic was natural, although in what way is not clear, and religiously licit, denying that it had anything to do with evil demons or necromancy.[86] He thought of the *Steganographia* as drawing upon a secret and occult wisdom related both to the secrets of creation in Genesis and the mysteries of the end of things in the Apocalypse, which he equates with kabbalah although he knew little of it, passed down from ancient wise men, thus evoking his version of the tradition of an ancient theology.[87] The appeal to spirits, which he does not deny are involved, is religiously legitimate because both good and bad spirits were created by God to aid in man's knowledge and perfection.[88] In addition to a religious sanction, this magic also has a religious function. In the letters, which Dee knew, defending himself and by implication the *Steganographia* against the charges of illicit magic, Trithemius urges the importance of the study of magic and presents it as a component in the mystical ascent of the soul to God, which at its higher stages is facilitated by communication with angels and angelic mediation between the soul and the creator. Thus, magic is a kind of mystical theology yielding a profound wisdom and spiritual perfection through knowledge of the natural and the metaphysical.[89]

At the same time as he was absorbing this dose of medieval demonic magic in the garb of Christian mysticism, Dee also actively studied another bivalent text of magic: the magical books of Pliny's *Natural History* summarizing ancient popular traditions of magic with a commentary derived from the Renaissance Neoplatonic interpretation of magic.[90] The most heavily annotated portion of the text is the commentary, the sections of Pliny being short and rather factual summaries of ancient magical practices, including demonology and divination.[91] The commentary itself, by Walter Riff, is a brief epitome of the Renaissance Neoplatonic theory of magic, referring to Jamblichus, Proclus, Psellus, Hermes Trismegistus, and Ficino.[92] What follows is not a summary of this text but a synopsis of material from the Pliny and some other things Dee was reading in the same period based on the indications his annotations give of what he was paying most attention to.[93] It is unlikely that Dee made any clear distinctions between these various kinds of magic on either philosophical or religious grounds. Jacques Gohory, whom Dee read the same year he read Trithemius and the Pliny, relates Trithemius to Ficino, Reuchlin, and Agrippa, recognizes the source of Agrippa's 'divine magic' in the magic of the *ars notoria* and the *Almadel*, which was officially condemned as diabolical and which Ficino had sought to avoid, and thereby reflects how easy it was to consider all kinds of magic as all of a piece.[94]

Echoing Pico, magic is said by Riff to be the consummation and active part of natural philosophy.[95] Magic, however, is not just an art derived from natural science; it is a sacred philosophy that is part of the divine wisdom of the ancient theology transmitted through a succession of sages. Just as the Persians equated magic with the worship of God, the sacred art of magic is a source of revelations and prophecies and the acquisition of a divine and spiritual wisdom through communication with spirits and angels.[96] Using the correspondences existing between the elemental, the celestial, and the supercelestial realms, magic can attain to celestial and even supercelestial power by uniting the virtues of lower things to their exemplars in the higher worlds.[97] As the microcosm, man can traverse the three realms and through reception of divine light, by which the soul is elevated and becomes adept, man becomes a great miracle with power and dominion over nature.[98] The interconnection between realms is based on the Neoplatonic idea that the seminal reasons of all things reflect the exemplary ideas in the divine mind, so that elemental things provide access to the celestial and supercelestial powers by means of the correspondence between the elemental seminal reason and its celestial, supercelestial, and ultimately divine exemplar.[99] The vehicle by which the occult virtues of these seminal reasons are propagated between the soul of the world and the physical world is Ficino's spirit.[100] One variety of magic thus implied by this view of nature is a 'natural' magic manipulating occult qualities and virtues propagated through the *spiritus mundi*, to which Dee applies the terminology of stellar radiation, apparently making associations with the ideas from the *Propaedeumata*, but also prominent is the possibility of magical action using individual spirits, demons, and angels in which Dee displayed an avid interest at this time.[101]

It is well-known that Dee sufficiently accepted demonic, or rather angelic, magic by 1581 actually to practise it, as is evident from the extensive records of the attempts beginning then and extending throughout the rest of his life to communicate with angels or spirits through the services of a succession of 'mediums' employing Dee's magical mirrors and crystals.[102] There are also indications, however, that Dee made his first tentative efforts in the practice of this more spiritual magic as early as the late 1560s, which is not surprising given the function of magic in the power Dee now proffered as an adept. In 1568, in some association with a W. Emery, Dee elicited by magic the very exact birth date for John Davis of May 3, 1552, at 2:42 p.m.[103] Dee's note does not say how this was done, and it is not clear what sort of magic might be able to yield the conviction of having obtained such exact information. This clearly involved some form of divination, of which many were known in the sixteenth century, but I have not found reference to any specific practice that would fit this situation. Mechanical forms of divination, such as the procedure given by Agrippa for determining the numerical equivalent of a person's planet and astrological sign by dividing the sum of the numerical equivalents of the letters in the names of the individual and of both parents by nine for the planet and twelve for the sign, will yield the foundations for a crude horoscope but not the precise information Dee obtained, which I suspect only the direct revelation of a spirit could supply.[104]

A number of things support this possibility. In 1581, when Dee's extensive practice of spirit magic began, he spoke of also practising this successfully on two occasions in the past, one of them apparently in the late 1560s.[105] Dee was never able to communicate with spirits directly, always needing the services of a scryer or 'medium', so the reference to W. Emery in association with this particular practice of magic in addition to the 'client' John Davis is also suggestive. Divination is often associated with foretelling the future, but in the literature Dee had available, divination with mirrors or other reflective surfaces is also associated with acquiring knowledge of the past. In the *Monas* Dee used the term 'Beryllisticus' for one who has visions in a crystal, a term, like 'gamaaea' for talisman, derived from Paracelsus, who characterized the 'ars berillistica' with visions in beryls, mirrors, glasses, and liquids of the past as well as of the present and the future.[106] Dee also had a manuscript of the *Ars sintrillia* of Artephius which also describes a practice employing the reflective surfaces of liquids to discover the past. His later interest in scrying, this indication that he was already appealing to angels in the 1560s, his careful annotation of the section in Pliny on divination with mirrors and bright objects with the term 'Berelistica' [*sic*], and his notation of the date 1567 in two places next to Psellus's discussion of aerial spirits, which are conjured by means of the reflective surface of a pitcher or pot of water, all point to the possibility of an active interest in this magic on Dee's part in the late 1560s.[107] If this was so, there was nonetheless nothing extraordinary about it. Crystal gazing was one of the most popular divination techniques to judge from the number of manuscript directions 'to see most excellent and certainlye in a christall stonne what secret thou wilt', and there are contemporary records of other spiritual séances, one at Cambridge in 1557 and a series of 'visions' of spirits in 1567.[108]

Part Three

THE *MATHEMATICALL PRAEFACE*, 1570

VI

VIA MATHEMATICA

Dee's practice of magic coincides with the beginning of one of the best documented periods in his life, a period in which he also pursued some of his most utilitarian scientific projects. After his return from the continent in the spring of 1564, and particularly from his establishment of residence at Mortlake by 1566, until he again left England in 1583, Dee was active in projects for exploration and providing advice to the government, as well as private instruction and consultation. The largest number of the works Dee claims to have written date from this period, and most of these are of a practical nature.[1] Clearly, neither magic nor the pursuit of adeptship detracted from Dee's interest and abilities in conventional mathematics and science or his interest in their practical uses.

In addition to being important for a consideration of Dee's natural philosophy and science, this period raises a number of issues. One set of issues clusters around the relationship of the Neoplatonism, numerology, mysticism, and magic that developed in the 1560s to his other scientific interests and activities. Did these things stimulate his work in the 1570s, did they detract from it, or were they of no consequence, being confined to a realm independent of normal mathematics and theoretical and applied science? The re-publication of the *Propaedeumata* in 1568, although with minor changes that coordinate with ideas that emerge in the *Monas*, indicates that he did not reject the fundamental ideas from the 1550s. Even more striking is the fact that in the *Praeface* he reaffirms the validity of the *Propaedeumata* in terms of his physics of radial emanations, quotations from Aristotle's natural works, and its conformity to the Aristotelian idea of demonstrative science (*MP*,b.j, b.iij–b.iiij). It may be anachronistic to perceive this as an inconsistency. Dee apparently saw no contradiction between the *Monas* and the *Propaedeumata* or the other things he does in the *Praeface*. It is nonetheless legitimate to ask what intellectual framework and strategies facilitated this reconciliation of positions that were inconsistent not only by our standards but also by those held by many of Dee's contemporaries. These issues will be the focus of the present chapter, which will be concerned with the *Praeface* to Euclid. Although not dedicated primarily or exclusively to natural philosophy, of all the works from the 1570s the *Praeface* is the one text that does provide some access to the intellectual framework in which Dee was performing at that time. The subsequent chapter will turn to Dee's activities in this same period.

Dee's *Mathematicall Praeface* has been his most noticed work among historians since it does the most to show Dee as a 'modern' of his time establishing one of the landmarks on the progressive road toward the scientific revolution. Frequently compared to Francis Bacon's *Advancement of Learning*, it seems a manifesto of modern science more farsighted than Bacon's because Dee combined an understanding of experimental method with an emphasis on the importance of mathematics and quantification for the study of nature.[2] Because it is in English and addressed to those outside the universities, the *Praeface* has also been judged of considerable influence in promoting the application of experimental method and mathematics to the activities of the middle classes, artisans, technical craftsmen, and mathematical practitioners who were important in the later development of science.[3]

Like his previous works, the *Praeface* bears signs of hasty composition, Dee lamenting that 'I haue been pinched with straightness of tyme: that, no way, I could so pen downe the matter (in my Minde) as I determined: hoping of conuenient laysure' (*MP*,A.iiij^v). So, 'still the Printer awayting, for my pen staying', the *Praeface* cannot be considered a systematic statement of Dee's ideas (*MP*,d.iiij^v). Dee indicates that he was invited, whether by the translator Henry Billingsley or the printer John Daye is not clear, to write the *Praeface* both to recommend the value of the mathematical arts and to justify the publication of Euclid in the vernacular for 'vnlatined people, and not Vniuersitie Scholars' (*MP*,A.iij^v). The role intended for Dee appears to have been to sanction a publication which it was feared would be perceived as a challenge to the claim of the universities to a monopoly on learning in the liberal arts by associating with the project Dee's multiple status as a university graduate, an associate of the court, and a mathematical practitioner.

The *Praeface* is nonetheless more than a catalogue of ways in which mathematics can be useful typical of many sixteenth-century introductions to mathematical works. Within the limits of this imposed role, Dee seems to have taken what liberties he could to incorporate ideas on mathematical and natural philosophy, digressions illustrating scientific applications of mathematics, and extended passages reflecting his personal views and enthusiasms. In addition to the format, Dee's ability to reveal the full extent of his thought was also limited by the very public forum of the vernacular *Praeface*. The long 'Digression Apologeticall' toward the end of the *Praeface*, in which he attempts to lay to rest his reputation, whether imagined or real, as a 'Caller, and Coniurer of wicked and damned Spirits,' calls attention to how extraordinarily sensitive Dee was about others misinterpreting his ideas and activities (*MP*,A.j–A.iij). As a result, he is quite cautious, being open when dealing with the 'exoteric' side of his philosophy and his public activities, and being guarded, oblique, or even silent regarding the mystical and magical 'esoteric' side of his thought. It is perhaps not accidental that much of the *Praeface* looks back to Dee's interests before 1560 and cites works that he had acquired before that date.[4] Thus, he mentions the *Propaedeumata* and its philosophy but not the *Monas*, although aspects of the philosophy of the *Monas* do show through and he even presents, in a very oblique fashion, his spirit magic as a part of his idea of 'Experimentall Science', which will be discussed below.

Dee acquitted himself of the charge to defend the translation with studied diplomacy. Far from harming the universities, which he calls the 'Storehouses & Threasory of all Sciences, and all Artes', he argues that making mathematics available in the vernacular will improve the preparation of students for university studies and stimulate those who ordinarily would not attend to seek 'the Perfection of all Philosophie' available in the universities after discovering how useful learning can be. In addition, both gentlemen and craftsmen who have no intention of studying philosophy in the universities should not be denied the means of furthering their knowledge of arts that will profit themselves and their country (*MP*,A.iiij). In this justification Dee presents mathematics under a double aspect as both a preparation for the higher intellectual study of philosophy and a foundation for arts of social utility, which is also a feature of how he makes his case for the value of mathematics.

Concerned that some among his audience might react like the student who fled Plato's academy after discovering that Plato's teaching was about the spiritual and eternal rather than wealth, health, and physical pleasure as he had expected, Dee's purpose is to prevent disappointment in those approaching Euclid by warning of the difficulties of mathematics but also to attract interest in the subject by describing the 'most plesaunt, and frutefull *Mathematicall Tree*'. Dee's intent is to promote mathematics among two audiences, intending the '*Pythagoricall*, and *Platonicall* perfect scholer, and the constant profound Philosopher' to find the intellectual and spiritual allure of mathematics, and Plato's 'fugitiue Scholers', the men of affairs interested only in material things, to find the 'commodity' and profit in the subject (*MP,☛.*iiij).

In its largest structure (Table 6.1), the beginning of the *Praeface* concerns pure mathematics and its philosophy and the later part, defining and describing the mathematical arts, concerns the practical applications of mathematics. Within the first section there is a substantial digression dealing with the utility of arithmetic since the mathematical arts he describes later, as befits an introduction to Euclid, are all in at least a remote way related to geometry. Within the sections dealing with the practical value of mathematics, the discussion ranges from instrumental uses, in which mathematical techniques are of service in technology, commerce, and the like, to intellectual uses, in which mathematical principles are the source or foundation for other kinds of knowledge as in physics.

Table 6.1   Outline of Dee's *Mathematicall Praeface*

1. Introduction, ☛.iiij
2. Philosophy of Mathematics, ☛.iiij–a.iij
   2.1. Pure number, arithmetic, *.j–*.ij
      2.1.1. Digression on vulgar arithmetic, *.ij–a.j
   2.2. Pure magnitude, geometry, a.j–a.iij
3. Mathematical arts, a.iij–A.iij
   3.1. Vulgar geometry, a.iij–a.iiij
   3.2. Derivative arts, a.iiij–A.iij
   3.3. 'Digression Apologeticall', A.j–A.iij
   3.4. Archemastrie, A.iij
4. Conclusion and defense of vernacular, A.iij^v–A.iiij^v

What follows will consider Dee's philosophy of mathematics and its general epistemological implications for the study and manipulation of the natural world. Following this, examples of the instrumental and the intellectual uses of mathematics will serve to illustrate how his philosophy of mathematics functioned in practice within natural philosophy. It will emerge, I believe, that different facets of his philosophy of mathematics and nature served to promote quite different approaches to knowledge and to nature. Finally, we shall consider how the *Praeface* reflects a framework in which Dee was able to encompass the rather disparate variety of epistemological and methodological approaches to knowledge revealed there and in his earlier works.

'THYNGES MATHEMATICALL'

Both instrumental and spiritual knowledge are appropriate for mankind because man is a microcosm made in the image of God. As the mid-point between the material and the spiritual realms, man embraces the entire range of creation, has dominion over the physical world, and also 'participateth with Spirits, and Angels' (*MP*,c.iiij). Mathematics is ideally suited to mankind because it also is a mid-point between the supernatural and the material and so can lead the mind to ascend to the contemplation of spiritual things and also to descend to conclusions about the natural world and the construction of useful inventions (*MP*,c.iij^v).

Dee's theoretical discussion of mathematics centers on a consideration of the '*Thynges Mathematicall*', number and magnitude. Number is a sum of units or monads, which are not numbers themselves but ideal indivisible entities, numbering being the mental union of these units into an idea of quantity. Magnitude is a notion according to which things are judged as long, broad, or thick, and is rendered as a geometric line. Such a line is a breadthless length, infinitely divisible in points. Points themselves are, like units, ideal indivisible entities, but also having position and capable of motion. While number is not produced by units but consists of an aggregate of units, a line is produced by the motion of a point but does not actually contain points. Just as points define the ideal line of one dimension, so lines define the ideal plane of two dimensions, and planes define the ideal solid of three dimensions (*MP*,*.j, a.j^v–a.ij). These definitions emphasize the totally abstract and conceptual character of number and magnitude, which are entirely devoid of any materiality and transcend any common sense notion of sensible multitude and dimension (*MP*,*.jᵛ–*.ij, a.jᵛ–a.ij).⁵

These 'mathematicals' are of interest to the philosopher, the scientist, and the practitioner because they are a unique third thing intermediary between supernatural things on the one hand and natural things on the other. Supernatural things are 'immateriall, simple, indiuisible, incorruptible, & vnchangeable', while natural things are 'materiall, compounded, diuisible, corruptible, and chaungeable' (*MP*,☞.iiijᵛ). Mathematicals, since they can be signified by material things and are by nature capable of division and aggregation, are not as simple or absolute as supernatural things, yet they differ from material things because their forms are immaterial and constant. As a result, mathematicals have a 'meruaylous newtralitie' and a 'straunge participation betwene thinges supernaturall, immortall, intellectuall, simple and indiuisile: and thynges naturall, mortall, sensible, compounded and diuisible' (*MP*,☞.iiijᵛ).

To this intermediary position of the objects of mathematics Dee attributes both epistemological and ontological significance. Ontologically, mathematicals are formal as they exist in the mind of the creator, rational as they exist in 'Spirituall and Angelicall Myndes, and in the Soule of man', or natural as they exist in created things. Formal numbers and magnitudes are those through which all things were created in number, weight, and measure. Formal number, for instance, as it is in the mind of the creator, is number numbering, while natural number in created things is number numbered. Number numbering is the discerning and distinguishing of things; and it is through this discrimination by number that God, 'in the beginnyng, produced orderly and distinctly all thinges', and by his continual numbering conserves them in being (*MP*,*.jᵛ, b.iiijᵛ, A.iiijᵛ). In addition to the commonplace that God created everything in number, weight, and measure, Dee also quotes the frequently cited passage from Boethius that all things were 'Formed by the reason of Numbers' as the 'principle example or patterne in the minde of the Creator' (*MP*,*.j).⁶ Unlike the formal exemplars, mathematicals as they exist in the reason do not create, but otherwise they are like the ideas in the divine mind and serve the mind for the numbering and measuring of multitude and magnitude (*MP*,*.jᵛ). Epistemologically, mathematics as it is in the reason also has an intermediary status between knowledge of natural things, which depends on sense perception and is limited to probability and conjecture, and knowledge of supernatural things which are directly and immediately apprehended by the mind and yield certainty. Mathematical knowledge is the product of the understanding, which makes use of sensible images in the imagination but extracts from them what is purely formal and elaborates a knowledge of these things that yields the certainty of truths derived from 'perfect demonstration' (*MP*,☞.iiijᵛ).[7] Mathematics thereby shares some of the limitations of sense knowledge and some of the perfection of pure intellection.

It is this intermediary status of mathematics, both ontologically in the place of the mathematicals between the divine exemplars and their created manifestation, and epistemologically in the place of mathematical knowledge between sense perception and direct intellectual apprehension, that gives mathematics its tremendous versatility and power. Although mathematics in the strict sense deals with the 'thynges mathematicall' and their inherent properties, besides dealing 'Speculatiuely in his own Arte', the 'Mathematicall minde' can also 'Mount aboue the cloudes and sterres: And thirdly, he can, by order, Descend, to frame Naturall thinges, to wonderful vses. . .' (*MP*,c.iijᵛ). Mathematics is thus next to theology in dignity and an indispensable aid in the attainment of 'Heauenly Wisedome' (*MP*,a.jᵛ, a.iij). Following Plato in the *Republic*, Dee urges that the study of mathematics leads the mind to abandon sense objects and prepares it to conceive intellectual and spiritual things (*MP*,*.ij, a.ijᵛ–a.iij).[8] In addition to its function in preparing the mind for divine knowledge, the divine mathematical ideas reflected in creation also provide a substantive view of divinity. The fact that God 'in the distinct creation of all creatures: in all their distinct parts, properties, natures, and vertues, by order, and most absolute number, brought from *Nothing*, to the *Formalitie* of their being and state', means that mathematics provides a glimpse of divine wisdom and the means to 'ascend, and mount vp (with Speculatiue winges) in spirit, to behold in the Glas of Creation, the *Forme* of *Formes*, the *Exemplar Number* of all things *Numerable*: both visible and inuisible: mortall and immortall, Corporall and Spirituall' (*MP*,*.j, b.iiijᵛ). The creation of the world in 'number, weight, and measure', also means that mathematics can descend to the world of nature and sense where it provides an 'inward and deepe search and vew, of all creatures distinct vertues, natures, and properties, and *Formes*', and endows natural knowledge with some of the certainty and precision inherent in mathematics but lacking in mere sense knowledge (*MP*,*.j*^{v}, b.iiij^v). To epitomize this omnicompetence of mathematics, Dee quotes Pico's *Conclusiones* that '*by Numbers, a way is had, to the searchyng out, and understandyng of euery thyng, hable to be knowen*' (*MP*,*.j*^{v}).[9]

The fundamentally Neoplatonic inspiration of Dee's philosophy of mathematics in the *Praeface* is unmistakable and has been noted by those who have argued that this Neoplatonic philosophy was important in justifying and stimulating the scientific study of nature in the Renaissance.[10] It is quite true that the idea that numbers were the first exemplar in the mind of God and that the universe was created in 'number, weight, and measure' were timeworn commonplaces of Pythagorean, Platonic, and Neoplatonic origin. They are commonly found in elementary textbooks of mathematics and were repeated by writers of various philosophical persuasions to advertise the importance of mathematics.[11] Frances Yates and Peter French have suggested that a Renaissance Hermetic magical philosophy provides a more specific impulse behind the active appreciation of the value of mathematics for the study of nature and the emphasis on the useful works of the mathematical sciences and arts that Dee expresses in the *Praeface*.[12] While we will see that Dee associated his ideas on mathematics with his ideas on magic, the textual basis for him deriving his mathematical philosophy from magical sources is very weak compared with the role of Neoplatonic sources, specifically Proclus's *Commentary* on Euclid which Dee had studied with care.[13] Dee's intermediary mathematicals reflect Proclus's elaboration of Plato's idea of the understanding as the epistemological intermediary between the Platonic dichotomy of the realm of pure being and simple intelligibles versus the realm of becoming and sensibles.[14] As in the *Monas*, Proclus's view of mathematics provided the foundation on which Dee was able in the *Praeface* to go well beyond the usual Pythagorean-Neoplatonic clichés about mathematics.

Proclus's concept of mathematical knowledge elaborates the intermediate place of mathematics in Plato's scale of knowledge. Between knowledge of sensible things, which is limited to belief and conjecture, and the purely rational knowledge of intelligible ideas or forms, stands the knowledge of the understanding (*dianoia*), which uses images from lower forms of knowledge and by reasoning discovers through them the reflection of intelligible forms.[15] The very name

152

of mathematics, derived as it is from *mathesis*, signifying learning, which is the recollection of eternal ideas in the soul, indicates the preeminent function of mathematics in purging the understanding, awakening the intellect, and arousing the innate knowledge of the soul.[16] Because of its intermediary position, mathematical knowledge operates at three different levels, just as it does for Dee. At its most intellectual level mathematics points to the region of genuine being and intelligible forms, in the middle region it unfolds and develops the ideas that are in the soul, and at the lower level it examines nature through the various sciences to discover the species of perceptible bodies by projecting upon them the ideas it has of the intelligible forms, thereby explaining their causes as these are contained in its ideas.[17] Mathematics and mathematical science are, for Proclus, the basis for an understanding of the intelligible structure that is the reality of the natural world.

More so than the reiterated commonplace about the divine use of number as the exemplar for creation, it was this epistemological consideration of the nature of mathematical knowledge and its relation to both the divine and the natural that yielded novel initiatives in the consideration of the function of mathematics in the understanding of nature during the Renaissance. Perhaps the earliest to exploit Proclus's ideas in this regard was Nicolaus Cusanus, whom Dee cites and whose ideas reinforced in a particular direction what Dee found in Proclus. Cusanus's primary concern was not with mathematics in itself but with the possibility of any rational theology given the unbridgeable chasm he perceived between the infinite of divinity and the finite human intellect. His central concern was, therefore, epistemological, and his ideas are of interest because of the role mathematics assumes in his epistemology. While direct and complete apprehension of the divine is impossible, the divine nature is reflected in creation both in material things and in the human mind, whose intellectual activity in elaborating sciences reflects the divine intellectual activity which was the exemplar of all creation. It is through considering human intellectual activity and particularly mathematical thought that Cusanus believed he could indirectly grasp aspects of the divine nature. Likewise, even though only God can know the infinite multiplicity of the sensible world with precision, the reflection of the divine intellect in human mathematical notions makes mathematics the prime instrument for discovering the reflection of divine intellectual activity in material creation as well. The intelligible structure of the universe of experience, therefore, can be interpreted by the human intellect because both the universe and the human mind are images of the divine mind. It is the ability of mathematical symbolization to reveal aspects of divinity that certifies that human mathematical science conforms to divine exemplars, and the conformity of aspects of the empirical world to human mathematical science in turn certifies the truth of conclusions based on mathematics.[18] Thus, in the *Idiota de staticis experimentis*, Cusanus argues the importance of the comparison of empirical quantitative measurements for the investigation of nature because all things were created in number, weight, and measure. From his essentially epistemological consideration of mathematics, Cusanus was led to see mathematics, combined with empirical experience and measurement, as the key to the understanding of the natural world.[19]

Others in the sixteenth century reflect an epistemological view of mathematics that echoes Proclus, Kepler being perhaps the most significant in his concern with establishing the grounds upon which it is legitimate to conclude that the mathematical images of the human mind truely reflect divine archetypes.[20] Like Cusanus's *De staticis experimentis*, what gives evidence to Kepler that mathematical conclusions are not arbitrary but represent a match between divine intelligibles and sensibles is that they correspond to measurable relations between physical things.[21] In the *Praeface*, Proclus's idea that mathematics is the medium for understanding the intelligible structure that is the reality of the natural world is reinforced by Cusanus. Dee introduces his discussion of statics by echoing Cusanus, picking up the theme that, although only God can know all things precisely and sense knowledge is limited to conjecture, the fact that God created all things in number, weight, and measure allows us to achieve some 'shaddow of perceiuerance' of divinity as that is reflected in creation (*MP*,b.iiij^v).[22]

PHILOSOPHY, MATHEMATICS, AND TECHNOLOGY

Following his theoretical discussion of mathematics, Dee indicates that

> from henceforth, in this my Preface, will I frame my talke, to *Plato* his fugitiue Scholers: or rather to such who well can, (and

154

> also will,) vse their vtward senses, to the glory of God, the
> benefit of their Countrey, and their owne secret contentation,
> or honest preferment, on this earthly Scaffold. To them, I will
> orderly recite, describe & declare a great Number of Artes,
> from our two Mathematicall fountaines, deriued into the fields
> of *Nature*. (*MP*,a.iij)

It is the virtue of mathematics that through these arts the potential
benefits that are latent in nature are brought forth and made to
yield fruit (*MP*,a.iij). The number of 'artes' is considerable and
at times bewildering, which is not helped by Dee's penchant for
distinguishing as separate arts rather narrow particular uses of
mathematics to which he must frequently assign names of his own
coinage from Greek roots. Along with the familiar geography,
perspective, astronomy, music, astrology, statics, architecture, and
navigation, we find, among others, things like 'trochilike' (properties
of circular motion), 'heliosophie' (properties of spiral lines), 'menandrie' (the multiplication of natural forces), 'horometrie' (measurement of time), 'zographie' (drawing), whose subjects may be
recognizable but whose names have fortunately passed into oblivion.

These are remarkable not only because the range of subjects is
so wide but because they are methodologically so diverse. Some,
such as astronomy, perspective (optics), and music (harmonics)
were recognized sciences by Aristotelian standards with a recognized place in the curriculum; and these, along with statics and
few others, are still recognized as sciences to which mathematical
principles and procedures are integral. Others, such as drawing,
architecture, 'thaumaturgike' (natural marvels), are less sciences
than crafts, arts, or technologies in which the fusion of principles
from several different sciences violates Aristotle's prohibition of
metabasis, and in which mathematical principles do not serve in the
derivation of new knowledge of nature even though they make use
of calculation and mensuration. After Dee's evocation of the
sublimity and purity of the mathematicals and the rigour of mathematical demonstration, we also find him praising the usefulness
of arithmetic and geometry for military commanders, surveyors,
lawyers, and merchants, and recommending mechanical proofs of
some of Euclid's propositions by weighing the contents of models
of cubes, cones, pyramids, and the like (*MP*,*.ij^v–a.j^v, a.iij^v–a.iiij,
c.j^v–c.iij^v).[23]

Dee is quite aware of this looseness. As he defines it an 'art mathematicall deriuative' will be any art whose teachings are ordered and confirmed by 'Mathematicall demonstratiue Method' 'as much & as perfectly' as the subject matter allows, which certainly admits great latitude (*MP*,a.iij). Bert Hansen has suggested that a social coherence, rather than any theoretical unity, is what is common to the arts treated in the *Praeface*. In this view, all of Dee's arts were among the competencies of mathematical practitioners whose main occupation was not the production of new theoretical knowledge but the provision of services, such as practical mathematical instruction, the design of instruments, engineering, and the staging of shows of marvels, that involved mathematical knowledge in one form or another. The *Praeface* is evidence of and a response to the growing demand for instruction in and application of established mathematical knowledge that served to diffuse and redistribute established information and techniques within society and in the process stimulated a familiarity with mathematics and science within a larger audience.[24] Dee himself certainly fits the role of mathematical practitioner, exemplified by his private teaching of a variety of mathematical subjects, his work as a navigational and astrological consultant, and his composition of popularizing scientific works for Edward VI and the Duchess of Northumberland, and he specifically addresses the section of the *Praeface* on the arts to the 'mechanicien' whose work involves the use of mathematics or rests on foundations established by mathematics (*MP*,a.iij^v). In terms of the purpose of this section of the *Praeface*, the issue of the theoretical and methodological coherence of these arts may be unimportant.

Although Dee may not have troubled himself about this issue, he nonetheless was more than only a mathematical practitioner and he had very clear aspirations to be considered a philosopher. In terms of this study, there are two issues regarding Dee's discussion of these arts and sciences. The first is whether they bear any relation to the mathematical philosophy of the early part of the *Praeface*. In other words, is the philosophy immaterial or does it support this apparent hodgepodge of things and inform the way Dee presents them? The second issue is whether any of these arts and sciences reflect magic in the sense that the magical leanings of his natural philosophy can be said to have promoted the mathematical sciences and the application of mathematics to the study of nature.[25]

The first point to note is that not only the treatment of mathematicals but even the presentation of the mathematical arts in the *Praeface* corresponds in more than an accidental way to Proclus's discussion in the Prologue to his *Commentary*. Dee's idea of the three-fold direction of mathematical thought as dealing with the inherent properties of mathematicals, ascending to the application of these to the supernatural and divine, and descending to their application to the natural, is explicitly based on Proclus.[26] In addition to repeating what became the familiar four-fold division of the 'species of mathematical science' into arithmetic and geometry and their derivatives, music and astronomy, that was attributed to Pythagoras, Proclus gives a more extensive division of mathematics based on a lost work of Geminus that reveals how geometry 'when it touches on the material world delivers out of itself a variety of sciences . . . by which it benefits the life of mortals'.[27] In this division, arithmetic and geometry as they deal with intelligibles are the primary and truly mathematical sciences, and as they deal with sensibles they yield a number of sciences and derivative arts. Dee's survey of the mathematical arts and sciences follows Proclus's discussion very closely. With rare exceptions his sciences and arts are either analogous to or subdivisions and compounds of those given in Proclus (Table 6.2).[28] In addition to their social coherence, Dee had the sanction of Proclus for his catalogue of useful mathematical subjects.

On the issue of whether Dee's philosophy of mathematics not only supported the inclusion of Dee's subjects within the scope of mathematics but also informed and guided the ways in which he suggested that mathematics could be of service in the study and exploitation of nature for human benefit we will look in detail at some specific examples from the *Praeface*. This will also serve to clarify to what extent Dee's magical interests and other elements of his natural philosophy may have not only served to stimulate a positive attitude toward the application of mathematics to nature but also contributed to actual scientific practice. I will look first at the mathematical arts, those things of practical benefit in the province of the 'Mechanicall workman', 'whose skill is, without knowledge of Mathematicall demonstration, perfectly to worke and finishe any sensible worke, by the Mathematicien principle or deriuatiue, demonstrated or demonstrable' (*MP*,a.iij^v). In these, mathematical techniques of calculation and mensuration may be used, and

Table 6.2 Schematic Comparison of Proclus's and Dee's Lists of Mathematical Subjects

Proclus's Division	*Dee's Sciences and Artes Mathematicall*
Concerning Intelligibles	Principall
Arithmetic	Arithmetic
Geometry	Geometry
Concerning sensibles	Derivative from arithmetic:
calculation	vulgar arithmetic of whole, proportional, circular (degrees, etc.), radicall, and cosike (algebra) numbers
tactics	tactics
Concerning Sensibles	Derivative from geometry:
geodesy (mensuration)	vulgar geometry, including:
	1. direct measurement of lines (mecometrie), planes (embadometrie), solids (stereometrie)
	2. indirect measure of distance (apomecometrie), heights (hypsometrie), area (planometrie)
	3. artes of indirect measure: geodesie (surveying), hypogeiodei (subterranean measure), geography, chorographie (measure of enclosed space), hydrographie
tactics	stratarithmetrie (ordering military forces)
canonics (musical ratios)	music
optics	perspective
catoptrics	perspective
scene painting	zographie
mechanics	trochilike (circular motion), heliosophie (spirals), pneumatithmie (pneumatics), hydragogie (aqueducts), menandrie (enhancement of power)
wonderworking	thaumaturgike
statics	statics
astronomy	astronomy
gnomics (time keeping)	horometrie
meterorology	astrology
dioptrics (astronomical instruments)	horometrie
	compound arts and sciences (all assume arithmetic and geometry plus other derivative arts equivalent to Proclus):
	Cosmography (astronomy, geography, hydrography, music)
	Anthropography (astronomy, geography, cosmography)
	Architecture (optics, music, cosmography, astronomy)
	Navigation (hydrography, astronomy, astrology, horometry)
No equivalent in Proclus	Archemastrie

mathematical principles may supply the foundation for the practice, but mathematical principles and demonstration do not serve to elicit new knowledge of the natural world. It is in these arts that mathematics is most closely associated with techniques used to control and manipulate nature, to gain power over and through nature, and to use nature to serve human purposes that are usually seen as the positive benefit that magic had on the approach to nature in the Renaissance.

The predominant theme in Dee's discussion of the mathematical arts is their usefulness in a socially productive sense, a theme inherent in the very purpose for which Dee was commissioned to write the *Praeface*. Thus he is at pains to show how merchants, lawyers, metalworkers, and military commanders can benefit from basic techniques of arithmetic computation and the role played by geometric techniques of mensuration in surveying and map making (*MP*,*.ij–a.j^v, a.iij^v–b.j). He emphasizes in particular the usefulness of a range of non-integer numbers, including fractions and irrational numbers in which the unit is not the common measure, and their application to continuous magnitudes (*MP*,*.ij). Euclid's *Elements*, however, goes far beyond these simple techniques, and Dee seems to have made some attempt to indicate the relevance of some of the more technical parts of Euclid as well as to make them accessible. In the section on statics, he indicates how hydrostatic principles can be used for comparing specific weights and the proportions of components of compounds. It is also here that he gives a variety of physical or mechanical techniques for determining the proportion of a circle to a square and a sphere to a cube, and for mechanically increasing the size of solid models. These techniques are not orthodox by Euclidean standards of mathematical demonstration, but Dee's point is that their correctness is sanctioned by mathematical demonstration and they make the results of mathematics available to workmen who do not know geometry (*MP*,c.j–c.iij^v).[29] The additions Dee made to some of the later books of Euclid are in a similar vein. Many are concerned with ancient unresolved problems, such as squaring the circle and doubling the cube, and Dee's treatment is perhaps noteworthy in his rather algebraic handling of geometrical proportions.[30] In this, as in his treatment of the non-integer numbers of vulgar arithmetic, he blurs the rigid Euclidean distinction between number, the province of arithmetic, and magnitude, the province of geometry, a distinction that had already been weakened in the Middle Ages.[31] For practical purposes, Dee considered numbers to refer to magnitudes, which had implications for the application of mathematics to nature in his discussion of the grading of compound medicines as we shall see in the next section. In addition to the pedagogical function of easing the comprehension of difficult material, Dee's additions, often drawn from Archimedes, extend Euclid's propositions in directions that make their mechanical relevance evident.[32]

It is this same emphasis on usefulness that runs through Dee's discussion of the 'Methodicall Artes' that are distinct in their principle subject matter from geometry but which 'vse the great ayde, direction, and Method' of geometry (*MP*,b.j). Some of these represent recognizable occupational fields, such as navigation, architecture, and zography (drawing, painting, sculpting, engraving). His aim in these is primarily to enhance the intellectual respect and dignity of these occupations by emphasizing their mathematical and, therefore, theoretical foundations. His discussion of navigation culminates with the observation that 'it doth appeare, by the premises, how *Mathematicall*, the *Art* of *Nauigation*, is . . .' (*MP*,A.j). It is mathematical perspective that is emphasized as central to drawing and the other pictorial arts, whose name has been changed to 'zographie' to disguise their demeaning association with manual skill, and in his discussion of architecture the quotation of Vitruvius on the broad intellectual learning of the architect in mathematics, the sciences, and the liberal arts, and the quotation of Alberti on architecture as abstract design serve to counter the usual valuation of architecture as a manual craft concerned only with material structures (*MP*,d.ij^v–d.iiij^v).[33] In fulfilling his charge to advertise the utility of mathematics, Dee thus tried to popularize in England the revaluation of the fine arts that was one of the accomplishments of Florentine *quattrocento* artists and humanists.[34]

Others, such as trochilike, heliosophie, pneumatics, menandrie, horometrie, hypogeiodei, and thaumaturgike, are more specific aspects of mechanics that lend themselves to application in a variety of engineering activities, among which Dee mentions mills, mining, pumps, cranes, bellows, gunnery, engines of war, mechanical clocks, and even the idea of a diving bell. Here Dee has made use of his library and his erudition to compile and communicate existing technological information from both classical sources and treatises on contemporary practice. Dee's main sources for these things seem to be Vitruvius and Hero of Alexandria among classical authors and Georg Agricola's *De re metalica* reflecting modern practice, as well as a number of sources repeating stories of noteworthy technological feats associated in legend with Archimedes, Archytas, Daedalus, and Roger Bacon. In this respect, Dee is serving as something of a vector, making accessible to a vernacular audience known materials that were often restricted to Latin treatises.

Dee also sought to indicate how practical technologies were founded in theory upon mathematical understanding, which served not only to indicate further the utility of mathematics to his audience but also to reduce the 'magical' stigma attached to the more unusual aspects of technology. Stories of Archytas's flying wooden dove, the brazen head of Bacon (or in some reports, Albertus Magnus), and other *automata*, including the statues of the Hermetic *Asclepius*, as well as optical effects, such as burning mirrors and optical illusions of men walking in air, were frequently retailed, often in association with the names of Archimedes and Roger Bacon, and commonly associated with magic (*MP*,d.j, A.j).[35] The mechanical scarab that Dee devised for the production of Aristophanes' *Peace* that he staged while at St John's College and his famous mirror that created the illusion of a life-size image of the viewer in front of the mirror are similar examples that did nothing to diminish Dee's reputation as a conjurer (*CR*,5–6; *MP*,b.j^v).

Although these types of marvels were associated with the name magic, as in Giambatista della Porta's *Magia naturalis*, and were absorbed into works of Renaissance Neoplatonic magic, such as Agrippa's *De occulta philosophia*, they are not genuinely magical in the usual sense associated with the popular Hermetica, late antique Neoplatonism, kabbalah, or their Renaissance manifestations.[36] Dee had been interested in this type of thing from his college days before his assimilation of Renaissance magic and they remained an interest associated with his activities as a mathematical practitioner. Rather than magic being the stimulus for an interest in scientific technology, Dee, following Roger Bacon, Nicole Oresme, and Claudio Celestino, attempted to make technology more widely accepted by removing its products from the realm of the magical by emphasizing that even the most marvellous feats of technology were 'Naturally, Mathematically, and Mechanically, wrought and contrived . . .' (*MP*,A.j^v). Mathematics, therefore, serves to de-mystify and to legitimate these activities. It is unlikely that Proclus's philosophy of

mathematics was a stimulus to Dee's positive valuation of technology, which most likely arose from Dee's early interest in Roger
Bacon with his emphasis on knowledge as socially useful and the
fact that one way Dee sought and found preferment was by making
the mathematical arts useful. Proclus's broad sense of what was
included in the mathematical arts, including the mechanics and
'wonder-working' of Archimedes, however, provided Dee with the
framework for extending the theoretical legitimacy of mathematics
to various technologies.[37] At the same time as he is illustrating the
usefulness of mathematics, Dee's emphasis on the mathematical
features of these arts and technologies functions to dignify
occupations that were denigrated, to de-mystify mechanics and
engineering, and, by defining them as separate disciplines with a
methodical foundation, to promote their concerted development and
application rather than haphazard and intuitive use.[38]

PHILOSOPHY, MATHEMATICS, AND SCIENCE

Beyond the arts in which mathematics contributes to practice, the
Praeface also includes examples of sciences in which mathematics is the
vehicle for learning something new about the intelligible structure
of the world and for the establishment of causal relations in scientific
explanations. In the sections on 'perspectiue', 'astronomie', and
'astrologie', Dee refers to the basic ideas and principles of the *Propaedeumata*, emphasizing the conformity of his theory of astrology
with Aristotle's natural philosophy and idea of scientific demonstration *propter quid* (*MP*,b.j–b.iiij). While Dee apparently has not abandoned Aristotle's idea of science, at least in the public forum of
the *Praeface* where he is also pitching the importance of mathematics
to the 'Vniuersitie Scholers' of '*Philosophie*, *Academicall*, or *Peripateticall*',
Dee's approach to astrology could also be accommodated to and
illustrate the Neoplatonic philosophy of mathematics that Dee presents in the *Praeface*. Proclus's idea that the fit between nature and the
mathematical ideas projected on nature by the mind as evidence that
those ideas correspond to the ideas of *Nous* supports Dee's approach
in the *Propaedeumata* that the fit between geometry and the propagation of light certifies the assumption that ray geometry is the pattern
for all propagation of force. From this structural assumption follows
Dee's elaboration of a mathematical theory of astral influences that
he believed met Aristotle's criteria for a demonstrative science.

Another instance Dee gives in which mathematics is critical to the study of natural philosophy is in the section on statics, which demonstrates the causes of heaviness and lightness and their motions through mathematical principles. Following quotation of the first six propositions from Archimedes' *On Floating Bodies*, Dee says 'by these verities, great Errors may be reformed, in Opinion of the Naturall Motion of things. . . . Which errors, are in Natural Philosophie (almost) of all men allowed: to much trusting to Authority: and false Suppositions'. He follows this by quoting Giambattista Benedetti's conclusion that the rate of fall of bodies of the same material, regardless of their weight, will be equal in the same medium (*MP*,b.iiij^v–c.j).[39] Statics and mechanics were areas in which Aristotle's prohibition of *metabasis* made the transference of principles between geometry and physics illegitimate, and clearly Dee was not only open to rejecting Aristotle's specific conclusions when not supported by mathematical reasoning, but also rejected the Aristotelian contention that mathematically derived conclusions, because they deal in things abstracted from matter, have no bearing on physics. Archimedes's example of introducing physical postulates into abstract geometry so that mechanics could be the subject of geometrical reasoning was important for bypassing the traditional Aristotelian reluctance to consider physics in mathematical terms.[40] Although Dee himself did no work in mechanics, he was sensitive to the value of mathematics in resolving questions of physical theory. Stimulus here again was not magic but the example of Archimedes, Cusanus's *De staticis experimentis* which he also quotes regarding statics, and even more generally Proclus's idea of applying mathematics to nature.[41]

Still another way in which Dee's conception of mathematics seems to have influenced the choice between competing theories in natural philosophy is illustrated in his discussion of the grading of compound qualities in pharmaceuticals. Here it is less mathematical reasoning confirming or falsifying an hypothesis than Dee's preference for one variety of mathematical computation leading to his endorsement of one of several competing theories of how qualities combine in compounds.[42] The traditional theory maintained that the four primary qualities – hot, cold, moist, and dry – were found in uncompounded medicines in four strengths or grades from one to four. The various theories advanced regarding the calculation of the strength of the resulting quality in a compound differed computationally because of different interpretations of what happened when qualities combined. These interpretations involved tricky issues in natural philosophy and metaphysics arising from the Aristotelian idea of the structure of material substance as the product of undifferentiated *prima materia* and a substantial form. Aristotle allowed that only one substantial form could be present in a substance at a time, raising the problem of what happens in mixtures; and while it was recognized that accidental qualities, such as heat as temperature, could increase and decrease, it was not clear how the essential qualities of medicinals which were tied to the substantial form of the substance could combine and change in strength.[43]

Dee presents a method of grading in the *Praeface* more as an illustration of the usefulness of practical arithmetic and particularly of algebra for physicians than as an independent treatment of the subject. Dee represents the idea of the gradation of qualities with a 'Crosse of Graduation' (figure 6.1), on which the perpendiculars represent the gradations between the two pairs of contrary qualities – hot–cold and moist–dry. Each arm is divided into four intervals designating the four degrees of intensity of each quality, and these in turn are divided 'into 10. or 12. smaller partes, equal'. Dee's willingness to subdivide each degree into fractions is an unusual feature of the method he presents and indicates an assumption of a continuity of intension and remission through all degrees from one contrary to the other (*MP*,*.iij).[44] Dee gives two verbal rules for computing the resulting quality in a compound. With components of equal quantities, the result is the mid-point between the constituent degrees, arrived at either by subtracting the lesser from the greater of the contrary qualities or by averaging the degrees in a mixture of one quality with a substance either of the same quality or of temperate (neutral) disposition. If, however, different quantities of the components are involved, the proportion of each quality by weight enters the calculation of the resulting quality, and it is here that Dee recommends and illustrates the use of algebra in the calculations. Finally, if more than two substances are combined, these computations are applied to pairs of substances and then to pairs of these results until a single quality results (*MP*,*.iij–*.iiijᵛ).[45]

As in other cases, what Dee presents is not original, except for the application of algebra to the calculations, but is based on a treatise attributed to Roger Bacon but most likely dating from the early fourteenth century (*MP*,*.iij).[46] What makes this interesting is that Dee presents Bacon's method in conscious preference to other methods, of which he mentions Galen, Averroes, Arnold of Villanova, and Ramon Lull (*MP*,*.iij).[47] Although Dee favors Bacon to Averroes, the Bacon treatise is actually a somewhat more philosophically sophisticated development of the Averroist approach in which substantial forms suffer intension and remission and the quality of a composite substance results from the neutralization of part of the stronger form by the weaker. It is this understanding of intension that underlies the analogy with the *linea intensionis* and the arithmetic rules for calculating resulting qualities as infinitely divisible magnitudes.[48]

It was for just this reason that the Averroist position was generally criticized on philosophical grounds in the Middle Ages. The acceptance of fractional degrees of forms and their qualities was unheard of, and the implication that they were infinitely divisible flew in the face of the predominant understanding of Aristotelian metaphysics and natural philosophy.[49] What became the dominant formulation, one addressing just these problems in Aristotelian philosophy, was that of Arnold of Villanova, which preserved the absolute character of qualitative forms so that they do not suffer intension or remission, change occurring only in the potency of the activity of their virtues in a new substance resulting from changes in their ratio to one another.[50] Lull's method is both complex and idiosyncratic, but is similar to Arnold's in considering the perceived qualities of substances to result from the interaction of component qualities and forms.[51]

In accepting Bacon's position, Dee ignores all the philosophical problems medieval thinkers found inherent in the issue of mixtures. In fact, Dee says that he need not discuss the concept of mixture since 'Common Philosophy' – Aristotle – has already defined it, apparently unconcerned with the difficulties medieval philosophers found with the definition of a mixture as the 'unification of the combinables resulting from their alteration' (*MP*,*.iiij^v).[52] Why Dee chose Bacon's method may only stem from his general intellectual loyalty to his countryman, but it may also be that his mathematical inclinations contributed to his preference. If, in Proclan fashion, understanding the structural realities of nature results from projecting upon natural things the mathematical ideas of the mind, the model of intension and remission based on the infinitely divisible magnitudes of Euclidean geometry and manipulated arithmetically in non-Euclidean fashion as numbers rather than as proportions may have taken precedence over philosophical commitments to the indivisibility of forms. It is perhaps significant that the discussion of grading comes in a section on the practical application of arithmetic in which Dee recommends the utility of numbers not strictly based on multiples of units, including fractions and irrationals (*MP*,*.ij).

PHILOSOPHY, MATHEMATICS, AND MAGIC

For none of the instances of the application of mathematics to nature in the *Praeface*, either in the form of technologies to exploit nature for practical benefits, or as sciences yielding new understandings of the natural world, did a magical philosophy serve either as the critical stimulus or to inform Dee's approach to the material. All of these things, presented in the *Praeface* in the framework of Proclus's philosophy of mathematics, reflect Dee's early practical and scientific interests and derive from non-magical sources. Although Dee would be understandably reticent about the magical interests he developed in the 1560s, the *Praeface* does hint at these, and the way it does so indicates both how he integrated them with his philosophy of mathematics and why they had little to do with the mathematical arts and sciences. He mentions that man 'participateth with Spirits, and Angels', which echoes the magical ascent of the soul to the 'horizon aeternitatis' of the *Monas* (*MP*,c.iiij). His reference to the '*Numbers Formall*' by which Joachim of Fiora prophesied, echoes his interest in the sciences 'de numeris formalibus,' 'de ponderibus mysticis', and 'de mensuris divinis' that he associated with Trithemius, alchemy, and magic in the context of discovering the mysteries of divinity (*MP*,*.j).

The most significant passage touching on Dee's magical interests in the *Praeface* is in the section on 'archemastrie' in which it is not a matter of 'echoes' of earlier statements but of direct albeit ingeniously veiled references to magic. Here Dee says that to the science of archemastrie

> doth the *Science Alnirangiat*, great service. Muse nothyng of this name. I chaunge not the name, so vsed, and in Print published by other: beyng a name proper to the Science. Vnder this, commeth *Ars Sintrillia*, by *Artephius*, briefly written. But the chief Science, of the Archemaster, (in this world) as yet known,

is an other (as it were) OPTICAL Science: wherof, the name shall be told (God willyng) when I shall haue some, (more iust) occasion, therof, to Discourse.[53]

While the references in this puzzling section are obscure, 'alnirangiat' and the 'ars sintrillia' are both explicitly magical, and I believe the 'other OPTICAL Science' refers to 'scrying', which Dee may have practised in the late 1560s.

Although Dee says we should 'muse nothyng of this name', 'alnirangiat' was far from a common term in the Latin West. 'Nīrangiyāt' was an Arabic term used to refer to various kinds of magic ranging from tricks to talismans and conjuring.[54] In the *Ghāyat al-hakīm* (the Arabic source of *Picatrix*), 'nīrang' refers to magical charms or spells, rendered at one point in the *Picatrix* as 'images' (talismans, amulets) for the attraction of celestial spirits.[55] Dee's source for the term was Andrea Alpago's translation of Ibn Sīnā's (Avicenna) *De divisionibus scientiarum*, in which a 'scientia *alnirangiat*' is listed among the subordinate branches of natural science.[56] Here 'alnirangiat' is defined as the science of the magic art that joins together the virtues of earthly things to produce strange and extra-ordinary effects. Thus, it is a form of natural magic for the manipulation of the hidden virtues of things.[57] Dee cited this edition when he quoted Ibn Sīnā's definition of algebra earlier in the *Praeface*, and Dee's copy of this work has the section on alnirangiat annotated in his hand, with 'magicae' in the margin and 'alnirangiat' and 'artis magicae' underlined (*MP*,*.ij^v).[58]

Artephius's *Ars sintrillia* involves a magic much less 'natural' than Ibn Sīnā's conception of alnirangiat. Artephius, whose identity is obscure and who may never have existed, was occasionally cited by medieval and Renaissance authors, being granted a reputation for deep and extensive knowledge in the occult, particularly alchemy and magic.[59] The name first appears in Europe in the twelfth century, and a number of works, some of apparently Arabic origin, were attributed to him.[60] The source for Dee's reference to Artephius was a manuscript codex he owned in 1556 that contained an *Ars sintrillia* among its constituent works.[61] While this codex has been identified, this portion of the manuscript is now missing and no other work with the title *Ars sintrillia* has, to my knowledge, been identified either in manuscript or in print.[62]

A clue to what the *ars sintrillia* might be is that William of

Auvergne (ca. 1180–1249), in the course of discussing revelations through the inspection of lucid objects, mentions the practice of an Artesius for obtaining visions of hidden things through the glittering of water placed below a polished sword. Significantly William calls this practice the 'ars triblia vel syntriblia'.[63] Derived from the Greek, 'triblia' means a bowl, pot, or deep vessel, and in the form 'syntri-blia' is the ultimate source of Dee's *Ars sintrillia* by means of a trivial clerical error through which 'syntriblia' became 'sintrillia'.[64] A reference to the art of Artephius in a twelfth-century manuscript makes clear the meaning of the bowls; this is an art of divination by the reflection of the sun's rays from a metal instrument into three vessels filled respectively with water, wine, and oil.[65]

The earliest surviving manuscript containing Artephius's *Ars sintrillia* is from the seventeenth century, titled *Artetii ac Mininii apologia in artem magicam*, under the heading 'De scientia praeteri-torum, praesentium, ac futuorum'.[66] This describes the use of three vases of different materials filled with water, wine, and oil in which there are semiprecious stones (figure 6.2). These are arranged in various ways with candles and, by the reflection of the rays of the sun, moon, and stars into the liquids from several instruments, including a sword, make possible various kinds of divination, especially knowledge of the past, present, and future. That this manuscript is a copy of a work with a continuous history from the twelfth-century reference to the three vases of Artephius's art and William of Auvergne's mention of Artephius's 'ars triblia vel syntri-blia', is suggested by Ristoro d'Arezzo's citation of it in the thir-teenth century, Gianfrancesco Pico della Mirandola's mention of an 'ars Artephij', yielding both knowledge of the past, present, and future and prophecies of hidden things through the gathering of celestial rays in a mirror, and Girolamo Cardano's lengthy summary and quotation from an 'Ars magica Artefii et Mihinii', which he says he found in an old parchment manuscript containing works by Euclid and Campanus, that is identical to this manuscript.[67]

Clearly, Artephius was associated with a magical technique involving divination by means of reflecting surfaces and celestial radiations, which would have suggested to Dee that it was a particular instance of the general science of magic, or alnirangiat, which is how Dee describes it. The fact that the central mechanism in Artephius's art is optical – the reflection and refraction of celestial rays – also indicates that Dee's final statement that the 'other (as it were) Optical Science', which is the 'chief Science, of the Archemaster' is some form of magic related to Artephius's divination (*MP*,A.iij^v). This is supported by Dee's conception of optics, which as we have seen in the *Propaedeumata*, was a general science of all radiated influence, including occult formal influences. In addition to optics itself and astrology, this 'other' optical science is most likely an additional method of investigating radiated influences. What suggests itself as this science is catoptromancy, or divination by mirrors, crystals, gems, and other reflecting surfaces, something frequently mentioned in the occult and magical literature of the Renaissance and which was the foundation of his extensive 'spiritual exercises' in communicating with angels in the 1580s.[68] It is also something to which he devoted perhaps more than a purely intellectual attention in the 1560s.

This magical dimension of the *Praeface* is not only cryptic but, I would argue, deliberately obscure. Artephius's *Ars sintrillia* could not have been well known, and alnirangiat is equally obscure without a reference to Ibn Sīnā's text. Since Dee gives an explicit reference to the same text of Ibn Sīnā earlier in the *Praeface*, I am inclined to think he deliberately concealed the alnirangiat reference by leaving the term in its Arabic form and giving no source. This intentional obscurity about the magical aspect of archemastrie is not surprising, considering that this section immediately follows a long apologia in which Dee attempted to lay to rest his reputation, whether real or imagined, as a conjurer (*MP*,A.j^v–A.iij).

Formal numbers, mystical weights, divine measures, and optical divination may not have much to do with Archimedean statics, grading compound qualities, or making a more powerful crane, but that may be the important point. Instead of a knowledge of created nature in its own right, magic for Dee was directed toward gaining an understanding of and acquiring knowledge through the supernatural world of spirits, the intelligible forms, and ultimately God himself. Magic, in the spiritual variety Dee assimilated in the 1560s, led away from nature, and while magic does not appear to have stimulated, conditioned, or influenced his ideas on the mathematical arts and sciences of nature it also does not seem to have hindered them. Yet in the *Praeface* Dee seems to consider these rather disparate forms of knowledge spanning technology, natural science, and mystical natural theology, encompassing his practical activities, the natural philosophy of the *Propaedeumata*, and the rather different thinking represented in the *Monas*, as all mathematical and as all science is some way. Significantly, the mystical and magical dimensions of mathematics seem to be sanctioned by the third dimension of Proclus' philosophy in which mathematics serves in the intellectual ascent to 'knowledge incomparable, and Heauenly Wisedome' through knowledge of the supernatural, the eternal, and the divine (*MP*,*.j^v–*.ij, a.iij). The mathematical philosophy based on Proclus that Dee articulated in the *Praeface* thus may well represent his attempt to integrate the range of his previous work, all of which he considered mathematical, within a coherent framework. How Dee considered all of these things to be sciences, however, is a different issue, and Dee's position, derived not from Proclus, but from Roger Bacon, comes in the section on archemastrie, the one division of the mathematical arts and sciences without a precedent in Proclus and the one Dee considered the capstone of all the rest.

ARCHEMASTRIE

Archemastrie has been at the focus of all arguments that Dee's *Praeface* looks forward to the scientific revolution because it is there that he seems to advocate the modern idea of experimental method in his discussion of 'Experimentall Science' (*MP*,A.iij^v).[69] Dee considered archemastrie the sovereign science because it builds upon and extends all other arts and sciences. As he defines it, archemastrie is both theoretical and practical. It certifies and makes useful the conclusions of all the mathematical arts and of natural philosophy, it extends the boundaries of the existing arts, and it also leads to experiences or accomplishments beyond the scope of other sciences. What has attracted the attention of commentators is Dee's emphasis on experience and experiment. In the crucial passage Dee says: 'And bycause it procedeth by *Experiences*: and searcheth forth the causes of Conclusions, by *Experiences*: and also putteth the Conclusions them selues, in *Experience*, it is named of some, *Scientia Experimentalis*. The *Experimentall Science*' (*MP*,A.iij^v). Since these experiences and accomplishments include not only the natural magic of alnirangiat but also Artephius's divination and some other optical science that may also be divinatory, this progressive reading of Dee is questionable. Rather than understand archemastrie by trying to see how it is prophetic of the future, it will be more effective to see what it meant to Dee and how it functioned for him in the context of the *Praeface*.

The term archemastrie itself is not original to Dee, being first used by Thomas Norton in the *Ordinal of Alchemy* to mean 'full of mastery'.[70] Dee significantly expands upon Norton, associating the term with ideas on 'scientia experimentalis' that he found in Cusanus and especially Roger Bacon. Cusanus uses the term 'experimentalis scientia' in his *Idiota de staticis experimentis*, in which he argues the importance of the comparison of empirical quantitative measurements for the investigation of nature.[71] This citation of Cusanus echoes Dee's earlier citation of the *De staticis experimentis* in the section on statics praising the value of experiments of the balance as revealing how the world was created in number, weight, and measure. Here, however, Cusanus provides little more than a locus for the use of the phrase 'scientia experimentalis'. What Dee intended by archemastrie becomes even clearer when it is realized that he is closely paraphrasing Roger Bacon's discussion in the sixth book of his *Opus majus*, entitled 'De scientia experimentalis'.[72] Bacon distinguishes two ways of knowing: one by argument and persuasion, by which he may mean Aristotle's syllogistic demonstration *quia* and *propter quid*; the other by 'scientia experimentalis', which alone removes all doubts.[73] 'Experiment' in this context, however, means nothing more than experience, not the controlled testing of hypotheses as in its modern connotation. In addition to the physical experience of the external senses, Bacon included within his idea of experience a range of 'interior illuminations', including divine inspiration and mystical rapture, which are of greater certainty than the experience of the exterior senses.[74] Bacon's 'scientia experimentalis' and, following him, Dee's archemastrie are methodologically, therefore, quite diverse and ambiguous.

This diversity and ambiguity is revealed by the three prerogatives experimental science has over all other sciences according to Bacon, each of which is paralleled by Dee both in his discussion of archemastrie and in his discussion of the various arts and sciences. First, it investigates by experience (*per experimentiam*) the conclusions that other sciences reach by reasoning. Second, it is the method of reaching truths in the other sciences that they cannot arrive at by their own methods. And third, it has the power that no other science has to investigate the secrets of nature; namely, the ability to acquire knowledge of the future, the past, and the present, the formation of judgments better than ordinary judicial astrology, and the production of wonderful works.[75]

Bacon's first prerogative of verifying conclusions derived from reasoning, and Dee's idea that archemastrie certifies the conclusions of other arts completely and fully by sensible experiences, whereas the arts themselves use only words and arguments that persuade but do not prove, are perhaps the closest of the three to a modern notion of experimental method.[76] Bacon's investigation of the cause of the rainbow, which he gives as a working illustration of this aspect of his concept of experimental science, suggests the verification or falsification of a mathematical model through arranged experimental tests.[77] Dee's proposal in the *Propaedeumata* to establish empirically the nature of the astrological effects resulting from his mathematical model of astrological influence based on Bacon's philosophy of the multiplication of species may be considered a similar example of this feature of Bacon's experimental science. In both cases, however, the premises of the model are not being tested; they are assumed to be valid. It is only conclusions not derived by syllogistic from these premises that must be certified through experience. In many instances Bacon's idea of this first prerogative pertains only to the impact of experience to induce conviction in the conclusions of rational arguments and has more the pedagogical purpose of convincing a novice of a truth than the testing of a hypothesis, which is also found in Dee's reference to the mechanical quadrature of the circle and doubling of the cube as 'Experimentall demonstration' (*MP*,c.ij^v).[78]

For both Bacon and Dee the second prerogative of this 'doctrine *Experimentall*' is that it can discover truths in the other sciences that they cannot arrive at by their own methods.[79] This aspect of archemastrie is of interest because it implies that the sciences can be extended by the introduction of principles from outside their normal boundaries. One of the refreshing features of the *Praeface* is the freedom and flexibility with which Dee seems to encourage the development of existing arts and sciences and the elaboration of new ones through the interaction of several distinct approaches, something we have also noticed in the radical redefinition of the disciplines in the *Monas*. Although when convenient Dee can evoke Aristotle's idea of a demonstrative science that is self-contained and is developed only from its own proper principles and methods with its implied prohibition of *metabasis*, he is more often interested in crossing the boundaries that separate the sciences to extend their development in new directions and to create new sciences. His proliferation of new names for various mathematically based activities, defining as distinct arts various combinations of mathematics and technology, his blurring of the classical Euclidean distinction between number and magnitude, and his exaltation of an Archimedean fusion of mechanics and mathematics all point in this direction.[80] He quite explicitly admits that

> I am nothing affrayde, of the disdayne of some such, as thinke Sciences and Artes, to be but Seuen. . . . They can not prescribe a certaine number of Artes: and in eche, certaine vnpassable bounds, to God, Nature, and mans Industrie. New Artes, dayly rise vp: and there was no such order taken, that, All Artes, should in one age, or in one land, or by one man, be made knowen to the world (*MP*,c.iiij).[81]

Although on the grounds of his philosophy of mathematics Dee is able to present all his arts and sciences as in some way mathematical, it is clear that in most of those he lists mathematics contributes only one dimension of the development of the science while principles from physics, optics, astronomy, anatomy, or practical engineering and the like also make a significant contribution. It is the archemaster who 'steppeth in, and leadeth forth on, the *Experiences*, by order of his doctrine *Experimentall*, to the chief and final power of Naturall and Mathematicall Artes', by establishing the connections of mathematical and natural principles. Like Bacon's 'scientia experimentalis', Dee's archemastrie is less a distinct science with its own subject matter and principles than a catchword for the experiential methods that can be applied in all sciences and a sanction for giving consideration to the diffuse body of lore reporting natural effects and secrets that had no disciplinary home.[82] What it provides is a bridge between mathematics and the natural sciences and, through its privilege of ranging across existing sciences and arts, a justification of interdisciplinary sciences, which are also the functions of Bacon's 'scientia experimentalis' in his project for a unified science.[83]

While Dee's discussion of archemastrie closely parallels Bacon's first two prerogatives, Bacon's third prerogative of experimental science, the power to investigate the secrets of nature, is only indirectly included by Dee. From the examples Bacon gives, the third prerogative seems largely to involve the practical application of theoretical science, including the discovery of unsuspected inventions and the production of marvels.[84] Archemastrie, in leading to 'the chief and finall power of Natural and Mathematicall Artes' as well as the feats of thaumaturgike and menandrie may reflect this. However, the occult overtones of some of Bacon's examples, reflecting his interest in natural magic, his citation of the occultist *Secretum secretorum*, and the suspiciously Artephian reference to these secrets of nature including knowledge of the future, the past, and the present, most likely suggested to Dee that Bacon's third prerogative was more than just simple technology.[85] Rather than being out of place, alnirangiat and the *Ars sintrillia* are in fact an integral part of Dee's experimental science as he understood it from Bacon. Alnirangiat both as a form of natural magic for the manipulation of the hidden virtues of things in order to perform the wonderful works of nature and art that Bacon included as the third aspect of his 'scientia experimentalis' but also, in Ibn Sīnā's division of the sciences, as a science derived from the theoretical sciences of nature whose attribute is certain knowledge corresponds to Dee's idea of Archimastrie.[86] Dee's citation of Artephius also parallels Bacon, since Bacon not only mentions Artephius a number of times as a natural philosopher who gained exotic knowledge through travel to the orient, used methods of concealing philosophical secrets from the multitude, and, in conjunction with his treatment of 'scientia experimentalis', acquired through experience such a knowledge of the occult properties of nature that he was able to prolong life.[87] As a procedure for obtaining knowledge of the past, the present, and the future, the *Ars sintrillia* also conforms to Bacon's third prerogative of 'scientia experimentalis'.[88] In Dee's usage, 'experimental science' clearly retains its traditional broad meaning of experiential knowledge resulting from some sort of practical trial. In fact, experiment in this sense of a practical trial had a wide currency in sixteenth-century English magical manuscript literature, where the term experiment is used for a variety of magical practices, including crystalgazing and raising spirits.[89]

Dee considered archemastrie to be a unique and autonomous activity, not original to him but unknown and unpractised at his time. Dee's archemastrie combines the practices of the mathematical arts and of magic, and the goals and theories of natural philosophy, with methods of experiential verification. The resulting fusion cuts across traditional disciplinary divisions and, in his terms, consummates these disciplines by verifying them, grounding them in experience, while extending them toward the fulfillment of the highest objective of all the sciences: knowledge of the most fundamental and hidden principles of the creator's work. It is not merely a composite of these components, nor can it be reduced to primarily one or another of them, such as experimental science or magic.

While isolated aspects of Dee's 'doctrine experimentall' may perhaps represent a fruitful method for the investigation of nature and look forward to modern experimental methods, these aspects are inextricably tied to the magical aspects of archemastrie. This magic is not a narrow practical or instrumental natural magic that rejects occult virtues or the special esoteric and mystical insight of the sage. Rather, it is a magic related to Dee's occult and esoteric interests as found in the *Monas* and the later spiritual exercises. Thus it points in a direction of a spiritual knowledge so opposed to natural science as later understood that it is impossible to cite Dee's concept of archemastrie as evidence that Renaissance magic and occultism unambiguously contributed to the evolution of a new science. While it is not unlikely that Dee's *Praeface* may have stimulated others to scientific pursuits, it is more doubtful that Dee's magic in the *Praeface* played any role in this. It is quite unlikely that the artisans and practitioners, 'being vnlatined people, and not Vniuersitie Scholars', whom Dee claims for his audience, could have perceived the magical dimension, which Dee has deliberately obscured (*MP*,A.iij^v). It may have been Dee's ironic fate to have contributed to the progress of science among those who were ignorant of the magical direction which Dee thought was the highest level of science.

Proclus's philosophy of mathematics and archemastrie together provide a framework for understanding Dee's activities and views in natural philosophy as manifestations of a personal direction of endeavour rather than in terms of some coherent philosophy that does little justice to his broad and idiosyncratic eclecticism. From the 1550s through the 1560s Dee assimilated some very different approaches to natural philosophy, yet even after the rather mystical philosophy of the *Monas* he rejected neither the practice of practical science and technology nor the natural philosophy of the *Propaedeumata*. When the *Propaedeumata* was republished in 1568 he grafted on to the text additions that reflect the developments of the 1560s, but in the *Praeface* he still presents his theory of astrology in the context of an Aristotelian science. The implication of the *Praeface*, in which practical mathematics, practical technologies, Archimedean mechanics, an optical physics of radiated influences, and a mystically oriented magic are all subsumed as natural sciences within the philosophy of mathematics and archemastrie, seems to be that these various approaches to a knowledge of and through nature were not mutually exclusive but complementary and related hierarchically. The philosophy of the *Monas* did not render that of the *Propaedeumata* obsolete or invalid. Rather, it represented the higher knowledge of religious insight and illumination. Although the mystical magic of the *Monas* was based on a philosophy of nature and yielded knowledge of nature, its objective was not, as in the *Propaedeumata*, a theory of causal relations in the physical world but a spiritual and religious knowledge of the creator through the discovery of the hidden reasons behind creation.

Mathematics thus functions as a kind of magical nexus linking the divine world with the created world and linking man to both through mathematical understanding. This function of mathematics in the *Praeface* also suggests a coherence to Dee's developing sense of his social function. Tapping into the divine and the divine in nature conferred power, and Dee sought to capitalize on his ability to tender power to solicit enhanced patronage. With the knowledge of the creator and the divine plan for the universe that Dee claimed in the *Monas* came moral insight, the spiritual transformation of the adept, and prophetic powers, which were the basis of his appeals to Cecil in 1562 and to Maximilian in 1564. Yet besides secret wisdom Dee had also offered Cecil practical knowledge that would rebound to the glory of the patron through its benefits to the commonwealth. It is also for their benefit to the commonwealth that Dee recommends the value of the work of the 'Common Artificer', benefits that will be enhanced through the 'good helpes and informations' he has provided in the *Praeface* (*MP*,A.iiij). Dee could function as an intermediary in the social hierarchy, tendering to both rulers and practitioners the benefits of the power of mathematics to range between the divine and the practical. The following chapter will explore his attempts to gain recognition and the attendant rewards for this status.

VII

THE VAGARIES OF PATRONAGE, 1565–1583

The impression given in the *Praeface* that magic neither encouraged nor detracted from practical and level-headed scientific work is reinforced by the record of Dee'a actual activities in the period between his return to England after publishing the *Monas* and 1583 when he dropped almost everything to pursue enlightenment and riches in the East. These activities spanned the broad range of interests that had emerged during the earlier years of his life, and included a number of mathematical works, alchemical experiments, consultation on English voyages of exploration, and continued interest in theology and spirit magic.

In mathematics, in addition to the annotations that he prepared for the English edition of Euclid, there are also two manuscript fragments from 1565 of purely mathematical work, one dealing with inscribing and circumscribing circles in and around various plane polygons, the other dealing with incommensurable lines (*CR*,25; *LA*,76).[1] The appearance of a super nova in Cassiopeia in 1572 was the occasion for his publication of a work on the determination of the parallax of a circumpolar object, and the title of another work he claims to have written, as well as other reports, indicate that he and Thomas Digges concluded, contrary to Aristotelian cosmology that the heavens are unchanging, that the nova was celestial rather than elemental and receding from the earth, although it is unlikely that Dee's method was practical for this purpose.[2] In mathematical navigation Dee devised by 1575 a solution to the nautical triangle which was the basis for the navigational tables he intended but never published because of their great expense.[3] Here, as in the case of his work on parallax, both his mathematical solution and the tables were not directly usable in practice. Of the greatest potential impact was Dee's work of 1583 on the reform of the calendar, which also turned out to be his last significant work in science. Prompted by the institution of the Gregorian calendar on the continent, Dee was commissioned by the government to study the issue (*CR*,22–3).[4] Although he considered it preferable to rectify the calendar on the basis of the date of the birth of Christ rather than the time of the Council of Nicea as the Gregorian reform did, thereby eliminating eleven rather than ten days, he recommended that England conform to the calendar being adopted elsewhere in Europe and provided a revised calendar for the remainder of 1583 incorporating the gradual elimination of the necessary days from May through August.[5] His proposals, despite their favourable reception by the government, were not instituted because of ecclesiastical opposition.[6]

During this same period there is evidence of continuous and considerable alchemical activity on Dee's part. Settlement at the family house in Mortlake in the later 1560s provided him with more space than he likely had when he lived in London, and by 1583 he had built three laboratories with a substantial amount of apparatus in several buildings on the property (*CR*,30–1). He reports beinging chemicals from Europe as early as 1571, and Roger Cook, who was serving Dee as an alchemical assistant when he left in 1581, had been with Dee since 1567, although it is not clear if he functioned as an alchemical assistant from the very beginning (*CR*,30–1).[7] There are very few indications of the nature of these alchemical activities, although the philosophers' stone and the elixir of transmutation were not unlikely Dee's ultimate concern since this was one of his main concerns in the 'angelic conversations' with Edward Kelley. Existing indications, however, suggest that he devoted considerable attention to practical chemical operations. In 1579 he noted showing visitors the manner of drawing aromatic oils.[8] A diary of chemical activities from June to October 1581 records a sequence of solutions and distillations. While it is difficult to determine exactly what was involved because the record is incomplete, what is notable is the absence of the metaphorical language of the *Monas* and the attention to quantitative precision, the exact quantities of ingredients and duration of various operations being noted quite exactly.[9]

The mystical and spiritual interests of the 1560s also continued to exert themselves. Dee discussed the mysteries provided by the

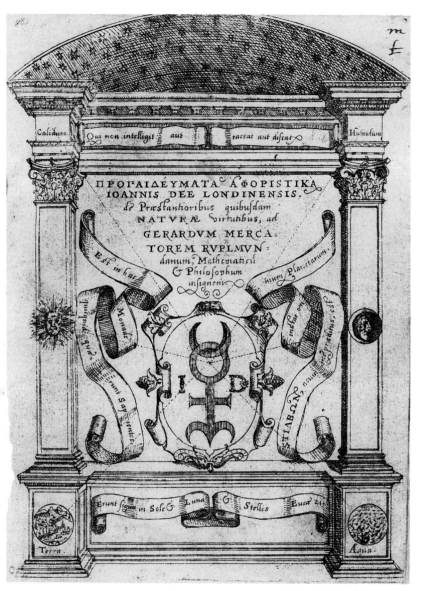

2.1 Title page, *Propaedeumata aphoristica*, 1558 (By permission of the Beinecke Rare Book and Manuscript Library, Yale University)

4.1 Monas hieroglyphica, Dee, *Monas hieroglyphica*,
fol.12 (Rare Book and Special Collections
Division, Library of Congress, Washington, DC)

MONAS
HIERO-
GLYPHI-
CA.

4.2 Title page, *Monas hieroglyphica*, 1564 (By permission of the Beinecke
Rare Book and Manuscript Library, Yale University)

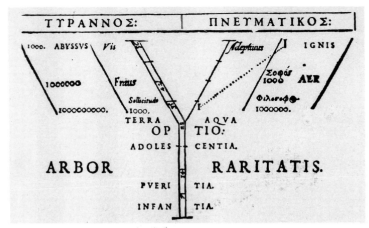

4.3 'Arbor raritatis', Dee, *Monas hieroglyphica*, fol.3 (Rare Book and Special Collections Division, Library of Congress, Washington, DC)

4.4 Pythagorean 'Y', Tory, *Champ fleury,* fol.127v (Lessing J. Rosenwald Collection, Library of Congress, Washington, DC)

4.5 Point, line, circle, Dee, *Monas hieroglyphica,* fol.12 (Rare Book and Special Collections Division, Library of Congress, Washington, DC)

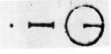

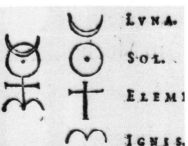

4.6 Monas and cosmos, Dee, *Monas hieroglyphica,* fol.13v (Rare Book and Special Collections Division, Library of Congress, Washington, DC)

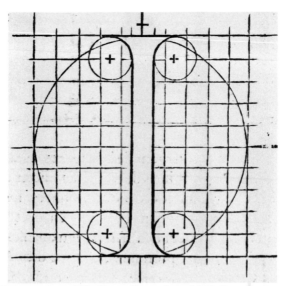

4.7 Construction of 'I', Tory, *Champ fleury,* fol.93 (Lessing J. Rosenwald Collection, Library of Congress, Washington, DC)

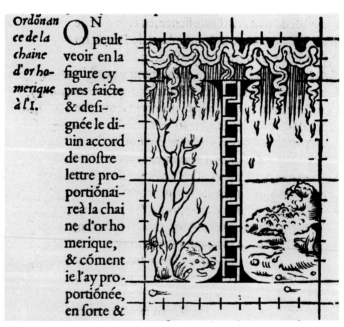

Ordōnance de la chaine d'or homerique à l'I.

ON peult veoir en la figure cy pres faicte & defignée le diuin accord de noftre lettre proportiónaire à la chaine d'or homerique, & cóment ie l'ay proportiónée, en forte &

4.8 'I' and the Golden Chain, Tory, *Champ fleury,* fol.53v (Lessing J. Rosenwald Collection, Library of Congress, Washington, DC)

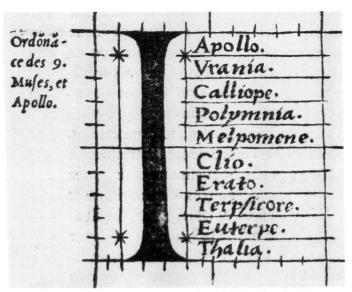

Ordōnā-
ce des 9.
Muſes, et
Apollo.

Apollo.
Vrania.
Calliope.
Polymnia.
Melpomene.
Clio.
Erato.
Terpſicore.
Euterpe.
Thalia.

4.9 'I' and the Muses, Tory, *Champ fleury,* fol.29v (Lessing J.
Rosenwald Collection, Library of Congress, Washington, DC)

Apollo.
Muſica.
Aſtronomia.
Arithmetica.
Geometria.
Rhetorica.
Dialectica.
Gramm.

4.10 'O' and the Liberal Arts, Tory, *Champ fleury,* fol.30v
(Lessing J. Rosenwald Collection, Library of Congress,
Washington, DC)

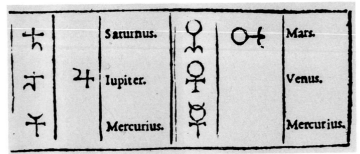

4.11 Signs of the planets generated from Monas, Dee, *Monas hieroglyphica*, fol.14 (Rare Book and Special Collections Division, Library of Congress, Washington, DC)

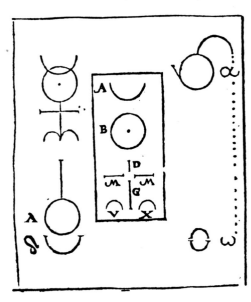

4.12 Alchemical vessels generated from Monas, Dee, *Monas hieroglyphica*, fol.22 (Rare Book and Special Collections Division, Library of Congress, Washington, DC)

4.13 The 'exaltation of the moon and the sun by the science of the elements', Dee, *Monas hieroglyphica*, fol.15 (Rare Book and Special Collections Division, Library of Congress, Washington, DC)

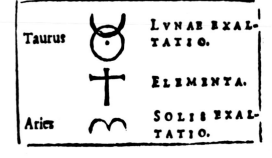

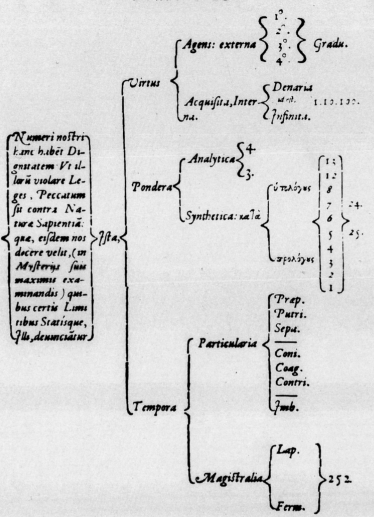

4.14 Numbers, weights, measures, Dee, *Monas hieroglyphica*, fol.26v (Rare Book and Special Collections Division, Library of Congress, Washington, DC)

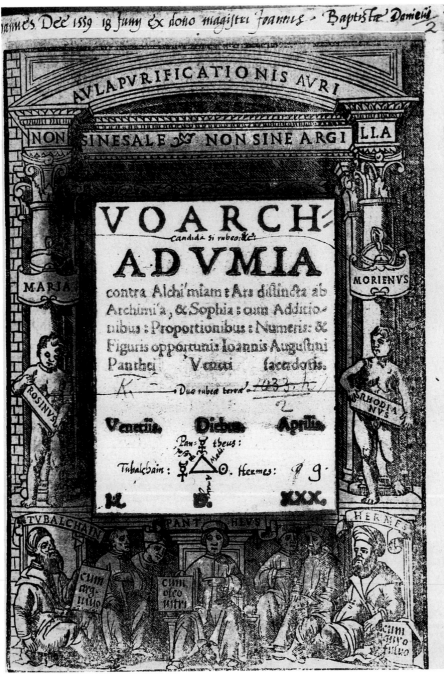

4.15 Title page, Joannes Pantheus, *Voarchadumia*, 1559
(By permission of the British Library)

Miſtio in radicibus unitatis ſeptuageſimiſecũdi Voarch‑
adúmicorum elementorum.   Caput quartum.

O . 14 . Lux minor: Inſertio reſpõdentiæ Charat‑
torum.xii.g.cp.1. in circa: ſeu.xxiii.g.cp.1. &, ½, in circa.
S . 18 . Ignis.i.Lux maior.
I . 9 . Cómerriſón.
R . 17 . Aer.i.Lux minor.
O' . 14 . Lux maior.

72 .

N . 13 . Oleum uitri.
G . 7 . Lux minor: Inſertio reſpondentiæ Charat‑
torum.xiii.g.cp.2. &, ½, ſeu.xxiii.g.cp.2. in circa.
A . 1 . Materia prima artis.
T . 19 . Ignis.i.Lux maior.
S . 18 . Aer.i.Lux minor.
O' . 14 . Lux maior.

72 .

4.16 Dee's notes, Pantheus, *Voarchadumia*, fol.18
(By permission of the British Library)

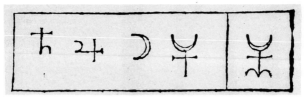

4.17 The genesis of lunar mercury, Dee, *Monas
hieroglyphica*, fol.14 (Rare Book and Special Collections
Division, Library of Congress, Washington, DC)

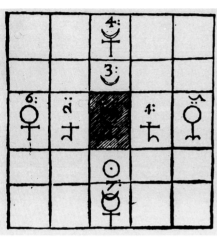

4.18 The seven stages, Dee, *Monas
hieroglyphica*, fol.14v (Rare Book and
Special Collections Division, Library
of Congress, Washington, DC)

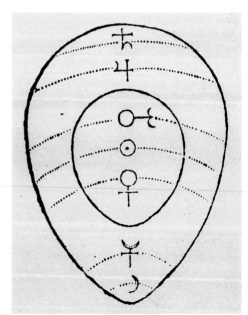

4.19 The celestial egg, Dee, *Monas
hieroglyphica*, fol.17 (Rare Book and
Special Collections Division, Library
of Congress, Washington, DC)

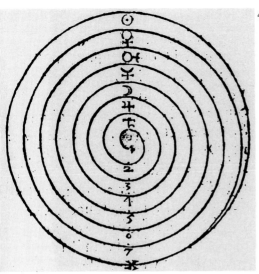

4.20 The seven celestial revolutions, Dee, *Monas hieroglyphica*, fol.18 (Rare Book and Special Collections Division, Library of Congress, Washington, DC)

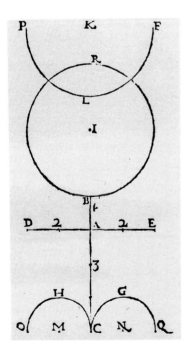

4.21 Geometrical construction of the Monas, Dee, *Monas hieroglyphica*, fol.24 (Rare Book and Special Collections Division, Library of Congress, Washington, DC)

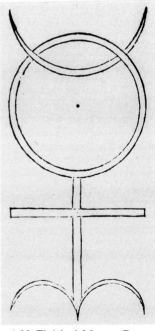

4.22 Finished Monas, Dee, *Monas hieroglyphica*, fol.25 (Rare Book and Special Collections Division, Library of Congress, Washington, DC)

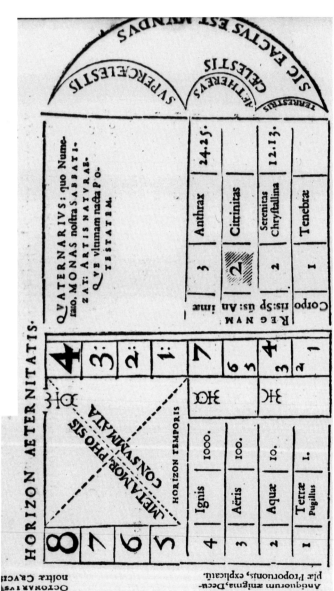

4.23 Cosmic correspondences, Dee, *Monas hieroglyphica*, fol.27 (Rare Book and Special Collections Division, Library of Congress, Washington, DC)

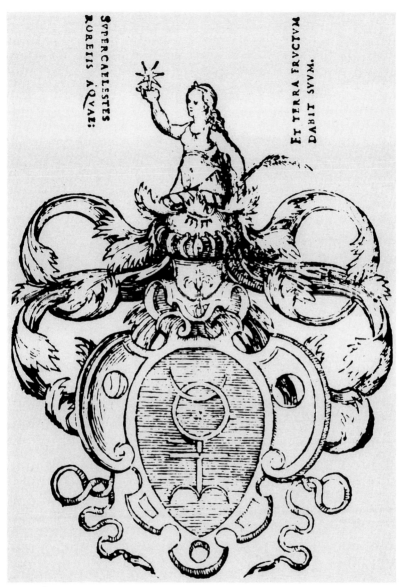

5.1 Colophon, Dee, *Monas hieroglyphica* (Rare Book and Special Collections Division, Library of Congress, Washington, DC)

Propædeumata Aphoristica

IOANNIS DEE, LONDINENSIS,

De Præftantioribus quibufdam

Naturæ virtutibus.

SVPERCAELESTES   ET TERRA FRVCTV
RORETIS AQVAE.   DABIT SVVM.

QVATER △ NARIVS

IN TERNARIO CONQVIESCENS.

Londini.

Anno. M.D.LXVIII.

5.2 Title page, Dee, *Propaedeumata aphoristica*, 1568
(By permission of Folger Shakespeare Library)

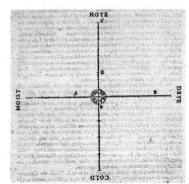

6.1 The 'crosse of graduation', Dee, *Mathematicall Praeface*, sig.*.iijv (By permission of the Folger Shakespeare Library)

6.2 'Ars sintrillia', *Artetii ac Mininii apologia in artem magicam*, Oesterreichische Nationalbibliothek, MS 11,294, fol.28 (Vienna, Oesterreichische Nationalbibliothek, Handschriften- und Inkunabelsammlung)

7.1 Title page, Dee, *General and Rare Memorials*
(By permission of the Folger Shakespeare Library)

A LETTER,

Containing a moſt briefe Diſcourſe Apologeticall, with a plaine Demonſtration, and feruent Proteſtation, for the lawfull, ſincere, very faithfull and Chriſtian courſe, of the Philoſophicall ſtudies and exerciſes, of a certaine ſtudious Gentleman : An ancient Seruaunt to her moſt excellent Maieſty Royall.

PARALLATICAE

Commentationis Praxeofq;

Nucleus quidam.

Authore Joanne Dee,
Londinenſi.

TIMEBO : Δ : IEOVA : FORTITVDO : MEA : A : QVO :

LONDINI
Apud Johannem Dayum Typo-
graphum. An. 1573.

7.3 Title page, Dee, *Parallaticae commentationis praxeosque*, 1573
(By permission of the Folger Shakespeare Library)

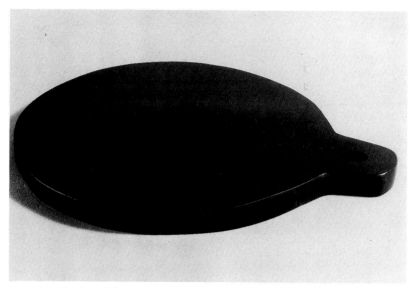

8.1 Dee's obsidian speculum
(Reproduced by courtesy of the Trustees of the British Museum)

8.2 Dee's 'crystal ball'
(Reproduced by courtesy of the Trustees of the British Museum)

8.3 Table from the 'Book of Enoch', Dee, *True and Faithful Relation*,
sig.[*.3]+[6]. (From author's copy.) After *Liber mysterium sextus et
sanctus*, British Library, MS Sloane 3189, fol.17

Liber Scientiae, Auxilij, & Victoriae Terrestris

Liber Scientiae

	91 Partium Terrae Nomina ab Hominibus imposita	91 Diuinae Impositionis Characteres Gymnetrici	30 Bonorum Primicapum Aereorum Ordines Speciarici	Bonorū Ministrantium vniuscuiusque Ordinis Numerus Tripartitus	Bonorū Ministrantium in singula Ordinibus Tripartitorum Numeri Totales	12 Angeli Reges, post 30 Ordines Trū bus praedominantes, qui 12 etiam Tribui Praesides sunt.	12 Tribus Populi Israelitici, in diuersone dispersae.	4 Plagae Mundi Tribubus Dispersis magna fūe.
Nonaginta et vnius Partium, Series Continua								
1 Aegyptus.	Occodon.	[symbol]	Ordo 1? LIL	1. 7209	14931	9. ZARZILG	Nephtalim	Orien. Aqstr.
2 Syria.	Pascomb.	[symbol]		2. 2360		11. ZINGGEN	Zabulon	Occid. dextr.
3 Mesopotamia	Valgars.	[symbol]		3. 5362		7. ALPUDUS	Isacamas	Occid. Sinistr.

8.4 Table of spirits, Dee, *Liber Scientiae, Auxiliae, Auxilij, & Victoriae Terrestris*. British Library, MS Sloane 3191, fol.16
(By permission of the British Library)

BBARNFL
BBAIGAO
BBALPAE
BBANIFG
BBROSNIA
BBASNOD

8.5 King Naspol, Dee, *De heptarchia mystica*, British Library, MS Sloane 3191, 42 (By permission of the British Library)

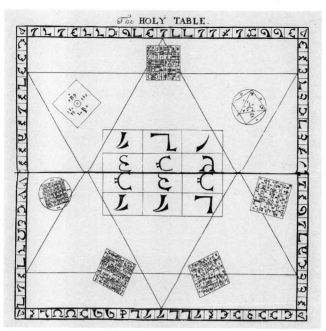

8.6 The Holy Table, or Table of Practice, Dee, *True and Faithful Relation*, sig.[*.3]+[5] (From author's copy)

8.7 Dee's Wax Disk
(Reproduced by courtesy of the Trustees of the British Museum)

VIGINTI QVATVOR SENIORVM (de quibus in Apocalypsi Beati Ioannis est mentio) ex Patris, Filij et Spiritus Sancti Imeis, collecta Nomina : Istoru Bonoru Angelorum Munus est, Hoibus, Reru humanarum Scientiam, Judiciumq impertire, &c

	Numen Diuinum BATAIVA, siue **BATAIVH**
	Abioro, siue Habioro
	Aaoxaif
ORINS	Htmorda
	Haozpi, siue Ahaozpi
	Hipotga
	Autotar
	Numen Diuinum ICZHHCA, siue **ICZHHCL**
	Aidrom, siue Laidrom
	Aczinor
MERIDIES	Lzinopo
	Lhctga, siue Alhctga
	Lbiansa
	Acmhcu
	Numen Diuinum RAAGIOS siue **RAAGIOL**
	Srahpm, siue Lsrahpm
	Saiihou
OCCIDENS	Laoaxrp
	Lgaiol, siue Slgaiol
	Ligdisa
	Soaixnt
	Numen Diuinum EDLPRNA, siue **EDLPRNA**
	Aetpio, siue AAetpio
	Adococt
SEPTENT.	Afndood
	Aphoce, siue Aaphoce
	Arinnap
	Anodoin

8.8 Twenty-four seniors, Dee, *De heptarchia mystica*, British Library MS Sloane 3191 (By permission of the British Library)

holy spirit for man's instruction and the nature of the last judgement in correspondence with Roger Edwards, reflecting themes from the *Monas*.[10] Most notable is evidence of a continuation or resumption of the practice of spirit magic. The earliest recorded spiritual conference is with Barnabas Saul on 22 December, 1581, but Dee had dealings with Saul from as early as October 1581 until March 1582 when Saul confessed that he no longer heard or saw spiritual creatures.[11] The note of a particular way of prayer in use since 1579 and Dee's reference that before his discovery of Saul he had 'perceived by some slight experience, with two diverse persons, that thou [God] hadst a special care to give me thy light, and truth, by thy holy and true ministers Angelicall and Spirituall' suggest earlier attempts.[12] In fact, in May 1581, before Saul appears in the *Diary*, he recorded that 'I had sight in *crystallo* offered me, and I saw', which is also noteworthy because Dee rarely saw any of the visions.[13] There is no record of who the two persons were prior to Saul, but there is no lack of possibilities, given Dee's weakness for somewhat shady characters offering secret knowledge. In 1579 John Davis and William Emery are again or still involved with Dee in some way, in the same year he met Bartholomew Hickman, who served Dee as scryer from 1591 until at least 1607, and in 1581 Robert Gardiner, who later revealed to Dee a great philosophical secret he had learned from a spiritual creature, briefly came to Dee's service.[14]

The fact that Dee's alchemical and spiritual pursuits were concurrent with his work on the calendar and extensive involvement in the planning of several voyages of exploration indicate that these activities were not mutually exclusive. While he could pursue these diverse activities without apparent conflict, the resurgence of spiritual magic is ominous since it is also difficult to ignore the fact that quite abruptly, and at a time when several projects were still incomplete, Dee left England with his recently discovered and most successful scryer to follow a Polish lord on his return to eastern Europe. The motivation behind this juggernaut is of considerable interest, since this absorption in spirit magic and eastern European adventure bring to an effective close his productive career and his intellectual development. Since he was interested, if not attempting to practise, spirit magic from the late 1560s, the answer is more complex than that he had discovered something new. This displacement seems to have resulted less because this spirit magic was intrinsically incompatible with the practice of 'normal' science than because Dee's activities turned increasingly to ideological and political issues in conjunction with his involvement with English projects of geographical exploration and because it was a compensation for the growing disappointment of his social and intellectual ambitions at the same time. Dee's activities during his Mortlake residence were explorations in exploiting his various intellectual accomplishments to define a role for himself within Elizabethan society and to secure reliable support for his intellectual pursuits.

EXPLORATION AND IMPERIAL IDEOLOGY

Dee's most persistent interest during this period was with various English projects for exploration. These projects included several attempts to discover a northern route to the Far East, resuming the efforts that had led to the founding of the Muscovy Company to which he contributed during Edward VI's reign, and the more novel attempts to colonize North America that originated with Humphrey Gilbert and culminated with Walter Raleigh's colony of Virginia. In this period his role was less that of technical consultant on navigation, as it had been earlier, and increasingly turned toward propagandizing particular objectives for English exploration in terms of his idea of a British Empire, a phrase he seems to have coined, making him seem prophetic of an immensely important feature of later English history. Dee's actual role in these various projects is neither well documented nor easy to determine.[15] Without pretending to solve all the problems involved or to give an account of English exploration in its own right, some consideration of Dee's activities related to these projects is of interest for what they reveal of his status in England and how he regarded his intellectual role.

With the establishment of trade relations with Russia and the foundation of the Muscovy Company in the early 1550s, the original objective of finding a northern route to the Far East (Cathay) fell into abeyance.[16] Interest in this project was revived, however, in the mid-1560s. In 1565 Anthony Jenkinson and Humphrey Gilbert made separate proposals to both Elizabeth and the Privy Council for support for resumption of exploration of a northern route to Cathay, eventually joining forces in favor of a Northwest passage around North America.[17] Although not published at the time, Gilbert wrote his *A Discourse of a Discovery* in 1566 arguing the practicality of such a route and the advantages to England of discovering it. Significantly, in addition to circumventing the Spanish and the Portuguese to take advantage of the wealth of trade with the Far East, Gilbert also suggested the possibility of establishing colonies in North America, and in a subsequent petition to the government in 1568 for a charter to explore, he asked for the grant of land in North American territories discovered as well as trading rights.[18]

Nothing concrete materialized from Gilbert's proposals at this time, but Dee was aware of them. Gilbert may have consulted Dee in preparing his arguments on the geographical feasibility of such a voyage, but the evidence is too meagre to determine their relationship in detail and it seems clear that the idea of colonization was original to Gilbert.[19] It was also at this time that Dee wrote a work at the request of Edward Dyer to which he refers as the 'Atlanticall Discourses' dealing with voyages of discovery.[20] This no longer exists but may be the same work as a *Reipublicae Britannicae Synopsis* of which only an outline dated 1570 exists.[21] If they are the same work, the outline indicates that Dee discussed the issue of voyages of discovery in the larger context of what factors would contribute to making England a flourishing kingdom. Dyer had come to court in 1565 as a protégé of the Earl of Leicester.[22] Since Leicester's father had been one of the promoters of Richard Chancellor's explorations and it was through his position in Dudley's household that Dee became associated with the early Muscovy voyages, it may be that Gilbert's new proposals prompted the consultation of Dee and that this, rather than any direct contact, may be how he learned of Gilbert's plans. Two things emerge from this. First, Dee was not an initiator in this renewed interest in exploration but he was consulted, perhaps because of his previous experience or because of his recognized expertise in navigation and geography. Second, when he was consulted he viewed his role as not limited to purely technical matters of geography and navigation but as extending to broader political issues as well.

This same pattern carries over to Dee's relation to subsequent exploration initiatives which proliferated in the 1570s. In 1576 Martin Frobisher began the first of three voyages to search for a Northwest passage. Planning for this had begun as early as 1574 when Frobisher and Michael Lok, a London merchant and the primary promoter of the project, approached the Muscovy Company, which held a monopoly for all northern exploration, for a licence for the voyage.[23] Dee does not seem to have been aware of these plans until 1576 when Dyer once again brought the matter to his attention by showing him Gilbert's recently published *Discourse of a Discovery* with a preface by George Gascoigne citing Dee's commendation of Gilbert's ideas in the *Mathematicall Praeface*.[24] This prompted Dee to make contact with Lok and Frobisher and as a result he provided some last minute and not very successful instruction in mathematical navigation to the sailors at the Muscovy House.[25] This was also the occasion that seems to have motivated Dee to prepare with great haste his *General and Rare Memorials pertayning to the Perfect Art of Navigation* setting forth his vision of a maritime British Empire.

This work actually comprised four distinct volumes, of which only two survive and one was published. The volume published in summer 1577 under the general title *General and Rare Memorials*, with the specific title *The Brytish Monarchie*, was written in early August 1576. Also referred to by Dee as *The Pety Navy Royall*, it urges Elizabeth to follow King Edgar and establish a standing Royal navy as the foundation for the re-establishment, security, and prosperity of the historic British Empire of King Arthur.[26] The second volume, written in autumn 1576, was *The Brytish Complement of the Perfect Art of Navigation* containing navigational tables. This was not printed because of the great expense and is now lost.[27] Of the third volume all Dee tells us is that he burnt it.[28] The final volume titled *Of Famous and Rich Discoveries* was written in the spring of 1577 and survives in manuscript.[29] This is a vast compilation of legendary and historical accounts of voyages in quest of the riches of the Far East beginning with that of Solomon to Ophir. In the course of this Dee proposes a rather unconventional map of northeast Asia above which he believed there was a very easy navigable route to Cathay, urging that England pursue this, and in conclusion Dee advances vast claims for Elizabeth's title to foreign lands. On the principle that territorial waters extend 100 miles from shore in conjunction with legendary reports of the foundation of the British monarchy by Brutus the Trojan and the conquests of the British kings Arthur and Malgo, Dee claims that Elizabeth has a legitimate claim to North America and to all territories within the 'oceanus brytannicus' extending from England north between North America and Norway.[30]

Much of this seems far-fetched, but so much of the world was unknown that contemporary geography allowed ample play for the imagination. He did not entirely lose touch with contemporary geography, consulting Abraham Ortelius and Mercator, whose reply Dee interpreted as confirming his ideas about Arthur's conquests, but his revision of the map of all of northeast Asia was so extraordinary that Richard Hakluyt, the emerging geographer of the next generation, found it hard to accept and could not get Mercator to confirm it.[31] The old British histories with their stories of Brutus and Arthur were coming under increasing scrutiny and attack, but they were an important element in Tudor political and religious ideology which Dee found useful to his purposes.[32] Dee's ideological purpose was so insistent that he marshalled any material from the historical record, no matter how legendary, to fill the gaps of contemporary geographical knowledge if it served that purpose.

It is unlikely that Frobisher's Northwest passage project was Dee's only concern in a work of this magnitude and scope, the first part of which was written only after Frobisher had departed, and the major objective of the fourth part was a Northeast passage. Rather, it would appear that Dee was either riding or being carried along by a wave of political activity that was the larger context of the voyages in the late 1570s to which the ideological content of the work was addressed. Frobisher's voyage was not the only one being planned in 1575 and 1576. Preparations were also being made for what became Francis Drake's famous voyage of circumnavigation and piracy of Spanish treasure that began in 1577. Ostensibly a private venture, Drake's voyage clearly had the support and encouragement of some elements in the government as an instrument of an anti-Spanish policy.

It is not inconsequential that some of those who were most active in supporting Drake's voyage – Francis Walsingham, the Earl of Leicester, and Christopher Hatton – were also the major proponents of an activist and aggressive policy opposing what they considered the very real threat to England posed by Spain.[33] On the continent this policy was aimed at creating a 'Protestant League' with the Dutch rebels and other princes to oppose Spanish power.[34] Another dimension of this policy involved the support of maritime enterprises directed against Spain in America on the theory that Spanish power rested on the importation of American treasure. This involved not only rather direct initiatives such as Drake's but also attempts to cut into the privileged trade routes of the Spanish and the

Portuguese and the exploration of territory and trade routes in areas Spanish and Portuguese power had not reached. Frobisher's Northwest passage project was, therefore, considered instrumental in this same policy, and it is no surprise that it also received support from Walsingham and other 'Protestant activists' at court.[35]

Humphrey Gilbert also became involved in these initiatives. He had some contact with Michael Lok in conjunction with Frobisher's voyage in 1575, and the publication of his *Discourse of a Discovery*, appearing well after the planning had begun, may well have served primarily as an advertisement for the enterprise.[36] Even more to the point, in 1577 he addressed a proposal to Elizabeth outlining 'how her Majesty may annoy the King of Spain', which under the pretext of expeditions of exploration and colonization would aim at attacking Spanish, Portuguese, and French fishing fleets off Newfoundland and piracy in the Caribbean.[37] This was followed in 1578 by the grant of letters patent for the establishment of colonies, granting Gilbert possession of all land, control over all trade, and full powers of justice and legislation with the proviso that the Crown receive a fifth of any gold and silver discovered, and that same autumn Gilbert led an expedition that disintegrated because of bad weather and dissension, and degenerated into some haphazard piracy.[38] Walsingham's influence was instrumental in securing Gilbert's patent, Gilbert being able to exploit the aggressive policy trend at court and Walsingham adding Gilbert's colonization scheme to the Drake and Frobisher expeditions in the offensive to 'annoy' the King of Spain.[39]

This aggressive anti-Spanish policy was not unchallenged within the government. Burghley favoured a much more cautious policy and Elizabeth inclined in that direction. She was distrustful of the efforts of Philip Sidney, another member of the activist group, to make contacts during his diplomatic trip to Europe in June 1577 with Protestant rulers, particularly William of Orange, as the foundation for a Protestant League, and annoyed when Sidney and other members of the group opposed her consideration of marriage with the Duke of Alençon.[40] In the context of this political debate, Dee's *General and Rare Memorials* served a clear ideological function, strikingly rendered in Dee's title-page illustration (figure 7.1).[41] In this 'British hieroglyphik', as the border calls it, the kneeling figure of 'Respublica Britannica' implores Elizabeth, at the helm of the 'Imperiall Monarchy' – or even of the 'Imperiall Ship, of the most part of Christendome: if so it be her Graces Pleasure' (labelled 'Europa') – to seize 'Occasio' (the figure on the fortress); an armed expedition under the benevolent disposition of the heavens and of God, who will send his 'Good Angell with sword and shield', will help Britain to make its citadel secure and gain 'Publik Commodities Innumerable, and (as yet) Incredible'.[42] The entire work urges upon Elizabeth, and implicitly the cautious voices in her councils, a policy of vigorous national self-assertion in which naval power was the instrument for securing Britain's peace and security, and implementing imperial claims, justifying this by evoking the British myth the Tudors had claimed as a sanction of their rights.[43] With regard to Europe, Dee is advocating that England should assume leadership of European affairs. With regard to America, his interpretation of the conquests of Arthur and other early Britons as well as later English explorers legitimated English colonization by challenging the Spanish claim to all of America through the assertion of England's right by prior conquest to North America. These territorial claims, further bolstered with the legend of a twelfth-century colony established in Florida by the Welsh Lord Owen Madoc, were the subject of several works Dee prepared specifically at Elizabeth's request and discussed with her as well as Walsingham and Burghley.[44]

Several observations with somewhat different levels of confidence emerge from this. Dee was neither an initiator nor a major planner of these projects for discovery, and while he may have attempted to exploit them as an opportunity to promote the adoption of his political views among the 'activist' group and so by Elizabeth, it seems more likely that he was not reluctantly drawn into the political arena by the partisans of an activist foreign and imperial policy to exploit his status as an expert in geography and navigation to advance their political programme.[45] Once again, it was Edward Dyer, an associate of Leicester and a close friend of Sir Philip Sidney, who made the first contact and was responsible for the dedication of the *General and Rare Memorials* to Dyer's close friend Sir Christopher Hatton, one of Elizabeth's most favoured courtiers, an associate of Leicester, and another advocate of the 'activist' policies with which Dyer was associated.[46] Dee indicates that the first volume of this work on *The Brytish Monarchie* was similar to the 'Atlanticall Discourses' and the 'Reipublicae Britannicae Synopsis' he had done for Dyer in the late 1560s, so Dyer certainly knew that

Dee's ideas would be favourable and useful in their cause.[47] Following this and just before he began work on the *Famous and Rich Discoveries*, in which he establishes the foundations for Elizabeth's imperial claims, Dee met with Leicester, Sidney, and Dyer.[48]

Since Dee gives no hint of the subject of the meeting and none of the other participants recorded it, a number of possibilities may be offered, all quite compatible with the message of his 'british hieroglyphic' and the 'Perfect Policie' urged in *General and Rare Memorials*. J. M. Osborn has suggested that it may have been for Dee's library and his science and learning, or merely out of curiosity, or as a preparation for Philip's forthcoming embassy to Europe through which he would test the diplomatic climate for the creation of a Protestant League.[49] E. G. R. Taylor has argued that it had something to do with the planning of Drake's voyage, since Leicester was one of the promoters of the voyage, and the Earl of Bedford, who was Drake's godfather, visited Dee several days later and because Dee refers in the *Famous and Rich Discoveries* to an imminent voyage that he suggests should test his theory of the location of the Straits of Anian separating Asia and North America in the Pacific.[50] Even if they were not consulting him on the matter of the voyage, Taylor's evidence indicates that Dee knew something of it, realized that it might serve to investigate his geographical theories, and perhaps attempted to urge upon them that this be done. To this list may be added the further possibility that the meeting had something to do with Dee's ideas on English territorial claims in North America and the North Atlantic which may well have been perceived as useful by the anti-Spanish 'activist' group at court.

The connection of Dee's ideas on these territorial claims with Humphrey Gilbert's colonization projects is stronger. Gilbert visited Dee on 26 May 1577, the very time when Dee was at work on the *Famous and Rich Discoveries*, and again on 6 November 1577.[51] Gilbert's proposals to 'annoy the King of Spain' are also dated 6 November 1577, suggesting that they were the topic of conversation, Dee either having some hand in their formulation or Gilbert seeking Dee's reactions or more likely his support, since it was at the end of the same month that Dee went to the court at Windsor where he 'declared' to Elizabeth her title to foreign territories and spoke with Walsingham and Hatton.[52] It is conceivable that these discussions and the written statement of 'her Majesties title Royall' in 1578 had some bearing upon the considerations that resulted in the grant to Humphrey Gilbert in June of 1578 of a charter for a colonization expedition.[53]

Except for the spectacular success of Drake, none of these projects yielded any tangible results. Frobisher's expedition to 'Meta Incognita' discovered what he believed to be the entrance of a Northwest passage and also brought back a sample of rock that was judged to contain gold, sparking a gold fever that stimulated new and larger subscriptions from the Queen, courtiers, and a number of others, including Dee, for two additional voyages which brought back tons of the ore but did little further exploration for a passage.[54] The ore turned out to be worthless and the entire project ended in scandal with the shareholders losing everything.[55] The indecisive results of Frobisher's expeditions concerning a Northwest passage led Gilbert to focus his attention toward exploration and colonization of the North American coast further south. Despite the failure of his first attempt in 1578, the year of Frobisher's last voyage, Gilbert attempted to keep his colonization scheme alive and Dee continued to play a role in this, largely by providing justification for English claims through his theories of Elizabeth's titles.

To finance a future voyage as well as to provide an incentive for others to mount expeditions that might result in claims under the terms of his charter, Gilbert exploited contemporary English land hunger by offering to others the assignment of large tracts of land and the delegation of commercial privileges to a mercantile corporation.[56] One particular group that took advantage of this were English Catholics who, faced with increased penalties beginning in 1581, saw colonization as a means to retain their religious convictions and their loyalty to England at the same time, a course encouraged by Walsingham.[57] One of the leaders of the Catholic group, George Peckham, and two of his associates visited Dee in 1582 regarding the English title to Norombega, roughly the New England–New York area of North America which Gilbert had offered them, in respect to Spanish and Portuguese claims to have divided the whole of the world's discoveries, since the Spanish ambassador to England, Don Bernardino de Mendoza, had made threatening remarks concerning English colonial plans. Dee must have satisfied them quite well because Peckham promised him 5000 acres from his own grant and a like amount from that of Sir Thomas Gerrard, another leader of the Catholic group.[58] Dee also prepared some maps and geographical descriptions of North America at this time, one apparently based on information he obtained from Simão Fernandez who visited Dee in 1580 after he had completed a reconnaissance voyage of the North American coast for Gilbert.[59] Since what remains of these are not adequate for navigational purposes, they probably also served Gilbert's promotional efforts by showing potential subscribers the location of the lands available and their proximity to trade routes.[60]

Not everyone abandoned the quest for a northern route to the East. A voyage to the northeast was planned in 1580, and once again Dee interjected himself at a late stage with instructions based on the unconventional theories of the *Famous and Rich Discoveries*, which were greeted with reluctance and scepticism.[61] The search for the Northwest passage was preserved through Dee himself, for in 1580 he received from Gilbert a grant of rights to all discoveries above the 50th parallel of latitude which, in addition to leaving almost all of what is now Canada for Dee to exploit, included all of the likely northern routes from the Atlantic to the Pacific.[62] Gilbert's willingness to assign these rights indicates that he had given up interest in the Northwest passage for colonization in middle latitudes and he may have granted them in consideration of Dee's services. Since it was with Humphrey's brother Adrian and the sailor John Davis, with whom Dee was already in contact in 1579, that he later attempted to exploit this grant, it may be that Dee sought the grant at their instigation or because the three had already begun to make plans.[63] At any rate, following on the failure of Humphrey Gilbert's second voyage in 1583, the three were planning a voyage to the northwest with the cooperation of Walsingham and Dyer, for which they petitioned for a charter of privileges and incorporation as the 'Fellowship of New Navigations Atlanticall and Septentrionall'.[64] John Davis sailed in June 1585, but Dee had left England in September 1583 before many of the details could be finalized and he was replaced by Sir Walter Ralegh in the charter for the company.[65]

In summary, Dee's major role in these projects for exploration was in the definition of the ideological context of ideas of a British Empire in which they took place and not that of a technical advisor let alone that of a leader in the movement. He seems to have quite enthusiastically stepped into this role, giving him an apparent intellectual importance in the formation of policy which was one of his aspirations. His investment in Frobisher's gold ore expeditions and his bargains for grants of land and other rights under the charters for exploration also indicate a concern to profit from them by securing some independent sources of wealth, which was the general objective of his efforts to secure patronage in this period.

ARISTOTLE IN SEARCH OF ALEXANDER

If the *Monas* was a bid to Maximilian II for patronage, it was without apparent effect, and when Dee returned to England in the Spring of 1564 he was still without any defined intellectual or financial position. Not that he was without means. He still held the two rectories of Upton and Long Leadenham bringing him £80 a year, which was not inconsequential. This he supplemented with the fees he undoubtedly received for astrological consultations and possibly other services of popular magic, and income from teaching.[66] He was also well considered at court. Elizabeth defended his *Monas*, which appears to have reached England before he did, and read the book with him after his return. She rewarded his gift of a copy of the 1568 edition of the *Propaedeumata* with £20, and, when her travels took her past Mortlake, she occasionally stopped to talk with him (*CR*,10, 18, 19, 22).[67] He was also consulted on a variety of matters. In addition to his work on calendar reform, which seems to have been requested by Lord Burghley, he was considered the appropriate person to reassure the government and the court that the comet of 1577 portended no great disaster and that a wax image of the Queen with a pin through its breast found in Lincoln's Inn field was harmless (*CR*,21–2).[68] He was consulted on Elizabeth's health in 1578 and sent to Europe briefly in that regard on the instructions of Walsingham and the Earl of Leicester, and the work he did on Elizabeth's titles to overseas territories was also done at the request of the government (*CR*,18, 22).[69]

Dee's aspirations, however, were far grander than this. He still sought and expected the kind of direct government support he had outlined in his letter to Cecil in 1562: sufficient unrestricted support to give him the leisure to pursue the secrets of science and philosophy to the glory and benefit of England and his patrons. This is the tenor of a further appeal in 1574 to his 'patron' Lord Burghley, asking for £200 yearly for life for his 'necessary maytenance' to reward his past efforts and continued zeal for 'the best and rarest matters mathematicall and philosophicall'.[70] Perhaps most revealing of Dee's conception of himself and of his role in England is his claim in 1577 at the conclusion of another long recitation of his neglect that 'yf in the foresaid whole course of his tyme, he had found a constant and assistant Christian Alexander, Brytan should not haue bin now destitute of a Christian Aristotle' (*NA*,63). That Dee was thinking of his role as Aristotle in terms of the *Secretum secretorum*, in which the secret knowledge of the imperial philosopher is the key to Alexander's political power and the source of public benefits is suggested later in the same work, when Dee calls for the public treasury to support four 'Christian philosophers' 'skilfull or to become skilfull, and also excellent, both in Speculation and also practice of *the Ancient and Secret Philosophy*' (*NA*,63).

It is significant that the context of this statement is the work in which Dee was advocating his ideas on the 'British Empire' buttressed with tales from the old British histories. Despite scepticism about these histories, of which Dee was aware, he accepted them not least because he himself was Welsh and because they were central to how he understood his endeavours.[71] His claim to special knowledge was based on his sense of having rediscovered the ancient wisdom of Enoch and the Adamic language that Roger Bacon associated in his notes to the *Secretum secretorum* with Aristotle's wisdom.[72] This was, moreover, a particularly British wisdom. Dee traced his descent from Roderick the Great, the legendary Prince of Wales, a descent he believed he shared with Roger Bacon, whose name before he became a Friar was, so he claims, David Dee of Radik.[73] Having inherited the mantle of British philosophy and claiming a distant relationship to Elizabeth and thus to the Welsh/British ancestry that led from Brutus to the Tudors, Dee was endowed with the intellectual authority to pronounce on matters of political policy.[74] Thus, if Elizabeth supported his studies and consulted his philosophical and political learning as Alexander did with Aristotle, she could succeed to the imperial stature of Alexander, and Britain could reclaim its imperial inheritance.

What Dee expected in terms of particular support is indicated in yet another appeal for Royal support, this time in 1592. Again he complains of poverty and unfulfilled promises of support and asks for a living worth £200 a year. What is most revealing are the detailed specifications he gives why the Mastership of St Cross's is preferable to several other possible livings. It is ideal because it has space in which to carry on his 'philosophicall exercises' and to establish a printing press to publish old manuscripts as well as his own works, it is close to supplies of fuel and to the glass-works in Sussex where he can obtain lenses and mirrors for his investigations, it has the facilities and the income so that he can lodge and support 'several mechanical servants' and learned visitors, and, since it is near the channel coast and relatively remote, it is a place where 'rare and excellent men' from all of Europe can come to dwell with Dee under Royal protection in freedom and security away from the prying public (*CR*,39–41). It very much seems that Dee wanted support to create a private research institute in which he not only could pursue his own private studies but would also be in a position to serve as patron to others by lodging them and by extending to them the Royal protection that he believed had been extended to him when Elizabeth granted him 'great security against any of her kingdome, that would, by reason of any my rare studies and philosophicall exercises, unduly seeke my overthrow' (*CR*,21). Dee's indication that these plans were intended to recreate what he had been doing at Mortlake, which he refers to as *Mortlacensis hospitalis philosophorum peregrinantium*, suggests that they were part of his aspirations in the 1560s and 1570s (*CR*,40). Dee's idea of an independent research institute, in which he would serve both as a practising philosopher-scientist and as a patron of other practitioners, students, and philosophers, is very similar to what Tycho Brahe created at Uraniburg.[75] It us unlikely that Dee's plans included the systematic astronomical observation programme for which Tycho is usually remembered, and his interest in spiritualist researches would have given his institute a considerably less scientific character, but we should not forget that Tycho pursued more than astronomy at Uraniburg, which also included an alchemical laboratory, so that comparison with Dee's multi-disciplinary institute is not entirely misplaced.[76]

Such plans were costly beyond Dee's ordinary income and the fact that he tried to fulfil them even in the absence of extensive assistance explains his frequent complaints of poverty. In 1592 his household included eight servants in addition to the nine members of the family and he estimated that he was spending over £200 a year (*CR*,36). Throughout the diaries, covering the period from the mid-1570s to the early 1600s, there are numerous records of household expenses and payments to various servants. Many of these are for maids, wet-nurses, butlers, and grounds-keepers that were part

of maintaining the social position of a landed gentleman to which
Dee aspired, but others relate to his scientific pursuits.[77] Dee's
alchemical assistants and scryers were paid, and often housed and
fed, Edward Kelley receiving the handsome arrangement of £50 a
year plus meals and lodging (*T&FR*,28–9).[78]

Achievement of his social ambitions came much easier to Dee
than the fulfilment of his aspirations for intellectual position. By
1570 Dee had adopted a coat of arms, not that his pretensions to
join the elite by tracing his lineage to the celtic ancestors of British
royalty, including Elizabeth, were seriously accepted (*CR*,26;
LA,76).[79] He seems to have acquired the reputation for being noticeably ambitious.[80] His marriage in February of 1578 to Jane
Fromond, who was a lady-in-waiting at court, was most likely a
social improvement on his earlier marriages and points to closer
contacts with the court.[81] The agreement of Edward Dyer, Blanch
Perry, and others at court to stand as godparents, albeit sending
proxies to the actual ceremony, for the christening of Arthur, born
in 1579, and Katherine, born in 1581, Elizabeth's visits to Mortlake
and requests that Dee spend more time at court, and the willingness
of courtiers as prominent as Francis Walsingham and the Earl of
Leicester to bring their business to Dee at Mortlake all reflect some
modest social success for the son of a London merchant (*CR*,18).[82]
It has often been assumed that Dee had a number of patrons among
the aristocracy, most notably the Earl of Leicester and the Sidneys
because of his close relationship with Northumberland and Sidney
in Edward's reign, and it is true that they and others at times
visited Mortlake, consulted with him, and served as his sponsors at
court, but it is unclear how far they served as patrons in the sense
of providing tangible support.[83] Dee himself does not record any
support from them, and if there was any his persistent appeals for
Royal support suggest that it was neither stable nor adequate
enough to suit his requirements.

The social mobility that marked Elizabethan society could accommodate Dee's social ambitions more readily than Elizabethan
patronage could meet Dee's demands for financial and intellectual
position.[84] Unlike continental courts, particularly those in Germany,
England did not have court scientists, and patronage either to
support or to reward research in itself was rare. Among aristocratic
patrons, science was considered as only one among a variety of
intellectual accomplishments and it was valued for its practical

utility or its capacity to delight through impressive astronomical instruments and clocks or the production of marvels. Patrons shunned too much indulgence in theory on their own part, and clients were expected to accommodate their talents and energies to the projects of the patron. Except to the extent that they could secure church livings for their clients, which was not the rule, patrons from Elizabeth down provided short-term rewards for the dedication of a book or particular projects but generally avoided long-term commitments, so that clients were commonly quite insecure.[85] Dee's expectation of sufficient long-term support to provide him with the leisure to pursue the secrets of philosophy and science without immediate practical justification was asking more than his society was accustomed or prepared to give. His insecurity was in fact quite routine. While Dee's 'mysticall and supermetaphysical philosophy' may have been acknowledged, and Elizabeth may indeed have 'vouchsafeth the name of hyr philosopher' to Dee as Richard Harvey reports, material rewards were rarer and usually reserved for tangible practical services.[86]

In 1564 and 1565 there was a flurry of proposals for Dee, one of which carried an income of £200, moved largely by the Marquess of Northampton, whom Dee had accompanied on his return from Europe, and Blanch Perry, none of which materialized (CR,12–13). Most of these were ecclesiastical livings, some of which Dee could not or would not take because they involved the care of souls, and, even where that was not an issue, Dee's history of rather flexible religious convictions and his reputation if not actual attachment to the occult and magic most likely assured that ecclesiastical authorities would prefer alternative candidates.

Dee was very sensitive about his reputation, complaining of numerous slanders and protesting his innocence of magic and 'unchristian' practices on many occasions.[87] These cannot all be dismissed as figments of his imagination. He is named as an atheist and conjurer in *Leicester's Commonwealth* and he was able to gain a judgement of £100 in damages against a Vincent Murphy, who apparently also spread abroad stories of Dee's conjuring that date back to Mary's reign.[88] There were other reminders of Dee's past which may well have made Dee's patrons wary and Dee uncomfortable with the atmosphere. The 1578 edition of the *Mirror for Magistrates* included two tragedies previously suppressed. Elianor Cobham's story was modelled on the episode of Dee's casting horoscopes for Elizabeth in 1555, for which he had been arrested. The author was none other than Dee's former accuser, George Ferrers, who now presented the incident in less unfavourable light, but the sore memory refused to die.[89] Ferrers's other contribution, Duke Humphrey of Gloucester's tragedy, in contrast presents another dimension of Elianor current at the time. Here she is guilty of engaging the services of a sorcerer against the life of the monarch. The method used was none other than pins stuck in an effigy.[90] Dee's sense of humble hurt surrounded by hosts of potential enemies, and his self-righteous need for divine vindication bordered on the melodramatic (figure 7.2), but was a feature of his personality that tinged all his perceptions of his social relations.

Besides his religious history and the fact that he expected rather too much from his patrons, he was also a less than effective proponent of his own cause because he either ignored or more likely disdained the normal rituals of patronage. Dee's long-standing connection with William Cecil should have placed him in a very advantageous position. Cecil, who became Lord Burghley in 1571, was one of the most important channels of patronage, including that of science, in Elizabethan England. While Cecil rewarded dedications and awarded commissions himself, and encouraged learning informally through his hospitality, he did not directly provide long-term settlements. Rather, he often provided the crucial introduction to court, after which the client was often on his own to seek the influence of others and the regard of the Queen, which might lead over the course of a long career to increasing rewards and eventually some permanent place.[91]

By 1564 Dee needed no introduction to court, but in 1568 after the republication of the *Propaedeumata* Cecil did advise Dee to have his other former patron, the Earl of Pembroke, present a copy of the work to Elizabeth, for which he received £20 (*CR*,19). The point of the advice, however, seems to have been lost on Dee; he appears to have been quite reluctant to dedicate published works to his English patrons. Addressing the *Propaedeumata* to Mercator in the last months of Mary's reign and the dedication of the *Monas* to Maximilian both make sense at times Dee may have been looking to the continent for other opportunities. In 1568, however, he might very well have dedicated the new edition of the *Propaedeumata* to an English patron in addition to adding a letter to the reader. Loyalty to his friend Mercator may have made him reluctant to add a new dedication, but the appearance of his work on parallax in 1573 with no dedication and his own arms on the title-page suggests a self-consideration quite in keeping with his image of himself as the British Aristotle who deserves to be sought out and supported (figure 7.3).[92] The only published work to bear a dedication to an English patron is the *General and Rare Memorials* of 1577, dedicated to Sir Christopher Hatton, and even that may have been a last-minute decision.[93] Only his manuscript works on Queen Elizabeth's title to foreign territories and on the reformation of the calendar, which were specifically commissioned by Elizabeth or for her by Burghley and Walsingham, does Dee dedicate to Elizabeth with any of the customary language intended to praise and glorify his patrons (*CR*,25; *LA*,74).[94] Another important consideration in securing Royal patronage was attendance at court, and although Elizabeth herself pointedly told him to spend more time there Dee seems only to have gone to the court when he had particular business, which was not often (*CR*,18).

Dee's approach to his patrons was less by these indirect, slow, and long-term methods than by making direct appeals based on his special expertise which met with little response. In his appeal to Burghley in 1574 Dee raised the matter of hidden treasure, saying that dreams, visions, and voices in the night have recently indicated to him possible locations and that he is able to discover it by natural means including the 'sympathy and antipathy of things'.[95] It was commonly believed that England was rich in buried treasure and that magic was useful in finding it, but such treasure belonged to the Crown and the use of magic for its discovery was a felony.[96] What Dee requests, should some other sinecure not be possible, is that he be granted for life letters patent to search for hidden treasure by the natural means that are legitimate by his 'Godly philosophy' despite the scruples of theologians and vulgar opinion, offering Burghley half the proceeds and assuring him that he would also discover by the same means mines of precious metals for the Crown that would more than compensate for relinquishing its rights to the treasure.[97] If Burghley replied it has not been recorded and there is no evidence that Dee received any patent.

Dee placed similar hopes on his advocacy of an imperial ideology and his claims regarding Elizabeth's titles. He coupled the *General and Rare Memorials* with a prefatory appeal for Royal support, perhaps thinking that the cause of the Walsingham, Leicester, and

Hatton group offered an opportunity to demonstrate his indispensable value to Elizabeth, but this opportunity was not without its pitfalls (*NA*,64–5). Burghley, who had actual responsibility for maintaining the Royal navy, was a more appropriate and powerful individual than Hatton for the dedication of Dee's work on a Royal navy, but Burghley was not sympathetic to the 'activist' group and their policies did not receive Elizabeth's whole-hearted support.[98] Although Elizabeth may have been flattered by the titles Dee bestowed on her, she was not an imperialist and there is no indication that she considered acting on them. Burghley himself was not impressed, Dee taking offence when Burghley ignored further requests for an audience (*CR*,18).[99] Dee's sense of slight was only assuaged when Elizabeth herself came by Mortlake to tell him Burghley had actually commended his work, and Burghley sent him a haunch of venison.[100] In 1597 Dee wrote again to Dyer on his ideas of British imperial sovereignty and expressed his puzzlement why his ideas had never been acted upon, indicating a naive obliviousness to political considerations.[101]

Thus during the 1570s and early 1580s Dee's hopes for preferment commensurate with his aspirations went largely unfulfilled. None of his appeals yielded any positive response, and if he had hopes to profit from any of his investments or rights in the voyages of exploration these were disappointed also. These disappointments were particularly trying because he was in fact experiencing financial difficulties, having to borrow money on several occasions.[102] Elizabeth's only positive gesture was to secure for Dee a dispensation from the Archbishop of Canterbury to hold his two rectories and any others subsequently bestowed for a period of ten years, which was later extended for the duration of his life (*CR*,12–13). The saddest twist came in 1582 when the Archbishop of Canterbury finally approved the request for Dee to hold his two rectories for life. Dee was so absorbed in his work on the reformation of the calendar that he neglected to get the great seal affixed to the grant in time, thereby losing the only secure livings he had (*CR*,13). It was at just this time that Edward Kelley, who proved to be Dee's most successful scryer, entered the picture, and in the next year, while Dee was pressing a desperate suit at court to replace the lost rectories, there arrived the Polish Prince Albrecht Laski, who seemed to promise Dee the kind of position in Poland that he could not achieve in England.

Edward Kelley, under the alias Edward Talbot, appeared at Mortlake on 9 March 1582 with tales of Barnabas Saul's ill dealings toward Dee just three days after Saul had told Dee he no longer heard or saw spiritual creatures and left.[103] Kelley had had some legal difficulties for forging or counterfeiting money, for which his ears had been cropped, and also figured in a story of necromancy involving a corpse he had helped to dig up.[104] Dee did not learn Kelley's real identity until the following November, and whatever he learned of Kelley's background did not permanently damage their relationship.[105] From the beginning Kelley proved to have vivid and rich visions and, once begun, their 'actions' with the spirits or angels as Dee referred to them were frequent, often once or twice daily, whenever Kelley was at Mortlake. These actions opened up to Dee a vast spiritual world, the angels offering revelations of divine mysteries, religious exhortations, and prophecies of the future. The next chapter will consider these actions more directly, but given Dee's aspiration to possess profound and secret philosophical wisdom these actions rapidly became an almost totally absorbing pursuit with Kelley essential to their continuance. Kelley likewise found Dee indispensable, both as an employer and possibly for his assistance in discovering the secret of alchemical transmutation he thought was hidden in an old manuscript and some red powder he had found.[106] Dee's captivation with these actions and his innocent faith in the revelations of the angels made it easy for Kelley to manipulate Dee, which he did both by threatening to quit the practice altogether and by directing the conversations to suit his purposes. Occasionally Dee would seek the pronouncement of the angels on personal matters, and it was through their often suitably vague replies, which were clearly Kelley's, that allowed Kelley to draw Dee away from England, breaking his ties with his more sober scientific work. The key element in this was the appearance of Albrecht Laski.

Laski, the Palatine of Siradia, was the head of a powerful Polish family with vast estates, although he was quite prodigal and, so, often wanting of money, a rather unorthodox Catholic, a partisan of the Habsburgs in Polish politics, having spent time at the courts of Maximilian II at Vienna and Rudolf II at Prague, and a patron of alchemists with a deep interest in magic and the occult.[107] The full purpose of his visit to England in 1583 is not clear, but while there he sought out those with a reputation for the occult, including

Dee.[108] He was brought to Mortlake by Sidney on 13 May, returned for dinner on 18 May, and visited frequently after that.[109] Laski very soon had intimations of the angelic conversations, for on 23 May Dee communicated to the angels Laski's questions about the life of King Stephen Báthory of Poland, whether Laski would succeed him as king, and whether he would gain the kingdom of Moldavia. Laski had a history of exploiting Polish politics with the apparent aim of securing the crown for himself which was not unfamiliar to some in England, and the angels obligingly replied with favourable prophecies that became increasingly definite as Dee's feelings for him warmed. The angels indicated their acceptance of Laski, eventually admitting him to the actions, fitting him out with a genealogy deriving from the Plantagenets through the English noble family of Lascy, and prophesying that he would achieve great victories and accomplish religious reunion among Christians, Jews, Saracens, and pagans in addition to ruling Poland.[110] In addition to being flattered by the angelic revelations, he may have been not a little interested in Kelley's alchemical powder, given his prodigality with cash.

In Laski Dee finally found someone who accepted him as a purveyor of secret wisdom and special political revelations. Laski was also quite congenial to Dee for reasons that carried great weight given his current condition in England. Laski, with his 'great good liking of all States of the people', may have displayed less social snobbishness than the court aristocracy Dee was accustomed to, and his 'favour' toward Dee and apparent efforts to 'suppresse and confound the malice and envie of my Country-men against me, for my better credit winning or recovering to do God better service hereafter thereby' cast him as Dee's long-sought protector who was willing, and apparently had the resources, to support Dee as he wished (*T&FR*,1). The implications of this were not lost on Kelley, whose prosperity at this time depended on Dee, and as Laski's favour with the angels rose, their view of Dee's English hopes declined. Before Laski arrived the angels were favourable to Adrian Gilbert's planned exploration, afterwards they were less so; Burghley and Walsingham with whom Dee was pressing some suit at the time, perhaps to replace his rectories, were declared to hate him and Laski, and were said to be conspiring against him. In contrast to them, whom he ought not trust, Laski was a true friend who would do much for Dee. On 21 September Dee and Kelley with their families joined Laski on his return to Cracow (*T&FR*,17, 22–3, 28–9, 30–1, 33).[111]

Part Four

THE *LIBRI MYSTERIORUM*, 1583–1589

VIII

THE MYSTICAL AND SUPERMETAPHYSICAL PHILOSOPHY

The body of material resulting from Dee's actions with spirits dwarfs, in its bulk, all of his other works combined, and it may well be the vehicle for the most intimate view of Dee's personality and spiritual and intellectual life. The topics of the actions range across religion, politics, the reformation of the church, cosmology, theology, eschatology, and natural philosophy, and both what the angels say and Dee's and Kelley's reactions provide a reflection of their deepest religious beliefs and concerns and their perceptions of and attitudes toward the world outside the closed room in which they carried on their practice. Thus far, however, this material has received little concentrated scholarly attention, providing rich resources for romantic biography and writers of occult sympathies but something of an embarrassment to any attempt to consider Dee as a significant figure in the history of philosophy and of science.[1] Whether or not his activities with Kelley are considered one of his productive endeavours, they represent such a large period of his life that they need to be considered for their bearing on Dee's natural philosophy and his intellectual career.

This material cannot be considered as science or natural philosophy in its own right, but there are elements that reflect Dee's concerns in natural philosophy and that draw upon and develop themes from his earlier writings. Some indication has already been given of how Dee's previous thinking may look forward to these angelic conversations considered as a kind of spirit magic. Since Dee's thinking changed in the course of his career and his mathematical and scientific interests often drew upon different influences, it is of interest to consider the relation of these activities to his previous thinking and to the varieties of magic current in the sixteenth century. Furthermore, while the circumstances of his disappointments with his fortunes in England and the apparent opportunity offered by Laski help to understand the particular shift in his career in 1582 and 1583, they do not fully explain why he was so amenable to the revelations offered through Kelley. It is also necessary to assess the motives that were influential in this kind of activity assuming such prominence in his consideration and becoming so addicting that even after separating from Kelley and returning to England in 1589 he never resumed any significant work in natural philosophy or science. This chapter will, therefore, provide the final elements in the consideration of Dee's intellectual development. The conclusion will then bring together our observations on the nature and development of Dee's natural philosophy and his conception of his intellectual role.

DEE, KELLEY, AND THE SPIRITS

The records of Dee's spiritual actions or angelic conversations comprise two distinct classes of material. The actual conversations are recorded in what amount to minutes of the séances. These are divided into a large number of 'books', each with a title that is usually some variation on *Liber mysteriorum*.[2] The second class of material comprises several books based on the angelic revelations, either directly dictated by the angels or abstracted from the minutes by Dee to represent the angels' teaching.[3]

Unlike Dee's published works we have considered, these records do not present the problem of discerning in the text a possibly esoteric level intentionally disguised from the uninitiated reader. Dee never intended this material for publication and never mentions it in public accounts of his writings. The revelations of the angels were private communications to Dee and Kelley, so there was little motive for secrecy. Other individuals were at times admitted to the actions, but only after Dee and Kelley had become confident, sometimes mistakenly, of their trustworthiness. The conversations do, however, present another problem, since the majority of the records consist of minutes of séances in which Dee neither saw nor heard the angels. It was through Kelley's account that Dee recorded what Kelley saw and what the angels said to Kelley, bracketed by Dee's record of his own opening and closing prayers and his and Kelley's comments, questions, and requests for clarification.

To what extent the revelations of the angels represent Dee's thinking presents a considerable problem that hinges on a judgement about what actually transpired in these séances and the role of Kelley as scryer. About Dee there is little difficulty. He never doubted that the spirits were real and was only rarely doubtful that they were good angels bearing genuine messages from God. Dee's records of noises, voices, apparitions, and prophetic dreams in his diaries quite independently of Kelley's influence, as well as his episodes with other scryers, indicate a personal belief in the reality of a spirit world, and while it may present interesting psychological issues, this belief was supported both by his readings and the broader cultural conditioning that spirits existed.[4] The closest Dee came to questioning the 'angelic' character of the spirits and the trustworthiness of Kelley's vision was near the end of their association when Kelley announced that the spirits commanded that they share everything in common, including their wives, but his scruples were soon put to rest when the spirits assured him that this was a special dispensation from God for them as his elect (*T&FR*,*10–12, *16–*21).

Kelley presents greater difficulties but a full assessment of his personality and motives will lead too far afield. He may well have consciously fabricated everything to deceive Dee, but his bouts of emotional anxiety and arguments with the spirits in the course of his visions, his reluctance to continue except for Dee's desperate pleadings, and his admission of the visions to religious authorities in Prague when that might have had serious consequences all suggest that more than conscious deception was involved (*T&FR*,64, 102, 370).[5] Although Kelley often questioned the divine character of the angels, he seems to have believed in their reality as firmly as did Dee, and while it is clear that the revelations of the angels through Kelley were often prejudiced in favor of Kelley's interests in particular circumstances, they also reflect what Kelley knew of Dee's interests. In a number of places in the minutes Dee has noted the similarity of the angelic revelations to material in Agrippa, Reuchlin, Trithemius, and Peter of Abano, and since Kelley lived with Dee and had access to his library, the revelations are very likely the joint product of Kelley's imagination and stock of knowledge and what he knew of Dee's thinking from their discussions and his reading among books of current interest to Dee.[6]

Dee, therefore, was more than just the passive recipient of the revelations. Keith Thomas's observation regarding séances and divination in popular magic that the client's imagination was the chief asset of the cunning men, whose services usually amounted to confirming the convictions of the client that were familiar to the seer, applies equally to Dee and Kelley.[7] Dee's interests determined the major themes of the revelations and his ideas as Kelley may have gleaned these from discussions and Dee's books contributed a considerable amount of their actual content. This, combined with Dee's abiding faith in their divinely inspired character, suggests that the records are evidence of Dee's and not just Kelley's thinking.

Dee did not consider these actions a type of magic but as a variety of religious experience sanctioned by the scriptural records of others to whom God or his angels imparted special illumination. In contrast to the 'wicked Conjurers' who 'have their Devils to write Books at their commandments', Dee thinks that as 'an honest Christian Philosopher' he should 'have the help of God his good Angels to write his holy Mysteries' (*T&FR*,27). The practice of the actions therefore takes place in the simple religious atmosphere of Dee's oratory following a period of silent prayer and ending with a short prayer of praise and thanksgiving. There is no element of invoking angels and compelling their services; rather it is a question of humbly petitioning God to send his angels, who are in no way thought to be doing Dee's or Kelley's bidding. The opening prayer Dee most often used was addressed to God and Jesus as the source and the embodiment of wisdom, and asks that he be worthy of their aid in philosophy and understanding and that they send their spiritual ministers to inform and instruct him in the arcana of the properties and use of all God's creatures.[8] There are no elaborate ritual preparations, quasi-sacramental ceremonies, or incantations that are part of the ceremonial magic of Agrippa's third book, nor are there the music and Orphic hymns, fumigations, candles, talismans, or foods and substances that figured in the magic of Ficino and Campanella for attracting the beneficent influences of the planets or planetary demons.[9]

The only piece of seemingly magical apparatus at the outset was the 'shew-stone' through which Dee's scryers had their visions. Dee eventually had several of these, one of which was supposedly brought by the angels themselves (figures 8.1 and 8.2).[10] Such polished translucent or reflective objects were the traditional instruments for catoptromancy.[11] Dee's earliest stone, which he says was given to him by a friend, was probably the circular flat black mirror of polished obsidian (figure 8.1). This was most likely brought by the Spanish from Mexico where the Aztecs deified obsidian and used it for divinatory mirrors.[12] It may have come to Dee with tales of mysterious or magical powers, for he says that he was informed that good angels were 'answerable' to it and associated it with the 'shew-stone' he believed had been used by 'high priests' of Israel at the order of God to seek his light in resolving their doubts and questions about his secrets.[13] Another significant distinction of Dee's practice from Ficino's and Agrippa's magic is that, except for rare requests for direct benefits, such as the alleviation of Arthur's or Jane's illness, Dee's objective is not the attraction of beneficial influences or the invocation and manipulation of spirits for specific purposes; rather it is to learn and follow God's will and to receive 'true knowledge and understanding of the laws and ordinances established in the natures and properties of his creatures'.[14]

The revelations often shift in their day-to-day focus and in their specific content, but there is an underlying coherence to the actions. What ties everything together is the notion that Dee and Kelley are the elect of God, specially chosen to received a divine revelation (*T&FR*,233, 370).[15] Despite the fact that they are apparently in God's special favour, they are not spared frequent homilies and exhortations on their sins, the nature of salvation, and the necessity of unflinching obedience to the angels as part of their obedience to God as a prerequisite to receiving the full revelation. These pronouncements often bear on issues of contemporary religious significance, and their tenor is most often Protestant and even Calvinist in the emphasis on the intrinsic sinfulness of mankind and the impossibility of salvation without God's gift of faith as a token of God's election (*T&FR*,7, 19, 54, 161–2, 189, 411). In keeping with earlier indications of Dee's flexibility in adapting to prevailing religious practice, the religious teachings of the angels do not have any specific denominational preference and in Prague they recommend that Dee and Kelley reconcile themselves to the Roman church and support a Catholic interpretation of transubstantiation and the Mass not unlike that Dee had defended when he was in Bishop Bonner's household (*T&FR*,237, 372–3). The investigation of Dee's religious views, for which there is much material in these records, is not germane to this study except to the extent that the atmosphere of his spiritual concerns conditioned his intellectual choices. He seems to have had a rather Protestant view of salvation by faith through God's grace and election that centred on the individual's direct relation to God independent of any organized church; yet he was quite latitudinarian in the acceptance of varying forms of religious observance and went beyond all the organized churches, both Protestant and Catholic, in accepting the validity of continuing divine revelation independent of scripture and church teachings.[16] The frequent concern with his spiritual worthiness and with the angelic revelations as a token of his special spiritual merit speaks to a profound sense of spiritual anxiety and insecurity.

The special revelations of the angels to Dee and Kelley fall into two large categories. In one category are prophetic revelations of often apocalyptic import regarding great religious and political changes in eastern Europe. These are closely tied to their personal fortunes with Laski and others with whom they became associated during their travels and will be dealt with later. In the other category is the reception of a revealed esoteric wisdom promising a universal knowledge of creation. From the point of view of Dee's intellectual career, this is by far his preeminent concern in the actions. It is the element that is most closely tied to his earlier concerns in natural philosophy, it is the issue that he unfailingly pursues to the very end of his association with Kelley, and it is the motive that originally prompted him to seek the aid of the angels.

THE BOOKS OF ENOCH

Dee is quite clear about his motive for initiating his actions with the spirits. The earliest record of angelic conferences is prefaced by a long prayer to God in which Dee confesses how he has prayed to God ever since his youth for 'pure and sound wisdome and understanding of your [God's] truthes naturall and artificiall' to be used for God's honour and glory and the benefit of Dee's fellow men. Although he has studied in many books and in many places and conferred with many men, Dee has concluded that 'I could find no other way to such true wisdome attayning but by thy extra-ordinary gift, and by no vulgar schole doctrine or humane invention', and cites the examples of Enoch, Moses, and others from scripture to whom God sent his angels and imparted special wisdom.[17] Likewise, when Edward Kelley first came to Mortlake and asked Dee to show him something in 'spiritual practice', Dee said that he was 'neyther studied, or exercised' in the 'vulgarly accounted magik', but that he had for a long time been 'desyrous to have help in my philosophical studies through the company and information of the blessed Angels of God'.[18] For Dee the angelic conversations were thus a continuation of his philosophical studies 'to fynde or get some ynkling, glimpse, or beame, of such aforesaid radicall truthes'.[19]

The 'pure and sound wisdome and understanding' of God's natural and artificial truths is delivered by the angels in a long and haphazard dictation of what are called the 'Books of Enoch'.[20] The historical Ethiopic Book of Enoch was unknown in Europe in the sixteenth century, but there was a long tradition in which the Patriarch Enoch was a pseudepigraph for a number of works in the Middle Ages. Some of these included occult hermetica, Arabic sources in particular equating Enoch with Hermes, and Christian mystical and visionary apocalyptic thought often drew upon the biblical account of Enoch as the recipient of God's special revelations and one of the two Old Testament figures to have been directly carried to heaven.[21] Enoch also figured in Jewish mysticism and kabbalah, identified following his metamorphoses as the angel closest to God, the celestial scribe, and the teacher of divine mysteries.[22] When appealing for the special instruction of God's angels Dee mentions the example of Enoch as enjoying direct conversation with God. Dee was certainly familiar with the biblical account of Enoch but his familiarity with Roger Bacon's notes on the *Secretum secretorum* and Guillaume Postel's *De originibus* are the likely source of a more elaborate idea of Enoch.[23]

Roger Bacon mentions Enoch as a recipient of an ancient, divine wisdom, and equates Enoch with Hermes.[24] Postel had met an Ethiopian priest from whom he had learned about the Ethiopic Book of Enoch, and in *De originibus* he presents Enoch as the first to record in writing an esoteric wisdom received by oral tradition from Adam and eventually dispersed. Significantly, Postel considers the various arts of magic and divination as fragments of this wisdom and considered that this wisdom could be attained through angels and spirits.[25] Likewise Dee's angels refer to Enoch as receiving and recording the wisdom of God that had been lost with Adam's sin. This wisdom was again corrupted and lost through men's unworthiness, but Dee and Kelley are now chosen to receive 'this Doctrine again out of darknesse' (*T&FR*,174). Dee's books of Enoch are therefore a restoration of the understanding of the creation that Adam had before his loss of innocence. In this prelapsarian state, Adam was a

> partaker of the Power and Spirit of God: whereby he not onely did know all things under his Creation and spoke them properly, naming them as they were: but also was partaker of our [the angels'] presence and society, yea a speaker of the mysteries of God; yea with God himself. (*T&FR*,92)

Dee and Kelley are not quite to recover the full 'innocency' of Adam; they are told that heavenly understanding and spiritual knowledge are closed to them in this life but that they shall have the keys to a knowledge of creation (*T&FR*,61, 94).

What this adamic understanding amounts to is difficult to grasp because of the haphazard way in which it was received over the course of many months of séances interrupted by sessions dominated by apocalyptic visions and homiletic exhortations. This is complicated by the fact that at several points the angels seem to repudiate everything and begin delivering their teaching in a new form. Some idea of what this teaching involved is nonetheless offered by the books Dee abstracted from the minutes of the séances. What all of these have in common is that they are catalogues of the angelic and spiritual hierarchies that govern the various regions of the earth and levels or domains of creation with descriptions of their characteristics, powers, their sigils, and the 'calls' or incantations by which they may be summoned. The *De heptarchia mystica*, drawing on the earliest revelations in 1582 and 1583, presents creation as divided into various sevens. There are seven kings, each with a subordinate prince and forty-two ministers, who rule various regions of the world and the affairs of men as well as being associated with each of the seven days of the week. There are also forty-nine good angels and, below them, other orders of angels whose purview seems to be physical nature, since there are groups for the cure of disease, for metals, for transformation, for the elements, for local change, for the mechanical arts, and for human knowledge of all secrets.[26]

Beginning in 1583 the angels introduced an entirely new language purporting to be the angelic language of Adam and of Enoch. This was dictated in the form of numerous grid-like tables of forty-nine rows by forty-nine columns in which letters, sometimes interspersed with numbers, occur in apparently random order (figure 8.3). These tables comprise the *Liber mysteriorum sextus et sanctus*, which is also referred to as the Book of Enoch.[27] By some method of selection the angels chose from these tables letters to form words and sentences, which amount to another set of calls pertaining to angels. These became the basis for the *48 Claves angelicae*, written in Cracow in 1584, which consists of a catalogue of the forty-eight angels, their characteristics and subordinate spirits, and their invocations in the 'Enochian' language with English translations.[28] A further catalogue from 1585, again different from the previous, is the *Liber scientiae auxilij et victoriae terrestris* listing the governing angels and their ministers for ninety-one different regions of the world (figure 8.4).[29] The spirits that most often figure in the séances – Annael, Michael, Gabriel, Raphael, and Urial – are the traditional arch-angels, although other less familiar names such as Salamian, Nalvage, and Madimi also appear. Nalvage and Madimi, who began as a young child and grew to maturity in the course of four years, played a particularly important role as time went on. It is through these spirits that Dee and Kelley learn of the hosts of lower angels and spiritual governors of the terrestrial realm such as King Naspol, his Prince Lisdon, and their forty-two ministers (figure 8.5). Some of these are also invoked during the actions and reveal their characteristics and powers.[30]

What this amounts to is a vast, overlapping, and confusing angelology or demonology compounded from a hodgepodge of sources. Various references to Peter of Abano, Trithemius, Reuchlin, and Agrippa indicate that Dee was aware of the similarity of these schemes both in general and in many details to their schemes.[31] At one point Kelley emerges from his study with Agrippa's *De occulta philosophia*, indicting the angels as frauds because they have plagiarized Agrippa, perhaps to forestall Dee's conclusion about who was the actual fraud (*T&FR*,158–9). There are also some figures with letters and numbers on concentric circles, perhaps reflecting some imitation of Ramon Lull's *ars combinandi* which Pico had associated with kabbalah (*T&FR*,5).[32] Dee, however, seems to have taken these similarities as confirmation of the validity of what other authors recorded. Another very likely source upon which Kelley drew for his visions of these angelic/demonic hierarchies were medieval manuals of ritual magic with their catalogues of demons, spirits, and angels and their sigils and incantations. Not all of these manuals consisted of 'black' magic directed at evil demons or diabolical agents; some present parallel spirit worlds in which a legitimate, or 'white', magic directed at divine angels is derived from God and may be used for pious purposes.[33] Kelley's personal expertise was more in the area of this 'vulgar magik' as Dee termed it. Not only was there the story of necromancy in Kelley's background, but at several points during his association with Dee he voiced his interest in practising magic from his own books and raising reprobate spirits, which he admitted doing on his own despite the prohibitions of Dee and the angels, who eventually command him to bury his own books of magic (*T&FR*,21, 64, 80, 115–16, 164).

The similarity of the books dictated by the angels to some of the medieval treatises of ritual magic is not surprising since we have already noted in Chapter V how dependent Renaissance magical works were on these sources for their specific content.[34] While Agrippa seemingly elevates this material by integrating it within the framework of a Neoplatonic and kabbalistic cosmology, Trithemius's *Steganographia*, with which Dee was particularly impressed, takes it over with little modification other than Christianizing it. Dee also notes a parallel to Arbatel, the pseudonym for the author of a work of doubtful provenance published in 1574 with the title *De magia veterum*.[35] This likewise presents a ritual magic in a Christian context as the revelation from God through his ministering angels as a means of restoring a lost wisdom and gaining knowledge of the secrets of nature.[36] It is perhaps noteworthy that shortly after Kelley's tenure began the angels not only dictate these tables of spirits, they also give directions for a 'table of practice' decorated with various mystical symbols (figure 8.6) and for a 'sigillum Dei' to be inscribed on wax disks (figure 8.7) to be placed under the legs of the table and beneath the shew-stone on the table.[37] The practice of the actions thus seems to take on a much greater aura of magic under Kelley's influence. One of the ironies of the angelic conferences is that, while Dee considered their conduct as in no way magical, what the angels deliver as the embodiment of the greatest and most arcane secrets of God's creation is essentially a system of demonic magic.

Sorting out in detail the sources of what the angels deliver is of little purpose since it pertains mostly to how Kelley constructed the visions. What is significant is that Dee accepted these revelations as legitimate. The angelic revelations never fulfilled Dee's desire for an understanding of the divine arcana, as we might expect given their source, but it is worth considering why he considered them his most promising medium for that knowledge. As the angels present it, the divine wisdom of Adam's innocence consisted of two interrelated aspects: his command of a divine language and his participation in the society of the angels. The language the angels impart to Dee is the '*Lingua Angelica, vel Adamica*', now for the first time since Adam's fall disclosed to mankind, and is the same as the discourse by which God created everything (*T&FR*,92). In this language every word signifies the essence of a substance so that this language contains the secrets and keys to the world because through it the true natures of all things are known (*T&FR*,92).[38] In reference to one of the tables of seemingly random letters, an angel explains that it embodies all human knowledge; physic (medicine); knowledge of all elemental creatures and why they were created; the nature of fire which is the secret life of all things; the discovery, virtues, and uses of metals and stones; the conjoining of natures and their destruction; movement from place to place; knowledge of all mechanical crafts; and, not least, *transmutatio formalis, sed non essentialis* (*T&FR*,179). The tables of letters the angels give are, however, not the *lingua adamica* itself because the letters are disorganized. The great secrets they contain are only revealed when the letters are selected and arranged according to some mystifying process involving the numerical values attached to the letters and their place in the tables (*T&FR*,79–80, 92, 364). In one instance a group of letters yield the sum 4723 which the angel calls both the 'Mystical roote in the highest ascendent of transmutation' and the 'square of the Philosophers work', and although Dee comments on the inconsistency between root and square he does not unduly trouble the angel (*T&FR*,80). The angels refer to this language as the 'cabala of nature' echoing the 'cabala of the real' of the *Monas*, and clearly the promises of the angels to reveal the original divine language of creation responds to the same interests that had been at work in the *Monas* (*T&FR*,65). This 'cabala' does not operate according to any apparent rules or key, so that even with the tables Dee was perpetually at the mercy of the angels for instruction which the angels never seem to complete although they continue to make promises to the very end (*T&FR*,*11).

The catalogues of angels and spirits with the calls by which they may be summoned serve to recover the second aspect of Adam's innocence: his society with the angels and command over all creatures. The knowledge of and ability to communicate with this vast spirit world is essential for an understanding of nature because the creation is presented in a vaguely kabbalistic fashion as the self-revelation of God through his attributes in the form of angels and spirits (*T&FR*,174–5, 370–1). The term kabbalistic may be ill-advised in this context because we have previously noted that Dee's knowledge of kabbalah was very slight and Kelley's was likely no better, but what little there is of cosmology and cosmogony in the conversations inclines in a vague and Christianized way more toward a kabbalistic than toward a Neoplatonic view.[39] These angels, spirits, and divine governors hold the secrets to the various realms of creation and by recovering their society, by means of magical conjurations, their knowledge will become available to Dee (figure 8.8). The recovery of the *lingua adamica* is the key to this because it is the language all God's creatures understand and through which they can be summoned. The calls derived from the tables thus have the power to call forth and make obedient the spirits so that they will open the 'mysteries of their creation' and their secret knowledge (*T&FR*,77, 88, 92, 139–40).

Thus magic, and a spirit/demonic magic of the most unabashed variety, becomes the key to the knowledge and understanding of the secrets of creation Dee sought. The situation is somewhat comical if we consider that, while Dee patiently recorded what he thought were divine revelations through the angels and not a kind of magic, Kelley was practising the only thing he knew, which was magic, and presented this demonic magic as the means to fulfilment of Dee's thirst for knowledge, Dee accepting in the end what he had set out to avoid. What the angels provided was a kind of knowledge but it was not the direct knowledge of the secrets of creation that Dee sought. Rather, it was a magic in the form of the angelic language and the description of the spiritual hierarchies and their calls that was the means to this knowledge. It is a magic that is far removed from both the philosophical magic and occult philosophy of the Renaissance and the natural magic he seems to have derived from Roger Bacon. Despite the similarity of the angelology and demonology to material in someone like Agrippa, there is no hint here of the Neoplatonic/Stoic theory of the spirit as the vehicle of magical influence, or of the role of the imagination, or of the sympathetic use of the divine qualities in lower things to draw down the influence of higher things. Nor is there any remnant of the quasi-physical concept of occult virtues as a mechanism of magical effects that is found in al-Kindī, Bacon, and the *Propaedeumata*. There is simply the idea of the world populated by hosts of spirits and magic as the straightforward theurgic conjuration of them.

The conversations do pick up on themes from Dee's earlier career and from his previous writings on natural philosophy, and it is worth looking at these both for what they reveal about the conversations and what the conversations reveal about his basic motivations in natural philosophy. Dee's idea of archemastrie clearly encompassed a variety of magic involving divination with optical devices, and his 'other optical science' may well have referred to a technique by which man might 'participateth with Spirits, and Angels' as he puts it elsewhere in the *Praeface* (*MP*,A.iij^v, c.iiij). The conversations are, in fact, very much a practical expression of the conception that had emerged in the 1560s of the philosopher as theologian who seeks out an esoteric wisdom of secret divine science that reveal a knowledge of God through his creation independent of scripture. He expresses this goal in his 1562 letter to Cecil and particularly in the *Monas* where the highest vocation of the philosopher as the *adeptiuus* is the exploration of 'supercelestial virtues and metaphysical influences' through a combination of kabbalah, magic, and alchemy. As with the *lingua adamica* of the conversations, in the *Monas* the key to this wisdom is Dee's recovery through divine inspiration of a sacred art of writing, his kabbalah of the real, hitherto lost or unknown. It is this holy language of divine creation that provides the medium for an intimate knowledge of God through his creation and for communication with God. The pursuit of knowledge in the *Monas* is a gnostic quest to overcome the fallen state of mankind in which a religious magic, which he absorbed in the 1560s both in a Neoplatonic form and in Trithemius's openly angelic/demonic form, provided the path for a mystical ascent to divine illumination. As a mysticism, the angelic conversations are odd in that Dee only participated in the visions vicariously through his scryers as a blind and deaf spectator.

The conversations as a quest for an understanding of the secrets of divine creation are therefore interwoven with themes that had already been of central importance to him when he wrote the *Monas* and that very directly build upon Dee's intellectual and spiritual aspirations of the 1560s. Like the *Monas*, what transpires in the conversations is not science. Even more so than in the *Monas*, the conversations are antithetical to science as both empirical investigation and rational inquiry with their emphasis on passivity and subservience in the reception of revelation. As knowledge the revelations are utterly banal, lacking even the redeeming value of ingenuity and inventiveness that give the *Monas* some interest. The greatest irony of Dee's career is that his attempts to get progressively closer to the truths of nature in fact lead to a progressive distancing from nature.

This, of course, was not Dee's perspective. For Dee they were the epitome and not the nadir of his 'philosophical exercises'. This centres on his fundamental intent in philosophy. We have previously touched on this in particular instances, but it is time to assemble the scattered indications. What these point to is that Dee considered all of his philosophical studies as having the ultimately religious purpose of knowing God and attaining 'heauenly wisedome' and an understanding of divine truths (*MP*,A.j^v; *LA*,71–2). Dee reiterates this theme, frequently embellished with a heart-rending recitation of the numerous years, the considerable expenses, the difficult travels, and the great personal sacrifices he has made in pursuit of his studies, in all of his pleas for patronage and all of his apologies defending the legitimacy of his studies against charges of conjuring.[40] The polemical and self-serving purpose to which Dee put these protestations should not, however, detract from his sincerity in making them. He presents natural philosophy as having this religious purpose in contexts where self-justificaion is not an issue, and in the private context of the minutes of the angelic conversations he uses identical terms to present that activity as the culmination of his life-long philosophical endeavour.[41]

Natural philosophy was, for Dee, preeminently a theology in which he sought

> by the true philosophicall method and harmony: proceeding and ascending (as it were), *gradatim*, from things visible, to consider thinges invisible: from thinges bodily, to conceive of things spirituall: from things transitorie, and momentarie, to meditate of things permanent: by thinges mortall (*visible and invisible*) to have some perceiverance of immortality, and to conclude, most briefely; by the most marvailous frame of the *whole World*, philosophically viewed, and circumspectly wayed, numbered, and measured (according to the talent, and gift of God, from

above allotted, for his divine purposes effecting) most faithfully to love, honor, and glorifie alwaies, the *Framer*, and *Creator* thereof. (*LA*,72)[42]

The notion of the book of nature as a divine revelation equivalent to scripture was a frequent common-place used to justify natural philosophy but Dee invested the idea with significant ramifications. He seems to have considered it not merely a parallel revelation to supplement scripture but a self-sufficient and adequate alternative to biblical theology with the advantage of greater certainty than scripture which was prone to varieties of human interpretation (*MH*,124/25, 200/201; *MP*,b.ij). He also invested this natural theology with considerable spiritual and emotional significance. The knowledge he sought through nature served a soteriologic as much as a noetic function; recovering the secrets of the creation would overcome original sin, heal and deliver the soul from distress, and lead 'from this vale of misery and the misery of this vale, and from this realm of shadoes and the shadows of this realm, to the sacred mount of Sion and to the heavenly temple' (*MH*,138/39, 198/99; *LA*,71). This last statement occurs in an apologetic piece to the Archbishop of Canterbury in which Dee defends his philosophical studies as fundamentally religious and Christian, but it is revealing that he uses almost identical terms in one of the prayers initiating the spiritual actions in which God is asked to guide him to 'Holy Mount Sion and to Thy celestial tabernacles'.[43] Thus, the stakes were high and Dee was willing to make a significant commitment, explaining to Cecil in 1562 that if necessary 'my flesh, blud, and bones shuld make the mechandyse' to acquire this divine wisdom.[44]

Despite his appeals to the study of natural phenomena in the *Propaedeumata* and the *Praeface* however, the letter to Cecil of 1562 indicates that Dee looked for this wisdom less in nature itself than in books and from other men and ultimately these never took him far enough. While he was quite confident in 1562 that he had found the precious books that would show him the way, and in the *Praeface* he is rhapsodic about the vision offered by the mirror of creation, by the 1580s he admitted that 'I found (at length) that neither any man living, nor any Book I could yet meet withal, was able to teach me those truths I desired, and longed for' (*T&FR*,231). The only alternative to human inquiry was the 'extra-ordinary gift' of angelic revelation, which was of such value that more than his 'flesh, blud, and bones' he now had, Faust-like, 'unto E.K. [Edward Kelley] offered my soul as a pawn, to discharge E.K. his crediting of them, as the good and faithful Ministers of Almighty God' (*T&FR,**12). In this context the frequent concern in the conversations with salvation and election, and the religious anxiety this speaks to, are of significance. While the angels voice the Protestant idea of salvation as God's individual election of individuals through the unmerited gift of faith and grace, the constant angelic reassurance that Dee and Kelley are elect and that the revelations represent a particular covenant between them and God indicates that Dee was less than comfortable with the reduction of the church as a source of supernatural sanctions and the sacramental dispensation of grace that resulted from the Protestant attempts to eliminate the magical elements in religion, thereby leaving the individual believer alone and often insecure in his relation to God.[45]

Keith Thomas has shown that religion was commonly considered in magical terms as a medium for obtaining supernatural powers and that religion and magic performed parallel functions in the sixteenth century, and he suggests that the many popular varieties of magic flourished at just this time because they filled the vacuum left as Protestantism diminished the magical functions of religion in favour of self-help.[46] Dee's allegiance to the Catholic Mass and to the conversations with their sacred and sacramental aura may well derive from the same emotional source. In his third book on 'theological magic' Agrippa includes Christian practices among prayers, sacraments, and rites that are elements of ceremonial magic, and Peter of Abano explicitly compares the Mass with magic, arguing that the magical effect of transubstantiation certifies the general effectiveness of incantations.[47] Like the popular magic studied by Thomas, the intellectual magic of the Renaissance also served an essentially religious function.

It is in its liturgies that religion is most similar to magic, and the fundamental element in the intellectual vogue of magic in the Renaissance was the ceremonial and ritualistic aspect of spiritual magic that made it an alternative form of religious life and path to salvation. This is most prominent in Reuchlin, Trithemius, Agrippa, and Arbatel, the authors explicitly cited in the *Libri mysteriorum* and to whose thinking Dee's angelic conversations bear the closest affinity. Not only do they present the idea of a vast spiritual world permeating and governing all creation and the theurgic techniques for invoking these spirits and angels from whom miraculous knowledge and power may be derived. They present magic as a vehicle for salvation through which the soul may escape the material realm and the limitations of human understanding and ascend to the supercelestial realm and union with the divine through divine illumination.[48] Significantly, magic in Reuchlin and Agrippa appears in the context of an explicit disillusionment with sense experience, natural knowledge, and human reason as sources of infallible religious knowledge and a concomitant dissatisfaction with both scholastic theology and humanist philology and rhetoric for the attainment of true wisdom. Both considered the mystical divine illumination and inspiration of the mind prepared by faith to be the only adequate source for an understanding of the deepest religious truths.[49] Such a revelation was typically considered to be embodied in the occult wisdom of the ancient theology and in the kabbalah where magic functioned as a sacramental rite for attaining direct and personal mystical illumination and gnosis. In Reuchlin and Agrippa magic was part of a broad occult philosophy considered both as a science of non-rational agents and as the science of their operation for the attainment of wondrous powers and religious knowledge.[50] For them magic was the key element in a fusion of philosophy, religion, and magic that would renew philosophy by making it operative and reform religion by infusing it, by means of a divine and angelic magic, with a reinvigorated ceremonial, ritual, and sacerdotal character.[51] With Trithemius divine illumination is also considered the necessary preliminary to any valid human knowledge, and magic is considered the vehicle by which the soul achieves mystical experience. Likewise in Arbatel the magical evocation of God's ministering spirits is the only way to the recovery of wisdom which is the necessary foundation for all other human knowledge.[52] While much of the intellectual magic of the Renaissance was derived as much from medieval demonic magical texts as it was from late antique Neoplatonic treatments of ancient theurgy, the cultural function of this philosophical revival of magic was as an instrument of religious regeneration that alleviated the often intense despair over the limits of human intellectual abilities, answered the quest for esoteric wisdom, and offered the spiritual assurance of direct illumination.

Although the angelic conversations reveal little of the Neoplatonic philosophical framework through which Reuchlin and Agrippa attempted to legitimate their presentations of magic, they have very strong affinities with the religious impulse that motivated the Renaissance interest in magic. The first indications of Dee's conception of the religious function of natural philosophy emerge in the early 1560s with Trithemius's idea of a mystical theology as a kind of magic. His discovery of Trithemius's *Steganographia* at the same time may well have established in his mind an association between mystical theology and spirit magic that continued through his later readings and the hints in the *Praeface*. Other than the serendipitous discovery of successful scryers, it is difficult to isolate the exact motivation for the angelic conversations, but Dee's definitive and all-absorbing turn to angelic revelation and spirit magic in the 1580s seems very likely to have resulted from the combination of an intensified religious anxiety and a growing pessimism about his ability either through books or his unaided abilities to achieve his goal of a natural theology.

THE PROPHETS OF PRAGUE

The second major theme of the angelic revelations is the prophecy of apocalyptic religious and political mutations encompassing all of Europe but largely centred on East European affairs. A thorough investigation of this theme is beyond the scope of this study. What I will consider is its relation to Dee's conception of his domain as a philosopher and his fortunes as a prophet, since it was largely on the basis of the prophetic revelations of the angels that he owed the invitation to accompany Laski and that he sought to make his way in realms of Rudolf II. Although in many ways the world of Rudolf II provided an atmosphere more receptive to the Dee of the angelic conversations, he was no more successful there than he had been with the court of Elizabeth for reasons that were fundamentally similar.

The prophecies and the dense allegorical imagery in which they are often couched are undoubtedly the product of Kelley's imagination, woven from the prophetic and apocalyptic books of the Bible, biblical commentaries, pulpit oratory, and the vast reservoir of contemporary apocalyptic imagery and expectations.[53] Typically, the angels preach the immanent coming of antichrist, great woes, and the overthrow of all existing political and religious arrangements as retribution for the wickedness of the world that has fallen from God and his commandments (*T&FR*,4, 22–3, 26, 43, 46, 60–1, 183–4, 215, 398, 411). From this divine judgement will emerge a general reformation in which all things will be restored to righteousness in a universal order marked by a unity of religious faith and organization, and the destruction of the Turk (*T&FR*,4, 22–3, 60–1, 187, 233–4, 240–3, 247). Hopes for the fulfilment of this great renovation are placed in a secular ruler, Albrecht Laski to begin with, but later the Emperor Rudolf II and even King Stephen of Poland (*T&FR*,22–3, 26, 183, 217, 233, 247, 400–5).[54] As in the revelation of the wisdom of Enoch, Dee and Kelley are divinely chosen as prophets through whom God's plans will be revealed and who are to serve as guides in the realization of those plans (*T&FR*,161, 187, 233).[55]

A substantial element from Dee's earlier intellectual development inclined him to an interest in prophecy and to casting himself in the role of prophet, so that these products of Kelley's imagination clearly responded to what Kelley knew of Dee's inclinations. As early as the *Monas* Dee presents the role of prophet of an esoteric religious wisdom as one aspect of the office of the adept. Although as yet there is no sense of impending doom and no clear political message, a secular ruler, in this case the future Habsburg Emperor, is considered the proper recipient of the secret knowledge of the philosopher. Further, in discussing astronomy in the *Praeface* Dee emphasizes that the heavenly bodies were made by God not just to provide knowledge of times as in the seasons, years, days, and the like, but 'for *Signes*' ('I wish, euery man should way this word, *Signes*') because astronomy also bears on the consideration of 'Sacred Prophesies' (*MP*,b.iij^v). Regarding the science of numbers as a vehicle of divine knowledge, he refers to the prophesies of Joachim of Fiora as derived from formal numbers, citing not only Pico della Mirandola's *Conclusiones* to that effect but also the works of Joachim himself (*MP*,*.j).[56]

Marjorie Reeves has indicated how an interest in prophecy and the prophetic expectation of a *renovatio mundi* was a part of the religiously motivated search for a divine esoteric wisdom and knowledge reflected in the Renaissance vogue of ancient theology, kabbalah, and other occult traditions.[57] Prominent among the divine revelations of the *Corpus hermeticum* is the apocalyptic prophecy of the *Asclepius* portraying the upheavals that will follow on religious and moral corruption and the eventual restoration of the world by

God; and, significantly, it is to this prophetic element in the Hermetic and other texts of Ficino's edition that Dee paid particular attention when he read them in the 1560s.[58] This connection of an esoteric ancient wisdom with an eschatological programme based on Joachimist inspiration for a general reformation leading to religious unity was particularly marked in Guillaume Postel, who was also one of the important sources of Dee's idea of an ancient wisdom.[59] Another form of prophetic thought with which Dee was familiar, and to which his mention of sacred prophecies in the *Praeface* may refer, centred on the astrological theory of history. The twelve signs of the zodiac were commonly divided into four trigons associated with the four elements, and in this theory major historical changes, usually marking the rise of new empires and religions, were thought to accompany the conjunction of the superior planets in a new trigon.[60] Dee's familiarity with these ideas is evident from his possession of the *De magis coniunctionibus* of Abū Ma'shar, who was the major source of the theory in the West, Trithemius's *De septem secundadeis*, in which a different angelic planetary governor is associated with a succession of historical cycles, and Cyprian Leowitz's *De coniunctionibus magnis*.[61]

In considering Dee's efforts in the 1570s promoting the idea of a British Empire we have already noticed that his conception of his role as a philosophical advisor to Elizabeth took on more explicit political and ideological overtones. In this same period, he dated the *General and Rare Memorials* and his work on calendar reform not according to the Christian chronology but with the 'world year' of 5540 and 5545 respectively from the beginning of time (*NA*,67).[62] Six-thousand years was often given as the terminus of historical development in these schemes, so this dating may indicate that Dee associated the realization of a British Empire under Elizabeth's rule with a new age in European history, with himself as the prophetic guide in the fulfilment of providence.[63] It is unclear that Dee associated his ideas on the British Empire in the 1570s with any general religious reformation in Europe at large, but by 1583 the political and religious renovation of Europe had become central elements in the prophetic office through which he sought better fortunes with Laski in Eastern Europe.

The astrological significance of 1583 may well have contributed both to sharpening his prophetic expectancy and to directing his attentions to the East. In that year the most momentous of the great conjunctions took place, marking not just the beginning of a new trigon but also the beginning of a new 'great year' in Aries, which prompted a spate of predictions portending political and religious upheavals including the coming of Christ and the end of time over the next few years.[64] Of particular note in this context is Leowitz's *De coniunctionibus magnis* which Dee acquired in 1564. Leowitz, who was associated with the Habsburgs, dedicated the work to Maximilian II, and devoted particular attention to relating the history of the Empire, his native Bohemia, and the Habsburgs to this astrological scheme of history up to 1564 and to his predictions for the subsequent years culminating in momentous changes centered on the Habsburg domains in 1584. Dee's annotations to Leowitz concentrate on the material relating to the Habsburg domains, so the portents of 1583 may well have revived his earlier interest in the Habsburgs.[65]

From the beginning of Dee's association with Laski his office as a prophet of a new religious and political order in Eastern Europe that would entail the destruction of the Turk and the restoration of religious unity assumed an importance equal to that of receiving the books of Enoch. When Laski's continued financial difficulties tarnished both his value as a patron and his prospects as the instrument of divine judgement, Dee's attentions turned increasingly to the Emperor Rudolf II and in August 1584 he and Kelley moved from Cracow to Prague, although his relations with Laski also continued for some time (*T&FR*,139, 145, 211–12).

In Prague Dee worked to gain an audience with Rudolf through the Spanish Ambassador, Guillén de San Clemente, with whom Dee established a friendly relationship, sending a copy of his *Monas* along with letters intimating that he had profound secrets for the Emperor alone (*T&FR*,218, 225, 245). He gained only one audience with Rudolf, on 3 September 1584, at which he told the Emperor of his search for knowledge and the aid he had received from the angels. Following the instructions of the angels, he proclaimed his status as God's chosen prophet, rebuked Rudolf for his sins, offered to make him a party to the conversations, and announced that if he believed Dee and his message he would triumph, defeat the Turk, and his seat would be the greatest that there ever was, otherwise he would be crushed (*T&FR*,217, 230–1). However grand Dee's ambitions and desperate his financial conditions were, he clearly was not about to compromise his convictions or abase himself in order to please. Something more of Dee's ambitions are revealed in a subsequent letter to Rudolf offering the revelation of divine mysteries and arcana, including the secret of the philosophers' stone and transmutation, which the angels promise to perform, and requesting that he grant Dee the title of Imperial Philosopher and Mathematician (*T&FR*,243, 246). Rudolf's response was to take the matter under consideration and, although he considered it to the extent of delegating Dr Jakob Kurz of his privy council to learn more from Dee, he seems to have remained uncertain about the angelic revelations (*T&FR*,231, 236, 247). In addition to having the Spanish Ambassador press his suit, Dee met with Kurz several times and showed him the records of the conversations, but he was reluctant to send Rudolf a Latin transcript of some of the actions, perhaps out of fear that they would fall into the wrong hands, and preferred a personal audience and a 'live' demonstration with Rudolf (*T&FR*,239–40, 246–9).

Prague should have offered Dee an ideal intellectual and spiritual home. Numerous strands of esoteric and occult thought thrived in an atmosphere of spiritual insecurity where the potential for confessional and political fragmentation made peace and unity seem brittle. Esoteric occult systems of thought, which offered the secret revelation of divinity in the harmony of the cosmos, were attractive alternatives to confessional arguments and disputes. The quest for personal salvation often took the form of an almost aesthetic contemplation of the cosmos, but the longing for the restoration of harmony within society frequently found expression in chiliastic expectations of a religious and political renovation leading to the establishment of a genuine *respublica Christiana*.[66]

Dee made contact with a number of the intellectual currents while in Prague. For a time Dee lived in a house lent to him by the imperial physician, Tadeáš Hájek, who is best known for his astronomical interests but also concerned himself with astrology and alchemy (*T&FR*,212).[67] In addition to his suit with Rudolf, Dee and Kurz found time to discuss their mutual interests in mathematics, and he consulted Hannibal Rosseli, a Catholic religious Hermetist currently at work on a monumental commentary on the *Corpus hermeticum*, as a confessor before communicating, although it is not evident whether he sought Rosseli out for his Hermetic scholarship as well (*T&FR*,248, 397).[68] He also found some similarity of interests with Francesco Pucci whom he met in Cracow in

1585.[69] Pucci had wandered through Europe, left the Catholic church, and developed a blend of personal mysticism aimed at discovering the fundamentals of a universal faith that could be accessible to all, chiliastic expectations of an immanent last judgement, and visions of a utopian Christian society.[70] Pucci may have sought out Dee in his quest for a true faith. He was admitted to the séances and had a long association with Dee, who considered him a part of his household by 1586.[71] By the time they met, Dee and Kelley had already reconciled themselves to the Roman church, and besides confirming Pucci's belief in an immanent renovation, the revelation of the angel Urial prompted Pucci likewise to return to the 'lap of the holy mother church'.[72]

Yet Dee's fortunes in Prague were as disappointing as they had been in England. Rudolf, despite his taste for secrets and the mystical bent of his religion, displayed considerable hesitancy regarding Dee's initiatives and eventually gave in to demands of the Papal Nuncio that Dee and Kelley be expelled from his territories. Dee's spiritual activities had not remained secret for very long in Prague, leading to rumours that he was a 'Conjurer, and a bankrupt alkimist' (T&FR,244, 247).[73] As early as 1584 the Nuncio Francisco Bonomo took an interest in them, and his successor, Germanus Malaspina, pursued the matter and pressed for a meeting with Dee and Kelley in March 1586 which only served to increase his hostility. The matter apparently even gained the attention of the Pope, and Malaspina's successor as Nuncio, Filippo Sega, not only secured Rudolf's order expelling Dee and Kelley in May of that year but also wanted them sent to Rome.[74] Since Pucci was at this time in contact with the Nuncio in his efforts to return to the Catholic church and also seems to have suggested to Dee that they accompany him to Rome, Dee became distrustful of Pucci, considered him a spy for the Nuncio, and broke relations with him (T&FR,419–20, 429–31, 433–4).[75] At the request of Vilém Rožmberk, Rudolf later granted permission for Dee and Kelley to stay in Rožmberk's lands and admitted regretting his order of expulsion, which he had granted only under pressure (T&FR,430, 435–6).[76] Rudolf seems to have been motivated less by opposition to Dee than by a desire to pacify Catholic authorities.

Rudolf's hesitancy regarding Dee's initiative was, however, apparent from the beginning before the emergence of ecclesiastical opposition, and this as well as his reluctant agreement to expulsion seems a part of his characteristically indefinite attitude toward religious questions. It is not clear what Dee's programme was; his utter reliance on the angels suggests that he may not have had one but expected the angels to reveal the course of events and the advice he was to give step by step. There are reports that he predicted the ruin of both Rome and Constantinople, but as his, or Kelley's, Catholic sympathies rose, the angels largely approve the institutions of the Papacy and the Roman church as the embodiment of the true apostolic tradition, and impute its failures to the sins of its personnel (*T&FR*,410–13).[77] A report of his visit to the court of Wilhelm IV of Hesse-Kassel indicates that he presented a pamphlet on the secrets of God related to the apocalypse, and let it be known that he disliked all religions and looked forward to a 'restorer of the house of Israel to his wanted terrestrial glorie'.[78] What seems clear is that Dee expected some temporal restoration and looked to a secular ruler to fulfil this role.

What Dee offered Rudolf was not just a personal contemplation of the esoteric harmonies of the cosmos and the revelation of divine secrets as a way to personal salvation. A response to Dee's initiative demanded of Rudolf commitment and decision both to trust Dee and the angelic revelations and potentially to follow some course of action, and this ran counter to Rudolf's personality and religious policy. Rudolf had no sympathy for the Protestant camp in his domains but he likewise did not actively support Papal efforts to promote counter-Reformation. He sought to maintain religious peace and balance by pursuing a middle course that would leave him free of both sides and avoid polarization in a situation that seemed so fragile. In Evans's perceptive analysis, Rudolf's irenism was not an activist policy but grew out of a mood of pessimistic resignation and spiritual uncertainty that made for vacillation and indecisiveness.[79] Dee's message may have been, as Evans puts it, 'relevant and meaningful' to his Prague audience, and his prediction of the destruction of the Turk may well have been welcome, but it asked too much of Rudolf.[80] It is perhaps revealing that what Kurz thought would best serve Dee's suit with Rudolf was Dee's mention of the 'secret of my glasse, for battering in a dark night, etc.', which was the mirror with which he had so amused Elizabeth (*T&FR*,255–6).[81] A clever divertissement was ideologically neutral. Although quite different in temperament, the hesitancy of Elizabeth and Burghley to countenance Dee's programme of British imperialism seems to have been predicated on the same reluctance to endanger England's freedom of action by polarizing a delicately balanced situation.

Even in such diverse courts as those of Elizabeth, Wilhelm IV of Hesse-Kassel, and Rudolf II, the common denominator of patronage was the glorification of the prince through the display of scientific and artistic wealth. Clients were expected to produce works that advertised the prince as patron, or that were of tangible practical utility, or that had aesthetic value.[82] Rudolf had no aversion to magic, having a servant cast a spell from the *Picatrix* on his brother Matthias; but clients, at least those aspiring to the title of Imperial Mathematician and Philosopher, were not expected to be political advisors or confessors as Rudolf seems to have presumed from Dee's chastisement of his sins during their meeting (*T& FR*,255).[83] Nor was patronage intended to glorify the client, and Dee's inflated sense of his self-importance cannot but have struck his prospective patrons as arrogant and presumptuous. In his discussions with Kurz, Dee made it clear that he did not come to Prague to live obscurely but expected to maintain and increase his fame and would be very injured if he were considered a trifler and not regarded (*T&FR*,255). Dee's conceit bordered on fantasy. Although he had knowledge of the displeasure of Elizabeth and others toward him in England, he magnificently appeared in Hesse-Kassel with a train of four coaches and presented himself as living at Elizabeth's charge, and as having departed her court because of the jealousies of some nobles and Rudolf's court, from which he had actually been expelled, because he was discontented with the Emperor's 'slender entertainment of him'.[84] The Landgraf of Hesse-Kassel recognized Dee's practical abilities, commissioning in 1587 some nautical charts to reflect information from Drake's voyage of circumnavigation, and they corresponded on political matters, but the figure Dee cut while at his court seems to have been the object of some ridicule.[85] When Dee returned to England in 1589, he travelled like a prince with three new coaches, wagons for his baggage, fifteen horses, and an assortment of soldiers and horsemen for protection, all of which he reckoned cost him close to £800 (*CR*,32–4).

Despite Dee's lofty claims to his prospective patrons, he in fact had little that was tangible to offer and produced almost nothing. The way of the world in courtly patronage was made abundantly clear when Kelley learned to make a facsimile of gold that convinced most observers that he had discovered the secret of transmutation. Alchemy seems to have been Kelley's major interest throughout, while his scrying may well have served only to gain Dee's support and, through him, the patrons to support his search for the secret of the powder he had discovered. In Vilém Rožmberk Dee and Kelley found a patron whose generosity matched his wealth, which may be the source of Dee's lavish funds for his trip home, and Rožmberk's interest in alchemy may well have provided the support and the encouragement that Kelley needed to become increasingly independent of Dee.[86] Dee's and Kelley's activities are less clear after spring 1586 because there are large gaps in the records of the spiritual actions. This may reflect only the vagaries of preservation, but it more than likely reflects a decline in the activity itself because of Kelley's reluctance. Kelley had perfected his technique of projection by fall of 1586 because in December Dee recorded that he performed a demonstration for two English visitors.[87] The following spring Kelley refused outright to scry any longer and, after Dee's attempt to have his son Arthur take Kelley's place failed to yield any visions, reluctantly agreed to resume scrying only to discredit the entire project through the scheme for sharing their wives (*T& FR*,*1–*31). During the same period the news of Kelley's alchemical feat brought him the attention and rewards Dee only dreamed about. Although he eventually came to a bad end, Kelley was much in demand by Rožmberk and Rudolf II, who made him a knight, and acquired considerable wealth.[88]

Word also reached England prompting Elizabeth to invite Dee and Kelley to return. When she received no response, Dee's friend, Edward Dyer, was sent to Prague, and when he arrived it became clear that he was interested not in Dee but in Kelley's transmutation and having Kelley return for the benefit of England.[89] Dyer returned without Kelley but made a highly favourable report to Elizabeth and Burghley, who wrote to Kelley commending his wisdom and learning and assuring him of rewards if he would put his abilities in the service of Elizabeth. In 1591 Dyer was again sent by Elizabeth and Burghley to try to get Kelley to return, but it was clear that Rudolf was not inclined to lose what he considered a valuable asset.[90] In contrast, Dee was offered nothing substantial when he returned. While Dee's reception by Elizabeth was cordial, and she and others made him occasional presents that eased his financial plight, his condition was little different than when he left.[91]

Dee returned to England to find that his library and laboratories had been despoiled by former associates, that other possessions had been dissipated by his brother-in-law, in whose safe keeping he had left them, and his financial condition was none too good (*CR*,27–32).[92] He gives no reason to think that his reception by Elizabeth was less than cordial, but the place he had so long sought still eluded him. Although the last twenty years of his life are not lacking in biographical interest, they have little further to offer the study of his career in natural philosophy.

In 1590 there appeared an anonymous almanac and prognostication for 1591 under the initials I. D. which was most likely Dee's since the almanac provides three calendars, the Julian, the Gregorian, and the 'true' based on calculations from the birth of Christ reflecting Dee's earlier ideas on calendar reform.[93] Little else of substance remains from this period. He claims to have written in 1591 on the microcosm as a compendium of all natural philosophy, and in 1592 on three ancient oracles, but neither work survives (*CR*,26–7; *LA*,76–7). In 1592 he also projected a large work, *De Horizonte Aeternitatis*, of which no trace remains, as a reply to Andreas Libavius's criticisms of his *Monas* (*LA*,77–8). He remained intellectually active for quite some time. He was acquainted with Thomas Harriot, entertained visitors and discussed philosophy and other affairs with them, and in 1604 met Richard Napier at dinner and discussed Ramon Lull and the transmutation of metals.[94] Alchemical practice still received some attention, but his experiences with Kelley seems to have somewhat soured him on this.[95] The pursuit of angelic revelations did not suffer the same fate and were seemingly his greatest devotion the rest of his life. There are records of séances as late as 1607, and he had relations with Bartholomew Hickman throughout this period. His reference to destroying some of these records indicates that what remain are only a fragment of an extensive and pervasive interest (*T& FR*,*32–*45).[96] These may well have been the source of the 'heavenly admonition' he delivered to Elizabeth, and the scrying activities also figure in the arrangements for the disposition of his library upon his death.[97]

His financial position continued to be as precarious as ever. His *Diary* records numerous gifts from Elizabeth and others that kept

him going, but he had a large family and maintained a large household, still hiring servants and assistants, so he also borrowed
frequently. In these last years he was still very much concerned
with defending his reputation and attempting to secure a living,
which were the motives behind his *Compendious Rehearsall*, written
for the commissioners appointed by Elizabeth to investigate his
request for support, and the *Letter Apologeticall*, written to justify the
religious legitimacy of his studies to the Archbishop of Canterbury
who had to pass on any ecclesiastical appointment.[98] In 1595 he
did receive the Wardenship of the Collegiate Chapter at Manchester, but this proved less than satisfactory in its rewards and an
administrative tribulation rather than the foundation for the private
research institute he sought.[99]

IX

CONCLUSION

JOHN DEE

This conclusion will look first at issues relating to John Dee and then draw together the strands pertaining to some of the broader issues that have arisen in the course of these studies. The main issue in previous discussions of Dee has centered on his intellectual filiaions and motivations. This has taken the form of associating him with a philosophical tradition, either the doctrines of Renaissance Neoplatonism, or the group of texts and ideas progressively elaborated in the Renaissance through a hermetic/kabbalist tradition in which Neoplatonism was associated with a strongly occult and magical philosophy. This latter approach is distilled in the idea of Dee as a *magus* and of magic as the central feature of his works and the motivation for both his work in science, and most notably his application of mathematics to the study of nature, and his religious life.

From the *Propaedeumata* through the *Libri mysteriorum*, and the *Monas* and the *Praeface* in between, however, the expression of Dee's intellectual life assumed considerable variation. His development over the course of his career was significant in terms of both intellectual content and motivation. Despite the abyss that separates the *Propaedeumata* and the *Libri mysteriorum*, there is a thread that ties the various manifestations of his natural philosophy together, a thread not of philosophical principles but of intellectual intent. This common intent was the desire to know nature, not superficially but through the 'preeminent virtues', the hidden springs and ultimate reasons behind the processes and very existence of the cosmos. In addition, he had a firm conviction that mathematical principles and procedures offered important aid in understanding nature. Dee considered that the understanding he sought was something not readily known even among scholars and that his acquisition of it would set him well above his contemporaries in learning. Further, the pursuit of this knowledge of nature was something of a religious quest because he thought of it as entailing an understanding of the divine. This appears as early as the *Propaedeumata*, although in muted form, in the idea that his theories were an explication of the first aphorism on the creation, and it became an ever more prominent feature of his intellectual endeavours.

The origins of this basic intellectual intent predate any records, but his trips to Louvain to study with other mathematically oriented philosophers in close proximity to his university studies suggests that it began at Cambridge and was reinforced by his contacts at Louvain. In pursuit of this goal Dee read. Dee's book of nature was, as in the case of many others of the time, found in the books of men. His reading was wide and eclectic, and encompassed not only the new culture of print but a deep reverence for medieval scribal culture. Other than a penchant for material that was 'occultist' in the broadest sense, including not only the occult arts and sciences of astrology, alchemy, and magic, but also writings of natural philosophy that posited a variety of hidden agencies as the key to understanding the fundamental substances and processes of nature, Dee worked in no clearly defined philosophical or intellectual tradition. His thinking was rather in a constant state of flux through the continuous assimilation of new material and the modulation of his earlier ideas. Rather than systematic statements of a carefully articulated position, the major expressions of his thinking, each composed hastily in response to some immediate and short-term occasion, represent momentary eruptions reflecting his current thoughts and material he had most deeply assimilated at that point brought to bear on issues of current concern.

His earliest philosophical studies were predominantly Aristotelian, although he showed little inclination toward being a professional Aristotelian. Rather, his equally early interest in mathematics and a variety of mathematical arts and sciences motivated him to seek avenues to integrate mathematical studies with natural philosophy leading him progressively to soften traditional Aristotelian divisions among the sciences and to appropriate quite eclectically increasingly non-Aristotelian materials into his natural philosophy. The central formative influence that may well have suggested the potentialities of integrating mathematics and natural philosophy and certainly guided his pursuit of his intellectual endeavour was Roger Bacon. Almost every significant feature of his intellectual development refers back in some way to the inspiration of Bacon and his progressive assimilation of Bacon's works. In some things he remained very close to Bacon; in others, while following the original impetus, he moved further away as he assimilated other materials that responded to changing intellectual appetites.

Bacon's influence on Dee's natural philosophy is most direct in the *Propaedeumata*. Here the main problem Dee addressed was 'occult' causality as it pertained to astrology. He developed what he considered were the foundations of astrology through a mathematical physics of radiated influences as the fundamental causal mechanism throughout the cosmos within an Aristotelian idea of demonstrative science. The central inspiration for this formulation came from the distinct interpretation of Aristotelian physics Dee found in al-Kindī, Grosseteste, and particularly Roger Bacon. In this interpretation of Aristotelian physics a crucial but 'occult' Neoplatonic element of emanationism provided the foundation for extending the model of geometric optics to the analysis of a broad range of causal relationships. This served both to provide an intelligible and non-spiritual, non-demonic treatment of the action of 'occult' qualities and influences and to facilitate the extension of mathematical treatment to domains of physics beyond those Aristotle had considered appropriate for mathematical study. This 'Baconian' approach toward understanding the behaviour of the physical world through a physical causality and mathematical models also carries through to analogous material in the *Mathematicall Praeface* in his treatment of astrology, perspective, grading, and statics.

The central issue that Dee addressed in the *Praeface* was the legitimacy and usefulness of mathematics for philosophy, the study of nature, and practical affairs. While his basic stance regarding the importance of mathematics echoes and probably derives from his early study of Bacon, and many of the specific examples he presents reflect similar material in Bacon, Dee drew from Proclus's theory of the ontological and epistemological status of mathematicals a framework in which to develop a coherent philosophy of mathematics. This philosophy not only indicated the intellectual status of the study of mathematics in and of itself but also provided the foundations for the extension of mathematical thought both into the realm of theological inquiry and into the arts and sciences dealing with physical nature. What is important is that the factor most prominent in the transition from pure mathematics to mathematics applied to the understanding of nature was not an ontological conception of mathematics associated with the 'Pythagorean' speculations of Renaissance Neoplatonic, kabbalist, or magical writers but Proclus's notion of the epistemological function of mathematics. Of equal or greater significance, when it comes to specific instances in the *Praeface* of the value of mathematics in scientific applications, the models for Dee's illustrations are Baconian and Archimedean.

A similar conclusion holds for whatever 'experimental' impulse is present in Dee's approach to the understanding of natural phenomena. His concept of 'experimental science' derives from Bacon, and his understanding of it was idiosyncratic and multifarious, encompassing a range of spiritual and magical 'experiences' beyond just the verification of theories by empirical test. Nevertheless, the aspect of his idea of archemastrie that came into play in the understanding of the behaviour of nature – the collection of empirical data both as a source of new information and for confirming theory – owed little if anything to Renaissance magical philosophies. This sense of the mutual and reciprocal role of theory and empiricism emerged very early, was prominent in the *Propaedeumata*, and continued into the *Praeface*.

To the extent that the radiated influences of the *Propaedeumata* were capable of manipulation by artificial means and of producing by design effects beyond those that occurred in nature's normal course, Dee's theory in the *Propaedeumata* also served to define as natural and technological a variety of effects that conventionally suffered the stigma of being magical. In this respect the *Propaedeumata* does involve a theory of 'natural magic'. The artificial manipulation of nature through technology, however, is only a small element in the *Propaedeumata*. It was not the central motivation behind the genesis of the theory; rather it was an implication of the physics and a technology through which the usefulness of mathematics and of this knowledge of the 'preeminent' virtues of nature became manifest. In the *Praeface*, when defending works of science and technology that were often confused with magic, Dee's tactic, like that of Roger Bacon, was not to isolate them within a special variety of magic called natural at one end of a continuum of magical practices but to disassociate them entirely from any imputation of magic. The marvellous effects that pertain to the art of thaumaturgik are sharply disassociated from the common pejorative sense of magic as the conjuring of demons. This may well have been a rhetorical ploy, but reserving the term magic for other sorts of things suggests that he considered magic different in important ways from technology.

Magic, including the term itself, does play a significant role in the *Monas*. Here it is associated with the miraculous transformation of the soul of the adept leading to spiritual ascent; that is, it is a religious experience. This mystical magic is grounded in natural philosophy in that this miraculous transformation is the culmination of a knowledge of the world. In the *Monas* this knowledge consists more in understanding the symbolic language that reveals the mathematical structural principles behind creation than in the laws of physical causality governing the behavior of nature. From this understanding comes a knowledge of the intrinsic associations and interrelations that hold in and between astronomy and alchemy, and with this is revealed the cosmic regenerative process epitomized in alchemical transmutation but pertaining equally to the soul.

Although the *Monas* marks a shift to a conception of natural philosophy very different from that of the *Propaedeumata*, the intent to know the hidden springs and ultimate reasons behind the processes and very existence of the cosmos was still Dee's fundamental motivation. In specific content the *Monas* is less indebted to Bacon than the *Propaedeumata*, but Bacon's idea of a universal science integrating all knowledge, of science as a path to divinity and moral regeneration, and of the natural philosopher as a servant of society in his capacity as a reformer of knowledge and advisor to the ruler was the important model that suggested to Dee this new direction. It was in the realization of this new direction that during the later 1550s and early 1560s Dee absorbed strands of occultism more characteristic of the Renaissance. Kabbalah, not as Hebrew studies or as a technique of scriptural exegesis but as the recovery of the divine language of creation, appealed to him as a key to a pristine religious wisdom and assumed a particularly natural philosophical cast through his study of Pantheus's union of kabbalah with alchemy. Trithemius's conception of alchemy as a magic expressed through numerology and of magic as a mystical ascent not only provided key elements in the cosmology but of equal importance suggested the idea of magic as a spiritual and mystical discipline with which Dee later associated the Florentine Neo-platonic theory of magic.

To somewhat varying degrees the somewhat different ideas of natural philosophy of the *Propaedeumata* and the *Monas* continued to find expression in the *Praeface* and in Dee's activities through the early 1580s. While more as points on a spectrum within his basic objectives than as mutually exclusive positions, these different ideas served significantly different functions. In contrast with the strands that stem from his early studies which relate primarily to under-standing the causal relations within the cosmos and the value of mathematics in the sciences and practical arts and technologies, the strand associated with the *Monas* was related to his interest in a natural theology revealing the creator's ideas through language and a mystical soteriology through a spiritual religious magic. Implicit in Dee's usage, magic had this exclusively religious connotation distinct both from conjuring and from technology. In the *Praeface* it was the multifarious ways of considering numbers and figures inherent in Proclus's philosophy of mathematics and the polysemous character of 'experience' within his idea of archemastrie through which these various strands were held together.

In the *Libri mysteriorum* Dee returned to his concern with discovering the divine language of creation as the vehicle for under-standing the divine reasons behind creation and with magic as a vehicle for spiritual illumination that first assumed expression in the *Monas*. At this point the substantive elements of the natural philosophy he had developed from Bacon, the mathematical philo-sophy from Proclus, and the concern with mathematical procedures for the investigation of nature recede to the point of disappearing. This is partially the result of relinquishing intellectual control largely to Kelley, but just as importantly it stems from the predomi-nance assumed by the religious desire for direct spiritual experience coupled with a despair of human capabilities and sources to lead him to ultimate things. It is here that Renaissance magical sources – Trithemius, Reuchlin, and Agrippa – assume predominance; sources in which the heritage of medieval ritual magic was strongest and in which a ceremonial spirit magic served a predominantly religious function.

Thus, Dee's work in natural philosophy was not a further progressive elaboration of Renaissance Florentine Neoplatonism, or of a 'hermetic' tradition, or of a Renaissance 'occult philosophy' with a hermetic, Neoplatonic, kabbalist core. He did come to share with others of his time the search for an 'ancient theology', a pristine divine language of things transcending the conventional character of human language, and a religious immediacy through magic as a religious mysticism, but his realization of these things came through his own personal development and an idiosyncratic blend of sources in which medieval Latin and Arabic writers were of as much importance as those of the Renaissance. The more these concerns became predominant, the more he moved toward natural philosophy as theology and magic as religion. Whatever the possibilities for science were within various kinds of magic, as Dee understood it and its Renaissance sources, magic was religious and not scientific. The only time he turned to magic as a source of natural knowledge was in the *Libri mysteriorum* out of despair of human capabilities.

Dee never advertised himself as a reformer of the organization of knowledge, but his approach to natural philosophy implied the redefinition of the organization of the sciences traditional within the universities, at times in quite startling ways. This redefinition took a variety of forms which, once again, reflect the different impulses at work in Dee's intellectual career. One theme motivating Dee's redefinition of disciplinary boundaries was his conviction of the value of mathematics for the study of nature. Under the influence first of Bacon and somewhat later of Proclus, Dee sought to articulate the foundations for the extension of mathematics to matters of physical science. In the *Propaedeumata* he did this through optics as an intermediary science between geometry and physics. In the *Praeface* he significantly broadened this; using Proclus's epistemological idea of mathematics to support the extension of mathematics to a broad range of arts and sciences, and the idea of archemastrie as a broad warrant to import new principles into sciences based on experience, he comes close to dissolving the entire notion of sciences having distinct boundaries. In demarginalizing alchemy and magic, and in projecting the claims of the adept to authority in theology and not just natural philosophy, the *Monas* was also quite radical. What supported this was the notion of an original language containing truths common to and thus unifying all sciences. Here Dee relied more heavily upon Renaissance magical and occult sources, and his motivation was less to find ways in which one discipline could enhance another than to support his claims as a mathematician and natural philosopher to theological authority.

A significant determinant in the course of Dee's career was his decision to reject university positions and to seek court patronage as the preferred alternative. This was undoubtedly closely related to his inclination to be free from disciplinary boundaries, to work outside the institutionally defined canon of texts and issues of academic philosophy, and to pursue studies in directions for which he had no sanctioned authority. To begin with, he had some success at court based on his possession of practical scientific expertise, and throughout his life his prospective patrons continued to value him in this regard. The *Propaedeumata* also indicates that he wished to be considered a natural philosopher, not just a technical advisor, and through his assimilation of new materials in the early 1560s his concept of his role as a philosopher expanded to include the possession of an arcane religious wisdom. Natural philosophy served as a vehicle for defining an intellectual role and acquiring status and position. He came to think of his status as a philosopher as entitling him to support and to special status as advisor to society's rulers.

His fortunes in this respect were rather disappointing. Courts did offer opportunities beyond the universities and might provide the context in which esoteric philosophies and ideas on the margins of institutionalized culture were recognized, yet courts were still role directive. Patrons had their own expectations and positions required negotiation.[1] Dee had contacts at several courts with very different approaches to scientific and cultural patronage, but he was not noticeably successful in negotiating a position suiting his aspirations at any, even at that of Rudolf II which was most receptive to the esoteric and the occult. Two things contributed to this. One was that he offered little in the way of services that were practical or that tangibly enhanced his patrons' glory. Second, and perhaps most important, he laid claim to offer politically and religiously ideological advice which not only was seen as dangerous but also impinged on a domain that princes were not accustomed to delegate to philosophers. In this he ran afoul of another set of institutional boundaries: those defining the professional domains of the courtier, the counsellor, and the ecclesiastic.

MAGIC AND THE OCCULT IN THE RENAISSANCE

The extent to which previous historiography has made of Dee a great *magus* and a follower of a Renaissance occult philosophy has entailed giving almost as much attention to the character of magic and the occult in the Renaissance as it has to their role in Dee's thinking. If Dee indicates anything about magic and the occult in the Renaissance it is that there were many varieties of magic available from a variety of sources and that there was hardly a single monolithic 'occult philosophy'. Generalizing about Renaissance magic, its character, sources, and relation to other developments including science is difficult and treacherous.

It may very well be that magic and other occult sciences acquired an enhanced intellectual status in the Renaissance. In the absence of any statistical surveys the intuitive impression at least is that magic and the occult were more frequently discussed, more favourably and with fewer reservations about types of magic employing non-physical agents, by more authors of intellectual stature than was the case in the Middle Ages. What is at issue is not that magic and the occult achieved a wider intellectual legitimacy in the Renaissance, it is rather characterizing how this took place. The Middle Ages and the Renaissance both had access to information on a wide range of magical practices and occult phenomena, extending from the occult properties of foods, plants, and minerals, through the sympathetic action of images, divinatory techniques, reports of marvels, to demonic and angelic ritual magic. Compared with the Middle Ages, when any phenomena or practice that could be suspected of demonic involvement was religiously suspect, what is noteworthy in the Renaissance is that the full range of magic and the occult were brought within the margins of respectability and endowed with both intellectual and religious legitimacy.

It is, however, important to recognize that there was a considerable range of approaches to magic and the occult in the Renaissance, that magic was legitimated in a variety of ways and for a variety of motives, and that different approaches were often preferential to different types of magic. The Hermetica were certainly not the only vehicle for the revaluation of magic in the Renaissance. A naturalistic Aristotelianism in the case of Oresme and Pomponazzi promoted an understanding of magical and occult phenomena as natural and rationally intelligible, and Roger Bacon's physics of radiated influence, as Dee indicates, could do much the same thing. In Ficino's case, the late Neoplatonists were of importance in providing the philosophical foundation for a variety of sympathetic magical effects motivated by a desire to extend the range of legitimate occult medical remedies while avoiding any imputation of demonic agents. Although quite different in their physics and therefore in the type of magical and occult phenomena considered legitimate, Ficino's effort was quite similar on a purely philosophical level to medieval attempts to 'naturalize' aspects of magic. More novel to the Renaissance than the strictly intellectual legitimation of magic was a religiously motivated interest in magic as a special wisdom and power delegated by God as a token of a special relationship between God and man and as a technique for restoring immediacy with God and the spiritual. This religious valuation of magic was especially encouraged by kabbalah, the Hermetica, and other texts in which magic was associated with the idea of an ancient theology, but also found support in Neoplatonic discussions of magic. It is largely in response to this religious impulse and through these sources that the more obvious forms of demonic/angelic ritual magic were brought into respectability, although Trithemius, who was less knowledgeable in kabbalah and Neoplatonic sources, indicates that the religious impulse was sufficient by itself.

This need to distinguish between different types of magic, both on the grounds of their content and theoretical presuppositions and on the grounds of the motivation behind the attention directed to each, also applies to the issue of the relation of magic to science in the Renaissance. Dee's case indicates that the different traditions of magic available in the Renaissance had different implications for science. In his case the Florentine/Neoplatonic approach, in which magic had a predominantly religious function, was quite separate from his use of the medieval tradition of a natural magic, with most of his scientific work that can be related to magic being related to the latter. Dee also suggests that the place of mathematics, usually as a mystical and symbolic view of numbers and figures as reflective of occult correspondences, in magical philosophies does not justify concluding that magic encouraged a mathematical approach to science preparatory to seventeenth-century science. While he shows considerable interest in mystical mathematical correspondences, this interest was quite separate from his actual work involving the application of mathematics and mathematical reasoning. The sources that encouraged the expression of a concrete approach to nature through mathematics were Proclus and Cusanus, not any magical texts.

If a sense of operational power, a curiosity to test the secrets of the occult tradition, a willingness to consider the occult as intelligible, and a confidence in finding explanations for insensible agents were ways that Renaissance magic prepared the ground for seventeenth-century science, these were more a central feature of natural magic independent of Hermetism, Neoplatonism, and kabbalah than of the more religiously motivated ideas of magic.[2] The existence of such an independent tradition of magic may well have been important in suggesting to a variety of writers of the later sixteenth century the possibility of disassociating magic as a technology from magic as a spiritual religion.[3]

NOTES

ABBREVIATIONS

Dee's published writings are referred to with the same abbreviations as in the text references. Other frequently cited sources are abbreviated as follows. References to other printed sources are to shortened forms of materials cited in the bibliography.

Calder	Calder, 'John Dee Studied as an English Neoplatonist'.
Diary	Dee's 'diary' consists of entries he made in various printed *Ephemerides*. The two surviving examples are Bodleian Library, MSS Ashmole 487 and 488. References will indicate the relevant MS followed by the date.
French	French, *John Dee*.
Roberts & Watson	Roberts and Watson, *John Dee's Library Catalogue*.
Yates, *GBHT*	Yates, *Giordano Bruno*.
Yates, *Occult*	Yates, *The Occult Philosophy*.
Yates, *Rosicrucian*	Yates, *The Rosicrucian Enlightenment*.
Yates, *Theatre*	Yates, *Theatre of the World*.

I. JOHN DEE AND RENAISSANCE INTELLECTUAL HISTORY

1 Roberts & Watson present evidence that Dee may have in fact lived until 1609.

2 To review this literature, which is quite extensive, would be to no purpose here. French, pp. 4–17, reviews the most important; Pritchard, *Alchemy*, lists additional items as does the bibliography.

3 Deacon, *John Dee*, draws on modern scholarly work but Dee as 'secret agent' dominates the interpretive framework, imaginative speculation and reconstruction playing as large a role as in Arnold Waldstein's *John Dee*, which is by the author's admission a novel. For similar elements in the work of an acknowledged historian, see Vickers, 'Frances Yates', pp. 304–6.

4 Taylor, *Tudor Geography*, and Taylor, *The Mathematical Practitioners*.
5 Johnson, *Astronomical Thought*.
6 Calder.
7 French, p. xi.
8 Yewbrey, 'John Dee'.
9 Calder, 1:i, 7–18, 25, 28, 43, 71–6, 865.
10 Calder, 1:142; following Burtt, *The Metaphysical Foundations*.
11 Calder, 1:14, 48–67, 124–42.
12 Calder, 1:44–8, 139, 2:5–7, n. 5; following Lenoble, *Mersenne*.
13 Yates, *GBHT*, p. 150; Yates, 'The Hermetic Tradition', pp. 259, 261–2.
14 Yates, *GBHT*, pp. 1–17; Garin, 'Magic and Astrology', pp. 149–53; on the Hermetic literature Festugière, *La révélation*, is fundamental; and Dannenfeldt, 'Hermetica Philosophica', pp. 137–56, surveys the transmission of that literature.
15 Yates, *GBHT*, pp. 20–43; Garin, 'Magic and Astrology', p. 153.
16 Yates, *GBHT*, pp. 17–18; Garin, 'Magic and Astrology', pp. 147, 153–7.
17 Yates, *GBHT*, pp. 13–14, 17–18, 44–58, 81; Garin, 'Magic and Astrology', pp. 148–54.
18 Yates, *GBHT*, pp. 17–18, 107–9, 144; Garin, 'Magic and Astrology', pp. 146–7.
19 For reviews assessing Yates's work see Schmitt, 'Reappraisals', pp. 200–14; Metaxopoulos, 'A la suite de F. A. Yates', pp. 53–65; and Tannier, 'Une nouvelle interprétation', pp. 15–33.
20 Yates, *GBHT*, pp. 107–9, 144, 155–6, 255; Garin 'Considerazioni', pp. 176–80.
21 Schmitt, 'Reappraisals', pp. 200–4.
22 Westman, 'Magical Reform', pp. 5–8.
23 Yates, *GBHT*, pp. 151–6, 235–49, 450–1; Yates, 'The Hermetic Tradition', pp. 268–71. This interpretation has been criticized in Rosen, 'Was Copernicus a Hermetist?' and most thoroughly in Westman, 'Magical Reform'.
24 Despite intimations by scholars, I am not aware of any records, such as Dee's minutes of his spiritual séances, of magical practices by Ficino, Pico, Agrippa, Reuchlin, Bruno, or others except for Campanella. See Walker, *Spiritual and Demonic Magic*, pp. 205–12.
25 Yates, 'The Hermetic Tradition', pp. 259, 261–2.
26 Yates, *GBHT*, pp. 146–7; Yates, 'The Hermetic Tradition', pp. 258–9, 261–2; Yates, *Theatre*, p. 5.
27 Yates, *GBHT*, p. 150.
28 Calder, 1:325, 2:168, nn.92–3.
29 Yates, *Shakespeare's Last Plays*, pp. 3–9.
30 Yates, 'The Hermetic Tradition', p. 263; Yates, *Rosicrucian*, pp. 222–3.
31 Yates, *Rosicrucian*, pp. 220–1.
32 Ibid., p. 221.
33 She prepared the ground for this view in *Shakespeare's Last Plays*, in

which she argues that Shakespeare reflects Renaissance magic and Dee, and in *Theatre of the World*, in which she explores the influence of Dee on English architecture and Robert Fludd and, through his memory theatres, on the construction of English theatres, including the Globe.

34 That is, after her *Giordano Bruno, Art of Memory*, essay on 'The Hermetic Tradition', and *Theatre of the World* but before *The Rosicrucian Enlightenment* and *The Occult Philosophy in the Elizabethan Age*.

35 French, pp. 2–3, 63–6, 87, 104–8, and chs 6 and 7.

36 Yewbrey, 'John Dee', pp. 13–14, 200, 337–42.

37 Calder, 1:247; French, p. 28. The issue is not the existence of Neoplatonic elements or Hermetist tendencies in some of Dee's works, but how these are used. Calder, because he considered Renaissance Neoplatonism to have had a positive relation to the development of early modern science, chose this element as the basis for developing an idea of Dee's philosophy and then interpreted Dee's writings in terms of this rather *a priori* construct (Calder, 1:7–14). French does the same thing with Hermetism, using almost exclusively among Dee's works the *Monas hieroglyphica* of 1564 and reading these ideas back into Dee's earlier works (French, 62–88, 93–103).

38 Skinner, 'Meaning and Understanding', pp. 4–11, 15–30, 48–9; cf. Lacapra, 'Rethinking Intellectual History', pp. 268–9.

39 This material was partially published posthumously as *T&FR*.

40 These are *Diary*.

41 In addition to *CR*, these are *LA*, *NA*, and the 'Digression Apologeticall' in *MP*,A.j^v–A.iij.

42 This is Dee, 'Catalogus librorum Bibliothecae'. An exhaustive and definitive edition of this is forthcoming as Roberts & Watson. While I regret that their work has not been completed in time for me to use it, both Julian Roberts and Andrew Watson have been generous in sharing aspects of their work with me.

43 Roberts & Watson.

44 Yates, *Theatre*, pp. 1–19, 33–7; and French, pp. 40–61, both make extensive use of Dee's library catalogue as a guide to his thinking. The use they make of it is flawed in significant ways. First, they give no consideration to when he acquired specific materials, implying that what he had in 1583 influenced him throughout his career. Second, they assume that what he had he in fact read and absorbed. Third, they ignore the bulk of material in the library, emphasizing as influential only selected authors and texts presumed to have been influential only on *a priori* grounds.

45 These are Bodleian Library, Corpus Christi College MS 191, fols 77^v–90; and British Library MS Add. 35213, fols 1–4^v. The latter list bears no date. It is later than 1556, including manuscripts from the 1556 lists, but contains no books published after 1559 at the latest.

46 Jamblichus, *Index eorum*. Dee's copy is in the Folger Shakespeare Library.

47 British Library MS Add. 35213, fol.2 or 2ᵛ.

48 Indications of the dating of the notes in Jamblichus are mention of the *Propaedeumata* (1558) on fol.48, mention of the 'kabbalah of the real' referred to in the *Monas* (1564) on fol.44, and the date 1567 in the margin on fol.52ᵛ.

49 Mary Hesse, 'Hermeticism and Historiography', pp. 147–57.

50 Some of the difficulties in defining magic in relation to religion and science are explored in Hammond, 'Magic', pp. 1349–56; Jarvie and Agassi, 'The Problem of the Rationality of Magic', pp. 55–74; Jarvie and Agassi, 'Magic and Rationality Again', pp. 236–45; Settle, 'The Rationality of Science', pp. 173–94; Geertz, 'An Anthropology of Religion and Magic', pp. 71–89; and Thomas, 'An Anthropology of Religion and Magic', pp. 91–109.

51 Important reappraisals are McGuire, 'Neoplatonism and Active Principles'; Westman, 'Magical Reform'; Garin, 'Divagazioni ermetiche'; Garin, 'Ancora sull'ermetismo'; Rossi, 'Hermeticism, Rationality'; Hall, 'Magic, Metaphysics and Mysticism'; and Schmitt, 'Reappraisals'. Collections of papers from two recent conferences which continue this reappraisal and point in some new directions are Vickers, *Occult and Scientific Mentalities*; and Debus and Merkle, *Intellectual History and the Occult*.

II 'OUTLANDISH AND HOMISH STUDIES AND EXERCISES PHILOSOPHICALL'

1 The 1558 edition has the title in Greek. For typographic convenience I will use the Latin title of the 1568 edition.

2 North, 'Celestial Influence', pp. 45–100, is a good general discussion of the theoretical basis of astrology. Thomas, *Religion and the Decline of Magic*, pp. 335–40, gives a summary of the general tenets of astrology in Dee's day and the types of predictive activity astrologers engaged in; and pp. 347–82, surveys the actual practices of a number of consulting astrologers. Thomas's discussion of the intellectual and social role of astrology, pp. 383–93, does much to explain the widespread interest in and recourse to astrology in the sixteenth and the seventeenth centuries.

3 Calder, 1:247; French, p. 28.

4 *MP*, A.iijᵛ–A.iiij; Dee, Letter to Sir William Cecil, 16 February 1562, *Bibliographical and Historical Miscellanies*, pp. 6–7.

5 Most scholars of English universities in the sixteenth century have taken as their starting point 1560 when some statutory, administrative, and religious stability was re-established. As a result, except for a work such as Simon, *Education and Society*, which covers more than just the universities, one is left with the older nineteenth-century historians and what remain of the pre-1550 university statutes and records. Recent work dealing with some aspects of the pre-Reformation universities are Rose, 'Erasmians and

Mathematicians'; Logan, 'The Origins of the so-called Regius
Professorships'; and Leader, 'Professorships and Academic Reform'.

6 Although the comments about universities in the *Praeface* do not refer
to Dee's education, I suspect they reflect his memory of his
experience rather than his knowledge of the situation in 1570.

7 Hackett, *Original Statutes*, p. 300. These date from ca. 1500 but there
is no evidence of significant statutory revision until after Dee left
Cambridge.

8 Leader, 'Professorships', pp. 216–18.

9 Hackett, pp. 298–303.

10 Simon, p. 200. On Greek studies, see Tilley, 'Greek Studies',
pp. 221–39, 438–56; on humanism in general at the universities,
see McConica, *English Humanists*, ch. 4.

11 Schmitt, *John Case*, pp. 17–20; Ashworth, 'The *Libelli sophistarum*',
p. 134; Jardine, 'Humanism and Dialectic', p. 147; also Jardine,
'The Place of Dialectic', pp. 31–62.

12 McConica, 'Humanism and Aristotle', pp. 296–327, indicates that
the old *Libelli sophistarum*, although not printed after 1530, continue
to show up in booksellers' inventories throughout the sixteenth
century. Jardine's ('Humanism and the Sixteenth Century
Cambridge Arts Course', pp. 16–17) examination of the book lists of
deceased BAs and MAs on the other hand indicates that humanist
dialectic grew to a position of prominence.

13 Schmitt, *John Case*, pp. 17–20.

14 Royal Commission, *Documents*, 1:384; Rose, 'Erasmians and
Mathematicians', pp. 48–9; Leader, 'Professorships', p. 224;
Fletcher, 'Change and Resistance', p. 13.

15 Johnson, *Astronomical Thought*, pp. 79–80.

16 Simon, pp. 81–2; McConica, *English Humanists*, pp. 78–80.

17 Mayor, *Early Statutes*, p. 104; Feingold, *Mathematician's Apprenticeship*,
pp. 35–6; on the regius professorships, see Logan, 'The Origins',
pp. 271–8.

18 Mayor, *Early Statutes*, pp. 36–7, 104, 244–6; Feingold, *Mathematician's
Apprenticeship*, pp. 35–6.

19 Mullinger, *The University of Cambridge*, pp. 36–44; Simon, pp. 207,
209–10; Logan, 'The Origins', pp. 271–8.

20 Mayor, *Early Statutes*, pp. 107–11, 245–7, 251–5.

21 Hackett, p. 277; *Documents*, 1:360.

22 Simon, p. 204.

23 Feingold, 'The Occult Tradition', p. 81; Strype, *John Cheke*, p. 105;
Heilbron, 'Introductory Essay', p. 8; Thomas, *Religion and the Decline
of Magic*, p. 343; Dewar, *Thomas Smith*, p. 14, n. 1; British Library
MS Sloane 325, contains numerous horoscopes of his family and
famous people recorded by Smith; Jordan, *Edward VI*, 2:409;
Jamblichus, *Index eorum*, note by Dee on fol.160 of copy in the Folger
Shakespeare Library, Washington, D.C., records Dee's recollection
of Cardano with Cheke.

24 Feingold, 'The Occult Tradition', pp. 75, 77–8.

25 Tilley, 'Greek Studies', p. 440; on Ascham at Cambridge, see McConica, *English Humanists*, pp. 208–13.

26 Roche, 'The Radius Astronomicus', pp. 18–23.

27 The date of Dee's return to England is uncertain. 1551 is indicated because Dee speaks of working with Mercator for three years (*PA*,110/11) and the earliest definite record of Dee back in England is December 1551 (*CR*,9).

28 Bartlett, 'Worshipful Gentlemen', pp. 235–48.

29 Simon, p. 206; Hudson, pp. 62, 81.

30 Vocht, *History of the Foundation*, 2:543, 545 and n. 2, 560–1.

31 Mercator, *Historia mundi*, pp. 26, 42.

32 Mercator to H. de Rantzau, May 1585, in van Durme, *Correspondence mercatorienne*, p. 192; and van Ortroy, 'Biobibliographie de Gemma Frisius', p. 23.

33 Heilbron, 'Introductory Essay', pp. 54–9.

34 *Cl. Ptolemaei . . . Operis quadripartiti. in latinum sermonem traductio: adjectis libris posterioibus . . . de sectione conica . . . quae parabola dicitur, deque speculo ustorio . . . cum praefatione D. Gemma Frisii*. The *De speculo ustorio* is actually a short Latin version of a treatise by Ibn al-Haytham on parabolic burning mirrors; see Heiberg and Wiedemann, 'Ibn al-Haitams Schrift', p. 231; and Clagett, *Archimedes*, 4:319–20. Gogava doubted Bacon's authorship of the *De sectione conica*, which is actually a version of an anonymous treatise later than Bacon that Clagett calls the *Speculi almukefi compositio*; see Clagett, *Archimedes*, 3:250–2; and Clagett, *Archimedes*, 4:99–100, 319–20.

35 These are al-Khayyāt, *De judiciis nativitatum*, bound with Hispalensis, *Epitome totius astrologiae*. The copy in the Royal College of Physicians, London, contains weather notes by Dee dated 1548.

36 Dee gives two dates in these two different places.

37 He describes this as *Prolegomena et dicta Parisiensia in Euclidis Elementorum Geometricorum librum primum et secundum in Collegio Rhemensi*. See *CR*,25; *LA*,74.

38 Calder, 1:293–303; French, pp. 29–31.

39 This lecture in mentioned only in *CR*, written in 1592. He claims that such a lecture was unprecedented in 'any University of Christendome' and that 'my auditory in Rhemes Colledge was so great, and the most part elder than my selfe, that the mathematical schooles could not hold them; for many were faine, without the schooles at the windowes, to be auditors and spectators. . . .'

40 Heilbron, 'Introductory Essay', pp. 6–8; Ross, 'Studies on Oronce Finé', pp. 212–16. These issues will be discussed more thoroughly in ch. VI.

41 The reference in the *Propaedeumata* does not mention the dedication to Edward of either work, but then Mary was still ruling at that time. The title of both works is given differently in the *CR* and *LA* than in the *Propaedeumata*.

42 Cooper, *Athenae Cantabrigiensis*, 2:497–510, 556; *Calendar of Patent Rolls, Edward VI*, 5:199; Calder, 1:302–3.

43 *Letters and Papers of Henry VIII*, 19(1):317, and 19(2):317, are the grants to supervise packing; *Calendar of Patent Rolls, Edward VI*, 3:201, is a licence to transfer property some of which formerly belonged to a monastery and a rectory; Calder, 2:90–1; Heilbron, 'Introductory Essay', p. 2.

44 Kearney, *Scholars and Gentlemen*, pp. 15, 19, 21–7; Stone, 'The Educational Revolution', pp. 41–80.

45 Simon, pp. 209–10; Hudson, *The Cambridge Connection*, pp. 3–4, 62; Strype, *John Cheke*, p. 22; Dewar, *Thomas Smith*, p. 24; McConica, *English Humanists*, pp. 215–18; Jordan, *Edward VI*, 1:41–2.

46 Simon, pp. 210–14.

47 *Letters and Papers of Henry VIII*, 21(2):342 & 344; *CR*,5.

48 Hudson, *The Cambridge Connection*, p. 62; Jordan, *Edward VI*, 1:41–2; Strype, *John Cheke*, p. 32; Collins, *William Cecil*, p. 76, Read, *Secretary Cecil*, pp. 24–30, and 37–61 passim.

49 Hudson, *The Cambridge Connection*, p. 76; Jordan, *Edward VI*, 2:21–2, 53.

50 Hoak, 'Rehabilitating the Duke', pp. 40–1.

51 Jordan, *Edward VI*, 2:419; Hoak, 'Rehabilitating the Duke', pp. 43–4.

52 McConica, *English Humanists*, p. 260; Feingold, *The Mathematician's Apprenticeship*, p. 262. William Pickering, whom Dee tutored in Louvain, sent a copy of Euclid to Cecil from Paris in 1551, indicating Cecil's personal interest in science. See Hudson, *The Cambridge Connection*, p. 81.

53 Calder, 1:305. The only evidence for Dee's relation with Pembroke at this time is a brief note by Dee in the copy of Cardano, *Libelli quinque*, in the Royal College of Physicians, London.

54 The full title of the second work is 'The Philosophicall and Poeticall Original occasions, of the Configurations, and names of the heavenly Asterismes'.

55 Jordan, *Edward VI*, 2:482–8; Quinn and Ryan, *England's Sea Empire*, pp. 21–22; Andrews, *Trade, Plunder and Settlement*, pp. 64–6.

56 Jordan, *Edward VI*, 2:489; Beer, *Northumberland*, pp. 193–4; Taylor, *Tudor Geography*, pp. 89–91; Andrews, *Trade, Plunder and Settlement*, pp. 65–7.

57 Dee presents Chancellor as an equal partner and has considerable respect for the instruments used, which were made by Chancellor. *LA*,75, lists a work written in 1553 as 'The Astronomicall, and logisticall rules, and Canons, to calculate the Ephemerides by, and other necessary accounts of heavenly motions: written at the request, and for the use of that excellent Mechanician Maister Richard Chauncelor, at his last voyage into Moschovia'. Taylor, *Tudor Geography*, pp. 90–1; Heilbron, 'Introductory Essay', pp. 9–10.

58 Quinn and Ryan, *England's Sea Empire*, p. 22; Andrews, *Trade, Plunder and Settlement*, pp. 68–9.

59 Taylor, *Tudor Geography*, pp. 95–6; *NA*,59. Dee describes a work, the 'Inventum mechanicum paradoxum de nova ratione delineandi circumferentiam circularem; unde valde rara alia dependent inventa',

written in 1556 which may relate to the 'Paradoxall Compas' that he claims to have invented in his work for the Muscovy Company. See *CR*,26; *LA*,75. Taylor, 'John Dee and the Nautical Triangle', pp. 318–25; and Waters, *The Art of Navigation*, pp. 209–12, 372–3, 526–7; attempt to reconstruct what Dee's invention was and its contribution to navigation.

60 These works are 1. 'De perspectiva illa qua peritissimi illustrissimique utuntur pictores' (1557) dealing with artistic perspective; 2. 'De Anuli astronomici multiplici usu' (1557) dealing with the astronomical instrument; and 3. 'Trochilica Inventa' (1558) dealing with what Dee later defined as '. . . the properties of all Circular motions', which amounts to the study of wheels and mills (*MP*,c.iiij^v). See *PA*,116/17; *CR*,26; *LA*,75.

61 Beer, *Northumberland*, pp. 165–7.

62 Strype, *John Cheke*, pp. 92–5.

63 Jordan, *Edward VI*, 2:501–3.

64 Calder, 1:309, cites a report that Dee declined the position because it was too public and did not allow enough freedom to travel, but the evidence is not contemporary with Dee, and Dee does not state what happened.

65 *CR*,20, is Dee's account. Calder, 1:310–18 and 2:157–65, gives a thorough account. In what follows, I have reviewed this episode because an adequate account is not available in any published work, although French, pp. 6, 8–9; and Heilbron, 'Introductory Essay', p. 11, briefly mention it.

66 *Acts of the Privy Council*, 1554–1555, pp. 137–8, 142–3; *Calendar of State Papers, Domestic, 1547–1580*, 5:67; *Register of the Privy Council, Mary*, 1:34 (Public Record Office PC/2/6); Foxe, *Acts and Monuments*, 7:77; *CR*,20; Campbell, 'Humphrey Duke of Gloucester', pp. 141–8. On Carye, see Watson, 'Christopher and William Carye', pp. 135–6. Others arrested whom I have not been able to identify are John Field and a Butler.

67 *Acts of the Privy Council*, 5:143; *Calendar of State Papers, Domestic, 1547–1580*, 5:67; Foxe, *Acts and Monuments*, 7:85. See Thomas, *Religion and the Decline of Magic*, p. 430, on the association of astrology and conjuring.

68 *Acts of the Privy Council*, 5:143, 176; Foxe, *Acts and Monuments*, 7:85. *NA*,57–8. In a note in Alexander, *Mathemalogium*, which he read while in Bonner's house, Dee refers to Bonner as a friend. Dee's signed copy of this is in the Royal College of Physicians, London.

69 Strype, *Thomas Smith*, pp. 27, 37–41; Dewar, *Thomas Smith*, pp. 42–3, 75; Jordan, *Edward VI*, 1:217, 2:246; Smith, *Tudor Prelates*, p. 282.

70 Thomas, *Religion and the Decline of Magic*, p. 307.

71 *CR*,20; *NA*,53; Foxe, *Acts and Monuments*, 7:349, 638, 641–2, 659, 734, 783, 784.

72 Jordan, *Edward VI*, 2:362–3.

73 Foxe, *Acts and Monuments*, 7:349 n.1, 641 n.6. 642, nn.2 & 3.

74 The work preceding Dee's is Leowitz, *Brevis et perspicio ratio*. The

title-page of this mentions not only the 'Admonitio' by Wolf but also the addition of Dee's work. The parent work is Leowitz, *Ephemeridum novum*. These connections have been noted by Calder, 1:501; and Molland, 'Mathematical and Angelic Astrology', p. 255.

75 Evans, *Rudolf II*, p. 221.

76 Dee's 'Regula' is at Leowitz, *Brevis et perspicio*, sig.R.ij.

77 Dee, *A Playne Discourse*, Oxford, Bodleian Library. MS Ashmole 179, pp. 18–19.

78 On Offusius see Thorndike, *A History of Magic*, 6:22–4, 108–11; Bowden, 'The Scientific Revolution in Astrology', pp. 78–89; Heilbron, 'Introductory Essay', pp. 53–4.

79 The fact that Dee does not mention these aphorisms in the list of writings he gives in the preface to the *Propaedeumata* indicates that they had been superseded by the more recent work. See *PA*,116/17.

80 These conclusions are based upon books and manuscripts that I have been able to identify as having been definitely owned by Dee and bearing a date. Roberts & Watson have undoubtedly found things in addition to those I am aware of, but they indicate that the material as they know it does not significantly depart from the pattern I have suggested.

81 Oxford, Corpus Christi College, MS 191, fols 77^v–90. This comprises several lists, headed variously: 'Libri antiqui scripti quos habeo anno 1556', 'Reddenda anno 1558 in festo Michaelis. Antiqua exemplaria quos habui a Collegio S. Petri Cantabrigiae 1556. 6 Maii', 'Recepi a doctore Hathar eodem tempore. reddenda in festo Michaelis 1558. ea quae sequuntur ut catalogus prefixus enumerat', 'Libri quos habeo in uno volumine in Collegio Reginali Oxoniae anno 1556. 12 Maii Magistro Morreno et Magistro Carie mecum praesentibus. Et Magister Knipe eiusdem collegii socius nobis tradidit, ita quod dicti magistri et episcopus Londiniensis pro eiusdem voluminis redditione onus omne in se susciperent.' 'Ex biliotheca Laelandi emi pro 30 solidis hos sequentes libros 1556. 18 Maii. Londinii', 'Authores alchymici quos perlegi anno 1556 a mense Julii.' The Carie mentioned is the same Christopher Carye arrested with Dee in 1555; see Watson 'Christopher and William Carye', p. 136. Dee was intensely interested in preserving manuscripts and proposed to Queen Mary in 1555 that the government establish a library to preserve as much as possible of what remained from the dissolution of the monasteries and their libraries; see Dee, 'A Supplication to Queen Mary'.

82 Some of the manuscripts listed in the later catalogue of his library, 'Catalogus librorum', are very similar to manuscripts in the Corpus Christi College lists, indicating that Dee may have failed to return some at all.

83 British Library, MS Add. 35213, fols 1, 1^v, 2, 2^v.

84 Dated survivors not on this list indicate that it does not include all the books Dee actually owned. See Roberts & Watson.

85 Since in the *Propaedeumata* he lists all three optical works, he was

undoubtedly mistaken in the later lists when he gives the date for one as 1559. Fragments of the *De speculis comburentibus*, and a work on perspective for artists based mainly on Dürer are preserved in British Library MS Cotton Vitellius C.VII.

86 The title is 'Speculum unitatis: sive Apologia pro Fratre Rogerio Bachone, in quo docetur, nihil illum per Daemoniorum auxilia fecisse, sed Philosophum fuisse maximum: naturaliterque, & modis homini Christiano licitis, maximas fecisse res: quas, indoctum solet vulgus in Daemoniorum referre facinora.'

87 Corpus Christi College MS 191, fols 77^{v}, 78^{v}, 79^{r-v}, 82, 83, 88^{v}; British Library MS Cotton Tiberius C.V.

88 Sixty-one of the seventy-six alchemical titles in the 1556 manuscript list are grouped in one list, 'Authores alchymici quos perlegi anno 1556 a mense Julii'. From this it is doubtful how carefully Dee could have considered them at that time.

III THE OUTSTANDING VIRTUES OF NATURE

1 *CR*,4–5. Dee's notes are on the two leaves following the last printed page in al-Khayyāt, *De iudiciis nativitatem* in the Royal College of Physicians. The table is headed 'Medii motus planetarum. 1548 primo Novembris in meridie'. The weather observations are headed 'Lovanii. Observationes factae de Aris variis affectionibus & mutationibus Ann. Domini 1548. Mense Aug.' Sections of this chapter were originally published as 'Astrology, Magic, and Optics'. Permission of the Renaissance Society of America to include them here is gratefully acknowledged.

2 See *Diary*, passim.

3 See the notes and underlinings in C. Plinius Secundus, *Liber II. C. Plinii de mundi historia*, British Library, shelf-mark C.107.d.22, fol.108^{v}. This work also contains an 'Oratio de dignitate astrologiae' by Milichus that presents a similar view of astrology on fols 213–14. This book is signed by Dee and dated 1550.

4 Ibid., fol.75$^{r/v}$.

5 See the long note in Dee's hand, dated 1551, on the flyleaf of Claudius Ptolemy, *Quadripartitum*, which is in the Royal College of Physicians, London. In the sense that man is strictly part of his environment, Dee's astrological theory included genethlialogy, or the casting of individual nativities, a practice in which Dee engaged all of his life. A number of horoscopes of nativities for the years 1564 to 1566 can be found in Oxford, Bodleian Library, MS Ashmole 337, fols 20–57^{v}; and Dee's diaries, Bodleian MSS Ashmole 487 and 488, contain references to the time and place of birth for numerous individuals, undoubtedly preparatory to casting horoscopes.

6 Aristotle, *Meteorologica*, 339a11–33.

7 Ibid., 340a25–35; Aristotle, *De generatione et corruptione*, 336a13–336b5.

8 Ptolemy, *Tetrabiblos*, pp. 5–9.

9 Ibid., pp. 9–11.

10 Lemay, *Abū Ma'shar*, pp. xxiii–v, 83–4. A 1506 edition of Abū Ma'shar, *Introductorium in astronomiam*, signed and dated by Dee in 1552, is in the University Library, Cambridge, shelf-mark R.* 4.55.

11 For the Harranians, see Pingree, 'Abū Ma'shar', 1:33–4, and the literature cited there.

12 Oxford, Bodleian Library, MS Ashmole 337, fols 51–7. Calder, 1:338–403, discusses these notes in great detail. These notes are undated, and Calder dates them later than the *Propaedeumata*. See Clulee, 'Astrology, Magic, and Optics', pp. 648–52, for the grounds on which I date them to this earlier period.

13 Bodleian Library, MS Ashmole 337, fols 51^v, 52^v, 56^v, citing the *Metaphysica*, the *Physica*, the *Meteorologica*, the *De anima*, and the *De generatione animalium*. The other author cited is apparently Agostino Nifo (fol.57^v), who defended the immortality of the soul against Pomponazzi; but Dee seems not to accept Nifo's view, since he immediately notes Aristotle's contradictory opinion.

14 Ibid., fols 51^v–52^v.

15 Ibid., fol.56^v, nos.1 & 4 of the notes representing his own thoughts, beginning 'Mea'.

16 Ibid., fols 56^v, 57, nos.9–11.

17 Ibid., fol.56^v, no.2.

18 Ibid., no.7.

19 See Dee's statement 'hominem ut fecit natura – corpus, spiritus, anima', in Ptolemy, *Quadripartitum*, fol.10^v (Royal College of Physician's copy).

20 *PA*, aphorisms XVI and XVII. Cf. Aristotle, *Meteorologica*, 339a11–33.

21 Cf. Aristotle, *Meteorologica*, 340a25–35, 341a15–25; Aristotle, *De generatione et corruptione*, 336a15–336b5.

22 John Dee, Letter to William Camden, 7 August 1574, Oxford, Bodleian Library MS Ashmole 1788, fol.71. In this letter he also indignantly denies charges that his aphorisms plagiarized the work of Urso. Dee did have an *Aphorismi Ursonis* in 1556 (Corpus Christi College MS 191, fol.83), but an examination of the text (von Jagow, *Die naturphilosophischen*) indicates that while Dee's first aphorism is similar in intent to the first aphorism of Urso, its wording is different and that the similarity of the two works ends at that point.

23 Cf. *MP*,b.ij^v–b.iij.

24 Dee clearly supposed that all celestial bodies were self-luminous, see *PA*, LIII, C.

25 Cf. *PA*, CXIX and Hermes, *IATPOMAΘHMATIKA*, 1:396 (11.29–30), 440 (11.31–32) [another version of the same treatise]. On the 'popular hermetica', see Festugière, *La révélation*, 1:1, 106–23.

26 Naturalism in this sense, however, should not imply a mechanical or physical causality to the exclusion of other influences that Dee considered natural. According to Dee, all influences were natural other than the intervention of angels or demons acting contrary to the laws of nature.

27 This was the general presupposition of all medieval optics. Species were not thought of as corpuscular, and rays had no real existence, but this diffusion could be described or represented by rays. See Lindberg, 'Introduction', pp. 39–40; and Lindberg, *Roger Bacon's Philosophy of Nature*, pp. viii, liv–vi. Also see the next section for a more detailed treatment of Dee's background on this issue.

28 Lindberg, 'The Genesis of Kepler's Theory', pp. 15–16. The major expressions of these ideas are found in Robert Grosseteste and Roger Bacon who will be discussed in the next section in conjunction with the sources upon which Dee relied for his ideas.

29 Lindberg, 'The Genesis of Kepler's Theory', pp. 16–17, 19.

30 Lindberg, 'Introduction', pp. 36–8.

31 The aphorisms dealing with basically astronomical issues and the determination of sizes, distances, and periods of planets and stars are scattered throughout. This material is discussed in detail in Heilbron, 'Introductory Essay', pp. 64–6, 73–90.

32 A spherical body clearly emits an infinite number of rays in all directions but the only rays that affect any one point will be those defined by the cone whose vertex is that point and whose base is the circular portion of the sphere visible from that point. The rays from an agent to the surface of a patient form an infinite number of such cones with vertices touching all points on the surface of the patient. Again, for any one point on the patient, only one of these cones is considered.

33 Planetary distances could be calculated with difficulty in Ptolemaic astronomy and more easily with Copernican models. Although planetary and stellar distances cannot be obtained directly with Ptolemaic models, the widespread adoption of the Ptolemaic system in medieval astronomy, both in Islam and later in the West, based on a part of Ptolemy's *Planetary Hypotheses* that survived only in Arabic, allowed for the computation of the absolute distances of all the planets and implied that the planets vary in distance from the centre of the universe and from the earth. See Toomer, 'Introduction', in Campanus of Novara, *Campanus of Novara*, pp. 53–6. Campanus adopts this system in detail, and Dee was most likely aware of it, since he had a copy of Campanus's work as early as 1556 (Corpus Christi College MS 191, fol.81ᵛ) in addition to a number of other medieval astronomical works. Dee clearly rejected the physical reality of the Copernican hypothesis at this point in time because he explicitly accepts the physical reality of the retrograde motion of the superior planets, which according to Copernicus were merely apparent motions resulting from the earth's motion (*PA*, LXXXVIII). This stance on Copernicus does not appear to have changed. In the *Monas hieroglyphica* of 1564 he assumed the reality of a geocentric and geostatic universe. See Zetterberg, 'Hermetic Geocentricity', pp. 385–93. This same aphorism remains unchanged in the 1568 edition of the *Propaedeumata*. The question of Dee's Copernicanism is also discussed in the larger context of the

relation of Hermetism to astronomical reform by Westman, 'Magical Reform', pp. 45–50. Although Dee's astrology and astronomy are thoroughly geocentric and Ptolemaic, he does mention Copernicus (*PA*,LXVII) in relation to the value of the length of the sidereal year. Dee, like many others at this time, were willing to adopt Copernicus's model for computational purposes but unwilling to accept his physical hypothesis. Thus, in his 'Epistola' to Field, *Ephemeris*, which are based on the rules of Copernicus and Reinhold, Dee recommends the work of Copernicus, Rheticus, and Reinhold for restoring astronomy, but does not discuss the heliocentric hypothesis. One attraction of Copernicus's model relevant to Dee's interests in the *Propaedeumata* is the ability to calculate planetary distances more readily than with the Ptolemaic model. See Heilbron, 'Introductory Essay', pp. 56–7, 85–6. Dee gives Copernicus's values for solar and lunar distances in the *MP*,b.ij, but there is no indication in the *Propaedeumata* which method he used.

34 In 1551 Dee wrote a work, which he did not publish and is now lost, in which he apparently dealt in greater detail with the determination of the type of measurements that he calls for in the *Propaedeumata*, entitled 'De Planetarum, Inerrantium stellarum, Nubiumque a centro terrae distaniis: & stellarum omnium veris inveniendis magnitudinibus. lib. 2. demonst.' *PA*,116/17; and, with a somewhat different title, *CR*,26; *LA*,74–5. This work clearly grew out of Dee's work with Mercator and Gemma Frisius at Louvain, therefore having some relation to his emerging astrological theories, and also looked forward to the method for finding stellar parallaxes that Dee published after the appearance of the nova of 1572 in *Parallaticae commentationis*. See Dee, *Parallaticae commentationis*, sig.D.iiij^v; and Heilbron, 'Introductory Essay', pp. 57–8. Since Offusius had worked with Dee in the early 1550s, Offusius's *De divina astrorum facultate* may reflect some of Dee's ideas. On Offusius's astrology and its relation to Dee see Heilbron, 'Introductory Essay', p. 54; and especially Bowden, 'The Scientific Revolution in Astrology', pp. 78–89.

35 Dee seems to intend what Roger Bacon says in more detail and more clearly in *Opus Majus*, 1:126–7.

36 See the discussion in the next section.

37 Dee is inconsistent here. At this point he implies that the speed of the moon increases its effects on humidity because he links humidity with motion on the analogy of the association of heat with light, but earlier he indicates that astral influences, as a general rule, are stronger in proportion to the length of time the influence is impressed, that is on the *slowness* of the motion. Perhaps we have a special case for the moon. If so, and the general rule still holds, the influence of the moon on humidity will increase as its speed increases but the total effect will be counteracted by the shorter duration through which the influence is impressed.

38 Dee lists the Bacon treatise among those manuscripts he possessed

in 1556 (Corpus Christi College MS 191, fol.78ᵛ), and he discusses
it in the *MP*,*.iij–*.iiij. For a discussion of Dee's treatment of Bacon's
grading, see Clulee, 'John Dee's Mathematics'.

39 Clulee, 'John Dee's Mathematics', pp. 180–1.

40 In these Dee solves several problems in permutations and
combinations. These are discussed by Heilbron, 'Introductory Essay',
pp. 90–1.

41 Dee, in Corpus Christi College MS 191 [1556], lists, at times several,
copies of Euclid's *Optics* (fols 78, 79); the medieval Latin Pseudo-
Euclid, *De Speculis* or *Catoptrica* (fols 77ᵛ, 79, 81, 83); al-Kindī's *De
radiis* (fol.81) and *De umbris et causis diversitatis aspectuum* (fol.81);
Grosseteste's *De impressionibus aeris* (fol.79ᵛ), *De iride* (fol.79), and *De
luce, calore, et frigide* (fol.82ᵛ); Bacon's *De multiplicatione specierum*
(fol.79), his *Perspectiva* (fols 77ᵛ, 79), and the following works in which
optics plays a major role in natural philosophy: *Magnum opus
communium naturalium* (fol.79) and *Summa ad Clementum* [*Opus Majus*]
(fol.83ᵛ). In addition, Dee acquired at this time a collection of the
Opus majus, *Opus minus*, and *Opus tertium* (British Library MS Cotton
Tiberius C.V.), and another collection attributed to Bacon with the
titles *Compendium philosophiae*, *De corporibus coelestibus*, and *De
mathematica* (Bodleian Library MS Digby 76). In Corpus Christi
College MS 191, Dee also lists Alhazen, *Perspectiva* (fols 78ᵛ, 79);
Witelo, *Perspectiva* (fols 80, 82ᵛ); Pecham, *Perspectiva communis* (fols 78,
81ᵛ); a copy of Pisanus [*sic*, Pecham], *Perspectiva communis* (fol.81); a
commentary on that by Domenico de Hassia [*sic*, Henry of Hesse/
Henry of Langenstein] (fol.81); an anonymous *Questiones super
perspectivam* (fol.81ᵛ); and treatises on burning mirrors (fols 78ᵛ,
82ᵛ).

42 The literature on 'light metaphysics', 'light symbolism', and 'light
speculation' is immense and beyond summary. For a general treatment
see Hedwig, *Sphaera lucis*. Discussion specific to the texts discussed
below are Lindberg, *Roger Bacon's Philosophy of Nature*, pp. vii–viii,
xxxv–xliv; Lindberg, 'The Origin of Kepler's Theory', pp. 5–42; and
d'Alverny and Hudry, 'Al-Kindī, *De radiis*', pp. 149–67.

43 Lindberg, 'The Genesis of Kepler's Theory', pp. 12–14.

44 Ibid., p. 13. *Theorica artium magicarum* is the proper title and more
adequately describes its content. A critical edition is in d'Alverny
and Hudry, 'Al-Kindī, *De radiis*', pp. 215–59. Additional notices of
manuscripts of al-Kindī's works are given in d'Alverny, 'Kindiana',
pp. 277–87. There are additional discussions of al-Kindī's *De radiis*
in Federici-Vescovini, *Studi sulla prospettiva medievale*, pp. 44–7; in
Lindberg, *Roger Bacon's Philosophy*, pp. xliv–xlvi; and in Lindberg,
Theories of Vision, p. 19.

45 Calder, 1:515–22, was the first to call attention to al-Kindī's treatise
as an important source of Dee's ideas. Note that Dee borrowed the
De radiis in 1556 and did not return it until 1558 (see above note
41). The similarity between the wording of passages in al-Kindī
and Dee make the dependence of Dee on al-Kindī unquestionable.

See the parallel passages cited in Clulee, 'Astrology, Magic, and Optics', p. 665, n. 98.

46 Al-Kindī, *De radiis*, pp. 216, 219–21.

47 Ibid., pp. 219, 244.

48 Al-Kindī was also interested in optics and was the author of an optical work entitled *De aspectibus* dealing with the mathematics and physics of the propagation of rays. There appears to have been little communication between his optics, in which there is no indication of an interest in astrology, and the theory in the *De radiis*. An explicit connection of mathematical optics with astrology had not, therefore, been made. The common attribution of the two works, however, was very significant because it was the likely foundation for the extension of geometrical optics to astral influences by Grosseteste and Bacon.

49 These were Grosseteste's *De impressionibus aeris*, *De iride*, and *De luce, calore, et frigide*. Thus, Dee had no direct access to works reflecting Grosseteste's epistemology, on which there has been less than total agreement regarding the place of Aristotelian, Neoplatonic, and Augustinian influences, and the role of empiricism, divine illumination, and deductive reasoning in Grosseteste's natural philosophy. In general, see McEvoy, *The Philosophy of Robert Grosseteste*, pp. 320–68; McEvoy, 'The Chronology', pp. 614–55; and Marrone, *William of Auvergne and Robert Grosseteste*, pp. 137–286; and specifically on Grosseteste's science, Crombie, *Robert Grosseteste*, passim; Eastwood, 'Medieval Empiricism', p. 309; and Eastwood, 'Grosseteste's "Quantitative" Law', p. 409.

50 Grosseteste's natural philosophy has been considered an example of a highly Neoplatonic 'light metaphysics'; see Crombie, *Robert Grosseteste*, p. 109; Eastwood, 'Medieval Empiricism', p. 308; and Eastwood, 'Metaphysical Derivations', p. 232. While Grosseteste does appeal to certain metaphysical principles – e.g., the uniformity and economy of nature (Eastwood, 'Grosseteste's "Quantitative" Law', pp. 409, 412–13) – and most likely was influenced by the tradition of light metaphysics, the *role* played by light in Grosseteste's *natural* philosophy is that of a physical agent that provides a mechanics describing the behaviour of the forms and virtues of heaven and earth; see Birkenmajer, 'Etudes', p. 356; McEvoy, *The Philosophy of Robert Grosseteste*, pp. 162–7; Hedwig, *Sphaera lucis*, pp. 121–2, 134–8; Lindberg, *Roger Bacon's Philosophy*, pp. xlix–liii; and Saccaro, 'Il Grosseteste e la luce', pp. 44–5.

51 Grosseteste, *De luce*, 51–2. This treatise is available in English translations by Riedl and Terrell.

52 Crombie, *Robert Grosseteste*, p. 106.

53 Grosseteste, *De luce*, pp. 52–7.

54 Crombie, *Robert Grosseteste*, pp. 59–60; Eastwood, 'Metaphysical Derivations', p. 235.

55 Eastwood, 'Metaphysical Derivations', pp. 307–8.

56 Crombie, *Robert Grosseteste*, p. 91; Hedwig, *Sphaera lucis*, pp. 121–2,

134–41; McEvoy, *The Philosophy of Robert Grosseteste*, pp. 168–70; Lindberg, 'On the Applicability', pp. 10–14.

57 Grosseteste, *Concerning Lines, Angles, and Figures*, pp. 385, 387. The Latin text of *De lineis, angulis et figuris*, is in *Die philosophischen Werke*, pp. 59–65. Crombie, *Robert Grosseteste*, pp. 104–6; Baur, *Die Philosophie des Robert Grosseteste*, pp. 92–3.

58 Dales, 'Robert Grosseteste's Views', pp. 357–60. It is interesting to note that Grosseteste moved away from traditional astrological theory under the influence of his interest in mathematics and his optical conception of astral influences just as did Dee.

59 Grosseteste, *Concerning Lines*, pp. 385–6; Grosseteste, *De impressionibus elementorum*, p. 87.

60 Grosseteste, *De impressionibus aeris (de prognosticatione)*, pp. 48–9; Grosseteste, *Concerning Lines*, pp. 386, 388.

61 Lindberg, *Roger Bacon's Philosophy*, p. liv. Bacon's major discussions of his theory of the 'multiplication of species', as he termed his doctrine, are found in the *Opus majus*, the *Opus tertium*, the *De multiplicatione specierum*, and the *Communia naturalia*, all of which are listed among the manuscripts in the 1556 lists and others Dee owned through 1558. One of these, British Library, MS Cotton Tiberius C.V., signed and dated 1558, contains the *Opus tertium* and the fourth part of the *Opus majus* in which the sections on perspective and burning mirrors are extensively annotated, in one place noting that Bacon's ideas apply to all virtues, not just to light rays (fol.52^v), which echoes his aphorisms XIIII & XXV. A critical edition with English translation of the *De multiplicatione specierum* is available in Lindberg, *Roger Bacon's Philosophy*, with an extensive analysis of the treatise on pp. liii–lxxi. The following discussion is intended only to indicate what Dee derived from Bacon for the *Propaedeumata* and emphasizes the astrological implications of Bacon's doctrine. Medieval perspective optics involved a theory of visual cognition as well as ray theory, as emphasized by Smith, 'Getting the Big Picture', pp. 568–89. Dee, however, seems to use only the ray theory in isolation.

62 Bacon, *Opus Majus*, 1:116, 120. On mathematics and nature in Bacon, see Lindberg, 'On the Applicability', pp. 16–24.

63 Bacon, *De multiplicatione specierum*, pp. 2–11; Bacon, *Opus Majus*, 1:130. Bacon was also clearly familiar with al-Kindī: see Bacon, *De multiplicatione specierum*, pp. 165, 173, 225, 253; and Easton, *Roger Bacon*, p. 104.

64 Bacon, *De multiplicatione specierum*, pp. 90–5; Bacon, *Opus Majus*, 1:131–13. See also Vescovini, *Studi*, pp. 57–62.

65 Bacon, *De multiplicatione specierum*, pp. 90–5, 244–7; Bacon, *Opus Majus*, 1:138.

66 Bacon, *Opus Majus*, 1:128–9; other sections dealing with astrology are 1:238–69, 376–403. Bacon, *Opus tertium*, pp. 107–9; Lindberg, *Roger Bacon's Philosophy*, pp. lxi–lxii.

67 Bacon, *De multiplicatione specierum*, pp. 208–11, 244–51; Bacon, *Opus*

Majus, 1:139–40; Lindberg, *Roger Bacon's Philosophy*, pp. lxiii–lxvi, lxx–lxxi.

68 In the 1556 lists of manuscripts, Dee cites Ibn al-Haytham's *Perspectiva* under Alhazen and lists several copies of Witelo's *Perspectiva* and Pecham's *Perspectiva communis*. Ibn al-Haytham's *Perspectiva* was published in the sixteenth century as the *Opticae thesaurus Alhazeni*, together with Witelo's *Perspectiva*. Crombie, pp. 165, 213–14; Lindberg, 'Introduction', pp. 29–32.

69 Lindberg, 'The Genesis of Kepler's Theory', pp. 22–9; Lindberg, *John Pecham*, pp. 25–7. The question of influences among Bacon, Witelo, and Pecham has been treated extensively in Lindberg, 'Lines of Influence', pp. 66–83.

70 Lindberg, 'The Genesis of Kepler's Theory', pp. 23–7; Walker, *Spiritual and Demonic Magic*, pp. 12–24; Yates, *GBHT*, pp. 119–20, 152–3.

71 Yates, *GBHT*, pp. 45, 63–70, 78–80, 131–2; Walker, *Spiritual and Demonic Magic*, pp. 12–24, 30–5, 112–19; Trinkaus, 'Ideals of Deification'.

72 Oresme, *De proportionibus proportionum*, pp. 304–7, 382–3, 424–7, and Grant's 'Introduction', pp. 61–3; Oresme, *Questio contra divinatores*, pp. 223–4; Caroti, 'La critica', pp. 597–8; Hansen, *Nicole Oresme*, pp. 18–21, 28–30.

73 Oresme, *The Medieval Geometry*, pp. 234–5, 298–9; Clagett, 'Introduction', p. 36; Oresme, *Questio contra divinatores*, pp. 274–6, 284–8; Caroti, 'La critica', pp. 596–606. See also Thorndike, *A History of Magic*, 3:413–14.

74 Oresme, *Questio contra divinatores*, p. 274.

75 Ibid., pp. 220–1, 268–76, 284–8, 291, 310; Oresme, *The Medieval Geometry*, pp. 374–5; Clagett, 'Introduction', p. 134; Caroti, 'La critica', pp. 587–611; Thorndike, *A History of Magic*, 3:414; Paschetto, *Demoni e Prodigi*, pp. 14, 22, 66, 68–9.

76 Bodleian Library, MS Corpus Christi College 191, fol.79ᵛ: 'Tractatus de proportionibus proportionum Nicolai de Oresme', fol.81: 'An futura possunt per astra praesciri. liber divinationum. Nicolai Oresme'. The latter is the *Questio*, the manuscript of which is lost; see James, *Lists of Manuscripts*, p. 20. A description of the manuscript containing the *De proportionibus* is in James, *A Descriptive Catalogue*, pp. 353–6, and indicates no annotations. The manuscript is actually Cambridge, Magdelene College, MS Pepys 2329, but was in Peterhouse when Dee borrowed it.

77 Cf. Oresme, *De proportionibus*, pp. 304–6.

78 Caroti, 'Nicole Oresme, Claudio Celestino, Oronce Finé', pp. 335–410, argues Finé's authorship and has the text on pp. 361–91; Thorndike, 'Coelestinus's Summary', pp. 629–35; and Céard, *La nature et les prodiges*, pp. 174–8, 340–3; accept a fifteenth-century Celestine Friar Claude as the author; Hansen, *Nicole Oresme*, pp. 120–2, presents evidence for the identification with Friar Claude Rapine.

79 Celestino, *De his quae mundo*, p. 632 (Finé's prefatory letter); Thorndike, 'Coelestinus's Summary', pp. 630–1; Caroti, 'La critica', p. 667.

80 Celestino, *De his quae mundo*, pp. 384–90; Caroti, 'Nicole Oresme, Claudio Celestino, Oronce Finé', pp. 358–9; Caroti, 'La critica', pp. 667–75.

81 Celestino, *De his quae mundo*, pp. 381–3.

82 *CR*,7–8; *MP*,A.j^v, where he quotes Celestino, *De his quae mundo*, p. 380.

83 Oresme, *Questio contra divinatores*, p. 299; Celestino, *De his quae mundo*, p. 387; cf. *PA*, XVII.

84 Celestino, *De his quae mundo*, p. 361 (Finé's prefatory letter explaining the inclusion of Bacon's treatise). This is the earliest printed edition of the Bacon *Epistola* that I have found in either the Library of Congress *National Union Catalogue of Pre-1956 Imprints* or the British Library *General Catalogue*. Finé's treatise on burning mirrors is Finé, *De speculo ustorio*.

85 Lindberg, 'On the Applicability', pp. 5–7; Wallace, *Causality and Scientific Explanation*, 1:11–13; Aristotle, *Analytica posteriora*, 78a23–79a16.

86 Alexander, *Mathemalogium*, Dee's copy of which is in the Royal College of Physicians, London. It bears his signature and the date 1551 as well as the note on reading it in 1555. Slight differences in the notes indicate that he may have read it twice, the heavier annotations apparently being the later of the two. On Alexander, who is rather obscure, see Lohr, 'Renaissance Latin Aristotle Commentaries', p. 242, and the slight literature indicated there.

87 Alexander, *Mathemalogium*, sig.A.j^v.

88 Ibid., sigs.A.ij^r/^{v}, E.ij^v–E.iij. On sig.E.ij^v next to the discussion of *quia* and *propter quid* Dee has once more noted the Greek terms τὸ ὅτι and τὸ διότι. Cf. Aristotle, *Analytica posteriora*, 71b9–16, 73a21–25, 75a13–19, 78a22–30.

89 Alexander, *Mathemalogium*, sigs.A.iij, D.iv, D.v–E.iij^v. Cf. Aristotle, *Analytica posteriora*, 75b8–20, 78a22–79a31; Wallace, *Causality and Scientific Explanation*, 1: 11–13, 37.

90 Livesey, '*Metabasis*', pp. 2–11, 19, 26–34.

91 Alexander, *Mathemalogium*, sig.E.iv^r/^{v}.

92 Livesey, '*Metabasis*', pp. 263–4, 267–88, 312–13.

93 Hutchison, 'What Happened to Occult Qualities', pp. 233–9.

94 Lindberg, 'On the Applicability', pp. 10–14, 16–21, 24.

95 It may be in conjunction with his reading of Alexander and consideration of the logic of demonstration that he wrote 'Περὶ Ἀκριβολογίας τῆσ Μαθηματικῆς. opus mathematice demonstratum. lib. 16,' which he claims to have written in 1555: *PA*,116–17; *CR*25; *LA*,75.

96 Westman, 'The Astronomer's Role', pp. 107–12, 117–21.

97 Ibid., pp. 121–2.

98 *PA*,116–17. The full title is 'Speculum unitatis: sive Apologia pro Fratre Rogerio Bachone Anglo, in qua docetur, nihil illum per

Daemoniorum auxilia fuisse, sed Philosophum fuisse maximum: naturaliterque, & modis homini Christiano licitis, maximas fecisse res: quas, indoctum solet vulgus in Daemoniorum referre facinora. lib. 1.' In *CR*,26; and *LA*,75, the date given for this is 1557.

99 Molland, 'Roger Bacon as Magician', pp. 445–7.

100 See, for example, British Library, MSS Sloane 3850, 3853, and 3884, which include a 'Thesaurus spiritum' and a 'Negromantiae' attributed to Bacon.

101 Bale, *Illustrium maioris Britanniae scriptorum*, fol.114ᵛ. Among the works Bale gives are 'De nigromanticis imaginibus', 'Practicas magiae', and 'De excantationibus'.

102 Bale, *Scriptorum illustrium maioris Brytanniae*, p. 342. The occult works listed are 'safe', dealing with astrology, alchemy, 'De operibus naturae occultis', and a 'Contra necromanticos'.

103 The 1557 edition of Bale's work is probably too late to have influenced Dee and during the late 1550s Bale, as a vigorous proponent of Protestantism, was in exile and so not personally in contact with Dee. It is therefore unlikely that it was Bale's shift that had any influence on Dee's opinions. On the other hand, Bale was connected with the strongly Protestant reforming party at court in the reign of Edward VI. This group included Northumberland and others with whom Dee was associated, so, unlikely as it may seem, it is possible that it was Dee who exercised a moderating influence on 'bilious' Bale.

104 Bacon, *Opus Majus*, 1:261–3; Bacon, *Opus tertium*, pp. 268–70. For the discussion of magic in the Middle Ages and the usage of 'natural magic', see Hansen, 'Science and Magic', pp. 483–506; Thorndike, *A History of Magic*, 2:242–3, 346–60, 548–59; Garin, 'Considerazioni', pp. 179–80; Zambelli, 'Il problema della magia', pp. 273–4. Molland argues that Bacon came very close to if he did not actually cross the border between natural and illicit magic ('Roger Bacon as Magician', pp. 458–60).

105 I cite the English translation *Roger Bacon's Letter*. For Dee's notes I will cite the edition in *Bibliotheca chemica curiosa*. All of the editions containing Dee's notes also contain additional notes. These are usually marked with a different set of initials and should not be confused with Dee's because they are the product of the same person who wrote the introductory letter addressed to the Rosicrucians. For Bacon's distinction, see Bacon, *Letter*, pp. 15–17.

106 Bacon, *Letter*, pp. 19–21; Bacon, *Opus Majus*, 1:133; Molland, 'Roger Bacon as Magician', pp. 452–8.

107 Bacon, *Letter*, pp. 28–9; Bacon, *Opus Majus*, 2:164–6.

108 Molland, 'Roger Bacon as Magician', pp. 452–8.

109 A critical edition and translation of Bacon's *De speculis comburentibus* is provided in Lindberg, *Roger Bacon's Philosophy*, pp. 271–341; which Lindberg discusses on pp. lxxi–lxxv.

110 Bacon, *Letter*, pp. 24–5; Bacon, *Opus Majus*, 1:395–6; Bacon, *Opus tertium*, pp. 96–8; Molland, 'Roger Bacon as Magician', pp. 459–60;

Molland, 'Roger Bacon: Magic and the Multiplication of Species', forthcoming in *Paideia*.

111 Two works Dee read and annotated in 1557 give further indication of his interest in magic. Ibn Sīnā, in *De divisionibus scientiarum*, discusses among the natural sciences the science of the magical arts which join the virtues of things together to produce strange and extraordinary effects. Dee's copy of this (in Avicenna, *Compendium de anima*, p. 142), signed and dated 1557, is in the Bodleian Library, pressmark Seldon 4⁰ A40 Art. Seld., and has 'artis magicae' underlined and 'magica' written in the margin. Likewise, in a section of Arnold of Villanova, *Opera*, in the Royal College of Physicians, London, which is signed by Dee and dated 1557, in which Arnold condemns witchcraft and incantations but accepts the impression of celestial influences on matter, Dee has written 'magia' and 'astrologia magia' in the margin.

112 This non-spiritual character of Dee's magic was perhaps reinforced by another source of Dee's astrology: al-Kindī's *De radiis*, pp. 230–4. Most of al-Kindī's treatise, which was also known as the *Theorica artium magicarum*, deals with various kinds of magic, including the power of images, the voice, incantations, and sacrifices. Although Dee does not explicitly discuss these types of magic, he may not have ignored them because al-Kindī presents all magical effects as the naturalistic result of the operation of rays.

113 Bacon, *Opus Majus*, 1:167–222.

114 *MP*,A.iij, b.iijᵛ; *PA*, VII, XXVI, LXXIII. The use of the term 'experimental' and 'experimental science' by Bacon and Dee should not be taken to indicate that either had a modern, or even seventeenth-century, notion of experiment. In their usage the term 'experiment' was little different from our sense of 'experience'. See the discussion of this issue below ch.VI.

115 *CR*,26; *LA*,75; give the date as 1559, but it must be from before 1558 since he lists it in the *Propaedeumata*. On the issue of the rainbow, which was considered by Grosseteste and Bacon among others, see Boyer, *The Rainbow*; Crombie, *Robert Grosseteste*, ch. 5; Lindberg, 'Roger Bacon's Theory of the Rainbow', pp. 235–48; Eastwood, 'Robert Grosseteste's Theory of the Rainbow', pp. 313–32; and Wallace, *The Scientific Methodology of Theodoric of Freiberg*.

116 This is listed in *PA*,116–17. *CR*,25; and *LA*,75 list it also with the date 1557. The fragment, of which the top and outside edges are fire damaged obliterating some text, is in British Library, MS Cotton Vitellius C.VII, fols 279–306. In addition to the title, the title page describes this as 'Inventa Joannis Dee londinensis, circa illam coni recti atque rectanguli sectionem quae ab antiquis mathematicis parabola appelabatur, Martij 8. 1558.' This text has been edited and translated in Clagett, *Archimedes*, 5(1):513–76, with introduction, pp. 489–512.

117 On burning mirrors see the literature given by Lindberg in Grant, ed., *Source Book*, pp. 413–14, nn. 104, 105; Wiedemann, 'Zur

Geschichte der Brennspiegel', pp. 110–30; and Lindberg's edition of Bacon's treatise in *Roger Bacon's Philosophy*. Among the numerous optical works in Dee's 1556 manuscript lists there are several works dealing specifically with burning mirrors as well as works of perspective containing discussions of burning mirrors.

118 Clagett, *Archimedes*, 5(1):489–512.

119 British Library, MS Cotton Vitellius, C.VII, fols 306ᵛ–9ᵛ.

120 *MP*,b.j. On the provenance of the mirror, see Calder, 1:296. In the Bodleian Library, MS Selden Supra 79, p. 150ᶜ, there is a description and measurement of this mirror that Thomas Allen had acquired from Dee. The description indicates that it was round and reflected from both the concave and the convex surfaces. The exact shape of the surface (spherical, parabolic, etc.) is not indicated.

121 Bourne, *A Treatise*, pp. 45–6.

122 See the note to ch. IX of Bacon, *Epistola de secretis operibus, Bibliotheca chemica curiosa*, 1:626. This note is an almost exact quote from Bacon, *Opus tertium*, pp. 39–40.

123 Bacon, *Opus tertium*, pp. 39–40. See also, Bacon, *Opus minus*, p. 359.

124 Bacon, *Opus tertium*, p. 40.

125 See below, ch. IV.

126 Schmitt, *Aristotle and the Renaissance*, p. 14.

127 Lindberg, *Roger Bacon's Philosophy*, pp. xliv–xlv; d'Alverny, 'La survivance', p. 164.

128 Peters, *Aristotle and the Arabs*, pp. 8–10, 158–9, 169–70.

129 Ibid., pp. xxiii, 222; Van Steenberghen, *Aristotle in the West*, pp. 113, 137.

130 Cf. Pomponazzi, *De naturalium effectuum*, pp. 98, 105–6; and Pico della Mirandola, *Conclusiones*, pp. 78–9.

131 Molland, 'Roger Bacon as Magician', p. 445, makes this point for Renaissance magical writers in general, noting that in addition to the *prisca magia* Renaissance magic also depended upon medieval sources, including Roger Bacon, al-Kindī, William of Auvergne, and Albertus Magnus.

132 Capp, *Astrology and the Popular Press*, pp. 19, 180–1.

133 For Kepler see Field, 'A Lutheran Astrologer', pp. 189–272; the literature cited there; Rosen, 'Kepler's Attitude', pp. 253–72; and Lindberg, 'The Genesis of Kepler's Theory', pp. 31–3. For Cardano, see his *Libelli quinque*, which contains five very traditional treatises on various aspects of astrology, over one thousand aphorisms, and one hundred sample genitures; and Heilbron, 'Introductory Essay', pp. 52–3.

IV THE HIEROGLYPHICS OF NATURE

1 The term 'monas' and its English equivalent, 'monad' or fundamental unit, are subject to a certain confusion in discussing Dee's *Monas hieroglyphica* because they can refer to several distinct things. To avoid this confusion, I have adopted the following conventions:

'monad' will refer generically to the fundamental unit or unity, 'Monas' will refer to Dee's symbol of the hieroglyphic monad, and '*Monas*' will refer to Dee's text about the 'Monas'.

2 *MH*,192/93. On Kepler, see Westman, 'Nature, Art, and Psyche', pp. 204–5.

3 Meric Casaubon, 'Preface', *T&FR*, p. 38; Debus, *The Chemical Philosophy*, 1:44.

4 Crosland, *Historical Studies*, p. 6, on *astronomia inferior*.

5 Tymme, *A Light in Darkness*. This is drawn from the materials in Bodleian Library MSS Ashmole 1459, pp. 469–81; and Ashmole 1440, pp. 170–1.

6 For the subsequent history and use of Dee's Monas as well as later editions of the *Monas*, see Josten, 'Introduction', pp. 90–9.

7 Calder, 1:570–90; and Josten, 'Introduction', pp. 84–90, 99–111, have the most extensive discussions of the *Monas*. French, pp. 76–80; Debus, *The Chemical Philosophy*, 1:44–5; and Nicholl, *The Chemical Theatre*, pp. 41–54, also discuss the *Monas* as alchemy. Luhrmann, 'An Interpretation of the *Fama Fraternitatis*', also assumes the alchemical interpretation.

8 Yates, *The Art of Memory*, p. 262; Yates, *Rosicrucian*, p. xii; Yates, *Occult*, pp. 83–4. In this she is followed closely by French, pp. 76–8; and Graham Yewbrey, 'John Dee', pp. 85, 88. Neither Yates, French, nor Yewbrey analyse the text of the *Monas* to any extent.

9 Yates, *Occult*, pp. 84–5, 87; van Dorsten, *The Radical Arts*, pp. 21–4; Yewbrey, pp. 74–6.

10 Walton, 'John Dee's *Monas hieroglyphica*', pp. 116–23.

11 Calder, 1:247, 544; Yates, *Occult*, pp. 83–4; Yewbrey, 'John Dee', p. 97.

12 Calder, 1:544–5, was struck by the noticeable difference between the *Propaedeumata* and the *Monas*, a feature overlooked by most subsequent commentators.

13 While Dee explains to his publisher, Willem Silvius, that he wants the *Monas* printed so that 'more people may enjoy them [the very excellent arcana] throughout the world', he specifically requests Silvius to guard against letting the book fall into the hands of the common people (*MH*,148–51). Elsewhere he is highly critical of the inability of the vulgar, from which he does not exclude academics and men of learning, to distinguish between shadows and the real thing, and their quickness to criticise things they do not understand (*MH*,140–7). He also frequently appeals to the wise and those whose 'eyes reside in their hearts' to perceive some particularly deep matter, while he disdainfully presents a clearer explanation in one place for those whose 'hearts are still projecting from their eyes' (*MH*,122/23, 124/25, 126/27, 128/29, 192/93). See Maclean, 'The Interpretation of Natural Signs', pp. 234–6.

14 Josten, 'Introduction', pp. 84–5; French, p. 80.

15 Calder, 1:619–20; Roberts & Watson, indicate that the earliest

surviving inscription in a book acquisition giving Mortlake as the location occurs in 18 September 1566.

16 Maximilian Habsburg (1527–1576) was crowned King of Hungary on 8 September 1563, at Pressburg, Hungary (now Bratislava, Czechoslovakia). From 1562 he had been King of Bohemia and King of the Romans, and in 1564 became Holy Roman Emperor as Maximilian II.

17 On the Pythagorean 'Y' and its treatment in the Renaissance, see Heninger, *Touches of Sweet Harmony*, pp. 269–71; and Panofsky, *Hercules am Scheidewege*, pp. 42–4, 64–8. Bacon, *Opus Majus*, 1:7–8. Tory, *Champ fleury*, the source of this figure, was very likely Dee's source.

18 *NA*,56. *CR*,10, also describes this meeting.

19 Dee's inclusion of some of these sciences may have been suggested by Norton, *Ordinall of Alchemy*, pp. 60–1, where he mentions grammar, arithmetic, music, astrology, perspective, the science *de pleno & vacuo*, and chiefly natural magic as sciences that to varying degrees illustrate or aid in alchemical processes.

20 The book is Pantheus, *Voarchadumia*, which Dee acquired in 1559.

21 *CR*,26; *LA*,75.

22 The *Speculum unitatis* listed in *PA*,116/17; *CR*,26; *LA*,75.

23 *PA*,116/17; *CR*,25–6; *LA*,75.

24 Calder, 1:534–40; Easton, 'The Early Editions', 515–32.

25 Roberts & Watson. In addition, most of the other books that Dee owned dealing with Hebrew and kabbalah have publication dates of 1560–1564, indicating that he could not have studied them before 1560 and may have acquired them before 1564. Although Dee collected noticeably little theology in general, what theology he did collect was mystical in its orientation, and there is a cluster of acquisitions in this area in the early 1560s. The other major new direction to emerge at this time is the collection of Paracelsian works which eventually constitute an imposing part of Dee's library. The earliest surviving work by Paracelsus dates from 1562, followed by a large number clustered through 1564. Jones, *The Discovery of Hebrew*, p. 168, briefly discusses Dee's Hebrew studies and pp. 275–7, lists the books on Hebrew and Oriental languages from Dee's 1583 library catalogue.

26 For an excellent survey of the idea of a natural language, see Coudert, 'Some Theories of a Natural Language', especially pp. 56–7, 64–91, for this discussion. See also Vickers, 'Analogy versus Identity', pp. 105–9.

27 Camporeale, 'Lorenzo Valla'.

28 Coudert, 'Some Theories', pp. 64–79. On Valla see Jardine, 'Lorenzo Valla', pp. 143–64; Waswo, 'The "Ordinary Language Philosophy"', pp. 255–71; and Waswo, 'Magic Words', pp. 76–90.

29 Coudert, 'Some Theories', p. 74–85.

30 Ibid., pp. 68–73, 75–85. On Jewish kabbalah, see Scholem, *Major Trends*; and Scholem, *On the Kabbalah*; Secret, *Les kabbalistes*; and Idel, 'The Magical and Neoplatonic Interpretation'.

31 Coudert, 'Some Theories', pp. 66–8, and the literature cited there

on hieroglyphics and emblems in the Renaissance. See Yates, *GBHT*, pp. 1–19, for the Hermetic texts, the legend of Hermes Trismegistus, and their impact in the fifteenth century.

32 Among Dee's books on Hebrew and Oriental languages are Ambrogio, *Introductio*; Cheradame, *Alphabetum*; and Postel, *De originibus*; see Roberts & Watson. Dee's copy of Postel is currently in the Royal College of Physicians, London. This last is not dated by Dee, but a marginal note mentions the Monas, thus, it is no earlier than 1557/58.

33 Cheradame, *Alphabetum*, pp. 4–6, 19–23; Postel, *De originibus*, pp. 13–34; Gohory, *De vsu & mysteriis notarum*, sig.A.ij. Dee's annotated copy of Gohory, dated 1562, is in University Library, Cambridge, shelf mark LE 19. 8².

34 On Pythagoreanism in the Renaissance, see Heninger, *Sweet Harmony*, pp. 78–84. For my purposes I have used 'Pythagorean' throughout to indicate the broad body of ideas and legend that was associated with Pythagoras in the Renaissance without any implication that these correspond with any body of doctrine of the historical Pythagoras.

35 Heninger, *Sweet Harmony*, pp. 158–77, discusses and illustrates a number of dimensions of tetradic correspondences.

36 Cornford, 'Mysticism and Science', pp. 1–3; Heninger, *Sweet Harmony*, pp. 87, 78–84, 146–94. Heninger provides extensive citations from Renaissance authors illustrating the pervasiveness of these ideas to the point that they can be considered almost a commonplace.

37 Dee eventually owned many classical, medieval, and Renaissance texts that presented Pythagorean ideas. Two texts that he clearly read before 1564 which have sections dealing with these matters heavily annotated are Alexander, *Mathemalogium*, acquired in 1551 and read and annotated in 1555, sig.B.ij^v; and Riffius [Rivius], *In Caii Plinii secundi naturalis historiae*, dated 1562, sig.C.ij–C.iij^v. Both of these are in the Royal College of Physicians, London. See Nauert, 'Caius Plinius Secundus', p. 419, on the correct form of Rivius and the authorship of this commentary.

38 I have not seen Dee's copy of Proclus, *Commentary*, but Dee mentions material from it in his 'Epistola' to Federico Commandino, sig.*.3^v–*.4, which was written in the Summer of 1563 when Dee visited Commandino at Urbino. On the issue of the chronology of Dee's visit to Commandino, see Rose, 'Commandino, John Dee', pp. 88–93.

39 Proclus, *Commentary*, pp. 14, 75, 80.

40 Ibid., pp. 79–80, 117.

41 Ibid., pp. 120, 123.

42 Ibid., pp. 123, 38.

43 See, for example, Torniello da Novara, *The Alphabet*. Ryder, *Lines of the Alphabet*, is a survey of the numerous Renaissance works of alphabet design, most of them geometrically constructed.

44 This is listed in Dee's pre-1560 inventory of books and manuscripts,

but no surviving copy has been identified that would indicate the exact date of acquisition. Roberts & Watson; British Library, MS 35213, fol.2.

45 Tory, *Champ fleury*, fols XXV^v, XI.

46 Ibid., fols XI–XII.

47 Ibid., fol.XXV^v.

48 The following discussion closely follows Walton, 'John Dee's *Monas Hieroglyphica*', pp. 119–21.

49 Scholem, *Jewish Mysticism*, pp. 100–1; Blau, *The Christian Interpretation*, p. 8; *Encyclopaedia Judaica*, 2:47; 7:369–74.

50 Lauterbach, 'Substitutes for the Tetragrammaton', pp. 41–9.

51 Ibid., p. 52.

52 For the alpha and omega of Greek, see *MH*,196–201.

53 The jargon of alchemy that served both to preserve secrets and to insulate the initiates from criticism from outside society appears very similar in function to the anti-language of criminal slang that Burke notes in 'Languages and Anti-Languages', pp. 25, 28; and Libavius considers membership in the society of alchemists as the same as associating with rogues and vagabonds, on which see Hannaway, *The Chemists*, p. 78.

54 Crosland, *Historical Studies*, p. 36.

55 Hannaway, *The Chemists*, pp. 117–51, presents Libavius's reform of chemistry as the provision of a common vocabulary and an orderly disposition of the subject in response to the confused and obscure character of existing chemical literature.

56 Bodleian Library, Corpus Christi College MS 191, fols 88^v–90.

57 Roberts & Watson.

58 Villanova, *Opera*, signed by Dee and dated 1557 is in the Royal College of Physicians, London; and British Library, MS Sloane 2128, signed and dated 1557.

59 Pantheus, *Voarchadumia*. Dee's copy is British Library shelf mark 1033. h. 1(2.).

60 Goltz, 'Versuch einer Grenzziehung', pp. 34–42.

61 Read, *Prelude to Chemistry*, pp. 9–10; Holmyard, *Alchemy*, pp. 21–4; Maier, *An der Grenze*, pp. 9–12. The exact nature of how qualities and elements combined in composite substances was never clear from Aristotle's texts and posed significant problems to Arabic and European philosophers in the Middle Ages. Alchemical texts, however, do not generally trouble themselves with these philosophical niceties. For instance, Arnold of Villanova devotes considerable attention to the philosophical issues in his work on grading compound medicines, but gives no attention to these issues in his alchemical texts. For a survey of these problems, see McVaugh, 'Introduction', pp. 3–136 passim; Newman, 'The *Summa Perfectionis*', 1:110–18; and Clulee, 'John Dee's Mathematics', pp. 182–94. It may be that the alchemical works that claim Arnold of Villanova as author are apocryphal, as suggested by Sarton, *Introduction*, 2:893–900; but Thorndike, *A History of Magic*, 3:52–84,

considers many of them as authentic, including the *Rosarius philosophorum* used in this discussion.

62 Read, *Prelude*, pp. 17–18; Holmyard, 'Introduction', pp. xi–xiii.

63 Read, *Prelude*, pp. 17–18, 119–20; Holmyard, *Alchemy*, pp. 74–5; and Holmyard, 'Introduction', pp. xi–xiii.

64 Holmyard, *Alchemy*, pp. 68–75, 86–8, 92–5; Newman, 'The *Summa Perfectionis*', 1:2–3, 74–6.

65 For influence of this theory and on these authors, see Holmyard, *Alchemy*, pp. 117–26, 134–48. The mystery of the identity of the Latin Geber seems finally to have been resolved in Newman's important 'The *Summa Perfectionis*'. He very convincingly demonstrates that the major Latin works that circulated under the name Geber were written by Paul of Taranto, a Franciscan active in the second half of the thirteenth century. Since some pseudoepigraphic texts were produced in the fourteenth century in imitation of Paul of Taranto's Geber, I have styled these as the Latin pseudo-Geber. See also Newman, 'New Light', pp. 76–90. Dee's aquisition of Villanova's *Opera* in 1557 has already been noticed. He also had access to Bacon's *Opus tertium* and the spurious *Speculum alchimiae*, Geber, and the *Pretiosa margarita novella* of Petrus Bonus. See, Oxford, Corpus Christi College MS 191, fols.88^{v}–90.

66 Newman, 'The *Summa Perfectionis*', 1:109–18, 269–71; Paul of Taranto, *Summa Perfectionis*, pp. 17–19, 42–3, 46–50; Paul of Taranto, *Investigatione Perfectionis*, pp. 19–20, 42–3, 48–9, 59–60; Bacon, *The Mirror of Alchimy*, p. 9; [pseudo]-Geber, *The Investigation*, in Geber, *The Works*, pp. 4–5.

67 Villanova, *Rosarius philosophorum*, in *Opera*, fol.333^{v}; Read, *Prelude*, pp. 130–33.

68 [pseudo]-Geber, *The Investigation*, pp. 9–11; Villanova, *Rosarius philosophorum*, *Opera*, fols 333^{v}–34^{v}; Bonus, *The New Pearl*, p. 190.

69 [pseudo]-Geber, *The Investigation*, p. 9.

70 Read, *Prelude*, pp. 136–42.

71 Read, *Prelude*, p. 136. Paul of Taranto, *Summa Perfectionis*, p. 66; and [pseudo]-Geber, *The Investigation*, p. 11, give eight without any clear relation to something else.

72 Villanova, *Rosarius philosophorum*, fols 335–38^{v}.

73 Dee lists Norton among the alchemical authors he read in 1556 (Oxford, Corpus Christi College MS 191, fol.89^{v}) and thought enough of it to make his own copy of it in 1577, which is now Oxford, Bodleian Library MS Ashmole 57.

74 Norton, *The Ordinall*, pp. 57–8.

75 Ibid., pp. 82–5.

76 In this scheme, one of the refreshing instances of uniformity of terminology in alchemy, sun=gold, the moon=silver, mercury=quicksilver, venus=copper, mars=iron, jupiter=tin, and saturn=lead. See Read, *Prelude*, pp. 88–93; Holmyard, *Alchemy*, pp. 153–54.

77 Bacon, *Part of the Opus tertium*, pp. 83–6; Villanova, *Rosarius philosophorum*, fol.334.

78 Bonus, *The New Pearl*, p. 146.
79 Villanova, *Rosarius philosophorum*, fol.335; Bonus, *The New Pearl*,
    pp. 123–4.
80 This has been suggested for Dee's *Monas* by Josten, 'Introduction',
    pp. 102–4. The literature on the interpretation of alchemical
    literature as expressing spiritual or psychological aspirations,
    experiences, and insights is too abundant to cite.
81 All references are to Dee's copy of the 1530 edition in the British
    Library, shelf mark 1033. h. 1(2.). Dee's annotations became so
    heavy that beginning between fols 37 and 38 he had the book
    interleaved to provide more space. See Thorndike, *A History of
    Magic*, 5:537–40; Ferguson, *Bibliotheca*, 2:166–7; and Duveen,
    Bibliotheca, pp. 449–50; for what little is known of Pantheus. Secret,
    Les kabbalistes, pp. 294–5, claims that he was the first in the West to
    amalgamate kabbalah and alchemy.
82 Calder, 1:611–13; and Josten, *MH*, p. 137, n. 27.
83 Pantheus, fols 6ᵛ–7ᵛ. Among the writers of archimia Pantheus
    mentions Hermes, Geber, Avicenna, Arnold, Raymond [Lull] and
    dismisses many other Arab, Chaldean, Greek, Hebrew, Indian, and
    Latin works.
84 Ibid., fols 7ᵛ–8.
85 Ibid., fols 8ᵛ, 11ᵛ.
86 Ibid., fols 11ᵛ–12.
87 Ibid., fol.40 are examples. For instance, the numerical value of the
    words 'NVTV DEI' is 90, which is equivalent to the combined
    numerical value of Putrefactio, Generatio, and Alteratio, the three
    operations that take place through the agency of fire and the
    command of God. By another calculation, these three processes yield
    the value 1154, which is found equivalent to the Greek equivalent
    of 'NVTV DEI'; and by yet another calculation they yield 1642,
    which is found equivalent to the same expression in Hebrew.
88 Ibid., fols 48ᵛ–9.
89 Ibid., fol.11ᵛ, cf. fols 38ᵛ–9.
90 Ibid., fol.18ᵛ.
91 Ibid., fols 15ᵛ, 37.
92 Ibid., fols 18ᵛ–22.
93 Ibid., fols 35–54.
94 Ibid., fols 34, 44; quoting Aristotle, *De generatione et corruptione*, 328b
    22.
95 Pantheus, fols 16, 60–1ᵛ.
96 John Dee to Sir William Cecil, 16 February 1562, *Bibliographical and
    Historical Miscellanies*, pp. 1–16.
97 Ibid., pp. 6–7.
98 The best treatment of Trithemius is Brann, *The Abbot Trithemius*. See
    also Arnold, *Johannes Trithemius*, and Behrendt, 'Abbot John
    Trithemius', pp. 212–29. The issue of the magical character of the
    Steganographia and its influence on Dee will be discussed in the next
    chapter.

99 On these letters and Trithemius's philosophy of magic and
   mysticism, see Brann, *The Abbot Trithemius*, pp. 18–20, 43–4; Brann,
   'The Shift from Mystical to Magical', pp. 147–59; and Brann,
   'George Ripley', pp. 212–20. The letters in question are to Johannes
   Westenburg of 10 May 1503, and to Germanus de Ganay of 24
   August 1505. The letter to Ganay is included in Trithemius,
   Epistolarum, pp. 89–94; and both are in Trithemius, *De septem
   secundadeis*, pp. 65–76, 81–100. Dee had both of these in 1583 (British
   Library, MS Harley 1879, fols 17, 18, 25^v) and his copy,
   unfortunately without a dated inscription, of the *De septem secundadeis*
   is in the Cambridge University Library, shelf mark Dd.* 4. 5.
   Although the date of his acquisition of these cannot be proven, his
   letter to Cecil indicates that the most likely time for him to have
   acquired them was during the trip to the continent in 1562 through
   1564. His access to the letter to Westenburg and to Trithemius's
   ideas, however, can be dated with certainty to this period because
   he acquired in January 1562 a copy of Gohory, *De vsu & mysteriis
   notarum*, which both discusses extensively Trithemius's numerology and
   includes extensive excerpts from the letter to Westenburg. Dee's copy
   of this with the dated inscription is in Cambridge University Library,
   shelf mark LE 19. 8^2. Trithemius was not alone in associating magic
   with alchemy. Dee may also have noticed that Norton, *The Ordinall
   of Alchemy*, p. 61, cited 'Magick Naturall' as the 'chiefe Mistris' among
   all sciences as an aid to alchemy.

100 Brann, 'The Shift from Mystical to Magical', pp. 154–5.

101 Trithemius, *De septem secundadeis*, pp. 67–70, 72–3, 82–3, 85–7, 92–7;
    Gohory, *De vsu & mysteriis notarum*, sigs.H.ij^v–H.i^v, I.i–I.iij^v; Brann,
    'George Ripley', pp. 213–15.

102 Trithemius, *De septem secundadeis*, pp. 82–6, 92–7.

103 Gohory, *De vsu & mysteriis notarum*, sig.H.iv.

104 Read, *Prelude*, p. 54. On the *Tabula smaragdina*, see Read, pp. 51–5;
    and Holmyard, *Alchemy*, pp. 97–100. Brann, 'The Shift from
    Mystical to Magical', p. 154; and Brann, 'George Ripley',
    pp. 213–14, discovered Trithemius's use of the Emerald Tablet.

105 Newman, 'Thomas Vaughn', pp. 129–30.

106 I borrow the phrase 'the writing of things' from Foucault, *The Order
    of Things*, pp. 34–42, because the concept and Foucault's exposition
    of it so clearly captures what Dee intends. Huppert, '*Divinatio et
    Erudatio*', pp. 191–207, has taken Foucault to task for implying that all
    Renaissance conceptions of language were inherently magical and
    that erudition was therefore a kind of divination. His point is well
    taken, but in the case of Dee's *Monas* and a significant portion of
    other Renaissance writing, Foucault has touched on an important
    point.

107 Likewise, what follows is intended only to illustrate the main
    dimensions of the *Monas* and not to explicate all aspects of the text.

108 See Pantheus, *Voarchadumia*, fols 49^v–52^v, where Dee notes these
    associations.

109 Cf. the Emerald Tablet in Read, *Prelude*, p. 54.
110 Bacon, *Part of the Opus tertium*, pp. 83–86; Bacon, *The Mirror of Alchimy*, p. 9.
111 Cf. Pantheus, *Voarchadumia*, fol.44, where Saturn and Jupiter both refer to the 'chyle' or corrupt body resulting from the dissolution of the elements in the first stage of the work, and fols 49ᵛ–50ᵛ, where the waxing of the moon is associated with the albification of this 'chyle' and the emergence of the mercury of metals.
112 Zetterberg, 'Hermetic Geocentricity', pp. 391–2.
113 Sheppard, 'Egg Symbolism', pp. 140–8.
114 Zetterberg, 'Hermetic Geocentricity', pp. 389–93, very perceptively used the evidence in the *Monas* to demonstrate Dee's positive commitment to a geocentric and geostatic universe. He also argues on the basis of the egg image and Dee's reference to Mercury's oval orbit that Dee's restoration of astronomy involved reviving an astronomical secret of the ancient *magi* in which Mercury travelled in an oval orbit around the Sun and not the Earth. While ingenious, there are significant problems with this interpretation. He himself recognizes that Dee's use of two different symbols for Mercury poses one problem. From quite early in the *Monas* Dee uses his unconventional symbol for Mercury to represent the planet and the conventional symbol to represent not a planet but the mercury of the philosophers that results from the total process. The parallel of the oval orbit of Mercury and the shape of the egg makes the egg in total an appropriate representation of philosophers' mercury but does not need to suggest, if we take the image too literally, that there is a second Mercury in the heavens orbiting the Sun. The second problem, which he ignores, is that the usual ancient alternative to the Ptolemaic order of the planets, which was well known in the sixteenth century and summarized by Copernicus, had both Mercury and Venus orbit the sun as the sun orbited the earth. On this, see Westman, 'Three Responses to the Copernican Theory', pp. 321–2. In addition to the astronomical difficulties of a scheme in which Mercury but not Venus orbits the sun, this would seem to make a shambles of the parallels between astronomy and the alchemical work that Dee seems to be at pains to make.
115 This order is found in Plato, *Timaeus*, 38C–D; and Plato, *Republic*, 616E–617B. See also Dreyer, *A History of Astronomy*, pp. 44, 168–9. This passage is potentially more interesting in terms of Dee reviving some ancient astronomy that involved Mercury orbiting the sun because this Platonic order was associated with the notion that Venus and Mercury orbited the sun, but by deferring treatment of this, Dee gives no grounds to form any conclusions. See Dreyer, pp. 126–30; Cohen and Drabkin, *A Source Book in Greek Science*, p. 107; and Eastwood, '"The Chaster Path of Venus"', pp. 146–8, 155–7.
116 Read, *Prelude*, p. 54.
117 See Proclus, *Commentary*, pp. 3, 45, on the concept of mathematical understanding.

118 Refering to Hippocrates, *Breaths* [*Liber de flatibus*], p. 229; 'opposites are cures for opposites. Medicine is in fact subtraction and addition. Subtraction of what is in excess, addition of what is wanting'.

119 Holmyard, *Alchemy*, pp. 27–8; Eliade, *The Forge and the Crucible*, pp. 151–3; Festugière, *La révélation*, 1:261–2, 282. The most explicit reflection of this in a work Dee knew is Bonus, *The New Pearl*, pp. 123–4.

120 Brann, 'The Shift from Mystical to Magical', pp. 154–5; Brann, 'Was Paracelsus a Disciple of Trithemius', pp. 76–81. See Trithemius, *De septem secundadeis*, pp. 69, 72–4, 82–3, 87–8, for the statement of these views in texts Dee had available.

121 Rivius, *In Caii Plinii*, sigs.A.iv^v–B.j.

122 Pico della Mirandola, *Conclusiones*, p. 79: 'Conclusiones Magicae . . . secundum opinionem propriam', nos. 26, 27, 28.

123 Grant, *Gnosticism*, pp. 7–9; Scholem, *Jewish Mysticism*, pp. 49–50.

V THE GREAT METAPHYSICAL REVOLUTION

1 Crosland, *Historical Studies*, pp. 4–7; and Goltz, 'Versuch einer Grenzziehung', pp. 33, 42–7, on alchemical language; and Vickers, 'Analogy versus Identity', pp. 95–163, on analogies and occult language in general.

2 Waswo, 'Magic Words', pp. 76–90.

3 Calder, 1:544; French, pp. 76–81, 93–6; Yates, *Occult*, pp. 83–4; Yewbrey, 'John Dee', pp. 91–110.

4 See *PA* (1568), XI (Macrocosm-microcosm analogy), XVIII (reference to alchemy and notarikon), XXVI (reference to Gamaaeas, the term in the *Monas* for the Monas as reconstituted in preparation for the 'great metaphysical revolution'), XLV (reference to magic), LXXIII consectarium 1 & 2 (microcosmic analogies), LXXVII (reference to the philosophers' stone as what has been separated and then seven times joined, which is the process in the *Monas*), and CXVIII (reference to mages).

5 The following discussion is indebted to the suggestions in Westman, 'The Astronomer's Role', pp. 105–47; his unpublished paper, 'Hermeticism and the Reform of the Disciplines' presented at a conference on Hermeticism in the Renaissance at the Folger Library in 1982; and his comments on a paper I presented on Renaissance magic at the History of Science Society Annual Meeting in 1979.

6 Hannaway, *The Chemists and the Word*, pp. 75–9, 89–90.

7 Johannes Radermacherus to Jacobus Colius, in Ortelius, *Epistolae*, no. 334, pp. 787–91. The letter is dated 1604 but refers to his frequent conversations with Dee forty years earlier in the bookshop of the Birkmanns in London.

8 See Livesey, '*Metabasis*', pp. 183–8, who points out that Aristotle's prohibition of *metabasis* was given as the rationale in the statutes that prohibited the arts faculty from discussing theological questions.

9 See Proclus, *A Commentary*, pp. 3–4, 10–14, 50–1.

10 Calder, 1:531.

11 Hudson, *The Cambridge Connection*, pp. 13, 25; Jordan, *Edward VI*, 2:501–3.

12 *CR*,21. Thomas, *Religion and the Decline of Magic*, pp. 493–4. Cecil's personal interest in astrology is reflected in some astrological notes in British Library, MS Landsdown 103, fol.297, and noted by Capp, *Astrology and the Popular Press*, p. 60. It has also been suggested that Dee may have been involved in the design of an astrolabe made by Thomas Gemini and presented to Elizabeth in 1559. See Gunther, 'The Astrolabe of Queen Elizabeth', pp. 65–72; and Gabb, 'The Astrological Astrolabe of Queen Elizabeth', pp. 101–3. There is, however, only indirect evidence of Dee's involvement.

13 *CR*,11. This Dr Willson may be the Thomas Wilson to whom the position went in 1560, he becoming Master of Requests at the same time, although this Wilson was not a doctor (*DNB*, 21:603–7).

14 *NA*,52–4; Foxe, *Acts and Monuments*, 7:349, 641–4, 681, 756–7, for the references to Dee which were explicit in the Latin edition of 1559 and the English edition of 1563, but suppressed in later editions.

15 Thomas, *Religion and the Decline of Magic*, pp. 430–1; *CR*,7–8; Larkey, 'Astrology and Politics', pp. 171–86.

16 John Dee, Letter to Sir William Cecil, 16 February 1562/63, *Bibliographical and Historical Miscellanies*, pp. 5–12.

17 Reconstructing Dee's travels is complex and based on numerous scraps of information. The Letter to Cecil, dated 1562, speaks of leaving England late the previous year; Elia Levita, *Composita verborum et nominum Hebraicorum*, Cambridge University Library, shelf mark K.* 6. 36., bears Dee's inscription at Louvain in 1562, and Dee's mention in the *Monas* (134/5) of his aphorisms to the Parisians, which may refer to the *Cabbalae Hebraicae* of 1562 (*CR*,26), indicates he may have visited Paris that year as well. For Dee's travels in 1563, see Rose, 'Commandino, John Dee', pp. 88–93. We have noted Dee's mention of his trip to Pressburg in the *Monas* (114/15). Some dates for the Italian part of Dee's trip are notes of the places and dates when items in an alchemical collection, British Library, MS Sloane 2006, were copied. These present some difficulty since the dates for Padua in late January 1564 and Venice in April 1564 conflict with his claim to have written the *Monas* in Antwerp from 13 to 30 January 1564. Andrew Watson believes that not all of the transcriptions and inscriptions in this volume are in Dee's hand, so that the later dates are most likely those of a scribe employed by Dee to complete the project after he left Italy for Antwerp. This fact, however, makes the dating of the end of Dee's stay in Italy uncertain.

18 Dee, Letter to Cecil, pp. 10–1.

19 Ibid., pp. 5, 10–12.

20 Evans, *Rudolf II*, pp. 52, 221; Evans, *Habsburg Monarchy*, pp. 19–22, 35; Bartolomeus de Rekingen, Letter to Dee, Vienna, 1564, Bodleian Library, MS Ashmole 1788, fols 134–5ᵛ. In 1564 Dee acquired Cyprian Leowitz's *De coniunctionibus magnis*, which was

dedicated to Maximilian, and heavily marked the detailed sections related to the Habsburgs, the Empire, and Bohemia (Cambridge University Library, shelf mark R.* 5. 21(E)).

21 Van Dorsten, *The Radical Arts*, pp. 21–4; Yewbrey, 'John Dee', pp. 74–84; each developing suggestions of Yates, *GBHT*, pp. 169–89; and Yates, *Occult*, pp. 84–8, on religious hermetism.

22 Van Dorsten (*The Radical Arts*, pp. 16–18, 21, 34, 37) supports the imputation of a political message to the *Monas* with a series of associations: (1) the similarity of Dee's fusion of science, philosophy, and theology to Giacomo Aconcio, who supported arguments for religius reconciliation and political toleration, and Guillaume Postel, who supported an ecumenical universal faith with cosmological theories; (2) Dee's residence and publication of the *Monas* with Willem Silvius who may have had connections with the Familist movement, which promoted religious toleration and unity and practised a Nicodemite strategy of religious simulation not dissimilar to Dee's behaviour with Bishop Bonner; in conjunction with (3) Maximilian's practice of religious toleration in his domains and search for a *politique* solution to the religious problem in the Netherlands where Dee was at the time. On Aconcio, see Rossi, *Aconcio*, pp. 9, 18–25; and O'Malley, *Aconcio*, pp. 10–12, 26–51, 123–6. On Postel, see Bouwsma, *Concordia Mundi*, pp. 24–5; and Kuntz, *Postel*, pp. 104–7, 139–42. On the Familists, see Moss, '*Godded with God*', pp. 7–8, 12–13, 23; and Hamilton, *The Family*, pp. 34, 43–8, 65–70. On Maximilian's religious policies, see Evans, *Habsburg Monarchy*, pp. 19–22; Evans, *Rudolf II*, p. 52; and Fichtner, *Ferdinand I*, pp. 244, 246–53. Aconcio accompanied some Marian exiles to England and was patronized by Elizabeth and Leicester as an engineer, but Dee never mentions him, and the only evidence of any connection is that Pierre de la Ramée wrote to both, asking Aconcio to forward the letter to Dee, yet neither letter suggests that Ramée considered the two acquainted. See Ramée, Letter to Jacobo Acontio, 14 Calends January 1565, and Letter to Joan. Dee, 14 Calends January 1565, in Ramée and Talon, *Collectiones*, pp. 173–4. Dee had met Postel in Paris in 1550, but Dee does not mention him later and it is difficult to determine if Dee could even have encountered him after his major religious shift in 1551. There is no positive evidence of Familist sympathies on Dee's part or on that of Silvius. See Clair, 'Willem Silvius', pp. 192–205. Yewbrey calls on later evidence to supply what the *Monas* lacks in explicit political content. On the basis of Dee's passing reference to his 'cosmopolitical theories' (*MH*,118/19), Yewbrey ('John Dee', pp. 42–4) argues that the 'wisdom' of the *Monas* is the 'wisdome' by which 'rulers rule' noted in a 1570 outline that Yewbrey claims is a summary of the no longer extant *Republicae Britannicae Synopsis* that Dee claims he wrote in 1565. See *CR*,26; *LA*,75; and British Library, MS Cotton Charter XIII, art. 39, which is 'Brytannicae Reipub. Synopsis: libris explicata tribus. Synopseos adumbratio a Joanne Dee L. designata Aº. 1570'.

23 *MH*,146/7, 218/19. Dee claims to have written the text in twelve days between January 13th and 25th, and the dedication to Maximilian in another five between January 25th and the 29th.

24 Easton, *Roger Bacon*, pp. 72–6.

25 Ibid., p. 179.

26 Livesey, '*Metabasis*', pp. 310–11, 325–6.

27 Bacon's ideas on mathematics are throughout his works. On the broad usefulness of mathematics including philosophy and theology, see Bacon, *The 'Opus Majus'*, 1:97–108, 175–80; on the division of the mathematical sciences including many physical sciences, see Bacon, *Communia mathematica*, pp. 38–51. Cf. Livesey, '*Metabasis*', pp. 312–17.

28 Bacon, *Opus Majus*, 2:167–8, 172–3, 202, 215–16; Livesey, '*Metabasis*', pp. 318–26.

29 Bacon, *Opus Majus*, 2:169–72; Easton, *Roger Bacon*, p. 176.

30 Easton, *Roger Bacon*, pp. 72–5. On the *Secretum secretorum* see Manzalaoui, 'The Secreta Secretorum', p. 83–106; Manzalaoui, 'The Pseudo-Aristotelian *Kitāb Sirr al-Asrār*', pp. 147–257; Grignaschi, 'L'Origine', pp. 7–112; Grignaschi, 'La diffusion', pp. 7–70; and Ryan and Schmitt, eds, *Pseudo-Aristotle*.

31 Bacon, *Secretum secretorum cum glossis et notulis*, and Bacon's commentary, *Tractatus brevis et utilis*, in Bacon, *Opera hactenus inedita*, fasc. 5:1–24 (Bacon's commentary), and 25–172 (text and Bacon's notes); Easton, *Roger Bacon*, pp. 72–82. Dee had a manuscript of Bacon's edition of the *Secretum secretorum* acquired in 1561 (Oxford, Corpus Christi College MS 149) and a printed edition acquired in 1563 (Cambridge University Library, shelf mark N.* 13. 6.). On Dee's manuscript as a copy of Bacon's edition, see Steele, 'Introduction', Bacon, *Opera hactenus inedita*, 5:vii. Both are too late to have influenced Dee's *Speculum unitatis*, but they may have played a role in the development of Dee's thinking in the 1560s.

32 Grignaschi, 'Remarques', pp. 9–11.

33 Bacon, *Secretum secretorum*, pp. 36–42, 157–172; Easton, *Roger Bacon*, p. 114; and Manzalaoui, 'The Secretum Secretorum', pp. 96–7. Bacon was one of the earliest in the Latin West to use the *Secretum* and he was noteworthy in attending more to the occult sections than to those concerned with political advice.

34 Bacon, *Secretum secretorum*, pp. 36–7, 62–3 (Bacon's notes); cf. Bacon, *The 'Opus Majus'*, 1:41–2, 45–56; and Bacon, *Opus tertium*, pp. 79–83. It is interesting to find an expression of the idea of an 'ancient theology' in the Middle Ages used in much the same way it was in the Renaissance. There were precedents among some of the patristic writers, so Bacon is not novel, and the Renaissance vogue of the ancient theology beginning with Ficino seems to be independent of medieval influence. See Walker, *The Ancient Theology*, pp. 1–3, 10–12.

35 Easton, *Roger Bacon*, pp. 30–1.

36 Bacon, *Opus tertium*, pp. 33–4, 73, 88.

37 Dee, Letter to Cecil, 16 February 1562, in *Bibliographical and Historical Miscellanies*, 1:6–7.

38 Walker, *The Ancient Theology*, pp. 1–3, 10–12; Walker, *Spiritual and Demonic Magic*, pp. 36–44. See Festugière, *La révélation*, chs 1–3, for a survey of late antique intellectual and cultural trends.

39 Walker, *Spiritual and Demonic*, pp. 3–24, 36–53, 75–84.

40 Ibid., pp. 75–6.

41 Yates, *GBHT*, pp. 40–1, 58, 65–6, 84–6.

42 Yates, *Occult*, pp. 1–5, 17–59.

43 Yates, *GBHT*, pp. 106–9, 144–56; Yates, *Occult*, pp. 80–4.

44 Culianu, 'Magia spirituale e magia demonica', pp. 363–5.

45 Copenhaver, 'Hermes Trismegistus'; Copenhaver, 'Scholastic Philosophy and Renaissance Magic', pp. 523–54.

46 Copenhaver, 'Hermes Trismegistus'; Copenhaver, 'Scholastic Philosophy and Renaissance Magic', pp. 550–4; Culianu, 'Magia spirituale', pp. 365–99.

47 Schmitt, 'Reappraisals in Renaissance Science', pp. 200–14; Copenhaver, 'Hermes Trismegistus'.

48 Recognizing a continuity between medieval and Renaissance magic acknowledged by earlier scholars (Garin, 'Considerazioni', pp. 171, 174–6; Nauert, *Agrippa*, pp. 224–5, 229–30) but obscured by the overemphasis on the novelty of Renaissance magic. A summary of the 'popular hermetica' would be impossible and some references to the secondary literature will have to suffice. Festugière, *La révélation*. 1:87, 355, distinguishes the philosophical hermetic treatises which are philosophical and theosophical from the treatises dealing with occult sciences of what he calls popular hermetism, and the bulk of his first volume covers this popular occult hermetica of late antiquity; d'Alverney, 'Survivance de la Magie Antique', pp. 154–78, considers evidence of survivals, as does Lynn Thorndike, 'Traditional Medieval Tracts', pp. 217–74, for one particular type of literature. Ryan and Schmitt, eds, *Pseudo-Aristotle, the 'Secret of Secrets'*, considers one prominent example. Thorndike, *A History of Magic*, vols I–II, passim, has numerous references to this literature as well as to medieval authors, such as William of Auvergne, Albertus Magnus, Arnold of Villanova, and Peter of Abano, whose works either report magical practices or incorporate magical elements to varying degrees.

49 The *Picatrix* is a Latin version of an Arabic treatise, *Ghāyat al-ḥakīm* (*The Aim of the Sage*), written in Spain in the mid-eleventh century. An edition of the Arabic is Ritter, ed., *Pseudo-Maǧrīṭī. Das Ziel des Weisen*, of which there is a German translation by Ritter and Plessner, '*Picatrix*'. A critical edition of the Latin is Pingree, ed., *Picatrix*, which appeared too late for me to use. I have used as an interim edition Compagni, 'Picatrix Latinus', pp. 237–337, text at 286–337, the preliminaries containing an extensive discussion of the philosophical content of the text. According to Pingree, 'Between the *Ghāya* and *Picatrix*', p. 27, the Latin version dates from shortly after the Spanish translation of 1256/8 on which it is based.

50 Garin, 'Considerazioni', pp. 174–6; Garin, 'Un manuale di magia',

pp. 414–17; and Garin, *Astrology in the Renaissance*, p. 46. Cf. Compagni, 'Picatrix Latinus', pp. 246–76, on the philosophy of *Picatrix* and, at p. 260, its relation to Ficino; and Compagni, 'La magia cerimoniale', pp. 283, 286–7, 296–7, 301.

51 This discussion is based on Pingree, 'Some Sources', pp. 1–15.

52 Pingree, 'Some Sources', pp. 1, 4–10; Festugière, *La révélation*, 1:137–210; Thorndike, *A History of Magic*, 2:281–8.

53 McCown, ed., *The Testament of Solomon*, pp. 2–4, 43–7, 52–68.

54 Ibid., pp. 48, 77.

55 Ibid., pp. 83–5, 100; Butler, *Ritual Magic*, pp. 49–65.

56 Yates, *GBHT*, pp. 9–12; Peters, *The Magician*, pp. 4–8, 15–16; Cohn, *Europe's Inner Demons*, pp. 155–7.

57 Thorndike, *A History of Magic*, 2:902–3; Cohn, *Europe's Inner Demons*, pp. 165–78, 193–5.

58 Hansen, 'Science and Magic', pp. 484–9; McAllister, *The Letter of Saint Thomas*, pp. 20–30 (text), 57–62 (commentary).

59 Thorndike, *A History of Magic*, 2:242–3, 346–7, 552–9, 660–2; Garin, 'Considerazioni', pp. 179–80; Zambelli, 'Il problema della magia', pp. 273–4.

60 Bacon, *Opus tertium*, 1:29.

61 Zambelli, 'Il problema della magia', p. 274; Bacon, *Part of the Opus tertium*, pp. 16–18, 44–8; Molland, 'Roger Bacon as Magician', pp. 457–60.

62 Bacon, *Opus tertium*, 1:96–8; Molland, 'Roger Bacon as Magician', pp. 459–60; Molland, 'Roger Bacon: Magic'.

63 Molland, 'Roger Bacon as Magician', p. 445; Walker, *Spiritual and Demonic Magic*, p. 107; Zambelli, 'Il problema della magia', pp. 279–80; Zambelli, 'Platone, Ficino', pp. 130–1; Nauert, *Agrippa*, pp. 224–5.

64 Garin, 'Considerazioni', p. 171; Garin, 'Un manuale di magia', pp. 393–8; Yates, *GBHT*, pp. 40–1, 58.

65 Walker, *Spiritual and Demonic Magic*, pp. 30–5, 45–7, 50–3; Zambelli, 'Il problema della magia', pp. 281–2; Zambelli, 'Platone, Ficino', p. 131.

66 On kabbalah, see Scholem, *Major Trends*.

67 Idel, 'The Magical and Neoplatonic Interpretation', pp. 188–200; Walker, *Spiritual and Demonic Magic*, pp. 90–6; Yates, *GBHT*, pp. 106–11, 137–41; Nauert, *Agrippa*, pp. 229–30, 245–8; Zika, 'Reuchlin's *De verbo mirifico*', pp. 110–20, 138.

68 Bodleian Library, MS Rawlinson D 868; British Library, MS Add. 36674, fols 23–45; Feingold, 'The Occult Tradition', p. 81.

69 Examples are many, of which the following are some: Bodleian library, MSS Ashmole 1515, fols 4–40; Ashmole 434, fols 114–37; Ashmole 1790, fols 116–19; British Library, MSS Add. 36674, fols 5–22; Sloane 1437; Sloane 3846, fols 103–63; Sloane 3847, fols 2–112; Sloane 3850; Sloane 3851.

70 For example, Bodleian Library MSS Douce 363, fol.40; Ashmole 244,

fols 1–22; British Library MSS Add. 36674, fol.47ᵛ; Sloane 3851, fol.6.

71 See Bodleian Library, MS Rawlinson D 253, 'A Treatise of Conjurations of Angels, with Experiments in Crystal, and Directions for Fumigation'; British Library, MS Add. 36674, fols 47ᵛ–58, 'An excellent book of the Art of Magic, first begun the 22 of March 1567', which is attributed to Simon Forman by a later owner. This is doubtful, Forman being aged fifteen in 1567. Forman did compose a treatise on geomancy and claims to have begun a general work on magic. Bodleian Library, MS Ashmole 354, fols 5–170, is his treatise on geomancy. See Forman, *The Autobiography*, p. 23.

72 Bodleian Library, Corpus Christi College 191, fols 77ᵛ–81. Roberts & Watson. See below, ch. VI, for a discussion of the probable nature of the *Ars sintrillia*.

73 British Library, MS Add. 35213, fols 1–4. Roberts & Watson. Also listed are the *Opera* of Synesius in Greek, and another collection, *Jamblichus cum multis alijs*, which may also contain the Neoplatonic texts on magic.

74 Dee, Letter to Cecil, p. 11, on the *Steganographia*; Gohory's *De vsu & mysteriis*, signed and dated 1562, is Cambridge University Library shelf-mark LE 19. 8²; the *Secretum secretorum*, signed and dated 1563, is Cambridge University Library shelf-mark N.* 13. 6.; and the Pliny, signed and dated 1562, is in the Royal College of Physicians, London. Dee also had two manuscripts containing the *Secretum secretorum*, Bodleian Library, Corpus Christi College MS 149, and Bodleian Library MS Digby 119, this last signed and dated 1551 and containing Bacon's edition of the text.

75 This is Jamblichus et al., *Index eorum quae hoc in libro habentur. Iamblichus de mysteriis aegyptorum, chaldaeorum, assyriorum* . . . (Venice, 1516), in the Folger Library, Washington, D.C. Fols 44 and 48 draw parallels with aphorisms of the *Propaedeumata*, and fol.44 mentions Paracelsus, the first work of whom Dee acquired in 1562, and the kabbalah of the real, which Dee dates to 1562. The date 1567 in the margin is found on fol.52ᵛ suggesting that he may not have read this before that year. The annotations are possibly in two slightly different inks, indicating two different dates of annotation, although a note on fol.45 in which the two inks occur in succession within the same sentence suggests one reading. In any case, the earliest of the two sets, if they are that, refer to the *Propaedeumata* and so are later than 1558, and the majority of the annotations are later than 1562.

76 Dee, Letter to Cecil, p. 11.

77 With the 1606 edition a *Clavis generalis triplex in libros steganographia* was also published, which presents the *Steganographia* as purely cryptographic, but it may not be Trithemius's own work. On the composition and reputation of the work, see Brann, *The Abbot Trithemius*, pp. 18–20. It was Charles de Bovelles to whom Trithemius showed the manuscript and who did much to further Trithemius's reputation for magic. See Victor, *Charles de Bovelles*, pp. 30–6.

78 Arnold, *Johannes Trithemius*, pp. 187–8; and Shumaker, 'Johannes Trithemius', pp. 95–100, 105; both argue that the work is simply cryptography. Walker, *Spiritual and Demonic Magic*, pp. 86–90, discusses the early cryptographic interpretation and concludes that it is partially cryptography and partially genuine demonic magic. Peuchert, *Pansophie*, pp. 47–55, 78–93, takes the *Steganographia* as fundamentally magical and indicates Trithemius's dependence on the traditional corpus of forbidden works of demonic magic. Brann, *The Abbot Trithemius*, p. 91, the most recent and authoritative student of Trithemius, also considers the *Steganographia* to be magical.

79 Not only did manuscripts of Trithemius's *Steganographia* circulate but late sixteenth and early seventeenth century manuscript collections also contain excerpts from his work and similar magical material from other sources attached to his name. See Bodleian Library, MS Ashmole 434, fols 1–24, for a 'Tractatus de angelis septem planetarun'; MS Ashmole 1460, fols 1–137, for a 'Liber experimentorum Johannis Trithemius'; and British Library, MS Sloane 3824, fols 121–40, for a 'Trithemius redivivus'.

80 Trithemius, *Steganographia*, sigs.):(.3ᵛ–):(.4, pp. 1, 58–60, and passim in bk. I.

81 Ibid., pp. 94–5, 160–3.

82 Ibid., pp. 160–3. Trithemius developed the astro-historical dimension of this idea in *De septem secundadeis*, pp. 3–5. In this light it is difficult to deny that the third book of the *Steganographia* is genuine, although that has been one argument used to absolve Trithemius of the undeniably magical character of Book three. See for example, Arnold, *Trithemius*, pp. 187–8.

83 Yates, *GBHT*, pp. 9–12; Thorndike, *A History of Magic*, 2:659–60; Peters, *The Magician*, pp. 4–8, 15–16; Zambelli, 'Il problema della magia', p. 273; Nauert, *Agrippa*, pp. 236–7; and Burke, 'Witchcraft and Magic', pp. 34–8, 42–4.

84 Peuchert, *Pansophie*, pp. 47–55; Thorndike, *A History of Magic*, 2:281–8.

85 Brann, *The Abbot Trithemius*, p. 91; Brann, 'Mystical to Magical Theology', p. 147; Peuchert, *Pansophie*, pp. 58–93; Compagni, 'La magia cerimoniale', pp. 318–20.

86 Trithemius, *Polygraphia*, sig.b.j.

87 Trithemius, *Steganographia*, sig.):(.2.

88 Ibid., sig.):(.3ᵛ–):(.4. The *Clavicula solomonis* and the *Ars notoria* distinguish different orders of spirits, some good and others evil, and different types of magic, illicit goetia being directed at evil infernal spirits and licit theurgy being directed at good celestial spirits. See for example British Library, MSS Sloane 1712, fols 1–37; and Sloane 3825 art. 2.

89 Trithemius, Letters to Germano de Ganay, Johannes Westenburg, and Joachim of Brandenburg, in Trithemius, *De septem secundadeis*, pp. 72–4, 85–6, 101–2, 105–6; Brann, 'Mystical to Magical Theology', pp. 148–55; and Dupèbe, 'Curiosité et magie', pp. 81–6.

90 Rivius, *In Caii Plinii*, also containing a *De fascinationibus disputatio*, a *De incantatione*, and a letter of Trithemius on the *Steganographia*. Nauert has shown that the commentary by Rivius (Walter Herman Ryff) is actually a plagiarism of the commentary of Stephanus Aquaeus (Etienne de L'Aique) to an earlier edition of Pliny, Ryff having eliminated Aquaeus's negative comments on magic, especially those on chapter II denouncing demonic magic for its dangers to religion. Ryff did not sign his name to the work, only including his initials on the title page, and the commentary in this edition was some times attributed to Trithemius. See Nauert, 'Caius Plinius Secundus', pp. 381–3 on Aquaeus, 419 on Ryff's edition; and Nauert, 'The Authorship', 282–5. Dee's annotated copy, dated 1562, is in the Royal College of Physicians, London. There is no indication to whom Dee may have attributed the commentary.

91 *In Caii Plinii*, sigs.D.ij^v–E.iij^v.

92 Ibid., sig.B.j^v.

93 Dee's annotated copy, dated 1562, of Gohory, *De vsu & mysteriis notarum liber* is Cambridge University Library shelf mark LE 19. 8². Dee's annotated copies of Postel, *De originibus* (Basel, [1553]); and Scaliger, *Exotericarum exercitationum*, are both in the Royal College of Physicians. Neither bears a date but I judge that they were acquired and annotated after the *Propaedeumata* and near in time to the *Monas* as follows. Neither appears in his 1557/59 book list, although that list does not invariably include everything he is known to have owned (British Library MS Add. 35213, fols 1–4^v; Roberts & Watson). The Scaliger of 1557, even if acquired soon after publication, was too late to have changed his thinking reflected in the *Propaedeumata* but the passages most heavily marked do relate to themes in the *Monas*. The Postel of 1553 is more problematic but Dee's marginal notation of 'monas nota' to a discussion of reduction of things to unity (p. 44) and his attention to Postel's discussion of original languages and notation of 'hieroglyphica literae' (p. 34) reflect Dee's interests in the 1560s rather than the 1550s.

94 Gohory, *De vsu & mysteriis*, sig.C.ij^v.

95 *In Caii Plinii*, sig.A.ij; cf. Pico della Mirandola, *Conclusiones*, p. 78 (Conclusiones magicae . . . secundum opinionem propriam, no. 3); and Pico della Mirandola, *Apologia*, 1:169.

96 *In Caii Plinii*, sig.A.ij–A.iij; Postel, *De originibus*, p. 67; Scaliger, *Exotericarum*, fols 10, 444^v–5; Gohory, *De vsu & mysteriis*, sig.F.ij; Synesius, *De somniis*, in Jamblichus *Index eorum*, fol.45; and Hermes Trismegistus, *Asclepius*, in Jamblichus, *Index eorum*, fols 127^v, 130.

97 *In Caii Plinii*, sigs.A.iv^v, B.j; Postel, *De originibus*, p. 59. Cf. Agrippa, *De occulta philosophia*, p. 1.

98 *In Caii Plinii*, sig.B.j. This idea of man as a great miracle is from the Hermetic *Asclepius*, see Yates, *GBHT*, pp. 28, 90.

99 *In Caii Plinii*, sig.B.iij; cf. Agrippa, *De occulta philosophia*, p. 18.

100 *In Caii Plinii*, sigs.B.j, B.iij; cf. Agrippa, *De occulta philosophia*, pp. 15–16, 19.

101 *In Caii Plinii*, sig.C.iv^v; Postel, *De originibus*, p. 67; Scaliger,
Exotericarum, fols 462–72, where the entire section 'De intelligentiis,
angeli, mentes' is underlined. See also Hermes Trismegistus,
Pimander, in Jamblichus, *Index eorum*, fols 115, 130; and Psellus, *De
daemonibus*, in Jamblichus, *Index eorum*, fol.50^v.

102 British Library MS Sloane 3188, fols 4–7, for the earliest preserved
record of his 'actions with spirits'. Besterman, *Crystalgazing*, is an
introduction to the subject of scrying with a not very good section
(pp. 17–25) on Dee.

103 Bodleian Library, MS Ashmole 423, fol.294, which is Ashmole's
transcription of an entry in Stöffler's *Ephemerides* for 1543–1558,
which was one of Dee's diaries, now lost. I am indebted to Julian
Roberts, Keeper of Printed Books at the Bodleian, for sharing this
information with me.

104 Agrippa, *De occulta philosophia*, pp. 143–4.

105 British Library, MS Sloane 3188, fols 7^v, 119^v–20.

106 Paracelsus, *Concerning the Nature of Things*, in Paracelsus, *The Hermetic
and Alchemical Writings*, 1:171. This discussion occurs in Book IX,
'Concerning the Signature of Natural Things', which circulated as a
separate work. This is significant because Bartholomeus de
Rekingen, the Imperial physician with whom bee became acquainted
at Maximilian's court, wrote to Dee in 1564 to continue their
discussion 'be signatura rerum', strengthening the evidence that Dee
was familiar with this work. See Bodleian Library, MS Ashmole 1788,
fols 134–5^v.

107 *In Caii Plinii*, sig.E.iij; cf. *MH*,136/37; Psellus, *De daemonibus*, in
Jamblichus, *Index eorum*, fol.50^v. One of the stones that Dee used in
his actions with spirits was of Spanish-American origin, Dee probably
acquiring it from a continental acquaintance on one of his trips, which
means that he could have had it by the late 1560s, although he did
make one brief trip to the continent again in the 1570s. See Tait,
'"The Devil's Looking-Glass"', pp. 195–212.

108 British Library MS Sloane 3848, fol.157; cf. also British Library MSS
Sloane 3849, fols 2–5; 3850, fol.89^v; 3853, fols 138–41; 3854, art. 5;
3884, fols 57^v–61; and MS Add. 36674, fols 38^v–9; Bodleian Library,
MS Add. B. 1, fol.3; MS Ashmole 1790, fol.118; and MS e Mus.
173, fol.26^v. The séance at Cambridge is Bodleian Library MS
Rawlinson D 253, p. 50; cf. Feingold, 'The Occult Tradition', p. 84.
British Library MS Add. 36674, fol.58, begins 'Certaine straung
visions, or apparitions of memorable note. Anno 1567', and contains
a series of these visions continuing from 24 February until 6 April of
that year. The possibility that Dee may have been connected with
this later practice is intriguing, but cannot be established.

VI *VIA MATHEMATICA*

1 The largest amount of Dee's writing to actually survive are the
records of his 'actions with spirits' in the 1580s. It is difficult to guess

how this would compare with all of his other writings if all of those had survived. In his own lists of his works (*CR*,24–7; *LA*,73–7) he does not list these records, and works from this period comprise close to half the works he claims for before 1583.

2 Taylor, *Tudor Geography*, p. 103; Johnson, *Astronomical Thought*, pp. 151–2; Calder, 1:640–5; Boas, *The Scientific Renaissance*, pp. 184–5. The original text of the *Praeface* is in Euclid, *The Elements of Geometry*, tr. Henry Billingsley (London, 1570), and is reproduced in facsimile in the edition by Debus. On the English Euclid, see Shenton, 'The First English Euclid'.

3 Taylor, *The Mathematical Practitioners*, p. 170; Calder, 1:640–5; Yates, *Theatre*, pp. 5, 40; French, pp. 160–87.

4 Roberts & Watson. Evidence from Dee's library is of less help in dealing with the *Praeface* and his later activities since he seems to have dated his acquisitions much less frequently after he moved to Mortlake, which makes it very difficult to determine what he acquired and read at a given time. This, however, is less of a hindrance with the *Praeface* than earlier works, since here he extensively quotes many of his sources. Although appearing too late to incorporate into the text, Knoespel, 'The Narrative Matter of Mathematics', offers some valuable observations on the rhetoric of Dee's *Praeface*.

5 Dee is so concerned to differentiate pure geometry from practical measurement that he proposes renaming geometry, denoting the measurement of land and therefore implying the limitation of the science to physical magnitudes, with '*Megathologia*' as more appropriate to the general and abstract science of magnitude (*MP*,a.ij). Dee's attention to the definition of point, line, surface, and solid, and his concern with replacing the misleading name geometry, in this case with 'megathoscopica', show up in notes in his copy of a Greek and Latin edition Euclid, *Euclidis Elementorum*, which is British Library, shelf mark b. 122 bb. 35. This is signed and dated August 1558, the notes occurring on the leaves preceding the title page and following the colophon. The note on megathoscopica is dated 1559.

6 Dee's translation of Boethius, *De institutione arithmetica*, p. 12.

7 Dee uses the expression '*Dianoeticall* discourse', derived from Proclus, rather than the term understanding, which I adopt following Proclus's translator. See Proclus, *A Commentary*, pp. xxxiv, 3, 9.

8 Cf. Plato, *Republic*, 525a–527c.

9 Cf. Pico della Mirandola, *Conclusiones*, p. 74.

10 Johnson, *Astronomical Thought*, pp. 151–2; Calder, 1:23, 630.

11 For indications of the pervasive repetition of these ideas, see Heninger, *Touches of Sweet Harmony*, passim.

12 Yates, *GBHT*, pp. 148–50; Yates, *Theatre*, pp. 30–2; Yates, *Rosicrucian*, pp. 76–80; Yates, *Occult*, pp. 75, 80–2; French, pp. 90–1.

13 John Dee, 'Epistola' to Federico Commandino, sig.*.3ᵛ–*.4. Dee's letter was written during his visit to Commandino in the summer

of 1563, and reveals a close reading of Proclus's *Commentary*. See Rose, 'Commandino, John Dee'.

14 Morrow, 'Introduction', Proclus, *A Commentary*, pp. xxxiii–xxxvi.

15 Proclus, *A Commentary*, pp. 3–4, 9–10, 13–14.

16 Ibid., p. 38.

17 Ibid., pp. 16–17, 50.

18 Cusanus, *De docta ignorantia*, *Opera*, 1:8–9, 110–11, 119–20, 126–7; Cusanus, *De coniecturis*, *Opera*, 3:4, 7–8; Cusanus, *Idiota de mente*, *Opera*, 5:63, 65, 67–72, 76–9. On Cusanus's epistemology see Cassirer, *The Individual and the Cosmos*, pp. 10–24, 36–45; and Cassirer, *Das Erkenntnisproblem*, 1:21–61.

19 Cusanus, *De staticis experimentis*, *Opera*, 5:119–20.

20 Westman, 'Nature, Art, and Psyche', pp. 201–7.

21 Ibid., p. 204.

22 This does not directly mention Cusanus, whose *De staticis* is only directly cited at A.iij^v, but the wording is a very close paraphrase of Cusanus, *De staticis experimentis*, pp. 119–20. Cf. *MP*,☞.iiij^v.

23 Bert Hansen, 'John Dee and Applied Mathematics', graphically called attention to these anomalies which have been overlooked by most commentators in their enthusiasm for Dee's promotion of the usefulness of mathematics.

24 Hansen, 'John Dee and Applied Mathematics'; Keller, 'Mathematics, Mechanics', pp. 348–52.

25 Yates, *GBHT*, pp. 148–9; Yates, *Occult*, p. 81; French, pp. 103–9, 161–2.

26 Cf. *MP*,☞.iiij^v–*.ij, a.iij; with Proclus, *A Commentary*, p. 50:

> At the upper and most intellectual height it looks around upon the region of genuine being. . . . In the middle region of knowledge it unfolds and develops the ideas that are in the understanding. . . . At the third level of mental exploration it examines nature.
> . . .

and pp. 16–17:

> The range of this thinking extends from on high all the way down to conclusions in the sense world, where it touches on nature and cooperates with natural science in establishing many of its propositions, just as it rises up from below and nearly joins intellect in apprehending primary principles. In its lowest applications, therefore, it projects all of mechanics, as well as optics and catoptrics and many other sciences bound up with sensible things and operative in them. . . .

27 Proclus, *A Commentary*, pp. 29–35, 50.

28 French, p. 108, claims that the *Praeface* is modelled on Agrippa's recommendation that the magician know arithmetic, music, geometry, optics, astronomy, sciences of weights, and mechanical sciences derived from these. Yates, *Theatre*, pp. 20–41; and Yates 'Renaissance Philosophers', p. 214; contends that the *Praeface* is based on the subjects Vitruvius urges the architect to know. In neither case is the parallel as close as that offered by Proclus.

29 Such techniques, which seem to be medieval additions to
Archimedean literature, were quite old and Dee could have derived
them from a number of medieval or Renaissance sources. See Clagett,
'Archimedes in the Late Middle Ages', pp. 44–5; and Clagett,
Archimedes, 3:311–12, 900.

30 Heilbron, 'Introduction', pp. 25–7.

31 Murdoch, 'the Medieval Euclid', pp. 86–90; Molland, 'The
Geometrical Background', p. 118; Livesey, *'Metabasis'*, pp. 53–8,
111–15, 455–7.

32 These 'inventions and annotations' are found in Euclid, *Elements*, fols
275, 311,325–6, 356^v–7^v, 359–62, 388^v–9^v. Dee says
> my intent in these additions is not to amend *Euclides* Method. . . .
> But my desire is somwhat to furnish you, toward a more general
> art Mathematical then *Euclides* Elements . . . can sufficiently helpe
> you vnto. . . . My Additions either geue light, where they are
> annexed to *Euclides* matter, or geue some ready ayde, and shew
> the way to dilate your discourses Mathematicall, or to inuent
> and practise thinges Mechanically. (fol.371)

Following two corollaries, Dee concludes
> the great Mechanical vse (besides Mathematicall considerations)
> which, these two Corollaryes may have in Wheeles of Mills,
> Clockes, Cranes, and other engines for water works, and for warres,
> and many other purposes, the earnest and witte Mechanicien
> will soone boult out, & gladly practise. (fol.357^v)

33 Gent, *Picture and Poetry*, p. 10.

34 Rossi, *Philosophy, Technology, and the Arts*, pp. 15–24, 29–30.

35 Zetterberg, 'The Mistaking of "the Mathematics" for Magic',
pp. 81–97; Zetterberg, ' "Mathematical Magic" ', pp. 2–5;
Molland, 'Roger Bacon as Magician', pp. 445–60; Eamon, 'Books of
Secrets', pp. 33–59.

36 della Porta, *Magia naturalis*, is largely a compilation of the more exotic
forms of technology.

37 Proclus, *A Commentary*, pp. 3–4, 51.

38 For a statement of this process as a general phenomenon in the
sixteenth century that emphasizes the importance of the example of
Archimedes and the texts of Vitruvius and Agricola similar to their
importance for Dee, see Rossi, *Philosophy, Technology, and the Arts*,
pp. 10–11, 15–18, 41–61.

39 The text of Benedetti is given in Drake and Drabkin, *Mechanics*,
pp. 147–53. On Benedetti, see Rose, *The Italian Renaissance of
Mathematics*, pp. 154–6; Drake and Drabkin, *Mechanics*, pp. 21–35,
38–41; Koyré, 'Giambattista Benedetti', pp. 98–102; Clagett,
Archimedes, 3:575–80, 582–3 (which treats Dee's discussion of
Benedetti); and Clagett, 'Archimedes in the Late Middle Ages',
p. 250; cf. Calder, 1:610.

40 Drake and Drabkin, *Mechanics*, pp. 5–6.

41 Dee, in his 'Epistola', to Federico Commandino (sig.*.3–*.4),
commends his work in making the works of Archimedes available.

42 The following is based substantially on my paper, 'John Dee's Mathematics', pp. 178–211. Although I have since revised my understanding of Dee's mathematical philosophy, the discussion there of the relation of various positions on the grading of compounds to medieval treatments of the structure of material substance and of the nature of the intension and remission of accidental forms provides the essential background to the following discussion. To this should now be added McVaugh's long introduction on the history of pharmaceutical theory in Arnoldus de Villanova, *Opera medica omnia*, vol. II, *Aphorismi de gradibus*, pp. 3–136, whose bibliography should be consulted for the materials on this subject. In addition to Arnold's work, this also presents al-Kindī's *Quia primos (Liber de gradibus)*, and the section 'De compositione medicarum' from Averroes's *Colliget*.

43 Clulee, 'Dee's Mathematics', pp. 178, 182–6.

44 Ibid., pp. 178–80; McVaugh, 'Introduction', pp. 4–5.

45 Clulee, 'Dee's Mathematics', p. 180.

46 Clulee, 'Dee's Mathematics', p. 180 & n.13, p. 194 & n.59; McVaugh, 'Introduction', p. 41 & n.20. This *Tractatus . . . de graduatione rerum compositarum* is attributed to Roger Bacon and found in many manuscripts in association with genuine works of Bacon. It was published in Bacon, *Opera hactenus inedita*, 9:144–49. Little and Withington do not doubt the correctness of the attribution, but McVaugh, 'Introduction', p. 41 & n.20 presents the arguments that it cannot be earlier than the fourteenth century. What matters here is that Dee considered it to be Bacon's. Dee refers to Bacon's method in the *Propaedeumata*. He had a manuscript of it in 1556 containing the *Expositio praedicti tractatus* that is not found in all manuscripts of the *Tractatus* (Bodleian Library, Corpus Christi College MS 191, fol.78^v), and made his own copy dated 1560, which is now Bodleian Library, Corpus Christi College MS 254, fols 194^v–206. For the purpose of the following discussion I will refer to the work as Bacon's, following Dee, with the understanding that the attribuion is doubtful.

47 The works of Galen, Averroes, and Arnold were published before 1570, and copies of these are listed in Dee's 1583 *Catalogue*. See Roberts & Watson, (British Library, MS Harley 1879, fols 57, 1, 39, 6^v, 8). Dee's copy of Arnold of Villanova, *Opera*, signed and dated 1557, with notes in Dee's hand throughout the *Liber aphorismorum de graduationibus medicinarum*, fols 250^v–262, is in the Royal College of Physicians, London. Dee's knowledge of Lull's theory of the elements and medicines most likely derived from manuscripts. Two pertinent works by Lull, an *Ars generalis medicina et astronomia* and a *De principijs . . . gradibus* are listed in the 1583 *Catalogue* (Roberts & Watson, [British Library, MS Harley 1879, fol.41]), although he may not have had these before 1570. Dee's 1556 manuscript list shows a *Physica seu medicina Raymundi* which may deal with Lull's method of grading. See Bodleian Library, Corpus Christi College MS 191, fol.80.

48 Clulee, 'Dee's Mathematics', pp. 194–6.

49 Ibid., pp. 184, 189; McVaugh, 'Introduction', pp. 61–8.

50 Clulee, 'Dee's Mathematics', pp. 187–92; McVaugh, 'Introduction', pp. 75–106.

51 Clulee, 'John Dee's Mathematics', pp. 192–3.

52 Quoting Aristotle, *De generatione et corruptione*, 328b 22.

53 *MP*,A.iij^v. The following discussion, containing additional manuscript evidence, is a revised version of a part of my paper, 'At the Crossroads of Magic and Science', pp. 60–4. Permission of Cambridge University Press to re-use this material from their book *Occult and Scientific Mentalities in the Renaissance*, ed. by Brian Vickers, is gratefully acknowledged.

54 Ullmann, *Die Natur- und Geheimwissenschaften*, pp. 360–3; Fahd, *La divination arabe*, p. 40. Nīranǧiyāt is found in various forms (nīranǧāt, nāranǧāt, nāranǧīyāt, nāringǐyyat, nīranǧiyyāt) and is a plural form of nīranǧ, a word of apparently Persian derivation.

55 Ullmann, p. 363; Ritter and Plessner, '*Picatrix*':, pp. 10, 155, 253; Compagni, 'Picatrix Latinus', p. 293.

56 Ibn Sīnā (Avicenna), *De divisionibus scientiarum, idem, Compendium de anima*, fol.142. See also Fahd, *La divination arabe*, p. 40; and *Dictionary of Scientific Biography*, 15:497, on Ibn Sīnā's use of the term.

57 Ibn Sīnā, *De divisionibus*, fol.142.

58 Dee's copy is in the Bodleian Library, Oxford, shelf mark Selden 4° A40 Art. Seld.

59 Artephius is also found as Artefius, Arthephius, Artepius, Artesius, and Artetius. Sarton, *Introduction*, 2:1, 219; Thorndike, *A History of Magic*, 2:353–4, give some information, not all of which can be accepted without question. Levi Della Viola, 'Something More about Artephius', p. 80 & n.6, has questioned the validity of identifying the name Artephius with any historical personality. For Artephius's reputation, see Levi Della Viola, pp. 80–1; Austin, 'Accredited Citations', pp. 368–76; Austin, 'Artephius-Orpheus', pp. 251–4; Thorndike, *A History of Magic*, 1:774, 2:353–4; and Delatte, *La Catoptromancie greque*, pp. 18–23.

60 See Rose, *Verzeichniss*, 14:1181–2 on Berlin MS 956(9). Works ascribed to Artephius are given in Borellius, *Bibliotheca chimica*, pp. 32–3; Sarton, *Introduction*, 2:1, 219; Ferguson, *Bibliotheca Chemica*, 1:51; and Singer, *Catalogue*, 1:128–30. Levi Della Viola, 'Something More about Artephius', pp. 82–5, reports the discovery of an Arabic original of the *Clavis*.

61 Dee, 'Libri antiqui scripti quos habeo anno 1556', Bodleian Liorary, Corpus Christi College MS 191, fol.77^v. This is still listed in the somewhat later list in British Library, MS Add. 35213, fol.4.

62 This codex is now Bodleian Library, Corpus Christi College MS 233, the contents of which date from the thirteenth through the fifteenth centuries. I am indebted to Andrew Watson for this information. Thorndike and Kibre, *A Catalogue of Incipits*, cols 9, 297, 774, give several citations, none of which appears to be the work in question.

Artephius's well known works, the *Clavis sapientiae* and the *Liber secretus* are alchemical with some magical overtones, but both had their own distinct historical identity so they cannot be considered the equivalent of the *Ars sintrillia*.

63 William of Auvergne, *De universo*, II, 3, p. 20, *idem*, *Opera*, 1:1057, fols 2C–D.

64 Forcellini, *Totius latinitatis lexicon*, 4:429: tryblium, ii, n. [gr. triblion]: catinus, paropsis, patina.

65 This description, in the margin of an alchemical manuscript, is transcribed in Rose, *Verzeichniss*, 14:1181–2.

66 Vienna, Oesterreichische Nationalbibliothek, MS 11,294, fols 25ᵛ–30ᵛ. This is followed (fols 31–39) by a chapter of thirteen 'experiments' related to the preceding section, which may or may not be part of the original *Ars* of Artephius. Borellius, *Bibliotheca chimica*, pp. 32–3, lists the same work. There are two French translations, Bibliothèque de l'Arsenal, MSS 2344 and 3009, the latter dated 1730, the former no earlier than the seventeenth century. These are discussed in Grillot de Givry, *La musée des sorciers*, p. 307.

67 Ristoro d'Arezzo, *La Composizione del Mondo*, pp. 166–7, referring to the beginning of Artephius's book, cites the 'mundus secundus' at the beginning of *De scientia praeteritorum*, Vienna, Oesterreichische Nationalbibliothek MS 11,294, fol.26, which indicates that this was a separate wrk at one time. Cf. Austin, 'Accredited Citations', pp. 368–75; Giovanni Francesco Pico della Mirandola, *De rerum praenotione*, *idem*, *Opera*, 1:426–7, 469; Cardano, *De rerum varietate*, *idem*, *Opera*, 3:312–16. There is a fifteenth-century manuscript in the British Library, Sloane 1118, fols 112–13ᵛ, referred to in the explicit as 'Arthephii de opere solis capitulum extractum de arte suttrillia', which is alchemical and bears no resemblance that I am aware of to any other works of Artephius. Since 'suttrillia' may be another corruption of 'sintriblia' or 'sintrillia', this may have been in some way associated with Artephius or a collection of works containing the *Ars sintrillia*.

68 Delatte, *La catoptromancie*, pp. 63, 69, 73, refers to a number of sixteenth-century discussions of catoptromancy.

69 Johnson, *Astronomical Thought*, pp. 151–2; Taylor, *Tudor Geography*, p. 103; Calder, 1:640–5; Boas, *The Scientific Renaissance*, pp. 184–5; French, pp. 160–2; all state in one way or another that Dee understood and advocated modern experimental method.

70 Norton, *The Ordinall of Alchemy*, p. 13; cf. *OED*, s.v. archemastry.

71 Cusanus, *De staticis experimentis*, pp. 129, 119–20. Dee obviously means this when he refers to Cusanus's work as the *Experimentes statikall*.

72 Dee does not mention Roger Bacon by name, but the 'RB' in the margin, in conjunction with the description of him as a philosopher native to England who wrote at the request of Clement, leaves no doubt whom he meant. Dee's text gives 'Clement the Sixt', but

clearly Clement IV (Pope 1265–8) is meant, for whom Bacon write the *Opus majus*, the *Opus minus*, and the *Opus tertium*.

73 Roger Bacon, *Opus Majus*, 2:167.

74 Ibid., 2:169–72.

75 Ibid., 2:167–8, 172–3, 202, 215–16. Bacon also discusses 'scientia experimentalis' in the *Opus tertium*. See Bacon, *Opus tertium*, pp. 43–7; and *idem, Part of the Opus tertium*, pp. 43–7.

76 Bacon, *Opus Majus*, 2:172–3; cf. *MP*,A.iij^v.

77 Crombie, *Robert Grosseteste*, pp. 139–43, 155–62, argues thus.

78 For more reserved discussions of the meaning of Bacon's 'scientia experimentalis', see Easton, *Roger Bacon*, pp. 7, 113, 181; Thorndike, *A History of Magic*, 2:658; and Lindberg, 'Roger Bacon's Experimental Science'.

79 Bacon, *Opus Majus*, 2:202; cf. *MP*,A.iij^v.

80 Livesey, '*Metabasis*', pp. 53–59, 69, on Euclid and Archimedes.

81 Cf. Rossi, *Philosophy, Technology, and the Arts*, pp. 10–12.

82 Livesey, '*Metabasis*', pp. 318–19; Lindberg, 'Roger Bacon's Experimental Science'.

83 Livesey, '*Metabasis*', pp. 314–17, 325–6.

84 Bacon, *Opus Majus*, 2:215–22.

85 Bacon's interest in natural magic is indicated in his *Epistola de secretis operibus*. The *Secretum secretorum* is cited in Bacon, *Opus Majus*, 2:215. See Molland, 'Roger Bacon as Magician', pp. 445–60; and Molland, 'Roger Bacon: Magic and the Multiplication of Species', forthcoming in *Paideia*.

86 Bacon, *Opus Majus*, 2:215–16; Bacon, *Opus tertium*, p. 44; Ibn Sīnā, *De divisionibus*, fols 139^v–40; cf. Goichon, *Lexique*, pp. 240–7, s.v. Ilm.

87 Bacon, *Epistola de secretis operibus*, pp. 540, 541, 545; Bacon, *Opus Majus*, 2:208, 209, 212–13.

88 Bacon, *Opus Majus*, 2:215; Bacon, *Opus tertium*, p. 44; Bacon, *Part of the Opus tertium*, p. 48.

89 See Bodleian Library, MS Rawlinson D 253, p. 50; British Library, MSS Add. 36674, fols 23, 58; Sloane 3824, fols 89–120; Sloane 3826, fol.97; Sloane 3848, fols 148, 157; Sloane 3849, fol.30; Sloane 3850, fols 23^v–25; Sloane 3851, fols 129–31^v; Sloane 3853, fol.54.

VII THE VAGARIES OF PATRONAGE, 1565–1583

1 The manuscript is Dee, *De trigono circinoque analogico. Opusculum mathematicum et mechanicum*, British Library, MS Cotton Vitellius C. VII, fols 270–3; the following fragment on incommensurables is fols 274–9^v and may be part of the same work.

2 Dee, *Parallaticae commentationis praxeosque nucleus quidam. CR*,25, and *LA*,76; also claims to have written in 1573 a *Hipparchus redivivus*, which may pertain to the star, and a *De stella admiranda in Cassiopeiae asterismo, coelitus demissa ad orbem usque Veneris, iterumque in coeli penetralia perpendiculariter retracta*, lib. 3, implying his conclusion about

its position and motion. Camden, *Annales rerum anglicarum*, pp. 231–3, 299–300, 315, mentions the work of Dee and Digges and quotes letters of Thomas Smith to Francis Walsingham reporting their conclusions. See Calder, 1:666–72; Johnson, *Astronomical Thought*, pp. 155–7; and Heilbron, 'Introduction', pp. 57–8. For Thomas Digges's work on the star, see Johnson and Larkey, 'Thomas Digges, the Copernican System', pp. 107–13.

3 Taylor, 'John Dee and the Nautical Triangle, 1575', pp. 319–25; Waters, *The Art of Navigation*, pp. 209–12, 525–6; Pepper, 'The Study of Thomas Harriot's Manuscripts: II', pp. 17–18, 21–3. Dee's table is 'Canon Gubernauticus'. This is most likely a model of the tables Dee (*CR*,25 and *LA*,74) indicates were to be part of *The British Complement of the perfect art of Navigation*, described as 'a great booke, in which are contained our Queene Elisabeth her tables gubernautik for longitudes and latitudes finding most easily and speedily'.

4 *Diary* (487), 26 February 1583.

5 Dee, *A Playne discourse*, Bodleian Library, MS Ashmole 1789, fols 3–32 (the treatise), and 36–41ᵛ (the 'Annus Reformationis'). Other copies are listed in the bibliography.

6 William Cecil, Lord Burghley, submitted Dee's proposal to three other mathematicians, Thomas Digges, Henry Savile, and a Mr Chambers, whose opinion was also favourable, and Francis Walsingham had the task of taking the issue to the bishops, who were not favourable. These documents are Bodleian Library, Corpus Christi College MS 254, fols 161ᵛ, 182–7ᵛ; British Library, MS Landsdown 39, art. 14; and British Library MS Add. 32092, fols 26–33. Although a proclamation of the reform was prepared on 28 April 1583 (*Calendar of State Papers, Domestic, 1581–1590*, p. 107), this was deferred, and a bill, introduced in Parliament in 1585, giving Elizabeth the authority to institute the reform also died. See also Calder, 1:724–34; 'Historical Notice', pp. 451–9; Read, *Mr. Secretary Walsingham*, 3:435, n. 1; Hoskin, 'The Reception of the Calendar', pp. 256–7; and Gingerich, 'The Civil Reception', pp. 269–71.

7 *Diary* (487), 12 July; 5, 7 September 1583.

8 Ibid., 10 June 1579.

9 Bodleian Library, MS Rawlinson D 241, fols 1–10.

10 Dee to Roger Edwards, 12 July 1580, British Library, MS Cotton Vitellius C. VII, fol.315.

11 British Library, MS Sloane 3188, fol.8; *Diary* (487), 9 October 1581; 27 January, 12 February, 6 March 1582.

12 British Library, MS Sloane 3188, fols 7ᵛ, 120.

13 *Diary* (487), 21 May 1581.

14 *Diary* (487), 18 October 1579; 22 June 1579; 29 September 1581; 20, 23 May 1582. On Bartholomew Hickman's later association with Dee, see *Diary* (487), 31 July 1591 to 29 September 1600, passim; and *T&FR*,*33–*45. In addition to Edward Kelley's clouded legal past, summarized in *DNB*, Dee mentions that Saul was indicted, but cleared, of some charge, and that Emery had been engaged in 'most

unhonest, hypocriticall, and devilish dealings and devises agaynst
me'.

15 Taylor, *Tudor Geography*, pp. 75–139; and French, p. 177; make Dee
the leading force in English expansion. Calder, 1:649–58, is more
cautious; and Quinn and Ryan, *England's Sea Empire*, pp. 19–45,
70–91, find it unnecessary to mention Dee at all.

16 Taylor, *Tudor Geography*, pp. 92–4, 97.

17 Quinn, *The Voyages*, 1:6–7; Taylor, *Tudor Geography*, p. 98; Andrews,
Trade, Plunder and Settlement, pp. 71, 167–8. The majority of Quinn's
volumes is the reproduction of much of the relevant documentation
relating to Gilbert's activities. Taylor also provides documentary
appendices.

18 Humphrey Gilbert, *A Discourse of a Discovery for a New Passage to Cataia*
(London, 1576), reprinted in Quinn, *The Voyages*, 1:129–64. See also
Quinn, *The Voyages*, 1:8–11; Taylor, *Tudor Geography*, p. 98.

19 *MP*,A.j, where he makes explicit reference to Gilbert's preparedness
to undertake a voyage only to be called away to deal with a rebellion
in Ireland. Quinn, *The Voyages*, 1:8–11, attributes the idea of
colonization to Gilbert. Quinn also suggests that Gilbert's colonial
ideas derive from discussions of colonization as part of the English
efforts to subdue Ireland, which he then extended to North America.
See Quinn, 'Sir Thomas Smith', pp. 543–60; Quinn, 'Ireland and
Sixteenth-Century European Expansion', p. 27; Quinn, *The
Elizabethans and the Irish*, pp. 106–13.

20 Dee, *General and Rare Memorials*, p. 2. Dee was writing this in 1576
and refers to the 'Atlanticall Discourses' as written 'almost ten yeres
sins', which dates it to the 1566–1568 period of Gilbert's proposals.

21 *CR*,26; *LA*,75; where he dates this *Synopsis* to 1565. This date is
certainly too early if this is the same as the 'Atlanticall Discourses',
but his recollection at this point in 1592 is likely to be less accurate
than it was in 1576. Either the *Synopsis* is a different work, or, if it
is the same, a date after 1566 is most likely. Cf. Yewbrey, 'John Dee',
pp. 42, 243–5. The 'Brytannicae Reipub. Synopsis: libris explicata
tribus. Synopseos Adumbratio a Joanne Dee. L. designata. A° 1570',
is British Library, MS Cotton Charter XIII, art. 39.

22 Sargent, *At the Court*, pp. 18–19.

23 Taylor, *Tudor Geography*, p. 107; Quinn, *The Voyages*, 1:29–30;
Andrews, *Trade, Plunder and Settlement*, pp. 168–9; Jones, *The Life of
Sir Martin Frobisher*, pp. 17–18; Thomson, *The North-West Passage*,
pp. 24–32.

24 Gilbert, *A Discourse*, in Quinn, *The Voyages*, 1:133; Dee, *General and
Rare Memorials*, p. 2.

25 Dee, *General and Rare Memorials*, pp. 2–3; Taylor, *Tudor Geography*,
pp. 107–9, 269–70; Andrews, *Trade, Plunder and Settlement*, p. 171.

26 *NA*,59–61; Dee, *General and Rare Memorials*, pp. 3–10, 56–8; Taylor,
Tudor Geography, p. 117; Gwyn, 'John Dee's *Art of Navigation*',
pp. 309–22.

27 *NA*,60–1; Cf. *CR*,25; *LA*,74.

28 *NA*,61; French, p. 183, suggests that it was suppressed 'possibly because it was politically dangerous', which evokes a conspiratorial aura in the absence of any evidence to that effect.

29 British Library, MS Cotton Vitellius C. VII, fols 25–267. This was fire damaged and lacks the first five chapters, which are referred to in Purchas, *Hakluytus Posthumus*, 1:93, 97, 105–6, 108–16. See also *NA*,61; *CR*,24–5; *LA*,74.

30 Dee, *Of Famous and Rich Discoveries*, British Library, MS Cotton Vitellius C. VII, passim, fols 249ᵛ–64ᵛ, for the British history and English territorial claims.

31 John Dee to Abraham Ortelius, 16 January 1577, in Ortelius, *Epistolae*, 1:157–60. *Diary* (487), 12 March 1577, records a meeting with Ortelius. For Dee, Mercator, and Hakluyt, see Taylor, 'A Letter Dated 1577 from Mercator', pp. 56–68; and Taylor, *Tudor Geography*, pp. 126–8, 130–4.

32 French, pp. 188–98; Williams, *Madoc*, pp. 34–5. On the subject of the British history in the Tudor period see Kendrick, *British Antiquity*, pp. 34–98; and on its function in Tudor ideology, see Yates, *Astraea*, pp. 38–59.

33 Read, *Walsingham*, 3:395; Quinn and Ryan, *England's Sea Empire*, pp. 81–6.

34 Howell, 'The Sidney Circle', pp. 31–3.

35 Read, *Walsingham*, 3:391–4; Quinn and Ryan, *England's Sea Empire*, pp. 31–5.

36 Quinn, *The Voyages*, 1:31; Taylor, *Tudor Geography*, p. 270.

37 Quinn, *The Voyages*, 1:32–5, 170–80; Andrews, *Trade, Plunder and Settlement*, pp. 186–7.

38 Quinn, *The Voyages*, 1:35–49, 188–94; Andrews, *Trade, Plunder and Settlement*, pp. 187–8.

39 Quinn, *The Voyages*, 1:199–200; Read, *Walsingham*, 3:398.

40 Howell, 'The Sidney Circle', pp. 31–4; McCoy, *Sir Philip Sidney*, pp. 1–2, 11–13.

41 Dee's drawing for the title page is Bodleian Library, MS Ashmole 1789, fol.50. Dee summarizes its meaning in *General and Rare Memorials*, p. 53.

42 Dee, *General and Rare Memorials*, p. 53.

43 Yates, *Astraea*, pp. 48–53; Trattner, 'God and Expansion', pp. 24–30.

44 These are 'Her Majesties title Royall to many forraine countrys, kingdomes, and provinces', 'written for her Majesties use, and by her Majesties commandment', of 1578; and 'De imperatoris nomine, authoritate, et potentia', 'dedicated to her Majestie' of 1579. See *CR*,25; *LA*,74. These no longer exist, but British Library, MS Cotton Augustus I, no. 1, has on the reverse of a map headed 'Ioannes Dee. Anno 1580' and a 'A brief Remembrance of sundry foreign Regions ... the lawful Title of our Soveraigne Lady Queen Elizabeth, for the due Clayme and iust discovery of the same disclosed'. *Diary* (487), 25–28 November 1577, records his discussion of these claims with Elizabeth and Walsingham; and

CR,18; and *Diary* (487), 3, 7 October 1580, records his discussion of the same with Elizabeth and Burghley. Despite the date on the map, Yewbrey, 'A Redated Manuscript of John Dee', pp. 249–53, argues on internal evidence that the 'Brief Remembrance' dates no later than May 1578. Thus it may reflect the ideas discussed with Elizabeth in November 1577 and later incorporated in 'Her Majesties title Royall', which she may have commissioned as a result of that meeting. On Dee's use of the Madoc legend, which he appears to have brought into currency, see Williams, *Madoc*, pp. 39–40, 55–64. A work Dee claims to have written in 1583, 'The Originals, and chiefe points, of our auncient Brytish Histories, discoursed upon, and examined', may also relate to his investigations on Elizabeth's titles; see *LA*,76.

45 Yewbrey, 'John Dee and the "Sidney Group"', pp. 228–31, 377, argues Dee's initiative in promoting his own political philosophy.

46 Sargent, *At the Court*, pp. 21, 46; Roberts, 'John Dee's Corrections', pp. 70–5.

47 Dee, *General and Rare Memorials*, p. 10.

48 *Diary* (487), 16 January 1577.

49 Osborn, *Young Philip Sidney*, p. 449.

50 Taylor, 'Master John Dee, Drake', pp. 125–30; Taylor, *Tudor Geography*, pp. 113–17; *Diary* (487), 22 January 1577.

51 *Diary* (487), 26 May 1577; 6 November 1577.

52 *Diary* (487), 22 November to 1 December 1577; Quinn, *The Voyages*, 1:32–5; Trattner, 'God and Expansion', p. 28.

53 *Diary* (487), 30 June 1578, indicates Dee was also discussing his ideas on Arthur's conquests and Elizabeth's titles with Daniel Rogers and Richard Hakluyt, Sr.

54 Thomson, *The North-West Passage*, pp. 33–43; Quinn and Ryan, *England's Sea Empire*, pp. 33–5; Andrews, *Trade, Plunder and Settlement*, pp. 173–4; Taylor, *Tudor Geography*, pp. 119–21; Sargent, *At the Court*, pp. 42–5; Read, *Walsingham*, 3:391–4. State Papers, Domestic, Elizabeth, PRO, SP 12/119, fols 76r/v, 79–83v; SP 12/123, fol.126.

55 The claim by Ward, 'Martin Frobisher and Dr. John Dee', pp. 453–5, that Dee accompanied Frobisher on the voyages and was, as an alchemist, the one who induced the search for gold, is wrong. Dee invested in but did not accompany any of Frobisher's voyages, and it was as one of the stockholders that he was appointed one of the commissioners responsible for overseeing the collection of unpaid subscriptions, the payment of the sailors, and the arrangements for assaying and refining the ore. See *Calendar of State Papers, Domestic 1547–1580*, p. 621.

56 Quinn, *The Voyages*, 1:49–50, 55–64; Quinn and Ryan, *England's Sea Empire*, pp. 39–43; Andrews, *Trade, Plunder and Settlement*, pp. 190–1.

57 Quinn, *England and the Discovery of America*, pp. 368–79; Read, *Walsingham*, 3:400–4; Merriman, 'Some Notes on the Treatment', pp. 480–500.

58 *Diary* (487), 16 July 1582, 1 November 1582; Quinn, *The Voyages*, 1:64.

59 *Diary* (487), 20 November 1580; Quinn, 'Simão Fernandes', pp. 8–9; Quinn, *England the the Discovery*, pp. 251–2; Quinn, *The Voyages*, 1:50–51; Taylor, *Tudor Geography*, p. 125. On the map based on Fernandes see 'The Gilbert Map of c. 1582–3', pp. 235–7; Bishop, 'The Lessons of the Gilbert Map', pp. 237–43. This is British Library, MS Cotton Roll XIII no. 48, and is the possible basis of Dee's map of 1580, British Library, MS Cotton Augustus, I no. 1. In 1580 Dee wrote a 'Atlantidis, vulgariter Indiae Occidentalis nominatae, emendatior descriptio', and in 1583 a 'Hemisphaerii Borealis Geographica atque Hydrographica descriptio' for use of English navigators along the coast of North America, which may be these maps. See *CR*,25–26; *LA*,76.

60 Quinn, *The Voyages*, 1:66–71.

61 *Diary* (487), 17 May 1580; Taylor, *Tudor Geography*, pp. 126–8; Andrews, *Trade, Plunder and Settlement*, pp. 72–5. Dee's instructions are 'Navigationis ad Cathayum per septentrionalia Scythiae et Tartariae litora delineatio Hydrographica: Arthuro Pitt et Carolo Jackmanno versus illas partes navigaturis in manus tradita', which he describes in *CR*,25; *LA*,76, and which are preserved in British Library, MS Landsdown 122, fol.30, and British Library, MS Cotton Ortho E. VIII, fol.77 (damaged).

62 *Diary* (487), 28 August 1580; 10 September 1580; Quinn, *The Voyages*, 1:52–3; Andrews, *Trade, Plunder and Settlement*, pp. 179–80.

63 *Diary* (487), 18 October 1579.

64 *Diary* (487), 23, 24 January 1583; 13 February 1583; 6 March 1583. Quinn, *The Voyages*, 1:96–9, 2:486–8; Taylor, *Tudor Geography*, pp. 137–9; Read, *Walsingham*, 3:404–10; Sargent, *At the Court*, p. 77; Thomson, *The North-West Passage*, p. 47. Among others, one of the purposes of the company was the conversion of the native peoples in discovered areas to Christianity, an evangelical interest on Dee's part that was already in evidence in 1581 when he claims to have written 'De modo Evangelii Jesu Christi publicandi, propagandi, stabiliendi inter Infideles Atlanticos'; see *CR*,26; *LA*,76.

65 Quinn, *The Voyages*, 1:99–100; 2:488–9.

66 Bodleian Library, MS Ashmole 337, fols 20–50ᵛ, is a notebook of horoscopes from 1564 through 1566, indicating astrological consultation, most of which was not nativities but horary questions. The *Diary* (487), passim, also has notes of the birth dates of numerous people, indicating that he also did nativities. Also noted in the *Diary* (487) are, the interpretation of a man's dreams on 11 February 1581; a student for dialling (time keeping) on 8 August 1579; and the arrival on 13 September 1580 of Benjamin Lok, son of the London merchant Michael Lok, who stayed until 31 August 1582, indicating that Dee took boarding students.

67 *Diary* (487), 17 September 1580, 18 April 1583.

68 Other accounts are *Acts of the Privy Council*, 1577–1578, pp. 309, 322, 326; *Calendar of State Papers, Spanish, 1568–1579*, p. 611.

69 *Diary* (487), 8, 16, 28, October; 4 November 1578 (consultations on Queen's health); 7 November through December 1578 (trip to Europe); November 1577 and October 1580 (Queen's title).

70 Dee to Lord Burghley, 3 October 1574, in Ellis, *Original Letters*, pp. 33–9.

71 Dee to William Camden, 7 August 1574, Bodleian Library, MS Ashmole 1788, fol.75.

72 Bacon, *Secretum secretorum*, pp. 36–7, 63–3.

73 On Dee's ancestry: Dee to William Camden, 7 August 1574, Bodleian Library, MS Ashmole 1788, fol.76; British Library, MSS Cotton Charter XIII, art. 38; Cotton Charter XIV, art. 1. Roger Bacon as David Dee: Dee, 'A Playne Discourse', Bodleian Library, MS Ashmole 179, art. 7, p. 55.

74 On Dee's and Elizabeth's shared ancestry: British Library, Cotton Charter XIV, art. 1. See also Williams, *Welsh Wizard*; Ashworth, 'The Sense of the Past', pp. 87–92.

75 Westman, 'The Astronomer's Role', pp. 122–5.

76 Dreyer, *Tycho Brahe*, pp. 93–102, 128–30.

77 *Diary* (487, 488), passim.

78 *Diary* (487), passim, on payments to his assistants.

79 Dee to William Camden, 7 August 1574, Bodleian Library, MS Ashmole 1788, fols 70–6; MacCaffrey, 'England: The Crown and the New Aristocracy', pp. 52–3.

80 Lilly, *Mr William Lilly's History*, p. 100, 'he was the most ambitious person living, and most desirous of Fame and Renown. . . .' Lilly does not appear to have known Dee himself and does not cite a specific source for this judgement, but he learned of Dee from Richard Napier who did know Dee, so his judgement may well reflect contemporary opinion.

81 *Diary* (487), 5 February 1578. Little is known of Dee's earlier marriage or marriages. Taylor, *Tudor Geography*, p. 75, found evidence that Dee was married first about 1565 to a Katherine Constable, a daughter of a London grocer. In his *Diary* (487), 16 March 1575, he mentions the death of a wife whose name and background are unknown. This may be the same Katherine Constable but was most probably a second marriage, the lack of any children before those of Jane Fromond pointing to rather brief marriages.

82 *Diary* (487), 16 July 1579, 17 September 1580, 10 June 1581, 18 April 1583.

83 Calder, 1:619–23; French, pp. 126–9. Other than Dee's own reports of various individuals at court, including the Marquess of Northampton, Blanch Perry, the Earl of Pembroke, Leicester, Dyer, and Sir Walter Ralegh, who sponsored him or requested favours for him from Elizabeth, there is little reliable evidence that Dee received any direct aristocratic patronage. Given Sir Philip Sidney's

less than flattering comment about Dee to Lanquet, Thomas Moffet's report that Sidney and Dyer studied chemistry with Dee should not be taken to indicate a close association between Sidney and Dee. See Osborn, *Young Philip Sidney*, pp. 146–7. Wood, *Athenae Oxonienses*, 2:542, includes Dee among those familiar with the Earl of Leicester and courted by Henry, the Earl of Northumberland, but Wood is quite late. The association of Dee with Leicester as his conjurer in *Leicester's Commonwealth* is easily more polemical than factual. See *A Copie of a Leter*, p. 80. The same holds for another polemic in which Dee may be the unnamed conjurer associated with Ralegh. See Strathmann, 'John Dee as Ralegh's "Conjurer"', pp. 365–72.

84 Stone, 'Social Mobility in England', pp. 16–55. A good introduction to the court is Loades, *The Tudor Court*.

85 Feingold, *The Mathematician's Apprenticeship*, pp. 190–6, 206, 210.

86 Gabriel Harvey, *Letter Book*, letter to Edmund Spenser, 1579, p. 71; Richard Harvey, *An astrological discourse*, p. 5.

87 *Diary* (487), 2 May, 19 June, 30 December, 1577; 28 April 1578; 18 October 1579; 30 June 1580; *MP*,A.j^v–A.iij; Dee to William Camden, 7 August 1574, Bodleian Library, MS Ashmole 1788, fols 70–6; *NA*,50–61; *LA*,71–83; Dee, *To the Kings most excellent Maiestie* (a petition to James I, that he be cleared of the slander that he has been a conjurer); Dee, *To the Honorable Assemblie of the Commons in the present Parlament* (a like petition).

88 *A Copie of a Leter*, p. 80; *NA*,51–3; *Diary* (487), 2 May 1577; 22 September, 20 October, 1580.

89 Campbell, 'Humphrey Duke of Gloucester', pp. 122–3, 125–6, 141–51.

90 Ibid., 124, 130, 151–5.

91 Feingold, *Mathematician's Apprenticeship*, p. 204; B. W. Beckingsale, *Burghley*, pp. 257–62; van Dorsten, 'Literary Patronage', p. 194; van Dorsten, 'Mr. Secretary Cecil', pp. 545–53; MacCaffrey, 'Place and Patronage', pp. 109, 112–14.

92 Dee's arms also appear in the initial 'D' beginning the *Mathematicall Praeface* of 1570, and in very elaborate form at the end of *LA* in 1599.

93 Roberts, 'John Dee's Corrections', pp. 70–5.

94 His works on Elizabeth's titles, which are no longer extant, are: *Her Majesties title Royall to many forraine countreys, kingdomes, and provinces*, 'written for her Majesties use, and by her Majesties commandment' (1578), and *De imperatoris nomine, authoritate, et potentia*, 'dedicated to her Majestie' (1579). Dedications inscribed on the calendar treatise are to Elizabeth and Burghley, Bodleian Library, MS Corpus Christi College 254, fols 163, 171; and MS Ashmole 1789, fol.35.

95 Dee to Burghley, in Ellis, *Original Letters*, pp. 35–7.

96 Thomas, *Religion and the Decline of Magic*, pp. 279–80, 292, 377.

97 Dee to Burghley, in Ellis, *Original Letters*, pp. 37–9.

98 Read, *Lord Burghley*, p. 410.

99 *Diary* (487), 3, 7, October 1580; Andrews, *Trade, Plunder and Settlement*, p. 11.
100 *Diary* (487), 10 October 1580, 2 November 1580.
101 Dee, *THALATTOCPATIA BPETTANIKH*, fol.12. This manuscript is dated 8 September 1597.
102 *Diary* (487), 18–20 June, November 18, 1577, records £117 in loans.
103 *Diary* (487), 9 March 1582; Dee, *Liber mysteriorum*, British Library, MS Sloane 3188, fol.7.
104 What is known of Kelley's background is summarized in Shumaker, 'John Dee's Conversations', pp. 25–6. Wood, *Athenae Oxonienses*, 1:639, reports without much conviction that he may at one time have been associated with Thomas Allen at Gloucester Hall, Oxford.
105 *Diary* (487), 10 November 1582.
106 Dee, *Libri mysteriorum*, British Library, MS Sloane 3188, fol.103^v.
107 Evans, *Rudolf II*, pp. 219–20; Osborn, *Young Philip Sidney*, pp. 112–13; Hubicki, 'Chemie und Alchemie', pp. 61–100, esp. p. 65.
108 In addition to Dee, Laski apparently sought out Thomas Allen, who declined an invitation to accompany him to Poland. See Wood, *Athenae Oxonienses*, 2:542; Watson, 'Thomas Allen', pp. 280–1.
109 *Diary* (487), 13 and 18 May 1583.
110 Dee, *Liber mysteriorum*, British Library, MS Sloane 3188, fols 107–8; *T&FR*, pp. 2–4, 17, 21–3. Sir Philip Sidney had eastern European contacts and was well aware of Laski's activities, and Walsingham also received a report on his background on the eve of his arrival in England. See Osborn, *Young Philip Sidney*, pp. 112–13, 398–403; Sir Henry Cobham (Brooke) to Walsingham, 11 May 1583, *Calendar of State Papers, Foreign, 1583 and Addenda*, p. 341.
111 *Diary* (487), 21 September 1583.

VIII THE MYSTICAL AND SUPERMETAPHYSICAL PHILOSOPHY

1 Calder, 1:739–833, devoted considerable space and careful attention to this material. Shumaker, 'John Dee's Conversations with Angels', pp. 15–52, is the only published scholarly attempt of which I am aware that attempts to deal with this material directly in its own right. Butler, *The Myth of the Magus*, pp. 160–72, and Butler, *Ritual Magic*, pp. 258–81, also deals with this material in a useful fashion.
2 A considerable amount of this material was published in 1659 by Meric Casaubon as *A True & Faithful Relation*. As this is generally more accessible than the manuscripts, I will cite this wherever possible. Casaubon's source is British Library, MS Cotton Appendix XLVI, in 2 volumes. Besides poor printing, Casaubon's edition does not scrupulously follow the manuscript, although the differences are generally minor. One British Library copy of the *T& FR*, shelf-mark 719. m. 12, has extensive annotations of these discrepancies made by William Shippen in 1683 based on a collation with the manuscript. Casaubon's edition begins only in May of

1583, the manuscript he used lacking the records from that point back to the earliest actions with Saul. These earlier records are British Library, MS Sloane 3188, which will be cited as the *Libri mysteriorum*. Casaubon's material must also be supplemented by the 'Praefatio latina in actionem primam ex 7'. It is one 'action' with a long preface by Dee, of which a translation has been published in Josten, 'An Unknown Chapter'.

3 These are the *Liber mysteriorum, sextus et sanctus*; and the *48 Claves angelicae*, the *Liber scientiae auxilij, & victoriae terrestris*, the *De heptarchia mystica*, the *Tabula bonorum angelorum*, and the *Fundamenta invocationum*.

4 *Diary* (487), 10 September, 9 December 1579; 13 January 1580; 8 March, 3 & 4 April 1581. It is impossible to cite the many works in Dee's library that present angels, spirits, and demons as real and accessible to human communication. An example of interest because it contains Dee's annotations of sections relating to spirits is Jamblichus, *Index eorum*, presently in the Folger Library. Dee was not alone among his contemporaries as is attested by other records of séances with spirits: British Library, MSS Add. 36674, fols 39, 58–9; Sloane 3884, fols 57ᵛ–61; Sloane 3853, fols 138–41; and Forman, *The Autobiography*, pp. 19–20. Also see Shumaker, 'John Dee's Conversations with Spirits', pp. 24–5; Thomas, *Religion and the Decline of Magic*, p. 229–30, 273, 559–62, 711.

5 Dee, 'Praefatio latina', pp. 225, 232–3, 235–6. See also Butler, *Ritual Magic*, pp. 259, 268.

6 Dee, *Libri mysteriorum*, British Library, MS Sloane 3188, fols 11ᵛ–3; and Dee, *T&FR*,158–9, are examples of citations.

7 Thomas, *Religion and the Decline of Magic*, pp. 248, 258.

8 Dee, *Libri mysteriorum*, British Museum, MS Sloane 3188, fol.5.

9 Walker, *Spiritual and Demonic Magic*, pp. 30–4, 92–5, 203–12.

10 Dee, *Libri mysteriorum*, British Library, MS Sloane 3188, fol.59ᵛ. This was most likely prearranged by Kelley since Dee only found it in the shadows between some books with Kelley's directions.

11 On catoptromancy see Delatte, *La catoptromancie*; much better than Theodore Besterman, *Crystalgazing*.

12 Tait, '"The Devils Looking-Glass"', p. 203.

13 Dee, *Libri mysteriorum*, British Library, MS Sloane 3188, fols 7, 9.

14 Ibid., fol.5; Dee, *De heptarchia mystica*, British Library, MS Sloane 3191, fol.45.

15 Dee, 'Praefatio Latina', pp. 226, 247.

16 Ibid., p. 227.

17 Dee, *Libri mysteriorum*, British Library, MS Sloane 3188, fol.7; cf. *T&FR*,231; and Dee, *De heptarchia mystica*, British Library, MS Sloane 3191, fol.45.

18 Dee, *Libri mysteriorum*, British Library, MS Sloane 3188, fol.9.

19 Ibid., fol.7.

20 Ibid., fols 79ᵛ–80.

21 Milik, *The Books of Enoch*, pp. v, 116–24.

22 Ibid., p. 125; Scholem, *Major Trends in Jewish Mysticism*, pp. 52, 67–70, 72.

23 Genesis, 5:22–24.

24 Bacon, *Secretum secretorum*, pp. 36–7, 62–3.

25 Postel, *De originibus*, pp. 13, 46–8, 54–67, all of which are sections underlined in Dee's copy in the Royal College of Physicians, London. Bouwsma, *Concordia Mundi*, pp. 13, 36, 61–2.

26 Dee, *Libri mysteriorum*, British Library, MS Sloane 3188, fol.25; Dee, *De heptarchia mystica*, British Library, MS Sloane 3191, fols 33–80^v.

27 Dee, *Libri mysteriorum*, British Library, MS Sloane 3188, fols 62^v, 63^v–4; Dee, *Liber mysteriorum sextus et sanctus*, British Library, MS Sloane 3189, fols 10–65.

28 Dee, *Liber mysteriorum sextus et sanctus*, British Library, MS Sloane 3189, fols 3–9; Dee, *48 Claves angelicae*, British Library, MS Sloane 3191, fols 3–13. For those inclined to seek the instruction of the angels, Laycock, *The Complete Enochian Dictionary*, attempts to provide instruction in the rudiments of this language.

29 Dee, *Liber scientiae auxilij et victoriae terrestris*, British Library, MS Sloane 3191, fols 15^v–31.

30 Dee, *Libri mysteriorum*, British Library, MS Sloane 3188, fols 8–14, 40, 45–8^v.

31 For some of these citations see Dee, *Libri mysteriorum*, British Library, MS Sloane 3188, fols 6, 11^v–3^v; *T&FR*,12.

32 Pico della Mirandola, *Apologia*, in his *Opera omnia*, fols 27^v–8; Yates, *GBHT*, pp. 95–6; Yates, *The Art of Memory*, pp. 188–90.

33 The *Clavicula Solomonis*, for example, covers good angels and their invocations as revealed to Solomon by the archangel Michael in addition to sections on evil spirits and planetary governors. See British Library, MS Sloane 1712, fols 1–37.

34 Some examples, although not identical, which illustrate the models Kelley had available are: *Ars notoria*, Bodleian Library, MS Ashmole 1515, fols 4–10; the *Book of King Solomon* (*Clavicula Solomonis*), British Library, MS Add. 36674, fols 1–20, which is found in numerous manuscripts; and *An excellent book of the Arte of Magic*, British Library, MS Add. 36674, fols 47^v–54^v, which was written in 1567 and is similar to the Dee material in being a sixteenth-century imitation of earlier exemplars.

35 Dee, *Libri mysteriorum*, British Library, MS Sloane 3188, fol.13^v; Thorndike, *A History of Magic*, 6:457–8; Peuchert, *Pansophie*, pp. 333–7.

36 Arbatel, *Of Magick*, pp. 179–217. I have not seen the original Basel edition. This translation contains only the 'Isagoge' and lacks certain preliminary material found in a sixteenth-century English manuscript translation, British Library, MS Sloane 3851, fols 6–50.

37 Dee, *Libri mysteriorum*, British Museum, MS Sloane 3188, fols 9^v–12^v, 30, 32^v–5^v. Casaubon, in his 'Preface', *T&FR*, sig.G.2, reports seeing the table in Cotton's library and includes an illustration of the designs

on the top at sigs.[*.3]+4ᵛ–[*.3]+5ʳ. On the wax disks see Dalton ['Notes on Dee's Wax Disks'], 380–3.

38 Dee, *Libri mysteriorum*, British Library, MS Sloane 3188, fols 62ᵛ–4, 70, 79ᵛ–80.

39 Scholem, *Jewish Mysticism*, pp. 208, 214–19.

40 Dee, Letter to Sir William Cecil, 16 February 1562, *Bibliographical and Historical Miscellanies*, pp. 6–11; *MP*,A.jᵛ–A.iij; Dee, Letter to Lord Burghley, 3 October 1574, Ellis, *Original Letters*, pp. 33–9; *NA*,62–3; *LA*,71–2.

41 *MP*,*.j, b.ij; Dee, *Libri mysteriorum*, British Library, MS Sloane 3188, fols 7, 9; Dee, *De heptarchia mystica*, British Library, MS Sloane 3191, fol.45; *T&FR*,231.

42 Cf. *MP*,*.j, b.ij.

43 Dee, 'Praefatio Latina', pp. 240–1.

44 Dee, Letter to Cecil, 1562, *Bibliographical and Historical Miscellanies*, p. 11.

45 Thomas, *Religion and the Decline of Magic*, pp. 78, 87, 327–8.

46 Ibid., pp. 27, 51–2, 89, 179, 636–8, 761–4.

47 Walker, *Spiritual and Demonic Magic*, pp. 36, 93–6; Thorndike, *A History of Magic*, 2:902–3.

48 Brann, 'The Shift from Mystical to Magical Theology', pp. 148–55; Zika, 'Reuchlin's *De verbo mirifico*', pp. 105–8, 115–20; Zika, 'Reuchlin and Erasmus', pp. 231–6, 242–3; Nauert, *Agrippa*, p. 262.

49 Zika, 'Reuchlin's *De verbo mirifico*', pp. 110–15; Zika, 'Reuchlin and Erasmus', pp. 244–5; Nauert, *Agrippa*, pp. 202, 214–20, 237, 265; Nauert, 'Magic and Skepticism', pp. 161–82; Spitz, 'Occultism and Despair of Reason', pp. 464–9; Zambelli, 'Cornelio Agrippa', pp. 109–14; Zambelli, '*Humanae Literae*', pp. 202–7; Zambelli, 'Agrippa von Nettesheim', pp. 273–7; Zambelli, 'Magic and Radical Reformation', pp. 84–7.

50 Zika, 'Reuchlin and Erasmus', p. 226.

51 Ibid., pp. 231–6, 241–3; Zika, 'Reuchlin's *De verbo mirifico*', p. 138.

52 Brann, 'Was Paracelsus a Disciple of Trithemius', pp. 76–8, 80; Arbatel, *Of Magick*, pp. 184–6, 196–8.

53 Shumaker, 'John Dee's Conversations', pp. 29–31. Of the growing literature on apocalyptic thought, prophecy, and millenarianism, both concerning its post-Reformation forms and functions and its sources in medieval traditions, see Christianson, *Reformers and Babylon*; Firth, *The Apocalyptic Tradition*; Patrides and Wittreich, *The Apocalypse*; Webster, *From Paracelsus to Newton*, pp. 15–47; Reeves, *The Influence of Prophecy*, pp. 96–125, 395–508; Reeves, *Joachim of Fiora*, pp. 83–165; Reeves, 'Some Popular Prophecies', pp. 107–34; and Cohn, *The Pursuit of the Millennium*.

54 Dee, 'Praefatio Latina', pp. 228, 230.

55 Ibid., p. 226.

56 He refers to Pico della Mirandola, 'Conclusiones de mathematicis secundum opinionem propriam' (no. 10), *Conclusiones*, p. 74. He gives no more specific reference to Joachim than to 'his books'. The

association of formal numbers with the prophecies of Joachim was a common element in the Renaissance idea of Joachim; see Reeves, *Joachim of Fiora*, pp. 90, 99, 150.

57 Reeves, *Joachim of Fiora*, pp. 84–5, 90.

58 Yates, *GBHT*, pp. 38–40; Jamblichus, *Index eorum*, fols 44ᵛ, 47, 127ᵛ, 128, 130ʳ/ᵛ, Dee's copy, Folger Library. On the essentially religious function of the Hermetic texts in Ficino's thought, see Copenhaver, 'Hermes Trismegistus, Proclus, and the Question of a Theory of Magic in the Renaissance'.

59 Reeves, *Joachim of Fiora*, pp. 121–4; Bouwsma, *Concordia Mundi*, passim.

60 Garin, *Astrology*, ch. 1, is good on the background on this theory and its fortune in the Renaissance; see also Aston, 'The Fiery Trigon Conjunction', pp. 161–6.

61 Dee's copy of Abū Ma'shar (Venice, 1515), signed and dated 1552, is Cambridge University Library, shelf-mark R.* 4. 23; of Trithemius (Frankfurt, 1545), signed, is Cambridge University Library, shelf-mark Dd.* 4. 5.; and of Leowitz (Lauingen, 1564), signed, annotated, and dated 1564, is Cambridge University Library, shelf-mark R.* 5. 21(E).

62 Dee, *A Playne Discourse*, Bodleian Library, Corpus Christi College MS 254, fol.163.

63 An interpretation most forcefully developed by Yewbrey, 'John Dee', pp. 27, 161, 183. See also Calder, 1:781–92.

64 Aston, 'The Fiery Trigon Conjunction', pp. 160–1, 166; Calder, 1:786–92.

65 See the annotations in Dee's copy of Leowitz, *De coniunctionibus magnis*, Cambridge University Library, shelf-mark R.* 5. 21.(E), passim; Evans, *Rudolf II*, p. 221.

66 Evans, *Rudolf II*, pp. 245–51, 275–84.

67 Ibid., pp. 203–4.

68 Yates, *GBHT*, pp. 179–80, 187–8.

69 Pucci, *Lettere, documenti e testimonianze*, 1:67–8, and 'Introduzione', 2:20; Firpo, 'John Dee', p. 50; Evans, *Rudolf II*, p. 102.

70 Firpo and Piattoli, 'Introduzione', Pucci, *Lettere, documenti e testimonianze*, 2:18–22; Firpo, 'John Dee', pp. 49–50; Eliav-Feldon, 'Secret Societies', pp. 139–59; Evans, *Rudolf II*, pp. 102–4.

71 Dee, 'Praefatio Latina', p. 231.

72 Pucci, *Lettere*, 1:67–70, and Firpo and Piattoli, 'Introduzione', 2:20–1; Firpo, 'John Dee', pp. 50–9; Dee, *T&FR*,409–17.

73 Dee, 'Praefatio Latina', pp. 227–30.

74 Dee, 'Praefatio Latina', pp. 230–4; *T&FR*,429–30; Firpo, 'John Dee', pp. 60–2; Evans, *Rudolf II*, p. 233.

75 Pucci, *Lettere*, 1:95–6; Firpo, 'John Dee', pp. 62–72. Pucci's intentions may have been quite sincere as part of a plan to carry the religious message of the angels to the Pope, but Dee and Kelley were clearly wise to stay clear of Italy.

76 On Rožmberk, see, Evans, *Rudolf II*, pp. 40, 65–6.

77 Dee, 'Praefatio Latina', pp. 227, 231–4.

78 Stephen Powle, Letter to Mr Secretary Walsingham, 8 April 1587; Stephen Powle, Letter to John Chamberlaine, 21 September 1587; Bodleian Library, MS Tanner 308, fols 67–8ᵛ, 53ᵛ–4; referring to the previous August, 1586; *T&FR*,429, 434, indicates that Kassel was one place Dee visited after he and Kelley had been expelled from Rudolf's domains.

79 Evans, *Rudolf II*, pp. 35–6, 54, 81–9, 96, 139.

80 Ibid., pp. 75–6, 233.

81 That this was the same mirror is indicated when *Diary* (488), 4 December 1588, mentions giving Kelley the mirror mentioned in the *Praeface* and esteemed by Elizabeth and Rudolf.

82 Westman, 'The Astronomer's Role', p. 122; Moran, 'Princes, Machines', pp. 209–28; Moran, 'German Prince Practitioners', pp. 253–74.

83 Evans, *Rudolf II*, p. 198.

84 Powle, Letters to Walsingham and Chamberlaine, Bodleian Library, MS Tanner 308, fols 67ᵛ–8, 53ᵛ–4; *T&FR*,247.

85 Moran, 'Science at the Court of Hesse-Kassel', pp. 32–4.

86 Evans, *Rudolf II*, pp. 40, 65–6.

87 *Diary* (488), 9 December 1586.

88 Evans, *Rudolf II*, p. 226.

89 Dee, Letter to Elizabeth, 10 November 1588, in Ellis, *Original Letters*, pp. 45–6; *Diary* (488), 1 & 3 June, 10 July, 1588; Sargent, *At the Court*, pp. 97, 103–4.

90 Strype, *Annals of the Reformation*, 3:131–6, 4:1–4; *List and Analysis of State Papers, Foreign, Elizabeth I*, 2:410–11, 414, 433, 3:457–8; Sargent, *At the Court*, pp. 105–7; Evans, *Rudolf II*, pp. 227–8.

91 *Diary* (488), 9 December 1589; 2 January, 18 April, 1590; *Diary* (487), 2 & 4 December 1590.

92 Roberts & Watson show that the story of the vandalism of his library by a 'mob' of local folk, which has become a stock episode of almost any account of Dee, is a myth.

93 I. D., *A Triple Almanacke for the yeere of our Lorde God 1591*, followed by I. D., *1591. A Prognostication for the same yeere* (London, n.d.), STC 435. The prefatory letters are dated April 1590.

94 Feingold, *The Mathematician's Apprenticeship*, pp. 136–7; *Diary* (487), 1590–1601, passim; Bodleian Library, MS Ashmole 1488, II, fol.21ᵛ.

95 Alchemical notes are Bodleian Library, MS Ashmole 1486, V. In a 1595 letter to Moritz of Hessen-Kassel, Dee emphasizes the difficulties of alchemy and warns Moritz against sophists who promise gold to princes. The relevant passage of the letter is in Moran, 'Privilege, Communication, and Chemistry', n.58.

96 These are the only séances from this period. See *Diary* (487), 29 September 1600, for the burning of Hickman's actions, and 1590–1601, passim, for his frequent relations with Hickman.

97 *Diary* (487), 3 May 1594; *T&FR*,*36–*8; Roberts & Watson.

98 See also Strathmann, 'John Dee as Ralegh's "Conjurer"', pp. 365–72, on one facet of his concern with his reputation.
99 *Diary* (487), 18 April, 26 May, 1595, 15 & 20 February, 1596, and passim; *Calendar of State Papers, Domestic, Elizabeth, 1595–1597*, p. 45; Dee, *THALATTOKPATIA BPITTANIKH* (1597), MS bound with Dee, *General and Rare Memorials*, British Library, shelf-mark C. 21. e. 12, fols 12–13. This is addressed to Edward Dyer and is a reiteration of his ideas on the British Empire, but its main intent is to complain of his situation in Manchester.

IX CONCLUSION

1 Tiryakian, 'Toward the Sociology of Esoteric Culture', p. 273; Westman, 'The Astronomer's Role', pp. 122, 133–4; Moran, 'German Prince-Practitioners', pp. 253, 267–72.
2 Eamon, 'Arcana Disclosed', pp. 134–5; Hutchison, 'What Happened to Occult Qualities', pp. 245–6, 249–50.
3 Gliozzi, 'Dalla magia naturale alla scienza', pp. 233–4; Anglo, 'Reginald Scot's *Discoverie of Witchcraft*', pp. 109–12; Rossi, *Francis Bacon*, pp. 18–19; Rossi, 'Hermeticism, Rationality, and the Scientific Revolution', pp. 255–6, 258–9, 262; Shapiro, *John Wilkins*, p. 54.

BIBLIOGRAPHY

A–JOHN DEE'S WRITINGS

The following is an attempt at a catalogue of Dee's extant writings. As such, it does not separate published and manuscript materials, but lists titles and items in chronological order. Writings with no determinate date have been listed separately, as are doubtful and spurious attributions. For each item all known manuscript locations and published editions are given.

Dated Writings

'A Supplication to Q. Mary . . . for the Recovery and Preservation of Ancient Writers and Monuments', 15 January 1556.
London, British Library, MS Cotton Vitellius C. VII, fol.310.
Oxford, Bodleian Library, MS Ashmole 1788, fols 80–2.
Oxford, Bodleian Library, MS Smith 96, art. 2.
Johannis Glastoniensis, *Chronica sive historia de rebus Glastoniensibus*. Edited by Thomas Hearn. 2 vols. Oxford, 1726. 2:490–2.
Dee, John. *Autobiographical Tracts*. Edited by James Crossley. Chetham Society, *Remains Historical and Literary of Lancaster and Chester Counties* 1 (1851): 46–7.
'Articles Concerning the Recovery and Preservation of the Ancient Monuments and Old Excellent Writers . . .', 15 January 1556.
Johannis Glastoniensis, *Chronica*, 2:493–5.
Dee, *Autobiographical Tracts*, pp.48–9.
'Epistola', 1556 [Prefatory Letter].
Field, John. *Ephemeris anni 1557*. London, 1556.
'Libri antiqui scripti quos habeo anno 1556'.
Oxford, Bodleian Library, Corpus Christi College MS 191, fols 77ᵛ–84.
Dee, John. *Lists of Manuscripts Formerly Owned by D. John Dee*. Edited by M. R. James. Supplement to the Transactions of the Bibliographical Society, 1. London, 1921.
Roberts, R. J. and Andrew G. Watson. *John Dee's Library Catalogue*. The Bibliographical Society, forthcoming.
'Authores Alchymici quos perlegi anno 1556, a mense Julij'.

Oxford, Bodleian Library, Corpus Christi College MS 191, fols 88ᵛ–90.
Dee, *Lists of Manuscripts*.
Roberts and Watson, *John Dee's Library Catalogue*.
'Canon Gubernauticus. An Arithmetical resolution of the Paradoxal
  Compass', 1556.
Oxford, Bodleian Library, MS Ashmole 242, fols 139–53.
Bourne, William. *A Regiment for the Sea, and other Writings on Navigation*.
  Edited by E. G. R. Taylor. Hakluyt Society, n.s. 121, pp.415–33.
  Cambridge, 1963.
Catalogue of books and manuscripts, 1557/59.
London, British Library, MS Add. 35213, fols 1–4.
Dee, *Lists of Manuscripts*.
Roberts and Watson, *John Dee's Library Catalogue*.
'Inventa Joannis Dee londinensis, circa illam coni recti atque rectanguli
  sectionem quae ab antiquis mathematicis parabola appelabatur,
  Martij 8, 1558' [De speculis comburentibus.]
London, British Library, MS Cotton Vitellius C. VII, fols 279–309.
Clagett, Marshall. *Archimedes in the Middle Ages*. Vol. 5.
  Quasi-Archimedean Geometry in the Thirteenth Century, pp.513–76.
  Philadelphia, 1984.
Propaedeumata aphoristica . . . de praestantioribus quibusdam naturae virtutibus.
  . . . London, 1558. Second edition. London, 1568.
Dee, John. 'Theoremata astronomica in recensione operis Joannis Dee
  Londonensis'. Milan, Bibliotheca Ambrosiana, MS S 97 supp.
Dee, John. *John Dee on Astronomy: 'Propaedeumata aphoristica' (1558 and
  1568), Latin and English*. Translated and Edited by Wayne
  Shumaker. Berkeley, 1978.
Additions to Recorde's *The Grounde of Artes*. 1561.
Recorde, Robert. *The Grounde of Artes: . . . now of late overtaken and
  augmented with new and necessary additions. I. D.* London, 1561.
  Reprinted. London, 1582, 1607, 1623, 1632, 1636, 1646, 1652, 1658,
  1662, 1668.
Letter to Sir William Cecil, 16 February 1562.
Philobiblion Society. *Bibliographical and Historical Miscellanies*, 1 (No. 12,
  1854):1–16.
Bailey, John E. 'John Dee and the *Steganographia* of Trithemius'. *Notes
  and Queries* 5th ser. 11 (May 1879):401–2.
'Epistola' to Federico Commandino, 1563.
Abu Bekr Muhammed ben Abdelbagi el-Bagdadi. *De superficierum
  divisionibus liber*. Edited by Federico Commandino. Pesaro, 1570.
Monas hieroglyphica. Antwerp, 1564. Frankfurt, 1591.
Florence, Bibliotheca Nazionale, Fondo Magliabechiano XVI 1 s. XVI
  65 misc. XVII.
Theatrum chemicum. Edited by Zetzner. Strasbourg, 1622. 2:191–230.
  Strasbourg, 1659. 2:178–215.
Le Monade hieroglyphique. Translated by Grillot de Givry. Paris, 1925.
  Reprinted. Milan, 1975.

The Hieroglyphic Monad. Translated by J. W. Hamilton-Jones. London, 1947. Reprinted. New York, 1975.

Josten, C. H. 'A Translation of John Dee's *Monas Hieroglyphica* (Antwerp, 1564), with an Introduction and Annotations'. *Ambix* 12 (1964):112–221.

Die Monas-Hieroglyphe. Edited by Agnes Klein. Interlaken, 1982.

The Hieroglyphic Monad. Edmonds, WA., 1986.

Horoscopes, 1564–66.

    Oxford, Bodleian Library, MS Ashmole 337, fols 20–57.

'De trigono, circino analogico', 1565.

    London, British Library, MS Cotton Vitellius C. VII, fols 268–78.

'Testamentum Johannis Dee Philosophi Summi ad Johannem Gwynn, transmissum 1568'.

    London, British Library, MS Harley 2407, art. 33.

    Oxford, Bodleian Library, MS Ashmole 1442, art. 1.

    Ashmole, Alias, ed. *Theatrum chemicum britannicum*, p.334. London, 1652.

Diary, 1540s–90s. [John Dee's 'diary' is comprised of entries he made in various ephemerides.]

    Oxford, Bodleian Library, MS Ashmole 423, fol.294. [Ashmole's extract of notes from Stöffler's Ephemerides.]

    Oxford, Bodleian Library, MS Ashmole 487. Stadius, Ioannes. *Ephemerides novae.* Cologne, 1570.

    Oxford, Bodleian Library, MS Ashmole 488. Maginus, Io. Antonius. *Ephemerides coelestium motuum.* Venice, 1582.

    Dee, John. *The Private Diary and Catalogue of his Library of Manuscripts.* Edited by James O. Halliwell. Royal Historical Society Publications, Camden Series, vol. 19. London, 1842. Reprinted. New York, 1968.

'Mathematicall Praeface' to Euclid, 1570.

    Euclid. *The Elements of Geometry of Euclid of Megara.* Translated by Henry Billingsley. London, 1570. Reprinted. London, 1651, 1661.

    Dee, John. *The Mathematicall Praeface to the Elements of Geometry of Euclid of Megara (1570).* Edited by Allen G. Debus. New York, 1975.

'Additions and Annotations' to Euclid, 1570.

    Euclid, *The Elements.* London, 1570.

    London, British Library, MS Sloane 15. [Copy from printed edition.]

Brytannicae Reipub. Synopsis: libris explicata tribus. Synopseos adumbratio a Joanne Dee. L. designata. A° 1570.

    London, British Library, MS Cotton Charter XIII, art.39.

Parallaticae commentationis praxeosque nucleus quidam. London, 1573.

Note to Burghley on the exchequer, 15 June 1573.

    London, British Library, MS Harley 94, art.3.

'Certaine verie rare observations of Chester: & some parts of Wales: . . .', 1574.

    London, British Library, MS Harley 473.

Letter to William Camden, 7 August 1574.

    Dublin, Trinity College, MS 392.

    London, British Library, MS Landsdown 19, fols 69–74.

Oxford, Bodleian Library, MS Ashmole 1788, fols 70–6.
Letter to Lord Burghley, 3 October 1574.
London, British Library, MS Landsdown 19, fols 81–3.
Halliwell-Philips, James O. ed. *A Collection of Letters Illustrative of the Progress of Science in England*, pp.13–18. London, 1841.
Ellis, Henry. *Original Letters of Eminent Literary Men of the Sixteenth, Seventeenth, and Eighteenth Centuries.* Camden Society Publications, 23:33–9. London, 1843.
'Correctiones e supplementa in Sigberti chronicon', 6 September 1576.
London, British Library, MS Cotton Vitellius C. IX, fols 2–55.
General and Rare Memorials Pertayning to the Perfect Art of Navigation. London 1577. Reprinted. The English Experience, no. 62. Amsterdam & New York, 1968.
Oxford, Bodleian Library, MS Ashmole 1789, fols 50–115.
Oxford, Bodleian Library, MS Douce, art. 3. Copy of printed edition by Dr Stephen Batman.
Dee, *Autobiographical Tracts*, pp.50–67. ['A Necessary Aduertisement']
Arber, Edward, ed. *An English Garner*, 2:61–70. London, 1879. Second edition, 6:45–54. Westminster, 1903. ['The Petty Navy Royal'.]
Hakluyt, Richard, ed. *The Texts and Versions of John de Plano Carpini.* London, 1903. [Selection on King Edgar's navigations.]
'Of Famous and Rich Discoveries', 1576.
London, British Museum, MS Cotton Vitellius C. VII, fols 25–267.
Johannis Glastoniensis, *Chronica*, 2:552–6. [Extracts]
Hakluyt, Richard, *Divers Voyages Touching the Discovery of America.* London, 1850. Pp.33–54. [Extracts]
Hakluyt, Richard, *The Principal Navigations, Voyages, Traffiques and Discoveries of the English Nation.* 12 vols. Glasgow, 1903–5. 2:159–81. [Extracts]
Purchas, Samuel, *Hakluytus Posthumus, or Purchas His Pilgrims.* 20 vols. Glasgow, 1905–7. 1:93, 97, 105–6, 108–16. [Summary of portions.]
Letter to a Radnorshire Cousin, 1577.
Dee, John. 'A Letter from Dr. John Dee to a Radnorshire Cousin, 1577'. Edited by F. Noble. *Transactions of the Radnorshire Society* 21 (1955):15–16.
'A brief Remembrance of sundry foreign Regions . . .', and Map, 1578/80.
London, British Library, MS Cotton Augustus I, vol.I, no. 1.
Map reproduced in Hakluyt, *The Principal Navigations*, 8:facing 486.
Notes on Drake's voyage.
London, British Library, MS Landsdown 122, art.4.
Correspondence with Roger Edwards, March–July, 1580.
London, British Library, MS Cotton Vitellius C. VII, fols 311–23.
Directions to Arthur Pitt and Charles Jackman for a voyage to Cathay, May 15/17, 1580.
London, British Library, MS Cotton Otho E. VIII, fols 77–9.
London, British Library, MS Landsdown 122, art.5.
Halliwell-Philips, *A Collection of Letters*, pp.20–1.

Diary of chemical experiments, 22 June 1581 to 6 October 1581.
  Oxford, Bodleian Library, MS Rawlinson D. 241.
'Mysteriorum libri', 1581–83. [Spiritual conferences at Mortlake]
  London, British Library, MS Sloane 3188.
  London, British Library, MS Sloane 3677.
  Oxford, Bodleian Library, MS Ashmole 1790, fols 34–56 [fragments].
'A Playne Discourse . . . concerning y needful reformation of ye vulgar
  kallender'. 25 March 1582.
  Oxford, Bodleian Library, MS Ashmole 1789, fols 1–40.
  Oxford, Bodleian Library, Corpus Christi College MS 254, fols 147–76.
  Oxford, Bodleian Library, MS Smith 35, art. 2.
  Oxford, Bodleian Library, MS Ashmole 179, art. 7.
Map for Humphrey Gilbert, 1582/83.
  London, British Library, MS Cotton Roll XIII No. 48.
Map of North America, 1583.
  Philadelphia, Free Library.
'Catalogus librorum bibliothecae (externae) Mortlacensis . . . 1583'.
  Cambridge, Trinity College, MS 0. 4. 20.
  London, British Library, MS Harley 1879, art. 5.
  Oxford, Bodleian Library, MS Ashmole 1142, fols 1–74.
  Oxford, Bodleian Library, MS Add. C. 194.
  Dee, *The Private Diary and the Catalogue of His Library of Manuscripts*.
  Dee, *Lists of Manuscripts*.
  Roberts and Watson, *John Dee's Library Catalogue*.
'Liber mysteriorum, sextus et sanctus', 1583 [Book of Enoch].
  London, British Library, MS Sloane 3189.
  London, British Library, MS Sloane 2575 [excerpts].
  London, British Library, MS Sloane 2599.
  London, British Library, MS Sloane 78 [excerpts].
  Oxford, Bodleian Library, MS Ashmole 422.
'Mysteriorum libri', 1583–1607. [Spiritual conferences from Mortlake to
  Bohemia.]
  London, British Library, MS Cotton Appendix XLVI.
  Dee, John. *A True and Faithful Relation of what passed for many yeers between
  Dr. John Dee and Some Spirits*. Edited by Meric Casaubon. London,
  1659. Reprinted. [A copy of this collated with British Library MS
  Cotton Appendix XLVI, Casaubon's source, is in London, British
  Library, shelf mark 719. m. 12.]
  Dee, John. *The Enochian Evocation of Dr. John Dee*. Edited and translated
  by Geoffrey James. Gillette, N.J., 1984. [Extracts]
Letter to Guillén de San Clemente, 28 September 1584.
  Dee, John. *A True and Faithful Relation*.
  San Clemente, Guillén de. *Correspondencia inedita*, pp.215–18. Edited by
  Margués de Ayerbe. Zaragosa, 1892.
'48 claves angelicae', 1584.
  London, British Library, MS Sloane 3191, art. 1.
  London, British Library, MS Sloane 3678, art. 1.
  Dee, *The Enochian Evocation*, pp.65–102.

BIBLIOGRAPHY

'Liber scientia auxilii, & victoriae', 1585.
  London, British Library, MS Sloane 3191, art. 2.
  London, British Library, MS Sloane 3678, art. 2.
  Dee, *The Enochian Evocation*, pp.103–16.
'Praefatio Latina in Actionem Primum ex 7 . . . 1586'.
  Oxford, Bodleian Library, MS Ashmole 1788, fols 37–60.
  Oxford, Bodleian Library, MS Ashmole 1790, art. 1.
  Josten, C. H. 'An Unknown Chapter in the Life of John Dee'. *Journal of the Warburg and Courtauld Institutes* 28 (1965):223–57.
'De heptarchia mystica', 'Tabula bonorum angelorum', 'Fundamenta invocationum', 1588.
  London, British Library, MS Sloane 3191, arts. 3–5.
  London, British Library, MS Sloane 3678, arts. 3–5.
  London, British Library, MS Add. 36674, fols 167–88.
  Oxford, Bodleian Library, MS Ashmole 1790, art. 2.
  Dee, John. *The Heptarchia Mystica of John Dee*. Edited by Robert Turner. Translated by Christopher Upton. Magnum Opus Hermetic Sourceworks 17. Edinburgh, 1983. Second enlarged edition. Wellingborough, 1986.
  Dee, *The Enochian Evocation*, pp.17–64, 117–77. [Extracts]
Letter to Edward Dyer, 1587.
  London, British Library, MS Harley 249, fol.95.
Letter to Elizabeth, 10 November 1588.
  London, British Library, MS Harley, 6986, art. 28.
  Ellis, *Original Letters*, pp.45–6.
Correspondence with Wilhelm of Hessen-Kassel, 1589.
  Marburg, Hessisches Staatsarchiv, 4A. 31. 39.
Letter to Elizabeth, 22 August 1589.
  London, British Library, MS Landsdown 61, fols 159–60.
Notes of household expenses, 22 January 1589 to October 1591.
  Oxford, Bodleian Library, MS Ashmole 337, art.3.
A Triple Almanacke for the yeere . . . 1591. London, 1590.
The Compendious Rehearsall of John Dee . . . made unto the two Honorable Commissioners . . . 1592.
  London, British Library, MS Cotton Vitellius C. VII, fols 1–13.
  Oxford, Bodleian Library, MS Ashmole 1788, fols 7–34.
  Oxford, Bodleian Library, MS Smith 96, art. 2.
  Glastoniensis. *Chronica*, 2:497–551.
  Dee, *Autobiographical Tracts*, pp.1–45.
A Letter, containing a most briefe discourse apologeticall . . . 1592. London, 1599.
  Another edition. London, 1603. Reprinted. The English Experience, no. 502. Amsterdam & New York, 1973.
  Dee, *A True & Faithful Relation*, sigs.I2ᵛ–K4ᵛ.
  Dee, *Autobiographical Tracts*, pp.69–84.
Letter to Camden, 22 May 1592.
  London, British Library, MS Cotton Julius Caesar V, fol.45.
Correspondence with John Stowe, December, 1592.
  London, British Library, MS Harley 374, fols 15–16.

307

Diary, 1595–1601.
　Dee, John. *Diary, for the Years 1595–1601, of Dr. John Dee, Warden of Manchester from 1595–1608*. Edited by John E. Bailey. Privately printed, 1880.
Letter to Moritz of Hessen-Kassel, 1595.
　Kassel, Murhardsche Bibliothek, 2° MS Chem 19, 1, fols 114–15.
　Moran, Bruce T., 'Privilege, Communication, and Chemiatry: The Hermetic-Alchemical Circle of Moritz of Hessen-Kassel', *Ambix* 32 (1985): n. 58. [Extract]
Letter to Camden, 17 October 1595.
　London, British Library, MS Cotton Julius Caesar III, fol.135.
Letter to Camden, 10 May 1596.
　London, British Library, MS Cotton Julius Caesar III, fol.136.
Letter to J. Caesar, 2 October 1596.
　London, British Library, MS Landsdown 158, fols 15–16.
'THALATTOKPATIA BPETTANIKH, sive de imperii brytannici Jurisdictione in mari'. 1597.
　London, British Library, MS Harley 249, fols 95–105.
　London, British Library, MS Royal 7 C. XVI, fols 158–65.
　Bound with Dee, *General and Rare Memorials*, London, British Library, shelf mark C. 21. e. 12.
'To the Kings most excellent maiestie'. London, 1604. [Broadside.]
　London, British Library, MS Landsdown 161, fol.178.
　Ellis, *Original Letters*, pp.47–8.
'To the Honorable Assemblie of the Commons in the Present Parliament'. London, 1604. [Broadside.]
Alchemical notes, 4 December 1607–21 January 1608.
　Oxford, Bodleian Library, MS Ashmole 1486, art. 5.

Undated Writings

On draining fens.
　Oxford, Bodleian Library, MS Ashmole 242, fols 156–4.
'Elegans et utilis libellus de arte mensurandi cum cercino et regula . . .'.
　London, British Library, MS Cotton Vitellius C. VII, fols 14–24.
'Epilogismus calculi diurnis planetarum, tum longitudinis, tum latitudinis'.
　London, British Library, MS Harley 588, art.14.
Geneology. Possibly 1570s because of the interest in this indicated in other writings at the time.
　London, British Library, MS Cotton Charter XIII, art. 39.
　London, British Library, MS Harley 5835, art. 2.
Geneology of Elizabeth and himself. Possibly 1570s because of the interest in this indicated in other writings at the time.
　London, British Library, MS Cotton Charter XIV, art. 1.
'Inventum Joannis Dee'. [Geometrical problems.]
　Oxford, Bodleian Library, Corpus Christi College MS 254, fols 188–90.

Notes on the soul. Before 1558. See Clulee, 'Astrology, Magic, and Optics', pp.650–2.
Oxford, Bodleian Library, MS Ashmole 337, fols 51–7.
Notes to Roger Bacon, *Epistola de secretis operibus artis et naturae, et de nullitate magiae.* Possibly 1558 or earlier because of his interest in Bacon's works at that time.
Bacon, Roger. *Epistola . . . de secretis operibus artis et naturae, et de nullitate magiae.* Hamburg, 1618.
Theatrum chemicum, 5:932–69. Edited by L. Zetzner. Strasbourg, 1622. Reprinted, Strasbourg, 1660.
Bibliotheca chemica curiosa, 1:616–26. Edited by Manget. Basel, 1702.
Deutsches theatrum chemicum. Edited by F. Roth-Scholtz. Nuremburg, 1732.
'A Table of Latitude . . . bearing from London'.
Oxford, Bodleian Library, MS Ashmole 174, art.16.
Treatise on fractions.
Oxford, Bodleian Library, MS Ashmole 242, fols 160–56.

Doubtful or Spurious Attributions

'Astrologie of Her Most Sacred and Illustrious Majestie Queene Elizabeth of Armada Renowne'. In Hippocrates Junior [pseud], *The Predicted Plague.* London, 1899. Pp.241–330.
El Hazzared [Abdul Alhazred]. *The Necronomicon or the Book of Dead Names.* Translated by John Dee. Antwerp, 1571. Reprinted St. Helier, 1978.
Tuba veneris. 1580.
London, Warburg Institute MS, shelf mark FBH.510.
Munich, Bayerische Staatsbibliothek, MS 27005.
The Rosie Crucian Secrets, their excellent method of making medicines of metals, also their lawes and mysteries.
London, British Library, MS Harley 6485.
Edited by E. J. Langford Garstin. Wellingborough, 1985.

B—PRINTED SOURCES

The following includes all published materials, other than writings of Dee, cited in the notes. A few items not cited dealing with Dee have been included because they are not in the bibliography to French, *John Dee,* or in Pritchard, *Alchemy,* which combined survey the extensive but not uniformly valuable literature on Dee. No attempt has been made to identify or to include surviving books owned by Dee as this will be done by R. J. Roberts in Roberts and Watson, *John Dee's Library Catalogue.*

Abū Ali Yahyā al-Khayyāt (Albohali). *De judiciis nativitatem liber vnus.* Nuremberg, 1546.
Acts of the Privy Council of England. Edited by J. R. Dasent. 32 vols. London, 1890–1907.

Agassi, Joseph, and Ian C. Jarvie. 'Magic and Rationality Again'. *British Journal of Sociology* 24 (1973):236–45.

Agrippa von Nettesheim, Henry Cornelius. *De occulta philosophia libri tres.* Cologne, 1533.

Alexander, Andreas. *Mathemalogium primae partis super novam et ueterem loycem Aristotelis.* Leipzig, 1504.

al-Kindī. *De radiis.* Edited by M. T. d'Alverny and F. Hudry. *Archives d'historie doctrinale et littéraire du moyen age* 41 (1974):139–260.

d'Alverny, M. T. 'Kindiana'. *Archives d'histoire doctrinale et littéraire du moyen age* 47 (1980):277–87.

d'Alverny, Marie-Therèse. 'La survivance de la magie antique'. In *Miscellanea Medievalia.* Vol. 1, *Antique und Orient*, edited by P. Wilpert, pp.154–78. Berlin, 1971.

Ambrosio, Teseo. *Introductio in chaldaicam linguam, syriacam, atque armenicam* . . . Pavia, 1539.

Andrews, Kenneth R. *Trade, Plunder and Settlement. Maritime Enterprise and the Genesis of the British Empire, 1480–1630.* Cambridge, 1984.

Anglo, Sydney. 'Reginald Scot's *Discoverie of Witchcraft*: Scepticism and Sadduceeism'. In Sidney Anglo, ed., *The Damned Art*, pp.106–39. London, 1977.

Arbatel [pseud]. *Of Magic.* In Agrippa of Nettesheim, Henry Cornelius [pseud]. *Fourth Book of Occult Philosophy.* Translated by Robert Turner. London, 1655.

Aristotle. *The Works of Aristotle.* Edited by David Ross. 12 vols. Oxford, 1908–1931.

Aristotle. *Analytica posteriora.* Translated by G. R. G. Mure. In idem, *The Works*, vol. 1.

Aristotle. *De anima.* Translated by A. J. Smith. In idem, *The Works*, vol. 3.

Aristotle. *De generatione animalium.* Translated by A. Platt. In idem, *The Works*, vol. 5.

Aristotle. *De generatione et corruptione.* Translated by H. H. Joachim. In idem, *The Works*, vol. 2.

Aristotle. *Meteorologica.* Translated by E. W. Webster. In idem, *The Works*, vol. 3.

Arnauld, Pierre. *Trois traitez de la philosophie naturelle.* . . . Paris, 1612.

Arnoldus de Villanova. *Opera.* Venice, 1527.

Arnoldus de Villanova. *Aphorismi de gradibus.* Edited by Michael R. McVaugh. Vol. 2 of idem. *Opera medica omnia.* Granada/Barcelona, 1975.

Arnold, Klaus. *Johannes Trithemius (1462–1516).* Würzburg, 1971.

Artephius [pseud]. *Clavis majoris sapientiae.* In *Theatrum chemicum*, 4:221–40. Strasburg, 1613–1622.

Artephius [pseud]. *Clavis majoris sapientiae.* In *Bibliotheca chemica curiosa*, 1:503–9. Edited by J. J. Manget. Geneva, 1702.

Ashworth, E. J. 'The *Libelli sophistarum* and the Use of Medieval Logic Texts at Oxford and Cambridge in the Early Sixteenth Century'. *Vivarium* 17 (1979):134–58.

Ashworth, Jr., William B. 'The Sense of the Past in English Scientific Thought of the Early 17th Century: The Impact of the Historical Revolution'. Ph.D. diss. University of Wisconsin, 1975.

Aston, Mrgaret E. 'The Fiery Trigon Conjunction: An Elizabethan Astrological Prediction'. *Isis* 61 (1970):159–87.

Aubrey, John. *Letters Written by Eminent Persons in the Seventeenth and Eighteenth Centuries*. 2 vols in 3. London, 1813.

Austin, Herbert Douglas. 'Accredited Citations in Ristoro d'Arezzo's "Composizione del mondo"'. *Studi Medievali* 4 (1913):334–82.

Austin, Herbert Douglas. 'Artephius-Orpheus'. *Speculum* 12 (1937):251–4.

Bacon, Roger. *Communia mathematica*. Edited by Robert Steele. In idem, *Opera hactenus inedita*, fasc. 16.

Bacon, Roger. *Epistola . . . de secretis operibus artis et naturae, et de nullitate magiae*. In idem, *Opera quaedam hactenus inedita*.

Bacon, Roger. *Letter Concerning the Marvelous Power of Art and of Nature and Concerning the Nullity of Magic*. Translated by Tenny L. Davis. Easton, 1923. Reprint. New York, 1982.

Bacon, Roger [pseud]. *The Mirror of Alchimy*. London, 1597.

Bacon, Roger. *Opera hactenus inedita*. Edited by Robert Steele. 16 fascicules. Oxford, 1909–1940.

Bacon, Roger. *Opera quaedam hactenus inedita*. Edited by J. S. Brewer. London, 1859.

Bacon, Roger. *The Opus Majus of Roger Bacon*. Edited by T. H. Bridges. 2 vols. Oxford, 1897. Reprint. Frankfurt/Main, 1964.

Bacon, Roger. *The Opus Majus*. Translated by Robert Belle Burke. 2 vols. New York, 1962.

Bacon, Roger. *Opus tertium*. In idem, *Opera quaedam hactenus inedita*.

Bacon, Roger. *Part of the Opus tertium of Roger Bacon*. Edited by A. G. Little. In British Society of Franciscan Studies. *Publications*. Vol. 4. Aberdeen, 1912.

Bacon, Roger. *Secretum secretorum cum glossis et notulis*. Edited by Robert Steele. In idem, *Opera hactenus inedita*, fasc. 5.

Bale, John. *Illustrium maioris britanniae scriptorum*. Wesel, 1548.

Bale, John. *Scriptorum illustrium maioris brytanniae . . . catalogus*. Basel, 1557.

Bartlett, Kenneth R. 'Worshipful Gentlemen of England: The Studio of Padua and the Education of the English Gentry in the Sixteenth Century', *Renaissance and Reformation* 18 (1982):235–48.

Baur, Ludwig. *Die Philosophie des Robert Grosseteste, Bichofs von Lincoln*. In *Beiträge zur Geschichte der Philosophie des Mittelalters*, 18 (1917): heft 4–6.

Beckingsale, B. W. *Burghley. Tudor Statesman, 1520–1598*. London, 1967.

Beer, Barrett L. *Northumberland. The Political career of John Dudley, Earl of Warwick and Duke of Northumberland*. Kent, 1973.

Behrendt, R. 'Abbot John Trithemius (1462–1516), Monk and Humanist'. *Revue Bénédictine* 84 (1974):212–29.

Besterman, Theodore. *Crystalgazing: A Study in the History, Distribution, Theory and Practice of Skrying*. London, 1924.

Birkenmajer, Aleksander. 'Etudes sur Witelo, II–III'. *Bulletin international de l'académie polonaise des sciences et lettres* année 1920, 354–60.

Bishop, R. P. 'Lessons of the Gilbert Map'. *The Geographical Journal* 72 (1928):237–43.

Blau, Joseph Leon. *The Christian Interpretation of the Cabala in the Renaissance.* New York, 1944.

Boas, Marie. *The Scientific Renaissance, 1450–1650.* New York, 1960.

Boethius. *De institutione arithmetica.* Edited by G. Friedlein. Leipzig, 1867.

Bonus, Peter. *The New Pearl of Great Price.* Translated by Arthur E. Waite. London, 1894.

Borellius, Petrus. *Bibliotheca chimica seu catalogus librorum philosophicorum hermeticorum.* Paris, 1654.

Bourne, William. *A Treatise on the Properties and Qualities of Glasses for Optical Purposes.* In *Rara mathematica,* edited by J. O. Halliwell-Philips. London, 1839.

Bouwsma, W. J. *Concordia mundi. The Career and Thought of Guillaume Postel, 1510–1581.* Cambridge, Mass., 1957.

Bowden, Mary Ellen. 'The Scientific Revolution in Astrology: The English Reformers, 1558–1686'. Ph.D. diss. Yale University, 1974.

Boyer, Carl B. *The Rainbow: From Myth to Mathematics.* New York, 1959.

Brann, Noel. *The Abbot Trithemius (1462–1516): The Renaissance of Monastic Humanism.* Studies in the History of Christian Thought, vol. 24. Leiden, 1981.

Brann, Noel. 'George Ripley and the Abbot Trithemius: An Inquiry into Contrasting Medical Attitudes'. *Ambix* 26 (1979):212–20.

Brann, Noel. 'Was Paracelsus a Disciple of Trithemius?' *Sixteenth Century Journal* 10 (1979):71–82.

Brann, Noel. 'The Shift from Mystical to Magical Theology in the Abbot Trithemius (1462–1516)'. In Western Michigan University Medieval Institute, *Studies in Medieval Culture* 11 (1977):147–59.

Burke, Peter. 'Languages and Anti-languages in Early Modern Italy'. *History Workshop* 11 (1981):24–32.

Burke, Peter. 'Witchcraft and Magic in Renaissance Italy: Gianfrancesco Pico and His *Strix*'. In Sydney Anglo, ed., *The Damned Art,* pp.32–52. London, 1977.

Burtt, Edwin Arthur. *The Metaphysical Foundations of Modern Science.* Revised edition. New York, 1924. Reprint. New York, 1954.

Butler, E. M. *The Myth of the Magus.* Cambridge, 1948.

Butler, E. M. *Ritual Magic.* Cambridge, 1949.

Calder, I. R. F. 'John Dee Studied as an English Neoplatonist'. 2 vols. Ph.D. diss. The Warburg Institute, London University, 1952.

Calendar of Patent Rolls, Edward VI, 1547–1553.

Calendar of State Papers, Domestic, Edward VI, Mary, Elizabeth, 1547–1580.

Calendar of State Papers, Domestic, Elizabeth, 1581–1590.

Calendar of State Papers, Domestic, Elizabeth, 1595–1597.

Calendar of State Papers, Foreign, Elizabeth, 1583 and Addenda.

Calendar of State Papers, Spanish, 1568–1579.

Campbell, Lily B. 'Humphrey Duke of Gloucester and Elianor Cobham His Wife in the *Mirror for Magistrates*'. *Huntington Library Bulletin* No. 5 (April, 1934):119–55.

Camden, William. *Annales rerum anglicarum, et hibernicarum regnante Elizabetha*. London, 1615.

Campanus of Novara. *Campanus of Novara and Medieval Planetary Theory: Theorica Planetarum*. Edited and Translated by Francis S. Benjamin, Jr. and G. J. Toomer. Madison, 1971.

Camporeale, Salvatore. 'Lorenzo Valla: the Transcending of Philosophy through Rhetoric'. Paper presented at the Colloquium on Renaissance Intellectual History, Humanities Center, The Johns Hopkins University, 28 February 1987.

Capp, Bernard. *Astrology and the Popular Press. English Almanacs, 1500–1800*. London, 1979.

Cardano, Girolamo. *Libelli quinque. Eiusdem . . . aphorismorum astronomicorm segmenta VII*. Nuremberg, 1547.

Cardano, Girolamo. *De rerum varietate*. In idem, *Opera omnia*, vol. 3. Lyon, 1662. Reprint. New York, 1967.

Caroti, Stefano. 'La critica contra l'astrologia di Nicole Oresme e la sua influenza nel Medioevo e nel Rinascimento'. *Atti della Accademia Nazionale dei Lincei. Classe di scienze morali, storich e filologiche. Memorie* ser. 8, 23 (1979):543–684.

Caroti, Stefano. 'Nicole Oresme, Claudio Celestino, Oronce Finé e i "mirabilia naturae"'. *Memorie Domenicane* 8–9 (1977–78):355–410.

Caroti, Stefano. 'Nicole Oresme, Quaestio contra divinatores horoscopios'. *Archives d'histoire doctrinale et littéraire du moyen age* 43 (1976):201–310.

Cassirer, Ernst. *Das Erkenntnisproblem in der Philosophie und Wissenschaft der Neueren Zeit*. 3d ed. 3 vols. Berlin, 1922–23. Reprint. Hildesheim, 1971.

Cassirer, Ernst. *The Individual and the Cosmos in Renaissance Philosophy*. Translated by Mario Domandi. New York, 1963.

Céard, Jean, *La nature et les prodiges. L'insolite au XVIe siècle en France*. Geneva, 1977.

Cheradame, Jean. *Alphabetum linguae sanctae, mystico intellectu refertum*. Paris, 1532.

Christianson, Paul. *Reformers and Babylon: English Apocalyptic Visions from the Reformation to the Eve of the Civil War*. Toronto, 1978.

Clagett, Marshall. 'Archimedes in the Later Middle Ages'. In Duane H. D. Roller, ed. *Perspectives in the History of Science and Technology*, pp.239–59. Norman, 1971.

Clagett, Marshall. *The Medieval Archimedes in the Renaissance, 1450–1565*. Vol. 3 of *Archimedes in the Middle Ages*. Philadelphia, 1978.

Clagett, Marshall. *Quasi-Archimedean Geometry in the Thirteenth Century*. Vol. 5 of *Archimedes in the Middle Ages*. Philadelphia, 1984.

Clagett, Marshall. *A Supplement on Medieval Latin Traditions of Conic Sections (1150–1566)*. Vol. 4 of *Archimedes in the Middle Ages*. Philadelphia, 1980.

Clair, Colin. 'Willem Silvius'. *The Library* 5th ser., 14 (1959):192–205.

Clulee, Nicholas H. 'Astrology, Magic, and Optics: Facets of John Dee's Early Natural Philosophy'. *Renaissance Quarterly* 30 (1977):632–80.

Clulee, Nicholas H. 'At the Crossroads of Magic and Science: John Dee's

Archemastrie'. In Brian Vickers, ed. *Occult and Scientific Mentalities in the Renaissance*, pp.57–71. Cambridge, 1984.

Clulee, Nicholas H. '"The Glas of Creation": Renaissance Mathematicism and Natural Philosophy in the Work of John Dee'. Ph.D. diss. University of Chicago, 1973.

Clulee, Nicholas H. 'John Dee's Mathematics and the Grading of Compound Qualities'. *Ambix* 18 (1971):178–211.

Cohen, Morris R. and I. E. Drabkin, eds. *A Source Book in Greek Science*. Cambridge, Mass., 1948.

Cohn, Norman. *Europe's Inner Demons*. New York, 1977.

Cohn, Norman. *The Pursuit of the Millenium*. London, 1970.

Collins, Arthur. *The Life of . . . William Cecil*. London, 1732.

Compagni, Vittoria Perrone. 'La magia cerimoniale del "Picatrix" nel Rinascimento'. *Atti dell'Accademia di scienze morali e politiche di Napoli* 88 (1977):279–330.

Compagni, Vittoria Perrone. 'Picatrix latinus: concezioni filosofico-religiose e prassi magica'. *Medioevo* 1 (1975):237–337.

Cooper, Charles Henry. 'John Dee'. In idem, *Athenae Cantabrigiensis*, II:497–510. Cambridge, 1861.

Copenhaver, Brian P. 'Hermes Trismegistus, Proclus, and the Question of a Theory of Magic in the Renaissance'. In Allen G. Debus and Ingrid Merkle, eds. *Intellectual History and the Occult in Early Modern Europe*. Forthcoming.

Copenhaver, Brian P. 'Scholastic Philosophy and Renaissance Magic in the *De vita* of Marsilio Ficino'. *Renaissance Quarterly* 37 (1984):523–54.

The Copie of a Leter Wryten by a Master of Arte of Cambridge . . . concerning . . . the Erle of Leycester and his friendes in England. N.p., 1584.

Cornford, F. M. 'Mysticism and Science in the Pythagorean Tradition'. *Classical Quarterly* 16 (1922):137–50; and 17 (1923):1–12.

Coudert, Alison. 'Some Theories of a Natural Language from the Renaissance to the Seventeenth Century'. In Albert Heinekamp and Dieter Mettler, eds. *Magia Naturalis und die Entstehung der Modernen Naturwissenshaften*, pp.56–113. Studia Leibnitiana, sonderheft 7. Wiesbaden, 1978.

Crombie, A. C. *Robert Grosseteste and the Origins of Experimental Science, 1100–1700*. Oxford, 1962.

Crosland, Maurice P. *Historical Studies in the Language of Chemistry*. London, 1962.

Culianu, Ioan Petru. 'Magia spirituale e magia demonica nel rinascimento'. *Revista di storia e letteratura religiosa* 17 (1981):360–408.

Cusanus, Nicolaus. *Idiota de sapientia, de mente, de staticis experimentis*. Edited by Ludwig Baur. In idem, *Opera omnia*. Edited by Ernst Hoffman. Vol 5. Leipzig, 1937.

Dales, R. C. 'Robert Grosseteste's Views on Astrology'. *Medieval Studies*, 29 (1967):357–63.

Dalton, O. M. [Notes on Dee's Wax Disks]. *Proceedings of the Society of Antiquaries, London*, 2d ser., 21 (1906–1907):380–3.

Dannenfeldt, Karl H. 'Hermetica Philosophica'. In F. Edward Cranz, ed.

Catalogus translationum et commentariorum, 1:137–56. Washington, D.C., 1960.

Deacon, Richard. *John Dee: Scientist, Geographer, Astrologer, and Secret Agent to Elizabeth I*. London, 1968.

Debus, Allen G. *The Chemical Philosophy: Paracelsian Science and Medicine in the 16th and 17th Centuries*. 2 vols. New York, 1977.

Debus, Allen G. 'Mathematics and Nature in the Chemical Texts of the Renaissance'. *Ambix*, 15 (1968):1–28.

Debus, Allen G., and Ingrid Merkle, eds. *Intellectual History and the Occult in Early Modern Europe*. Forthcoming.

Delatte, Armand. *La catoptromancie grecque et ses dérivés*. Bibliothèque de la Faculté de Philosophie et Lettres de l'Université de Liége, fasc. 48. Liege/Paris, 1932.

della Porta, Giambattista. *Magia naturalis, sive de miraculis rerum naturalium libri IIII*. Naples, 1558.

de Smet, Antoine. 'John Dee et sa place dans l'histoire de la cartographie'. In Hellen Wallis, ed. *My Head is a Map: Essays and Memoirs in Honor of R. V. Tooley*, pp.107–13. London, 1973.

Dewar, Mary. *Sir Thomas Smith, A Tudor Intellectual in Office*. London, 1964.

van Dorsten, Jan. 'Literary Patronage in Elizabethan England: The Early Phase'. In Guy Fitch Lytle and Stephen Orgel, eds. *Patronage in the Renaissance*, pp.191–206. Princeton, 1982.

van Dorsten, Jan. *The Radical Arts. First Decade of an Elizabethan Renaissance*. Leiden, 1970.

van Dorsten, Jan. 'Mr. Secretary Cecil, Patron of Letters'. *English Studies*, 50 (1969):545–53.

Drake, Stillman, and I. E. Drabkin, eds. and trans. *Mechanics in Sixteenth-Century Italy*. Madison, 1969.

Dreyer, J. L. E. *A History of Astronomy from Thales to Kepler*. 2d ed. New York, 1953.

Dreyer, J. L. E. *Tycho Brahe*. New York, 1963.

Dupèbe, Jean. 'Curiosité et magie chez Johannes Trithemius'. In Jean Céard, ed., *La curiosité à la Renaissance*, pp.71–98. Paris, 1986.

van Durme, M. ed. *Correspondence Mercatorienne*. Anvers, 1959.

Duveen, Denis I. *Bibliotheca Alchemica et Chemica*. London, 1949.

Eamon, William. 'Arcana Disclosed: The Advent of Printing, the Books of Secrets, and the Development of Experimental Science in the Sixteenth Century'. *History of Science* 22 (1984):111–50.

Eamon, William. 'Books of Secrets and the Empirical Foundations of English Natural Philosophy, 1550–1660'. Ph.D. thesis. University of Kansas, 1977.

Easton, Joy B. 'John Dee'. In *Dictionary of Scientific Biography*, 4:5–6.

Easton, Joy B. 'The Early Editions of Robert Recorde's *Ground of Arts*'. *Isis* 58 (1967):515–32.

Easton, Stewart C. *Roger Bacon and His Search for a Universal Science*. New York, 1952.

Eastwood, Bruce S. '"The Chaster Path of Venus" (orbis Veneris castior) in the Astronomy of Martianus Capella'. *Archives Internationales d'Histoire des Sciences* 32 (1982):145–58.

Eastwood, Bruce S. 'Grosseteste's "Quantitative" Law of Refraction: A Chapter in the History of Non-experimental Science'. *Journal of the History of Ideas* 28 (1967):403–14.

Eastwood, Bruce S. 'Medieval Empiricism: The Case of Grosseteste's Optics'. *Speculum* 43 (1968):306–21.

Eastwood, Bruce S. 'Metaphysical Derivations of a Law of Refraction: Damianos and Grosseteste'. *Archive for History of Exact Sciences* 6 (1970):224–36.

Eastwood, Bruce S. 'Robert Grosseteste's Theory of the Rainbow'. *Archives Internationales d'Histoire des Sciences* 19 (1966):313–32.

'Edward Kelley'. *Dictionary of National Biography*, 10:1230–2.

Elias Levita. *Composita verborum et nominum hebraicorum*. Basel, 1525.

Eliav-Feldon, Miriam. 'Secret Societies, Utopias, and Peace Plans: The Case of Francesco Pucci'. *The Journal of Medieval and Renaissance Studies* 14 (1984):139–58.

Euclid. *Evclidis elementorum libri XV*. Paris, 1557.

Euclid. *Optica & catoptrica*. Greek with Latin translation by Joannes Pena. Paris, 1557.

Evans, R. J. W. *The Making of the Habsburg Monarchy, 1550–1700. An Interpretation*. Oxford. 1979.

Evans, R. J. W. *Rudolf II and His World. A Study in Intellectual History, 1576–1612*. New York, 1973.

Fahd, Toufic. *La divination arabe. Etudes religieuses, sociologiques et folkloriques sur le milieu natif de l'Islam*. Leiden, 1966.

Federici–Vescovini, Graziella. *Studi sulla prospettiva medievale*. Università di Torino Pubblicazioni della Facoltà di Lettere e Filosofia, 16, 1. Turin, 1965.

Feingold, Mordechai. *The Mathematician's Apprenticeship. Science, Universities, and Society in England, 1560–1640*. Cambridge, 1984.

Feingold, Mordechai. 'The Occult Tradition in the English Universities of the Renaissance: A Reassessment'. In Brian Vickers, ed. *Occult and Scientific Mentalities in the Renaissance*, pp.73–94. Cambridge, 1984.

Ferguson, John. *Bibliotheca chemica*. 2 vols. London, 1906.

Festugière, A. J. *La révélation d'Hermès Trismégiste*. 4 vols. Paris, 1944–54.

Fichtner, Paula Sutter. *Ferdinand I of Austria: The Politics of Dynasticism in the Age of the Reformation*. New York, 1982.

Field, Judith V. 'A Lutheran Astrologer: Johannes Kepler'. *Archive for History of Exact Sciences* 31 (1984):189–272.

Finé, Oronce. *De speculo ustorio*. Paris, 1551.

Firpo, Luigi. 'John Dee, scienzato, negromante, e avventuriero'. *Rinascimento* 3 (1952):25–84.

Firth, Katherine R. *The Apocalyptic Tradition in Reformation Britain, 1530–1645*. New York, 1979.

Fletcher, John M. 'Change and Resistance to Change: A Consideration of the Development of English and German Universities during the Sixteenth Century'. *History of Universities* 1 (1981):1–36.

Forcellini, Aegidii. *Totius latinitatis lexicon*. Padua, 1773.

Forman, Simon. *The Autobiography and Personal Diary . . . from 1552–1602*. Edited by J. O. Halliwell. London, 1849.

Foucault, Michel. *The Order of Things. An Archaeology of the Human Sciences*. New York, 1973.

Foxe, John. *Acts and Monuments*. Edited by George Townsend. 8 vols. Reprint. New York, 1965.

French, Peter J. *John Dee: The World of an Elizabethan Magus*. London, 1972.

Garin, Eugenio. 'Ancora sull'ermetismo'. *Revista critica di storia della filosophia* 32 (1977):342–7.

Garin, Eugenio. *Astrology in the Renaissance: The Zodiac of Life*. Translated by Carolyn Jackson and June Allen, revised by Clare Robertson. London, 1983.

Garin, Eugenio. 'Considerazioni sulla magia'. In idem, *Medioevo e Rinascimento*, pp.170–91. Bari, 1954.

Garin, Eugenio. 'Divagazioni ermetiche'. *Revista critica di storia della filosophia* 31 (1976):462–6.

Garin, Eugenio. 'Magic and Astrology in the Civilization of the Renaissance'. In idem, *Science and Civic Life in the Italian Renaissance*, trans. by Peter Munz, pp.146–65. New York, 1969.

Garin, Eugenio. 'Un manuale di magia: *Picatrix*'. In idem, *L'etá nuova: ricerche di storia della cultura del XII al XVI secolo*, pp.387–419. Naples, 1969.

Geertz, Hildred. 'An Anthropology of Religion and Magic, I'. *Journal of Interdisciplinary History* 6 (1975):71–89.

Geber. *The Works of Geber*. Translated by Richard Russell. London, 1928.

Gent, Lucy. *Picture and Poetry, 1560–1620*. Leamington Spa, 1981.

Gilbert, Humphry. *A Discourse of a Discovery for a New Passage to Cataia*. London, 1576.

'The Gilbert Map of 1582–3'. *The Geographical Journal* 72 (1926):235–7.

Gingerich, Owen. 'The Civil Reception of the Gregorian Calendar'. In G. V. Coyne, M. A. Hoskin, and O. Pedersen, eds., *Gregorian Reform of the Calendar: Proceedings of the Vatican Conference to Commemorate its 400th Anniversary, 1582–1982*, pp.265–79. Città del Vaticano, 1983.

Gliozzi, Mario. 'Dalla magia naturale all scienza'. *Cultura Scuola* 7 no. 28 (1968): 232–6.

Gohory, Jacques. *De vsu & mysteriis notarum liber*. Paris, 1550.

Goichon, A.-M. *Lexique de la langue philosophique d'Ibn Sīnā (Avicenna)*. Paris, 1938.

Goltz, Dietlinde. 'Versuch einer Grenzziehung zwischen "Chemie" und "Alchemie"'. *Sudhoffs Archiv für Geschichte der Medizin und der Naturwissenschaften* 52 (1968):30–47.

Grant, Robert M. *Gnosticism and Early Christianity*. Revised ed. New York, 1966.

Grignaschi, Mario. 'La diffusion du "Secretum Secretorum" (Sirr al-Asrār) dans l'Europe Occidentale'. *Archives d'histoire doctrinale et littéraire du moyen age* 47 (1980):7–70.

Grignaschi, Mario. 'L'origine et les métamorphoses du "Sirr al asrār"'. *Archives d'histoire doctrinale et littéraire du moyen age* 43 (1976):7–112.

Grignaschi, Mario. 'Remarques sur la formation et l'interprétation du *SIRR AL-'ASRĀR*'. In W. F. Ryan and Charles B. Schmitt, eds., *Pseudo-Aristotle, The 'Secret of Secrets': Sources and Influences*, pp.3–33. London, 1982.

Grillot de Givry, Emile A. *La musée des sorciers*. Paris, 1929.

Grosseteste, Robert. *Concerning Lines, Angles, and Figures*. Translated by David C. Lindberg, in Edward Grant, ed., *A Source Book in Medieval Science*, pp.385–8. Cambridge, Mass., 1974.

Grosseteste, Robert. *De impressionibus aeris (de prognosticatione)*. In idem, *Die philosophischen Werke des Robert Grosseteste*, Edited by Ludwig Baur. *Beiträge zur Geschichte der Philosophie des Mittelalters* 9 (1912):41–51.

Grosseteste, Robert. *De impressionibus elementorum*. In idem, *Die philosophischen Werke*, pp.87–9.

Grosseteste, Robert. *On Light*. Translated by Clare C. Riedl. Milwaukee, 1942.

Grosseteste, Robert. *On Light*. Translated by C. F. Terrell. *Paideuma* 2, no. 3 (1973):455–62.

Gunther, R. T. 'The Astrolabe of Queen Elizabeth'. *Archaeologia* 86 (1936):65–72.

Gwyn, David. 'John Dee's *Art of Navigation*'. *The Book Collector* 34 (1985): 309–22.

Hackett, M. B. *The Original Statutes of Cambridge University*. Cambridge, 1970.

Hall, A. Rupert. 'Magic, Metaphysics and Mysticism in the Scientific Revolution'. In M. L. Righini Bonelli and William R. Shea, eds. *Reason, Experiment, and Mysticism in the Scientific Revolution*, pp.275–82. New York, 1975.

Hammond, Dorothy. 'Magic: A Problem in Semantics'. *American Anthropologist* 72 (1970):1349–56.

Hannaway, Owen. *The Chemists and the Word. The Didactic Origins of Chemistry*. Baltimore, 1975.

Hansen, Bert. 'John Dee and Applied Mathematics in Elizabethan England'. Paper presented at the American Historical Association Annual Meeting, December 29, 1981.

Hansen, Bert. *Nicole Oresme and the Marvels of Nature*. A Study of his *De causis mirabilium* with Critical Edition, Translation, and Commentary. Toronto, 1985.

Hansen, Bert. 'Science and Magic'. In David C. Lindberg, ed., *Science in the Middle Ages*, pp.483–506. Chicago, 1978.

Harvey, Gabriel. *Letter Book of Gabriel Harvey, A.D. 1573–1580*. Edited by E. J. L. Scott. Camden Society Publications no. 22. London, 1884.

Harvey, Richard. *An Astrological Discourse*. London, 1583.

Hedwig, Klaus. *Sphaera lucis: Studien zur Intelligibilität des Seinden im Kontext der mittelalterlichen Lichtspekulation. Beiträge zur Geschichte der Philosophie und Theologie des Mittelalters* Neue Folge Bd. 18. Münster, 1980.

Heiberg, J. L. and E. Wiedemann. 'Ibn al-Haiṯams Schrift über parabolische Hohlspiegel', *Bibliotheca Mathematica* 3rd ser., 10 (1910):201–37.

Heilbron, J. L. 'Introductory Essay'. In John Dee, *John Dee on Astronomy*, edited by Wayne Shumaker, pp.1–99. Berkeley, 1978.

Heninger, Jr., S. K. *Touches of Sweet Harmony. Pythagorean Cosmology and Renaissance Poetics*. San Marino, 1974.

Hermes. *The Learned Work of Hermes Trismegistus Intituled: Iatromathematica*. Translated by John Harvey. London, 1583.

Hermes. *IATPΘMAOHMATIKA*. In Julius Ludwig Ideler, ed., *Physici et Medici Graeci Minores*, vol. I. 2 vols. Berlin, 1841.

Hesse, Mary. 'Hermeticism and Historiography: An Apology for the Internal History of Science'. In Roger H. Stuewer, ed., *Historical and Philosophical Perspectives of Science*, pp.134–62. Minneapolis, 1970.

Hippocrates. *Breaths*. In Hippocrates, *Works*, translated by W. H. S. Jones, vol. II. London, 1923.

'Historical Notice of the Attempt Made by the English Government to Rectify the Calendar, A. D. 1584–1585'. *The Gentleman's Magazine* n.s. 36 (1851):451–9.

Hoak, Dale. 'Rehabilitating the Duke of Northumberland: Politics and Political Control, 1549–1553'. In Robert Tittler and Jennifer Loach, eds., *The Mid-Tudor Polity, 1540–1560*, pp.29–51. Totowa, 1980.

Hoffmann, Ann. 'John Dee'. In idem, *Lives of the Tudor Age, 1485–1603*, pp.123–5. New York, 1977.

Holmyard, E. J. *Alchemy*. Baltimore, 1957.

Holmyard, E. J. 'Introduction'. In Geber. *The Works of Geber*. Translated by Richard Russell. London, 1928.

Hoskin, Michael A. 'The Reception of the Calendar by Other Churches'. In G. V. Coyne, M. A. Hoskin, and O. Pedersen, eds., *Gregorian Reform of the Calendar: Proceedings of the Vatican Conference to Commemorate its 400th Anniversary, 1582–1982*, pp.255–64. Città del Vaticano, 1983.

Howell, Jr., Roger. 'The Sidney Circle and the Protestant Cause in Elizabethan Foreign Policy'. *Renaissance and Modern Studies* 19 (1975): 31–46.

Hubicki, W. 'Chemie und Alchemie des 16. Jahrhunderts in Polen'. *Annales Universitatis Mariae Curie-Skladowska. Sectio AA, Physica et Chemica* 10 (1955):61–100. Lublin, 1957.

Hudson, Winthrop S. *The Cambridge Connection and the Elizabethan Settlement of 1559*. Durham, 1980.

Huppert, George. '*Divinatio et Eruditio*: Thoughts on Foucault'. *History and Theory* 13 (1974):191–207.

Hutchison, Keith. 'What Happened to Occult Qualities in the Scientific Revolution'. *Isis* 73 (1982):233–53.

Ibn Sīnā (Avicenna). *De divisione scientiarum*. In idem, *Compendium de anima*, translated and edited by Andrea Alpago. Venice, 1546. Reprint, Farnborough, 1969.

Idel, Moshe. 'The Magical and Neoplatonic Interpretation of the Kabbala in the Renaissance'. In Bernard Dov Cooperman, *Jewish Thought in the Sixteenth Century*, pp.186–242. Cambridge, Mass., 1983.

319

Ioannes Hispalensis. *Epitome totius astrologiae*. Nuremburg, 1548.

Iskander, Albert Z. 'Ibn Sīnā'. In *Dictionary of Scientific Biography*, XV: 494–501.

Jagow, Gebhard von, ed. *Die naturphilosophischen, ausführlich konnentierten Aphorismen des Magister Urso von Calabrien aus der medizinischen Schule von Salerno*. Leipzig, 1924.

Jamblichus et al. *Index eorum quae in hoc libro habentur. Jamblichus de mysteriis Aegyptiorum, Chaldaeorum, Assyriorum . . .* Venice, 1516.

James, M. R. *A Descriptive Catalogue of the Manuscripts in the Library of Peterhouse*. Cambridge, 1899.

Jardine, Lisa. 'Humanism and Dialectic in Sixteenth-Century Cambridge: a Preliminary Investigation'. In R. R. Bolgar, ed., *Classical Influences on European Culture, A.D. 1500–1700*, pp.141–54. Cambridge, 1976.

Jardine, Lisa. 'Humanism and the Sixteenth-Century Cambridge Arts Course'. *History of Education* 4 (1975): 16–31.

Jardine, Lisa. 'Lorenzo Valla and the Intellectual Origins of Humanist Dialectic'. *Journal of the History of Philosophy* 15 (1977):143–64.

Jardine, Lisa. 'The Place of Dialectic Teaching in Sixteenth-Century Cambridge'. *Studies in the Renaissance* 21 (1974):31–62.

Jarvie, I. C. and J. Agassi. 'The Problem of the Rationality of Magic'. *British Journal of Sociology* 18 (1967):55–74. Reprinted in Bryan R. Wilson, ed., *Rationality*, pp.172–93. Oxford, 1970.

Jarvie, I. C. and J. Agassi. 'Magic and Rationality Again', *British Journal of Sociology*, 24 (1973):236–45.

Jesi, Furio. 'John Dee e il suo sapere'. *Comunità* no. 166 (April 1972):272–303.

Johannet, Renée. 'La vie mouvementée d'un astrologue'. *Revue de Paris* 5 (1932):909–29.

'John Dee'. *Dictionary of National Biography*, 5:720–29.

Johnson, Francis R. *Astronomical Thought in Renaissance England. A Study of the English Scientific Writings from 1500 to 1645*. Baltimore, 1937.

Johnson, Francis R. and Sanford V. Larkey. 'Thomas Digges, the Copernican System, and the Idea of the Infinity of the Universe in 1576'. *Huntington Library Bulletin* 5 (April, 1934):69–117.

Jones, Frank. *The Life of Martin Frobisher*. London, 1878.

Jones, Gareth Lloyd. *The Discovery of Hebrew in Tudor England: A Third Language*. Manchester, 1983.

Jordan, W. K. *Edward VI*. 2 vols. London, 1968, 1970.

Josten, C. H. 'Introduction'. In 'A Translation of John Dee's *Monas hieroglyphica* (Antwerp, 1564), with an Introduction and Annotations'. *Ambix* 12 (1964):84–111.

Josten, C. H. 'An Unknown Chapter in the Life of John Dee'. *Journal of the Warburg and Courtauld Institutes* 28 (1965):233–57.

Kearney, Hugh. *Scholars and Gentlemen. Universities and Society in Pre-Industrial Britain, 1500–1700*. Ithaca, 1970.

Keller, Alexander. 'Mathematics, Mechanics, and the Origins of the Culture of Mechanical Invention'. *Minerva* 23 (1985):348–61.

Kendrick, T. D. *British Antiquity*. London, 1950.

Kiesewetter, Karl. *John Dee: ein Spiritist des 16 Jahrhunderts.* Leipzig, 1893.

Knoespel, Kenneth J. 'The Narrative Matter of Mathematics: John Dee's Preface to the Elements of Euclid of Megara (1570)'. *Philological Quarterly* 66 (Winter, 1987):26–46.

Koyré, Alexandre. 'Giambattista Benedetti, Critic of Aristotle'. In Ernan McMullin, ed., *Galileo, Man of Science*, pp.98–117. New York, 1967.

Kuntz, Marion L. *Guillaume Postel, Prophet of the Restitution of All Things: His Life and Thought.* Boston, 1981.

Lacapra, Dominick. 'Rethinking Intellectual History and Reading Texts'. *History and Theory* 19 (1980):245–76.

La Ramée, Pierre de. *Scholarum mathematicarum.* Basel, 1569.

La Ramée, Pierre de, and Omar Talon. *Collectaneae, Praefationes, Epistolae, Orationes.* Marburg, 1599. Reprinted Hildesheim, 1969.

Larkey, Sanford V. 'Astrology and Politics in the First Years of Elizabeth's Reign'. *Bulletin of the Institute of the History of Medicine* 3 (1935):171–86.

Lauterbach, J. Z. 'Substitutes for the Tetragrammaton'. American Academy for Jewish Research, *Proceedings* (1930–1931):39–67.

Laycock, Donald C. *The Complete Enochian Dictionary. A Dictionary of the Angelic Language as Revealed to Dr. John Dee and Edward Kelley.* London, 1978.

Leader, Damian Riehl. 'Professorships and Academic Reform at Cambridge: 1488–1520'. *Sixteenth Century Journal* 14 (1983):215–17.

Lemay, Richard. *Abū Ma 'shar and Latin Aristotelianism in the Twelfth Century.* Beirut, 1962.

Lenoble, Robert. *Mersenne ou la naissance du mécanisme.* Paris, 1943.

Leowitz, Cyprian. *Brevis et perspicva ratio iudicandi genituras.* London, 1558.

Leowitz, Cyprian. *De conivnctionibus magnis . . .* London, 1573.

Leowitz, Cyprian. *Ephemeridum novum.* Augsburg, 1557.

Letters and Papers, Foreign and Domestic, Henry VIII.

Levi Della Viola, G. 'Something More About Artephius and his "Clavis Sapientia"'. *Speculum* 13 (1938):80–5.

The Life of Dr. John Dee . . . Containing an account of his studies . . . his travels . . . his various prophecies, among which may be noticed an earthquake to destroy London in the year 1842. London, 1842.

Lilly, William. *Mr. William Lilly's History of His Life and Times. . . .* London, 1715.

Lindberg, David C. 'On the Applicability of Mathematics to Nature: Roger Bacon and His Predecessors'. *British Journal for the History of Science* 15 (1982):3–25. Reprinted in David C. Lindberg, *Studies in the History of Medieval Optics.* London, 1983.

Lindberg, David C. 'The Genesis of Kepler's Theory of Light: Light Metaphysics from Plotinus to Kepler'. *Osiris* n.s. 2 (1986):4–42.

Lindberg, David C. 'Introduction'. In John Pecham, *John Pecham and the Science of Optics: perspectiva communis*, edited and translated by David C. Lindberg, pp.1–58. Madison, 1970.

Lindberg, David C. 'Lines of Influence in Thirteenth-Century Optics: Bacon, Witelo, and Pecham'. *Speculum* 46 (1971):66–83. Reprinted in

David C. Lindberg, *Studies in the History of Medieval Optics*. London, 1983.

Lindberg, David C. 'Roger Bacon's Experimental Science: A Reappraisal'. Paper given at the History of Science Society Annual Meeting, 24 October 1986.

Lindberg, David C. *Roger Bacon's Philosophy of Nature*. Oxford, 1983.

Lindberg, David C. 'Roger Bacon's Theory of the Rainbow: Progress or Regress?' *Isis* 57 (1966):235–48. Reprinted in David C. Lindberg, *Studies in the History of Medieval Optics*. London, 1983.

Lindberg, David C. *Theories of Vision from al-Kindī to Kepler*. Chicago, 1976.

List and Analysis of State Papers, Foreign, Elizabeth I.

Livesey, Steven J. '*Metabasis*: The Interrelationship of the Sciences in Antiquity and the Middle Ages'. Ph.D. diss. University of California, Los Angeles, 1982.

Loades, David. *The Tudor Court*. Ottawa, N.J., 1987.

Logan, F. Donald. 'The Origins of the so-called Regius Professorships: an Aspect of the Renaissance in Oxford and Cambridge'. In Derek Baker, ed., *Renaissance and Renewal in Christian History*, pp.271–8. Studies in Church History, vol. 14. Oxford, 1977.

Lohr, C. H. 'Renaissance Latin Aristotle Commentaries: Authors A-B'. *Studies in the Renaissance* 21 (1974):228–89.

London, Institute of Historical Research. *Corrections and Additions to the Dictionary of National Biography*. Boston, 1966.

Luhrmann, T. M. 'An Interpretation of the *Fama Fraternitatis* with Respect to Dee's *Monas Hieroglyphica*'. *Ambix* 33 (1986):1–10.

McAllister, Joseph B. *The Letter of Saint Thomas Aquinas 'De occultis operibus naturae'*. Washington, D.C., 1939.

McCaffrey, W. T. 'England: The Crown and the New Aristocracy, 1540–1600'. *Past and Present* 30 (1965):52–64.

McCaffrey, W. T. 'Place and Patronage in Elizabethan Politics'. In S. T. Bindoff, et al. *Elizabethan Government and Society*, pp.95–126. London, 1961.

McConica, James K. *English Humanists and Reformation Politics under Henry VIII and Edward VI*. Oxford, 1965.

McConica, James K. 'Humanism and Aristotle in Tudor Oxford'. *English Historical Review*, 94 (1979):291–317.

McCoy, Richard C. *Sir Philip Sidney: Rebellion in Arcadia*. New Brunswick, 1979.

McEvoy, James. 'The Chronology of Robert Grosseteste's Writings on Nature and Natural Philosophy'. *Speculum* 58 (1983):614–55.

McEvoy, James. *The Philosophy of Robert Grosseteste*. Oxford, 1982.

McGuire, J. E. 'Neoplatonism and Active Principles: Newton and the *Corpus Hermeticum*', In Robert S. Westman and J. E. McGuire, *Hermeticism and the Scientific Revolution*, pp.93–142. Los Angeles, 1977.

Maclean, Ian. 'The Interpretation of Natural Signs: Cardano's *De subtilitate* versus Scaliger's *Exercitationes*'. In Brian Vickers, ed., *Occult and Scientific Mentalities in the Renaissance*, pp.231–52. Cambridge, 1984.

McVaugh, Michael R. 'Introduction'. In Arnoldus de Villanova,

Aphorismi de gradibus. Edited by Michael R. McVaugh. Vol. 2 of idem, *Opera medica omnia.* Granada/Barcelona, 1975.

Maier, Anneliese. *An der Grenze von Scholastik und Naturwissenschaft,* 2d ed. Rome, 1952.

al-Majrītī, Maslama ibn Aḥmad [pseud]. *Das Ziel des Weisen.* [Arabic of *Picatrix*]. Edited by Hellmut Ritter. Studies of the Warburg Institute, vol. 12. Berlin, 1933.

al-Majrītī, Maslama ibn Aḥmad [pseud] *'Picatrix'. Das Ziel des Weisen von Pseudo-Maǧrītī.* [German translation of above]. Translated by Hellmut Ritter and M. Plessner. Studies of the Warburg Institute, vol. 27. London, 1962.

Manget, Johannes Jacobus, ed. *Bibliotheca chemica curiosa.* 2 vols. Geneva, 1702.

Manzalaoui, Mahmoud A. 'The Pseudo-Aristotelian *Kitāb Sirr al-Asrār:* Facts and Problems'. *Oriens* 23–24 (1970–1971):147–257.

Manzalaoui, Mahmoud A. 'The Secreta Secretorum. The Medieval European Version of "Kitāb Sirr al-Asrār"'. Alexandria University, *Bulletin of the Faculty of Arts* 15 (1961):83–106.

Marrone, Steven P. *William of Auvergne and Robert Grosseteste: New Ideas of Truth in the Early Thirteenth Century.* Princeton, 1983.

Mayor, J. E. B., ed. *Early Statutes of the College of St. John the Evangelist in the University of Cambridge.* Cambridge, 1859.

Mercator, Gerard. *Correspondence mercatorienne.* Edited by M. van Durme. Anvers, 1959.

Mercator, Gerard. *Historia mundi: or Mercator's Atlas. Containing his Cosmographical Description of the Fabricke and Figure of the world.* Englished by W. S. [William Sparke]. London, 1635.

Merriman, Roger B. 'Some Notes on the Treatment of the English Catholics in the Reign of Elizabeth'. *American Historical Review* 13 (1908):480–500.

Metaxopoulos, Emile. 'A la suite de F. A. Yates. Débats sur le rôle de la tradition hermétiste dans la révolution scientifique des XVIᵉ et XVIIᵉ siècles'. *Revue de Synthèse* 103 (1982):53–65.

Milik, Jósef T., ed. *The Books of Enoch.* Oxford, 1976.

The Mirrour for Magistrates. Edited by Lily B. Campbell. Cambridge, 1938.

Molland, A. G. 'The Geometrical Background to the "Merton School"'. *British Journal for the History of Science* 4 (1968):108–25.

Molland, A. G. 'Mathematical and Angelic Astrology'. *British Journal for the History of Science* 13 (1980):255–58.

Molland, A. G. 'Roger Bacon as Magician'. *Traditio* 30 (1974):445–60.

Molland, A. G. 'Roger Bacon: Magic and the Multiplication of Species'. Forthcoming in *Paideia.*

Moran, Bruce T. 'German Prince-Practicioners: Aspects in the Development of Courtly Science, Technology, and Procedures in the Renaissance'. *Technology and Culture* 22 (1981):253–74.

Moran, Bruce T. 'Princes, Machines, and the Valuation of Precision in the 16th Century'. *Sudhoffs Archiv* 61, no. 3 (1977):209–28.

Moran, Bruce T. 'Privilege, Communication, and Chemiatry: The

Hermetic-Alchemical Circle of Moritz of Hessen-Kassel'. *Ambix* 32 (1985):110–126.

Moran, Bruce T. 'Science at the Court of Hesse-Kassel: Informal Communication, Collaboration, and the Role of the Prince-Practicioner in the Sixteenth Century'. Ph.D. diss. University of California, Los Angeles, 1978.

Moss, Jean Dietz. '*Godded with God*: Hendrik Niclaes and His Family of Love. American Philosophical Society, *Transactions*, vol. 71, pt. 8. Philadelphia, 1981.

Mullinger, James Bass. *The University of Cambridge, from the Royal Injunctions of 1535 to the Accession of Charles the First.* Cambridge, 1884.

Murdoch, John E. 'The Medieval Euclid: Salient Aspects of the Translations of the *Elements* by Adelard of Bath and Companus of Novara'. XII^c Congress International d'Histoire des Sciences, *Acts* 1 (1970):67–94.

Nauert, Jr., Charles G. *Agrippa and the Crisis of Renaissance Thought.* Urbana, 1965.

Nauert, Jr., Charles G. 'The Author of a Renaissance Commentary on Pliny: Rivius, Trithemius or Aquaeus?' *Journal of the Warburg and Courtauld Institutes* 42 (1979):282–5.

Nauert, Jr., Charles G. 'Caius Plinius Secundus'. In F. Edward Cranz, ed., *Catalogus Translationum et Commentariorum*, 4:297–422. Washington, D.C., 1980.

Nauert, Jr., Charles G. 'Magic and Skepticism in Agrippa's Thought'. *Journal of the History of Ideas* 18 (1957):161–82.

Newman, William. 'The Genesis of the *Summa perfectionis*'. *Archives internationales d'histoire des sciences* forthcoming.

Newman, William. 'New Light on the Identity of "Geber"'. *Sudhoffs Archiv* 69 (1985):76–90.

Newman, William. 'The *Summa perfectionis* and Late Medieval Alchemy: A Study of Chemical Traditions, Techniques, and Theories in Thirteenth Century Italy'. Ph.D. diss. 4 vols. Harvard University, 1986.

Newman, William. 'Thomas Vaughn as an Interpreter of Agrippa von Nettesheim'. *Ambix* 29 (1982):125–40.

Nicoll, Charles. *The Chemical Theatre.* London, 1980.

Noble, F. 'Dee's Connections with Radnorshire'. *Transactions of the Radnorshire Society* 26 (1956):40–2.

North, John D. 'Celestial Influence – the Major Premiss of Astrology'. In Paola Zambelli, ed., '*Astrologi hallucinati*'. *Stars and the End of the World in Luther's Time*, pp.45–100. Berlin, 1986.

North, John D. 'The Western Calendar – "Intolerabilis, horribilis, et derisibilis;" Four Centuries of Discontent'. In G. V. Coyne, M. A. Hoskin, and O. Pedersen, eds., *Gregorian Reform of the Calendar: Proceedings of the Vatican Conference to Commemorate its 400th Anniversary, 1582–1982*, pp.75–113. Città del Vaticano, 1983.

Norton, Thomas. *The Ordinall of Alchemy.* In *Theatrum Chemicum Britannicum.* Edited by Elias Ashmole. London, 1652.

Offusius, Joannes Franciscus. *De divina astrorum facultate.* Paris, 1570.

O'Malley, Charles Donald. *Jacopo Aconcio.* Translated by Delio Cantimori. Rome, 1955.

Oresme, Nicole. *Nicole Oresme and the Medieval Geometry of Qualities and Motions.* Edited and translated by Marshall Clagett. Madison, 1968.

Oresme, Nicole. *De proportionibus proportionum and Ad pauca respicientes.* Edited and translated by Edward Grant. Madison, 1966.

Ortelius, Abraham and Jacob. *Abrahami Ortelii . . . Epistolae.* Edited by John Henry Hessels. Ecclesiae Londino-Batavae Archivum, vol. 1. Cambridge, 1887.

van Ortroy, F., ed. 'Biobibliographie de Gemma Frisius, fondateur de l'école belge de géographie, de son fils Cornaille et de ses neveux les Arsenius'. Académie royal de belgique, Classe des lettres et sciences morales et politiques, *Mémoires* 11 no. 2 (1920).

Osborn, J. M. *Young Philip Sidney, 1572–1577.* New Haven, 1972.

Panofsky, Erwin. *Hercules am Scheidewege, und andere Antike Bildstoffe in der Neueren Kunst.* Studien der Bibliothek Warburg, vol. 18. Leibzig, 1930.

Pantheus, Ioannis Augustini. *Voarchadvmia contra alchemiam: ars distincta ab archimia, & sophia: cum additionibus: proportionibus: numeris: & figuris opportunis.* Venice, 1530.

Paracelsus, Aureolus Phillipus Theophrastus Bombast. *The Hermetic and Alchemical Writings.* 2 vols. Edited and translated by Arthur Edward Waite. London, 1894.

Paschetto, Eugenia. *Demoni e Prodigi. Note su alcuni scritti di Witelo e di Oresme.* Turin, 1978.

Patrides, C. A., and Joseph Wittreich. *The Apocalypse in English Renaissance Thought and Literature.* Ithaca, 1984.

Paul of Taranto. *Summa perfectionis.* Edited by William Newman. In William Newman, 'The *Summa perfectionis*', Vol. 4, pt. 1.

Paul of Taranto. *Investigatione perfectionis.* Edited by William Newman. In William Newman, 'The *Summa perfectionis*', Vol. 4, pt. 2.

Pecham, John. *John Pecham and the Science of Optics: Perspectiva communis.* Edited and translated by David C. Lindberg. Madison, 1970.

Pepper, Jon V. 'The Study of Thomas Harriot's Manuscripts: II. Harriot's Unpublished Papers'. *History of Science* 6 (1967):17–40.

Peters, Edward. *The Magician, the Witch, and the Law.* Philadelphia, 1978.

Peters, F. C. *Aristotle and the Arabs. The Aristotelian Tradition in Islam.* New York, 1968.

Peuchert, Will-Erich. *Pansophie. Ein Versuch zur Geschichte der weissen und schwarzen Magie.* 2d ed. Berlin, 1956.

Pickering, Chris. 'The Conjurer John Dee: The Myth, 1555–1608'. *The Hermetic Journal* no. 33 (Autumn, 1986):5–15.

Pico della Mirandola, Giovanni. *Conclusiones sive theses DCCC Romae anno 1486 publice disputandae, sed non admissae.* Edited by Bohdan Kieszkowski. Travaux d'humanisme et renaissance, no. 131. Geneva, 1973.

Pico della Mirandola, Giovanni. *Opera omnia.* 2 vols. Basel, 1572–1573.

Pico della Mirandola, Ioannis Franciscus. *De rerum praenotione.* In idem,

Opera omnia. 2 vols. Basel, 1573. Reprint. Monumenta Politica Philosophica Humanistica Rariora, series 1, no. 14a. Turin, 1972.

Pingree, David. 'Abū Ma'shar'. *Dictionary of Scientific Biography*, 1:32–9.

Pingree, David. 'Between *Ghāya* and *Picatrix* I: The Spanish Version'. *Journal of the Warburg and Courtauld Institutes* 44 (1981):27–56.

Pingree, David. *Picatrix: The Latin Version of the 'Ghāyat Al-Ḥakīm.* Studies of the Warburg Institute, 39. London, 1986.

Pingree, David. 'Some Sources of the GHĀYAT AL-ḤAKĪM'. *Journal of the Warburg and Courtauld Institutes* 43 (1980):1–15.

Plato. *Republic.* Translated by Paul Shorey. In idem, *The Collected Dialogues of Plato.* Edited by Edith Hamilton and Huntington Cairns. Bollingen Series vol. 71. New York, 1961.

Plato. *Timaeus.* Translated by F. M. Cornford. In idem, *Plato's Cosmology.* Indianapolis, 1937.

Plinius secundus, C. *Liber II C. Plinii de mundi historia, cum commentariis Iacobi Milichii.* Frankfurt, 1543.

Pomponazzi, Pietro. *De naturalium effectuum admirandorum causis, seu de incantationibus.* In idem, *Opera.* Basel, 1567.

Postel, Guillaume. *De originibus.* Basel, 1553.

Prideaux, W. R. B. 'Books from John Dee's Library'. *Notes and Queries*, 9th ser., 8 (1901):137–8; 10th ser., 1 (1904):241–2.

Pritchard, Alan. *Alchemy. A Bibliography of English Language Writings.* London, 1980.

Proclus. *A Commentary on the First Book of Euclid's Elements.* Translated by Glenn R. Morrow. Princeton, 1970.

Ptolemy, Claudius. *Quadripartitum.* Venice, 1519.

Ptolemy, Claudius. *Operis quadripartiti: . . . adjectis libris posterioribus . . . de sectione conica . . . quae parabola dicitur, deque speculo ustorio.* Edited and translated by Gemma Frisius. Louvain, 1548.

Ptolemy, Claudius. *Tetrabiblos,* tr. E. E. Robins. Cambridge, Mass., 1940.

Pucci, Francesco. *Lettere, documenti e testimonianze.* 2 vols. Edited by Luigi Firpo and Renato Piattoli. Florence, 1955–1959.

Purchas, Samuel. *Hakluytus Posthumus, or Purchas His Pilgrims.* 20 vols. Glasgow, 1905–1907.

Quinn, David Beers. *The Elizabethans and the Irish.* Ithaca, 1966.

Quinn, David Beers. *England and the Discovery of America, 1481–1620.* New York, 1974.

Quinn, David Beers. 'Ireland and Sixteenth Century European Expansion'. *Historical Studies* 1 (1958):20–32. Edited by T. Desmond Williams. London, 1958.

Quinn, David Beers. 'Simão Fernandes, A Portuguese Pilot in the English Service, *circa* 1573–1588'. Congresso International de Historia dos Descobrimentos, *Actas* 3 (1961):3–19.

Quinn, David Beers. 'Sir Thomas Smith (1513–1577) and the Beginnings of English Colonial Theory'. *Proceedings of the American Philosophical Society* 89 no. 4 (1945):543–60.

Quinn, David Beers, ed. *The Voyages and Colonising Enterprises of Sir Humphrey Gilbert.* 2 vols. Hakluyt Society, n.s. vol. 83. London, 1940.

Quinn, David B., and A. N. Ryan. *England's Sea Empire, 1550–1642.* London, 1983.

Rashed, Roshdi. 'Le "Discourse de la Lumière" d'Ibn al-Haytham (Alhazen)'. *Revue d'histoire des sciences et de leurs applications* 21 (1968):197–224.

Read, Conyers. *Lord Burghley and Queen Elizabeth.* London, 1960.

Read, Conyers. *Mr. Secretary Cecil and Queen Elizabeth.* London, 1955.

Read, Conyers. *Mr. Secretary Walsingham and the Policy of Queen Elizabeth.* 3 vols. Oxford, 1925.

Read, John. *Prelude to Chemistry. An Outline of Alchemy, its Literature, and Relationships.* London, 1961.

Reeves, Marjorie. *The Influence of Prophecy in the Later Middle Ages.* Oxford, 1969.

Reeves, Marjorie. *Joachim of Fiore and the Prophetic Future.* London, 1976.

Reeves, Marjorie. 'Some Popular Prophesies from the Fourteenth to the Seventeenth Century'. *Studies in Church History* 8 (1971):107–34.

'A Relic of Dr. John Dee'. *Isis* 34 (1943):365.

Ristoro d'Arezzo. *La composizione del mondo (1282).* Edited by Alberto Morino. Florence, 1976.

Rivius, Gualterus Hermenius. *In Caii Plinii secundi naturalis historiae. . . .* N.p., 1548.

Roberts, R. J. 'John Dee's Corrections to his "Art of Navigation"'. *Book Collector* 24 (Spring 1975):70–5.

Roberts, R. J., and Andrew G. Watson. *John Dee's Library Catalogue.* The Bibliographical Society, forthcoming.

Roche, John J. 'The Radius Astronomicus in England'. *Annals of Science* 38 (1981):1–32.

Rose, Paul Lawrence. 'Commandino, John Dee, and the *De superficierum divisionibus* of Machometus Bagdedinus'. *Isis* 63 (1972):88–93.

Rose, Paul Lawrence. 'Erasmians and Mathematicians at Cambridge in the Early Sixteenth Century'. *Sixteenth Century Journal* 8 (No.2, 1977):47–59.

Rose, Paul Lawrence. *The Italian Renaissance of Mathematics: Studies on Humanists and Mathematicians from Petrarch to Galileo.* Geneva, 1975.

Rose, Valentin. *Verzeichniss der Lateinischen Handschriften.* Vols. 12, 13, 14 of Preussische Staatsbibliothek, Berlin, *Die Handschriften-Verzeichnisse der Königlichen Bibliothek.* Berlin, 1893.

Rosen, Edward. 'Was Copernicus a Hermetist?' In Roger H. Stuewer, ed., *Historical and Philosophical Perspectives of Science*, pp.163–71. Minneapolis, 1970.

Rosen, Edward. 'John Dee and Commandino'. *Scripta Mathematica* 28 (1970):321–6.

Rosen, Edward. 'Kepler's Attitude Toward Astrology and Mysticism'. In Brian Vickers, ed., *Occult and Scientific Mentalities in the Renaissance*, pp.253–72. Cambridge, 1984.

Ross, Richard P. 'Studies on Oronce Finé'. Ph.D. diss. Columbia University, 1971.

Rossi, Paolo. *Francis Bacon, From Magic to Science*. Translated by Sacha Rabinovitch. Chicago, 1968.

Rossi, Paolo. *Giacomo Aconcio*. Milan, 1952.

Rossi, Paolo. 'Hermeticism, Rationality and the Scientific Revolution'. In M. L. Righini Bonelli and William R. Shea, eds., *Reason, Experiment, and Mysticism in the Scientific Revolution*, pp.247–73. New York, 1975.

Rossi, Paolo. *Philosophy, Technology, and the Arts in the Early Modern Era*. Translated by Salvator Attanasio. Edited by Benjamin Nelson. New York, 1970.

Rowse, A. L. *The Elizabethan Renaissance. The Life of the Society*. London, 1971.

Royal Commission. *Documents Relating to the University and Colleges of Cambridge*. 3 vols. London, 1852.

Ryan, W. F., and Charles B. Schmitt, eds. *Pseudo-Aristotle, the 'Secret of Secrets': Sources and Influences*. Warburg Institute Surveys, vol. 9. London, 1982.

Ryder, John. *Lines of the Alphabet in the 16th Century*. London, 1965.

Saccaro, Giuseppa Battisti. 'Il Grosseteste e la luce'. *Medioevo* 2 (1976):21–75.

Sargent, Ralph M. *At the Court of Queen Elizabeth. The Life and Lyrics of Sir Edward Dyer*. New York, 1935.

Sarton, George. *Introduction to the History of Science*. 3 vols. Washington, D.C., 1927–1948.

Scaliger, Julius Caesar. *Exotericarum exercitationum . . . de subtilitate ad Hieronymum Cardanum*. Paris, 1557.

Schmitt, Charles B. *Aristotle and the Renaissance*. Cambridge, Mass., 1983.

Schmitt, Charles B. *John Case and Aristotelianism in Renaissance England*. Buffalo, 1983.

Schmitt, Charles B. 'Reappraisals in Renaissance Science.' *History of Science* 16 (1978):200–14. Reprinted in idem, *Studies in Renaissance Philosophy and Science*.

Scholem, Gershom G. *Major Trends in Jewish Mysticism*. New York, 1954.

Scholem, Gershom G. *On the Kabbalah and its Symbolism*. Translated by Ralph Manheim. New York, 1965.

Secret, François. *Les Kabbalistes Chrétiens de la Renaissance*. Paris, 1964.

Settle, Tom. 'The Rationality of Science *versus* the Raionality of Magic'. *Philosophy of Social Science* 1 (1971):173–94.

Shapiro, Barbara J. *John Wilkins, 1614–72: An Intellectual Biography*. Berkeley, 1969.

Sheppard, H. J. 'Egg Symbolism in Alchemy'. *Ambix* 6 (1958):140–8.

Shenton, Walter F. 'The First English Euclid'. *American Mathematical Monthly* 35 (1928):505–12.

Shumaker, Wayne. *Renaissance Curiosa*. Medieval and Renaissance Texts and Studies, vol. 8. Binghamton, 1982.

Simon, Joan. *Education and Society in Tudor England*. New York, 1966.

Singer, Dorothea Waley. *Catalogue of Latin and Vernacular Alchemical Manuscripts in Great Britain and Ireland*. 3 vols. Brussels, 1928.

Skinner, Quentin. 'Meaning and Understanding in the History of Ideas'. *History and Theory* 8 (1969):3–53.

Smith, A. Mark. 'Getting the Big Picture in Perspective Optics'. *Isis* 72 (1981):568–89.

Smith, Lacey Baldwin. *Tudor Prelates and Politics, 1536–1558*. Princeton, 1953.

Southern, R. W. *Robert Grosseteste: The Growth of an English Mind in Medieval Europe*. Oxford, 1986.

Spitz, Lewis W. 'Occultism and Despair of Reason in Renaissance Thought'. *Journal of the History of Ideas* 27 (1966):464–9.

van Steenberghen, Fernand. *Aristotle in the West. The Origins of Latin Aristotelianism*. Translated by Leonard Johnston. Louvain, 1955.

Stone, Lawrence. 'The Educational Revolution in England, 1560–1640'. *Past and Present* 28 (1964):41–80.

Stone, Lawrence. 'Social Mobility in England, 1500–1700'. *Past and Present* 33 (1966):16–55.

Strathmann, Ernest A. 'John Dee as Ralegh's "Conjurer"'. *The Huntington Library Quarterly* 10 (1947):365–72.

Strong, Edward W. *Procedures and Metaphysics. A Study in the Philosophy of Mathematical-Physical Science in the Sixteenth and Seventeenth Centuries*. 1936. Reprint. New York, 1976.

Strype, John. *Annals of the Reformation*. New ed. 4 vols. in 7. Oxford, 1924.

Strype, John. *The Life of Sir John Cheke*. Oxford, 1821.

Strype, John. *The Life of Sir Thomas Smith*. Oxford, 1820.

Szöny, György E. 'John Dee, an Elizabethan Magus and His Links with Central Europe'. *Angol Filológiai Tanulmányok (Hungarian Studies in English)* 13 (1980):71–83.

Tait, Hugh. '"The Devil's Looking-Glass": The Magical Speculum of John Dee'. In Warren Hunting Smith, ed., *Horace Walpole: Writer, Politician, and Connoisseur*, pp.195–212. New Haven, 1967.

Tannier, Bernard. 'Une nouvelle interprétation de la "philosophie occulte" a la Renaissance: L'oeuvre de Frances A. Yates'. *Aries* 2 (1984):15–33.

Taylor, E. G. R. 'John Dee and the Nautical Triangle, 1575'. *Journal of the Institute of Navigation* 8 (1955):318–25.

Taylor, E. G. R. 'A Letter Dated 1577 from Mercator to John Dee'. *Imago Mundi* 13 (1956):56–68.

Taylor, E. G. R. 'Master John Dee, Drake, and the Straits of Anian'. *The Mariner's Mirror* 15 (1929):125–30.

Taylor, E. G. R. *The Mathematical Practitioners of Tudor and Stuart England*. Cambridge, 1954.

Taylor, E. G. R. *Tudor Geography, 1485–1583*. London, 1930.

The Testament of Solomon. Edited by Chester Charlton McCown. Leipzig, 1922.

Thomas, Keith. 'An Anthropology of Religion and Magic, II'. *Journal of Interdisciplinary History* 6 (1975):91–109.

Thomas, Keith. *Religion and the Decline of Magic. Studies in Popular Belief in 16th and 17th Century England*. Harmondsworth, 1973.

Thomson, George Malcolm. *The North-West Passage*. London, 1975.

Thorndike, Lynn. *A Catalogue of Incipits of Medieval Scientific Writings in Latin*. Revised and augmented edition. London, 1963.

Thorndike, Lynn. 'Coelestinus's Summary of Nicolas Oresme on Marvels'. *Osiris* 1 (1936):629–35.

Thorndike, Lynn. *A History of Magic and Experimental Science*. 8 vols. New York, 1922–48.

Thorndike, Lynn. 'Traditional Medieval Tracts Concerning Engraved Astrological Images'. *Mélanges Auguste Pelzer* 3d series, fasc. 26 (1947):217–74.

Tilley, Arthur. 'Greek Studies in England in the Early 16th Century'. *English Historical Review* 53 (1938):438–56.

Tiryakian, Edward A. 'Toward the Sociology of Esoteric Culture'. In Edward A. Tiryakian, ed., *On the Margin of the Visible. Sociology, the Esoteric, and the Occult*, pp.257–80. New York, 1974.

Torniello da Novara, Francesco. *The Alphabet of Francesco Torniello da Novara, 1517*. Verona, 1971.

Tory, Geoffrey. *Champ Fleury, ou l'art et science de la proportion des lettres*. Paris, 1529. Reprint. Paris, 1931; and Geneva, 1973.

Trattner, Walter I. 'God and Expansion in Elizabethan England: John Dee, 1527–1583'. *Journal of the History of Ideas* 25 (1964):17–34.

Trinkaus, Charles. 'Ideals of Deification, Autonomy, and Stellar Power in Marsilio Ficino'. Paper presented at the Colloquium on Renaissance Intellectual History, Humanities Center, The Johns Hopkins University, 28 February 1987.

Trithemius, Johannes. *Epistolarum familiarum libri duo*. Haganau, 1536.

Trithemius, Johannes. *De septem secundadeis, id est intelligentiis sive spiritibus orbis post deum moventibus*. Nuremberg, 1522.

Trithemius, Johannes. *Steganographia*. Frankfurt, 1606.

Tymme, Thomas. *A Light in Darkness, which illumineth for all the Monas Hieroglyphica. . . .* Oxford, 1963.

Ullman, Manfred. *Die Natur- und Geheimwissenschaften im Islam*. Leiden, 1972.

Vickers, Brian. 'Analogy versus Identity: The Rejection of Occult Symbolism, 1580–1680'. In Brian Vickers, ed., *Occult and Scientific Mentalities in the Renaissance*, pp.95–163. Cambridge, 1984.

Vickers, Brian. 'Frances Yates and the Writing of History'. *Journal of Modern History* 51 (1979):287–316.

Vickers, Brian, ed. *Occult and Scientific Mentalities in the Renaissance*. Cambridge, 1984.

Victor, Joseph M. *Charles de Bovelles, 1479–1553: An Intellectual Biography*. Geneva, 1978.

de Vocht, Henry. *History of the Foundation and the Rise of the Collegium Trilingue Lovaniense, 1517–1550*. 4 vols. Louvain, 1951–1955.

Waldstein, Arnold. *John Dee, le sorcier de la reine Elizabeth*. Paris, 1974.

Walker, D. P. *The Ancient Theology. Studies in Christian Platonism from the Fifteenth to the Eighteenth Century*. London, 1972.

Walker, D. P. *Spiritual and Demonic Magic from Ficino to Campanella*. London, 1958.

Wallace, William. *Causality and Scientific Explanation* 2 vols. Ann Arbor, 1972–74.

Wallace, William. *The Scientific Methodology of Theodoric of Freiberg*. Studia Friburgensia, n.s. no. 26. Freibourg, 1959.

Walton, Michael T. 'John Dee's *Monas Hieroglyphica*: Geometrical Cabala'. *Ambix* 23 (1976):116–23.

Ward, B. M. 'Martin Frobisher and Dr. John Dee'. *The Mariner's Mirror* 12 (1926):453–5.

Waswo, Richard. 'Magic Words and Reference Theories'. *Journal of Literary Semantics* 6 (1977):79–90.

Waswo, Richard. 'The "Ordinary Language Philosophy" of Lorenzo Valla'. *Bibliothèque d'Humanisme et Renaissance* 41 (1979):255–71.

Waters, D. W. *The Art of Navigation in England in Elizabethan and Early Stuart Times*. 2d ed. Greenwich, 1978.

Watson, Andrew G. 'Christopher and William Carye, Collectors of Monastic Manuscripts and "John Carye"'. *The Library* 5th ser. 20 (1965):135–42.

Watson, Andrew G. 'A Merton College Manuscript [of John Dee] Reconstructed: Harley 625; Digby 178, fols 1–14, 88–115; Cotton Tiberius B. IX, fols 1–4, 225–35'. *Bodleian Library Record* 9 (1976):207–17.

Watson, Andrew G. 'Thomas Allen of Oxford and His Manuscripts'. In M. B. Parkes and Andrew G. Watson, eds. *Medieval Scribes, Manuscripts, and Libraries: Essays Presented to N. R. Ker*, pp.279–314. London, 1978.

Webster, Charles. *From Paracelsus to Newton. Magic and the Making of Modern Science*. Cambridge, 1982.

Westman, Robert S. 'The Astronomer's Role in the Sixteenth Century: A Preliminary Study'. *History of Science* 18 (1980):105–47.

Westman, Robert S. 'Magical Reform and Astronomical Reform: The Yates Thesis Reconsidered'. In Robert S. Westman and J. E. McGuire, *Hermeticism and the Scientific Revolution*, pp.1–91. Los Angeles, 1977.

Westman, Robert S. 'Nature, Art, and Psyche: Jung, Pauli, and the Kepler-Fludd Polemic'. In Brian Vickers, ed., *Occult and Scientific Mentalities in the Renaissance*, pp.177–229. Cambridge, 1984.

Westman, Robert S. 'Three Responses to the Copernican Theory: Johannes Praetorius, Tycho Brahe, and Michael Maestlin'. In Robert S. Westman, ed. *The Copernican Achievement*, pp.285–345. Berkeley, 1975.

Wiedemann, Eilhard. 'Zur Geschichte der Brennspiegel'. *Annalen der Physik und Chemie* n.s. 39 (1890):110–30.

William of Auvergne. *Opera Omnia*. 2 vols. Paris, 1674.

Williams, Gwyn A. *Madoc: The Making of a Myth*. London, 1979.

Williams, Gwyn A. *Welsh Wizard and the British Empire: Dr John Dee and a Welsh Identity*. Cardif, 1986.

'Thomas Wilson (1525?–1581)'. *Dictionary of National Biography*, 21:603–7.

Wood, Anthony à. *Athenae Oxonienses*. Edited by Philip Bliss. 5 vols. London, 1813–1820.

Yates, Frances A. *The Art of Memory*. Chicago, 1966.

Yates, Frances A. *Astraea. The Imperial Theme in the Sixteenth Century*. London, 1975.

Yates, Frances A. *Giordano Bruno and the Hermetic Tradition*. Chicago, 1964.

Yates, Frances A. 'A Great Magus'. In Frances A. Yates, *Ideas and Ideals in the North European Renaissance. Collected Essays*. Vol.3, pp.49–59. London, 1984.

Yates, Frances A. 'The Hermetic Tradition in Renaissance Science'. In Charles S. Singleton, ed., *Art, Science, and History in the Renaissance*, pp.255–74. Baltimore, 1968. Reprinted in Frances A. Yates, *Ideas and Ideals in the North European Renaissance. Collected Essays*. Vol.3, pp.227–46. London, 1984.

Yates, Frances A. *The Occult Philosophy in the Elizabethan Age*. London, 1969.

Yates, Frances A. 'Renaissance Philosophers in Elizabethan England: John Dee and Giordano Bruno'. In Hugh Lloyd-Jones et al., eds., *History and Imagination: Essays in Honor of H. R. Trevor-Roper*, pp.104–14. New York, 1982. Reprinted in Frances A. Yates, *Lull and Bruno. Collected Essays*. Vol.1, pp.210–21. London, 1982.

Yates, Frances A. *The Rosicrucian Enlightenment*. London, 1972.

Yates, Frances A. *Shakespeare's Last Plays: A New Approach*. London, 1975.

Yates, Frances A. *Theatre of the World*. London, 1969.

Yewbrey, Graham. 'John Dee and the "Sidney Group": Cosmopolitics and Protestant "Activism" in the 1570's'. Ph.D. thesis, University of Hull, 1981.

Yewbrey, Graham. 'A Redated Manuscript of John Dee'. *Bulletin of the Institute of Historical Research* 50 (1977):249–53.

Zambelli, Paola. 'Agrippa von Nettesheim in der neueren kritischen Studien und in dem Handschriften'. *Archiv für Kulturgeschichte* 51 (1969):264–95.

Zambelli, Paola. 'Cornelio Agrippa di Nettesheim, testi scleti'. In Eugenio Garin et al., *Testi Umanistici su l'Ermetismo*, pp.107–62. Rome, 1955.

Zambelli, Paola. '*Humanae literae, verbum divinum, docta ignorantia* negli ultimi scritti di Enrico Cornelio Agrippa'. *Giornale Critico della Filosofia Italiana* 46 (1966):101–13.

Zambelli, Paola. 'Magic and Radical Reformation in Agrippa of Nettesheim'. *Journal of the Warburg and Courtauld Institutes* 39 (1976):69–103.

Zambelli, Paola. 'Platone, Ficino, e la magia'. In *Studia humanitatis. Festschrift für Ernesto Grassi*, pp.121–42. Munich, 1973.

Zambelli, Paola. 'Il problema della magia naturale nel Rinascimento'. *Rivista Critica di Storia della Filosofia* 28 (1973):271–96.

Zetterberg, J. Peter. 'Hermetic Geocentricity: John Dee's Celestial Egg'. *Isis* 70 (1979):385–93.

Zetterberg, J. Peter. '"Mathematical Magic" in England: 1550–1650'. Ph.D. diss. University of Wisconsin, 1976.

Zetterberg, J. Peter. 'The Mistaking of "the Mathematics" for Magic in Tudor and Early Stuart England'. *Sixteenth Century Journal* 11 (1980):83–97.

Zika, Charles. 'Reuchlin and Erasmus: Humanism and Occult Philosophy'. *Journal of Religious History* 9 (1977):223–46.

Zika, Charles. 'Reuchlin's *De verbo mirifico* and the Magic Debate of the Late Fifteenth Century'. *Journal of the Warburg and Courtauld Institutes* 39 (1976):104–38.

C–OTHER MANUSCRIPTS CITED

Included below are all manuscripts cited other than those of Dee's writings. Many were cited only in passing, and for each is indicated the items of interest for this study. No attempt has been made to identify or to include all surviving manuscripts that Dee owned as this will be done by Andrew Watson in Roberts and Watson, *John Dee's Library Catalogue*.

Cambridge, Magdelene College
    MS Pepys 2329. Nicole Oresme, *Tractatus de proportionibus proportionum*

Dublin, Trinity College
    MS 382. Report on Dee's calendar reform.

London, British Library
    MS Add. 32092. Reports on Dee's reform of the calendar.
    MS Add. 36674. Collection of magical texts.
    MS Cotton Tiberius C. V. Roger Bacon, *Opus majus, Opus minus, Opus tertium.*
    MS Landsdown 39, art. 4. Burghley's summary of Dee's calendar reform.
    MS Landsdown 103. William Cecil's astrological notes.
    MS Landsdown 109, art. 27. Robert Cecil's notes on Dee's calendar reform.
    MS Sloane 325. Thomas Smith horoscopes.
    MS Sloane 1118. Artephii *De opere solis.*
    MS Sloane 1437. *Liber de divinatione.*
    MS Sloane 1712. *Ars notoria.*
    MS Sloane 2006. Alchemical collection.
    MS Sloane 2128. Alchemical collection.
    MS Sloane 3824. *Trithemius redivivus.*
    MS Sloane 3825. *Clavicula Solomonis.*
    MS Sloane 3826. 'Experiments' [conjurations].
    MS Sloane 3846. *Cepher Raz'iel.*
    MS Sloane 3847. Key of Solomon.
    MS Sloane 3848. Magical texts.
    MS Sloane 3849. 'Experiments' [conjurations].
    MS Sloane 3850. Collection of magical texts.

MS Sloane 3851. Collection of magical texts.
MS Sloane 3853. [pseudo] Roger Bacon, *Thesaurus spiritum. Tractatio de speculo.*
MS Sloane 3854, art. 5. 'Experimenta de speculo'.
MS Sloane 3884. [pseudo] Roger Bacon, *De operatione magiae.* 'Ad includendum in speculo spiritu'.

London, Public Record Office
PC 2/6. Register of the Privy Council, Mary, I.
SP 12/119. State Papers, Domestic, Elizabeth.
SP 12/123. State Papers, Domestic, Elizabeth.

Oxford, Bodleian Library
MS Add. B. 1. Medical recipes, charms, incantations, directions for making a magic crystal.
MS Ashmole 57. Thomas Norton, *Ordinall of Alchemy.*
MS Ashmole 244. Simon Forman, *Book of Cabala.*
MS Ashmole 354. Simon Forman, *Treatise on Geomancy.*
MS Ashmole 434. *Summarum de geomantia. Tractatus de angelis planetarum.*
MS Ashmole 1440. Thomas Tymme, *A Light in Darkness.*
MS Ashmole 1459. Thomas Tymme. *A Light in Darkness.*
MS Ashmole 1460. [pseudo] Trithemius, *Liber experimentorum.*
MS Ashmole 1515. *Ars notoria.*
MS Ashmole 1788. Bartolomeus de Rekingen to Dee, Vienna, 1564.
MS Ashmole 1790. *Cepher Raz'iel.* 'Experiments with a crystal'.
MS Ashmole 1819. Thomas Tymme, Epistle Dedicatory [to Dee's *Monas*].
MS Digby 76. Works by Roger Bacon.
MS Digby 119. Roger Bacon's edition of *Secretum secretorum.*
MS Douce 363. *Ars notoria.*
MS e Mus. 173. Magical formulae and 'experiments'.
MS Rawlinson D. 253. *A treatise of conjurations.*
MS Rawlinson D. 868. Catalogue of magical texts.
MS Selden Supra 79. Description of Dee's mirror. Extracts from books and manuscripts belonging to Dee.
MS Tanner 308. Letters of Stephen Powle about Dee.

Oxford, Corpus Christi College [Deposited at the Bodleian Library]
MS Corpus Christi College 149. *Secretum secretorum.*
MS Corpus Christi College 233. Codex containing Artephius, *Ars sintrillia,* when Dee owned it.
MS Corpus Christi College 254. Works by Roger Bacon, al-Kindī, etc. Burghley and Walsingham on Dee's calendar reform.

Paris, Bibliothèque de l'Arsenal
MS 2344. Artephius, *L'art magique d'Artephius et de Mihinius.*
MS 3009. Artephius, *L'art magique d'Artephius et de Mihinius.*

Vienna, Oesterreichische Nationalbibliothek
MS 11,294. Artephius, *Artetii ac Mininii apologia in artem magicam.*

INDEX

Abū Ma'shar, 41, 222

Adam, 210; language of, 88, 213

Agricola, Georg, 160

Agrippa, Henry Cornelius, 5, 8, 131, 135, 136, 139, 141, 161, 205, 206, 207, 211, 212, 214, 218, 219, 236; Fourth Book of, 135; and magic, 129, 134

Alberti, Leon Battista, 160

Albertus Magnus, 133, 161

Albumazar or Albumasar, see Abū Ma'shar

alchemy, 96–105; Arabic, 98; Aristotle's theory of elements and, 97–8; astrology and, 106–10; as astronomia inferior, 69; celestial influences in, 98, 100; Dee and Kelley practice in Prague, 228; Dee's practice of, 178, 229; disciplinary status of, 119–20; elixir/philosophers' stone, 98–100; as the hermetic science, 26, 83; language of, 117; Latin, 98; as magic, 103–5, 110–14, 127, 235; mercury–sulphur theory of, 98–100; as mystical religion, 100, 101, 111–14; Norton and, 100; in Pantheus' Voarchadumia, 101–3; rhetoric of, 96; transmutation, 97; see also Dee, John, Monas hieroglyphica

Alençon, Francis, Duke of, 184

Alexander, Andrea: and metabasis, 62;

on scientific demonstration and mathematics, 61–2

algebra, 159, 164, 167

Alhazen, see Ibn al-Haytham

al-Kindī, 55, 58, 64, 135, 215, 233; on light as corporeal, 53; on optical physics and astrology, 52–4, 57; and magic, 66, 132, 134

Almadel, 139

alnirangiat, 166–70, 174

Alpago, Andrea, 167

alphabet: geometrical construction of, 92; of nature, 86, 95; see also language

al-Rāzī, 98

amulet, see talismans

ancient theology, 116, 237; Bacon and, 126; magic and, 128, 130, 139, 219, 240; in Renaissance, 221

angelic magic, see magic, spirit/demonic

angels, see magic, spirit/demonic

antipathy, see sympathy and antipathy

Antwerp, 77, 103, 104

Apocalypse, 138

Aquinas, Thomas, see Thomas Aquinas

Arabs: alchemy of, 98; Aristotelian philosophy and, 71; magic of, 167; natural philosophy, magic, and the occult sciences, 130, 133

Arbatel, 212, 218, 219

archemastrie, see Dee, John, Mathematicall Praeface

Archimedes, 160, 161, 162, 163

Archytas, 160, 161

337

Aries, constellation, 106, 223
Aristophanes, 161
Aristotle, aristotelianism, 4, 71–2, 155, 163, 165, 171, 232; Arabic, 71; Arabic astrology and, 41, 71; in the Cambridge curriculum, 23–6; element theory and alchemy, 97–8; and mathematics in science, 163; and *metabasis*, 62, 119; natural philosophy and natural magic, 133; and occult qualities, 62; physics and astrology, 40–1; and scientific demonstration, 61–3, 67; *see also* Pseudo-Aristotle
Arnold of Villanova, 164–5; and alchemy, 96, 97, 98, 100
ars berillistica, see divination
ars notoria or *ars notaria*, 132, 135, 138, 139
ars sintrillia, see Artephius; Dee, John, *Mathematicall Praeface*
Artephius, 167–70, 174; *ars sintrillia*, 135, 141, 166–9, 174
Arthur, King, 182, 183, 185
Asclepius, see Corpus hermeticum
Ashmole, Elias, 11
astrological influences, *see* influences astrological
astrology, 21, 36, ch. III *passim*; alchemy and, 106–10; al-Kindī on, 53–4; Aristotelian physics and, 40–1; Bacon and, 55–6; clerical attitude toward, 122; as conjuring, 34; Ficino and, 57; Grosseteste and, 54–5; judicial, 21; Louvain group and, 28; medieval and Renaissance, 71–2; as physics, 28, 42, 233; as science, 62; theory of history, 222–3; weather prediction by, 39–40; *see also* cones; Dee, John, *Propaedeumata aphoristica*; influences, astrological; rays; species; virtues
astronomia inferior as alchemy, 69, 78, 100
Averroes, 164, 165
Avicenna, *see* Ibn Sīnā
Aztecs, 207

Bacon, Francis, 146
Bacon, Roger, 18, 52, 60, 81, 160; 161, 170, 209, 214, 215, 233, 234, 235, 236, 239; alchemy, 69, 98; on ancient theology, 126; and Artephius, 174;

art of graduation, 51, 164–5; and astrology, 56; on the importance of languages, 126; *integritas sapientiae*, 125–7; on language, 84–5; Louvain group and, 28; magic, 64–6, 133; mathematics and natural philosophy, 55, 62, 125; multiplication of species, 56, 65–6, 172; and physics of light, 55; *scientia experimentalis*, 67, 125, 171–4; and *Secretum secretorum*, 126, 190; on strength of rays of influence, 55
Bale, John, 64
Báthory, Stephen, King of Poland, 198, 221
Benedetti, Giambattista, 163
Benger, Thomas, 34
Billingsley, Henry, 146
Boethius, 150
Bohemia, 9, 223
Bonner, Edmund, Bishop of London, 34, 121, 122, 207
Bonomo, Francisco, Papal Nuncio, 225
Bonus, Petrus, 98
book of nature, 87–8, 217, 232
Bouelles, Charles de, 92
Bourne, William, 69
Brahe, Tycho, 191
British Empire, 180, 182, 188, 190, 222
British Histories, 183, 190
Bruno, Giordano, 6
Brutus as founder of British monarchy, 182, 183, 190
burning mirrors, 28, 66, 68, 161
Burtt, Edwin, 3–4

Caius, John, 135
Calder, I. R. F., 2–4, 7, 8, 9
calendar, reform of, 178
Cambridge group, 27; and Edward VI, 30; and Elizabeth, 121
Cambridge Platonism, 4
Cambridge University: curriculum at, 23–6; humanism at, 24; medieval dialectic at, 24; St John's College, 25; scientific and mathematical teaching at, 24–5
Campanella, Tommaso, 206
Cardano, Girolamo, 26, 73, 168
Carmina aurea, 128
Carye, Christopher, 33
Casaubon, Meric, 78, 80
Cathay, 32, 180, 182

catoptrics: applied to celestial rays, 48; and astral magic, 66, 67; as means of investigating celestial influences, 68; *see also* optics

catoptromancy, *see* divination

causality: astrological, light, rays, and optics, 45–6, 54–5, 62–3; mechanistic and seventeenth-century science, 4; naturalistic, in Dee's astrology, 43; occult, 58–61, 233; and science, 62–3

Cecil, William, Lord Burghley, 1, 27, 31–3, 103, 111, 127, 137, 176, 189, 195, 198, 215, 217, 226, 228; and anti-Spanish party, 184; and Dee's imperialism, 185, 196; as Dee's patron, 30–1, 123, 189, 194–6; position in Elizabeth's court, 122

celestial influences, *see* influences, astrological

celestial magic, *see* magic, spirit/demonic

Celestino, Claudio, 59–60, 161

Chaldean Oracles, see *Oracula chaldaica*

Chancellor, Richard, 32, 36, 181

Chapman, George, 8

Charles V, Emperor, 27

Cheke, John, 33; at Cambridge, 25, 26; position in Edward VI's court, 30, 31

Cheradame, Jean, 88

chiromancy, *see* divination

Clavicula Solomonis, 132, 138

Commandino, Federico, 123

condemnations of 1277, 60

cones: of astral influence, 48 & n. 32, 49–50; define rays of influence, 55, 56; and strength of rays, 49–50, 55, 56; *see also* rays

conjunctions, 'great', and historical cycles, 222–3

conjuring/conjurations, 34, 132, 135, 137, 141, 167, 235, 236; *see also* magic, ceremonial/ritual; magic, spirit/demonic

Cook, Roger, 178

Copenhaver, Brian P., 130

Copernicus, Nicholas, 4, 6

Corpus hermeticum, 4–6, 45, 71, 88, 128, 135, 224; *Asclepius*, 130, 135, 161, 221; correct dating of, 6; Ficino's translations of, 13; magic and, 5,

130; and Renaissance magic, 129–30; revival in Renaissance, 5

cosmos, cosmology: as mathematical, 89–91

creation: as alchemical process, 102, 105; as mathematical, 90; reflects divinity, 15, 86–7, 90, 111, 114, 118, 151, 153–4, 176, 213, 214, 215, 217, 236

Crosland, Maurice, 96

cryptography, 136, 137

crystalomancy, *see* divination

Culianu, Ioan Petru, 129, 130

Cusanus, Nicolaus, 163, 241; on mathematics, 153–4; *scientia experimentalis*, 171

Cyranides, 132

Daedalus, 160

Davis, John, 140, 141, 179, 188

Daye, John, 146

Dee, Arthur, 192, 207, 228

Dee, Jane, 192, 207

Dee, John: adeptship and philosophy as theologian and prophet, 215, 220–1; alchemical practice, 178, 229; alchemy, 38; and ancient theology, 190; and anti-Spanish party, 183–6; Aristotelian influences, 40–2, 232; arrested, 33; as astrological consultant, 123, 189; astrological studies at Louvain, 39; astrology, 21, 22, 28, 34, 39–42; astronomical observations, 35; calendar reform, 178, 229; at Cambridge, 22–6; and Cecil, 123–5; *Compendious Rehearsall*, 12; diaries, 11, 179, 191, 205, 229; and ecclesiastic authorities, 122; and Elizabeth, 121–3; and English exploration and navigation, 31–3, 180–9; and experimental science, 234; fellow of Trinity College, 30; final years, 228, 229; foreign travel, 123; and H. Gilbert, 181–2, 186–7; hieroglyphic monad, 21, 69, ch. IV *passim*; inspired by R. Bacon, 18, 28, 37, 64, 69, 72, 81, 84–5, 121, 125–8, 232–4, 237; intellectual/social ambitions and role, 9, 11, 15–17, 33, 63, 116, 119, 121, 123–5, 156, 176, 180, 188, 189, 190, 192, 196, 220, 223–8, 237–8; interpretations, 1–10; introduces astronomer's staff to

England, 27; and Kelley, 196; laboratories at Mortlake, 80, 178; and Laski, 196, 198; lectures on Euclid in Paris, 29; at Louvain, 26–9; magic and science, 177, 179; magic and Trithemius, 136–9; magic as religious experience, 235–7; on magic to find buried treasure, 195; as magus, 4, 9, 231; as mathematical practitioner, 256, 161; mathematics, 232–4; mathematics and natural philosophy, 176; Maximilian II, 125; naturalism of, 40, 41–2; natural philosophy, 7, 10–11, 15–17, 22, 38, 42, 66, 70–2, 114, 120–1, 125–8, 175–6, 215–17, 231–8; natural philosophy as theology, 231–8; on nautical triangle, 177; notes on the soul, 41–2; on nova of 1572, 177; optical works, 68; optics and natural philosophy, 70; patronage, 27, 29–33, 35, 63, 120–5, 176, 189–98, 223–8, 238; private teaching, 123, 189; promotes imperial ideology, 180, 182–3, 184–6, 187, 190, 195–6, 222, 226; and reform of disciplines, 118–21, 237–8; relation of magic and science, 234–6; religious position, 34, 122, 178, 179, 193, 207–8, 218, 226; reputation as conjurer, 34, 35, 122, 147, 161, 169, 193, 225; residence at Mortlake, 80, 96, 145, 189, 191, 192; revision of Recorde's *The Grounde of Arts*, 85; services to Elizabeth's government, 189; science as religious quest, 103, 112; spiritual magic, 18, 140–1, 167, 169, 178–9, 196–7; studies, 52, 85, 86, 88, 96, 97, 118, 127, 136, 139, 232; trick mirror, 69; weather observations, 39, 67; *see also* entries for individual works

Dee, John, *General and Rare Memorials*, 182–3, 186, 195; as bid for patronage, 195–6; and British imperialism, 184–6; and Northeast passage, 188; plans for British navy, 182, 185

Dee, John, library, 12, 13, 17, 37, 160, 229; acquisitions, 12, 28, 36, 86, 96, 123, 135, 136, 167; catalogues, 6, 12–13, 36, 37, 96, 97, 135; Paracelsian materials, 12, 13; reading

and annotations, 12–13, 16, 28, 36, 37, 38, 56, 58, 60, 61, 63, 64, 65, 69, 71, 86, 90, 91, 92, 96, 97, 98, 101, 111, 112, 120, 135, 136, 139, 152, 167, 205, 222–3, 232

Dee, John, *Libri mysteriorum*, 11, 15; catalogues of angels/demons, 210, 211, 213, 214; character of, 203–8; Kelley's role in, 204–5; as magic, 212, 214, 215; natural philosophy, 236; prophetic dimension, 220–3, 226; and Pucci, 224–5; recovery of adamic language and divine wisdom, 208–15; relation to Dee's natural philosophy, 208–10, 214–17, 219–20; religious/political programme, 226

Dee, John, lost works: on astrology, 36; *Cabbalae Hebraicae*, 83, 85; *De Caelestis Globi*, 29; on constellations, 31; on Elizabeth's titles, 182, 185, 186; on exploration, 181; on incommensurables, 177; on inscribed and circumscribed circles, 177; *De itinere subterraneo*, 85; on logic, 24; *Mercurius Caelestis*, 28; on navigation, 182; *De nova navigationum ratione*, 29; on planetary distances, 29; on refraction and rainbow, 68; on tides, 31; *Speculum unitatis*, 64, 70, 84, 126; *De triangulorum areis libri demonstrati 3*, 85

Dee, John, *Mathematicall Praeface*, 7, 9, 10, 15, 136, 182, ch. VI *passim*; additions to Euclid, 159–60 & n. 32, 177; algebra, 159, 164, 167; alnirangiat, 166–9, 174; archemastrie, 166, 170–5, 215, 234, 236, 237; *ars sintrillia*, 141, 166–9, 174; on art of graduation, 51, 163–6; on astrology, 40, 61; audience and composition, 146–9, 175; and Bacon, 171–4; demystifies the marvellous, 161–2; enhances status of mathematical arts, 160–1; experimental science, 67, 170–5; interpretations, 146, 152, 170; library, use of in, 160; magic and science, 157–62, 163, 166, 169–70, 173–6; magic as religious, 169–70, 176; magic in, 166; on mathematical arts, 154–62; on mathematics, 233–4; mathematics, creation, and divinity, 150–1; on mathematics and science, 162–6; mechanical methods in geometry, 159–60; on mechanics, 160–1; and *metabasis*, 155, 163, 172; natural philosophy, 233–4. on number and magnitude, 149–50, 159, 166; on optics, 47, 69; optics and magic, 168–9; on perspective and astrology, 68; philosophy of mathematics and mathematical knowledge, 149–54, 170, 175–6; and Proclus's philosophy of mathematics, 152–4, 157–8, 161–2, 170, 175–6; and prophecy, 221; quotes Celestino on marvels, 59; reform of disciplines, 172–3; and scientific demonstration, 61, 162; on statics, 159, 162–3; utility of mathematics, 155–6, 159–62

Dee, John, *Monas hieroglyphica*, 7, 8, 10, 15, 69, 77–96, 105–15, 136, 166, 169, 213, 215, 229; alchemy and astrology, 106–10; alchemy as magic, 83, 110–14; alchemy as religion, 111–14; astronomia inferior, 78, 106–10; beryllisticus (*see also* divination), 141; dedication to Maximilian II, 121, 124–5; and Emerald Tablet, 107, 109; *gematria* in, 92, 94–5; geocentric astronomy of, 108 & n. 114; as hieroglyphic writing, 82, 86, 87, 109; horizon aeternitatis, 114, 166; horizon temporis, 113; idea of adeptiuus, 81–3, 111–14; interpretations, 77, 78, 117, 124; and kabbalah, 83; as kabbalah of the real, 83, 86, 95; and language, 117, 127; as magical amulet, 111, 114; and magic, 127–8; mathematical structure of creation, 89–91; mathematics in, 117, 124; mercury–sulphur theory, 106–7; natural philosophy, 235–6; natural philosophy as theology, 111–15; *notarikon* in, 92, 93; and patronage, 121–5; philosopher as prophet, 221; reform of disciplines, 82–6, 110, 115, 118–21, 172; relation to *Propaedeumata*, 78, 116–21; religious magic of, 127–8; rhetorical strategies of, 120; and rhetoric of occultism, 79–80 & n. 13; supposed political/religious message, 124 & n. 22; symbol as language of creation and cosmology, 86–96, 106, 109;

tetractys and elements, 90; *tsiruf* in, 92–4, 107; unity of knowledge, 77, 114; voarchadumia, 83, 85; on writing and language, 84–5

Dee, John, *Propaedeumata aphoristica*, 7, 10, 15, 21–2, 37, 42–52, 136, 162, 169, 215; addressed to Mercator, 26–7; alchemy in, 38, 69; astral magic, 64–9; astral magic and alchemy, 69; catoptrics in, 66, 68; and Celestino, 59–60, 60; and experiment, 172; ideas reaffirmed in *Praeface*, 145; identifying astrological influences, 63–7; and Louvain group, 28; magic in, 127; mathematics in, 117; and medieval optical natural philosophy, 52–7; natural philosophy of, 22, 38, 70–73; optics and, 46–51; and Oresme's critique of astrology, 57–8; and patronage, 35, 63; rays as mechanism of astrological causality, 45; reform of disciplines, 118; relation to *Monas*, 116–21; and scientific demonstration, 61; scientific objective, 60; and studies, 22, 30; 1568 revisions, 118, 145

Dee, Katherine, 192

Dee, Rowland, 30

della Porta, Giambattista, 129, 161

demonology, 5, 132, 136, 139, 211, 214; *see also* magic, spirit/demonic

demons, *see* magic, spirit/demonic

demonstration, scientific, 233; Aristotle and, 61–2; Bacon and, 171; Dee and, 60–1, 62–3, 162

de Rekingen, Bartholomeus, 124

Descartes, René, 4

Diacceto, Francesco Cattani da, 134

Digges, Thomas, 27, 177

distances, of planets, 28, 48

divination, 135, 136, 139, 141, 168, 169, 170, 206, 215; catoptromancy, 141, 169, 206; crystalgazing, 141, 174; in Dee's *Monas*, 83

Drake, Francis, 183, 184, 186, 187

Dudley, Jane, Duchess of Northumberland, 31, 33, 156

Dudley, John, Duke of Northumberland, 31–3

Dudley, John, Earl of Warwick, 31, 33

Dudley, Robert, Earl of Leicester, 1, 33, 122, 181, 183, 185, 186, 189, 192, 195, 196

Dyer, Edward, 181, 182, 185, 186, 188, 192, 196, 228

Edgar, King, 182
Edwards, Roger, 179
Edward VI, King, 27, 29, 30, 64, 156, 180
elements, *see* alchemy
elixir, *see* alchemy
Elizabeth, Queen, 9, 12, 16, 33, 82, 121, 182, 185, 186, 189, 190, 193, 194, 195, 196, 220, 222, 226, 227, 228, 229, 230; anti-Spanish party at court, 183–6, 196; and Dee, 121–3; Dee's expectations of, 190–1; and Dee's *Monas*, 120; and exploration, 180; and imperialism, 196
emanation, 54, 71; Neoplatonic idea of creation as, 53
Emerald Tablet: and Dee's *Monas*, 107, 109; Trithemius on, 105
Emery, William, 140–1, 179
Enoch, 126, 190, 208, 209, 210, 221; and divine language, 88, 102; Ethiopic Book of, 209
Euclid, 92, 155, 159; English translation of *Elements*, 7; *see also* Dee, John, *Mathematicall Praeface*
Evans, R. J. W., 226
experiment, 171–4; as magical experience, 174
exploration, English, 32, 180–9; colonization projects, 180–1, 184, 186–8

Faust, 217
Feingold, Mordechai, 26
Fernandez, Simão, 188
Ferrers, George, 34, 194
Ficino, Marsilio, 8, 13, 18, 26, 135, 138, 139, 140, 206, 207, 222, 240; and astrology, 57; and Renaissance magic, 128–31, 134; revives Hermetica, 5
Finé, Oronce, 59–60
Fisher, John, 25
Foxe, John, 34, 35
France, 184
French, Peter J., 2, 3, 9, 152
Friar Claude Rapine, *see* Celestino, Claudio
Frobisher, Martin, 181–2, 183, 184, 187, 188

Fromond (Dee), Jane, *see* Dee, Jane

Galen, 164
Galileo, 4
gammaaea (talisman), 114, 141
Ganay, Germanus de, 105
Gardiner, Robert, 179
Garin, Eugenio, 131
Gascoigne, George, 182
Gaspar à Mirica, 27
Geber (Latin pseudo-), 98–9
gematria, *see* kabbalah
Geminus, 157
Gemma Frisius, 27–8, 32; and astrology, 28
Genesis, 107, 138
Gerrard, Thomas, 187
Gesner, Conrad, 123
Ghāyat al-ḥakīm, *see* Picatrix
Gilbert, Adrian, 188, 198
Gilbert, Humphrey, 182; and anti-Spanish policy, 184; colonization projects, 180–1, 184, 186–8
Giorgi, Francesco, 8, 136
gnosticism, 114, 134
Gogava, Antonio, 27, 28; edition of Ptolemy, 28
Gohory, Jacques, 88, 136, 139
graduation, art of, 163–6; in astrology, 51–2
grammar, *see* language
Green, Bartlet, 34
Gregorian calendar, 178, 229
Grosseteste, Robert, 52, 233; and light, 54; mathematics and natural philosophy, 62; optics, natural philosophy, and astrology, 54–5; on strength of rays of influence, 55

Hájek, Tadeáš, 224
Hakluyt, Richard, 183
Hansen, Bert, 156
harmony, cosmic, 43
Harranians, 41
Harriot, Thomas, 229
Harvey, Gabriel, 26
Harvey, Richard, 193
Hatton, Christopher, 183, 185, 186, 195, 196
heat, celestial bodies as causes of, 50
Herbert, William, Earl of Pembroke, 31, 33, 122, 194
Hermes Trismegistus, 4, 5, 105, 126,

139; antiquity denied, 6; Dee cites, 45; inventor of writing and sciences, 91
hermetic science, *see* alchemy
Hermeticism, *see* Hermetism
Hermetism: Renaissance, 4–5; Renaissance, and magic, 129–31, 134; Renaissance, magic and science, 6, 17–18; Rosicrucian, 8
Hero of Alexandria, 160
Hickman, Bartholomew, 179, 229
Hippocrates, 84
horoscopes, 39
humanism: English, and science, 24; in the Cambridge curriculum, 23–4

Iatromathematica, 45, 135
Ibn al-Haytham, 56, 58
Ibn Sīnā, 98, 167, 169, 174
Idel, Moshe, 134
images, magical, 66, 132, 167
incantations, 65, 66, 131, 133, 134, 137, 138, 206, 210, 211, 218; *see also* magic, ceremonial/ritual; magic, spirit/demonic
Indies (East), *see* Cathay
influences, astrological, 40–1, 44–52; and alchemy, 98, 100; al-Kindī on, 53–4; Bacon on, 56; calculating strength of, 50, 51; as cones of rays, 48–50; Louvain group on, 28; not absolute, 45; Oresme and, 58; as rays according to Robert Grosseteste, 55; strength of, determined by cone of rays, 49–50, 55, 56; *see also* astrology; virtues; species

Jābir ibn Hayyān, 98
Jamblichus, 128, 135, 139
Jenkinson, Anthony, 180
Joachim of Fiora, 166, 221
Johnson, Frances R., 2

kabbalah, 118, 138, 219, 221; and Dee's *Monas*, 83–4, 86, 92–5; as gnostic magic, 134; *gematria*, 92, 94–5, 102; Hebrew, 87–8; and magic in Renaissance, 134; *notarikon*, 92–3; Pantheus and, 102; *tsiruf*, 92–4, 107
Kelley, Edward, 1, 11, 178, 192, 196, 198, 203, 204, 208, 214, 217–18, 220, 221, 223, 225, 226, 236; and alchemy,

197, 227–9; and magic, 197; role in Dee's spirit magic, 205–6, 211–12
Kepler, Johannes, 4, 73, 77, 154
Kurz, Jakob, 224, 226, 227

laboratory, alchemical, 178
language: of Adam, 190; in alchemy, 117; ancient, as having magic power, 88; of creation and angelic, 210; Dee on, in *Monas*, 83–4; Dee's Monas as, 86–96; divine, of creation, 84, 87, 213, 235, 236, 237; 'Enochian', 211; Hebrew as divine, 88; hieroglyphs, 82, 88; humanist idea of, 87; Neoplatonic idea of, and magic, 87
Laski, Albrecht, 16, 196, 197–8, 204, 208, 220–1, 222, 223
Lazarelli, Lodovico, 134
Leicester's Commonwealth, 193
Lenoble, Robert, 4, 7
Leowitz, Cyprian, 35, 222, 223
Libavius, Andreas, 96, 119, 229
Liber Raziels, see Sefer Razi'el
light, 46; metaphysics of, 53; metaphysics of, Neoplatonic in Renaissance, 56–7; as physics according to Bacon, 55; physics and astrology, 42, 46–8; physics of, and al-Kindī, 53; physics of, and demonstrative science, 62; physics of, and Grosseteste, 54
Lok, Michael, 181–2, 184
Louvain, 26–9, 232
Lull, Ramon, 8, 164, 165, 211, 229

Machometus Bagdadinus, 123
macrocosm–microcosm analogy, 118, 131, 140, 149
Madoc, Owen, 185
magic, 64–7, 127–41, 227; alchemy and, 103–5, 110–14; al-Kindī and, 66; astral, 66; and Bacon, 64; ceremonial/ritual, 66, 131–4, 206, 211–15, 218–19, 236; Christianization of, 128; condemned by Christianity, 133; as divine wisdom, 209; finding buried treasure by, 195; and the Hermetica, 5; kabbalah and, in Renaissance, 134; and language, 87; and mathematics, 240; in the Middle Ages, 5; natural, 18, 65, 128–9, 133–4, 140, 167, 170, 234–5; Neoplatonic, 128–32, 139–40; power of words, 66; religious

character and function, 7, 127,
128–34, 135, 138–9, 215–16,
218–20, 235, 236–7, 240;
Renaissance, 5–6, 17, 18, 239–41;
Renaissance, and science, 6–7, 14; as
rival to religion, 133; and science,
161–2, 166–70, 175, 177, 179, 234–5,
236–7, 240; sources and assimilation
of, 130, 132–5; spirit/demonic, 18,
128–35, 137–41, 179, 211–15,
218–19; sympathetic, 130–2, 134,
135; as technology, 161; *see also*
conjuring/conjurations; divination
magnet, as emitting rays, 44
magus, 112; as adept, 140; Dee as a, 4,
9; medieval religious idea of, 132;
Renaissance idea of, 5–6
Malaspina, Germanus, Papal Nuncio,
225
maleficium, 133
Malgo, British king, 182
Marlow, Christopher, 8
marvels, 133, 161
Mary, Queen, 33, 121
mathematics, 120, 149–52; character of,
in *Propaedeumata* and *Monas*, 117; and
nature, 54, 56; relation to magic, 240;
and science, 153–4, 162–6; suspect
as magic, 122; *see also* ch. VI *passim*
Maximilian II, emperor, 77, 81, 116,
120, 121, 123, 124, 176, 189, 194,
197, 223; and Dee's *Monas*, 120–1; as
patron, 124
medicine, astrological, 45
Mendoza, Bernardino de, 187
Mercator, Gerard, 26–8, 32, 35, 183,
194; and astrology, 28
Merchant Adventurers, 32
mercury, *see* metals, mercury–sulphur
theory of
Meta Incognita, 187
metabasis: Andrea Alexander on, 62;
Aristotle on, 62; in Dee's *Monas*, 119;
in Dee's *Praeface*, 155, 163, 172;
Grosseteste and Bacon ease
restriction on, 62
metals: Aristotle on formation of, 98;
mercury–sulphur theory of, 98, 102
meteorology and astrology, 39
microcosm, *see* macrocosm–microcosm
analogy
Mirror for Magistrates, 193
mirrors, 48, 65, 161; Dee's trick, 226;

magic, 140, 168, 207; *see also* burning
mirrors; divination
Molland, A. G., 64
monad, 89; in creation, 89–91; as
principle of number, 90, 149; *see also*
number
Moses, 208
multiplication of species, 46–7, 55–6,
65–6, 172
Murphy, Vincent, 193
Muscovy Company, 32, 33, 180, 181,
182

Napier, Richard, 229
nautical triangle, Dee and, 177
navigation, *see* Dee, John; Dee, John,
General and Rare Memorials;
exploration
necromancy, 138, 212
Neoplatonism, 71; late antique, 72; and
mathematical science, 152;
Renaissance, 3–4, 128, 236;
Renaissance, and magic, 128–32, 134,
139–40; Renaissance, and magic and
science, 72, 3–7
Norombega, 187
Northampton, Marquess of, 193
Northeast passage, 32, 183, 188
Northwest passage, 32, 180–2, 183, 184,
187–8
Norton, Thomas, 104; on archemastrie,
171; and Dee's *Monas*, 100, 110
notarikon, *see* kabbalah
notory art, *see* ars notoria
nova of 1572, 177
number: fractional and irrational, 159;
as magnitude, 159, 166
numerology, *see* Pythagoreanism
Nuñez, Pedro, 27, 32

occult, qualities and influences, 233;
Aristotle and, 62; in magic, 140
occultism: Aristotelian vs Neoplatonic
and hermetic, 72; Renaissance,
129–32, 239; Renaissance, and
science, 14, 18; rhetoric of, 80, 96
Offusius, Joannes Franciscus, 36
Ophir, 182
optics: and astrology, 28; and
mathematical astrology, 233, 46–52;
and mathematical physics, 237;
medieval, and astrology, 52–9; and

science, 62–3; and scientific demonstration, 61; *see also* catoptrics
Oracula chaldaica, 128
Oracula sibyllina, 128
Oresme, Nicole, 161, 239; critique of astrology, 57–9; incommensurability of celestial motions, 57
Orphica, 128
Orphism, 5
Ortelius, Abraham, 183
Osborn, J. M., 186

Pantheus, Joannes, 97, 127, 235; and alchemy, 101–3
Paracelsus, 141
Parr, Catherine, 30
patronage, 9, 27, 31–2, 64, 120, 121–3, 189–98, 223–8, 229–30, 238
Paul of Taranto, 98
Pecham, John, 56
Peckham, George, 187
Perry, Blanch, 192, 193
perspective, *see* catoptrics; optics
Peter of Abano, 135, 205, 211, 218; on magic and the Mass, 133
philosophers' stone, *see* alchemy
physics: astrological, 42–52; qualitative, 40–1
Picatrix, 130–2, 134, 138, 167, 227
Pickering, William, 27, 69
Pico della Mirandola, Gianfrancesco, 168
Pico della Mirandola, Giovanni, 5, 8, 26, 72, 131, 135, 136, 138, 139, 152, 211, 221; horizon aeternitatis and magic, 114; kabbalah and religious magic, 129, 134
Pingree, David, 131
planets: in alchemy, 106–10; emit species as rays, 44; Mercury's oval deferent, 108; moon as governor of humidity, 51 & n. 37; sun, heat of, 50
Plato, 128, 148, 151, 152, 154
Pliny the Elder, 112, 136, 139, 141
Plotinus, 128
Pomponazzi, Pietro, 72, 239
popular hermetica, 45, 130–1
Porphyry, 128, 135
Portugal, 181, 183, 184, 187
Postel, Guillaume, 88, 209, 222
Prague: culture in the age of Rudolf II,

224–6; Dee and Kelley in, 205, 207, 223–8
Pressburg, Hungary, 81
Proclus, 18, 128, 135, 139, 163, 166, 175, 233, 234, 236, 237, 241; classification of sciences, 120, 157–9; geometry as cosmology, 90–1; on mathematicals, 152–4; mathematics and science, 153; and Neoplatonic magic, 130, 131
prophecy, 220–1; and magic, 140
Psellus, Michael, 135, 139, 141
Pseudo-Aristotle, *Secretum secretorum*, 190, 126, 174, 209
Pseudo-Dionysius, 5
Ptolemy, Claudius, 28, 40, 41
Pucci, Francesco, 224–5
Pythagoreanism, 3, 4, 6, 7, 81, 128, 157; numerology and cosmology, 89–92, 103–4; tetractys, 89–90, 104, 110, 118

qualities, primary, in elements, 97

Radermacher, Johan, 119
rainbow, 61, 172
Raleigh, Walter, 180, 188
Rapine, Friar Claude, *see* Celestino, Claudio
rays: al-Kindî on, 53; of astral influence, 44–52; celestial, in divination, 168; as cones, 48–9, 55–6; conjunctions of, as unique, 45; determination of strength of, 49–50, 55–6; emitted by all substance, 44; as mechanism of magic, 134; as occult, 44, 46, 48; stellar, and magic, 140; *see also* cones
Recorde, Robert, 85
Reeves, Marjorie, 221
religion: alchemy and magic as, 104–5; and magic, 133–5, 138, 218; and magic in Renaissance, 134, 240; and science, 14; science as, 103; science as religious quest, 111–14
religious unity, 198
renovatio mundi, 221
Reuchlin, Johann, 134, 135, 139, 205, 211, 218–19, 236
Revelation, 114
Riff, Walter, 139
Ristoro d'Arezzo, 168
rituals, *see* ceremonial magic
Roberts, Julian, 12

Rosicrucian: manifestos, 8; movement, 8, 9
Rosseli, Hannibal, 224
Rožmberk, Vilém, 225, 228
Rudolf II, Emperor, 9, 16, 197, 220, 221, 223–6, 227, 228, 238
Russell, Francis, Earl of Bedford, 186
Russia, 32, 180

Sabaeans, 41
San Clemente, Guillén de, Spanish Ambassador, 223, 224
Saul, Barnabas, 179, 197
Schmitt, Charles, 71
science: confused with magic, 133; and magic, 161–2, 166–70, 175, 177, 179, 234–5, 236–7, 240; relation to religion and magic, 14; as religious for Dee, 15–16; Renaissance magic and, 6–7, 17, 129, 134
scrying, see divination
Secretum secretorum, see Pseudo-Aristotle
Sefer Razi'el, 132, 134, 138
Sega, Filippo, Papal Nuncio, 225
Seymour, Edward, Duke of Somerset, 31
Shakespeare, William, 8
Sibylline Oracles, see Oracula sibyllina
Sidney, Henry, 32
Sidney, Philip, 1, 8, 184, 185, 186, 192, 198
sigils, 137, 138, 210, 211
Skinner, Quentin, 10
Smith, Thomas, 26, 30
Solomon, 182; as magician, 132, 135
Spain, 181, 183, 184, 185, 187; English policy against, 184–6
species, 44–6, 54; Dee's sense of, 46; differing effects of, 44; light and, 46; see also virtues
Spenser, Edmund, 8
spirits, 197; see conjuring/conjurations; magic, ceremonial/ritual; magic, spirit/demonic
spiritus mundi, 140; in Ficino's magic, 128; Neoplatonic/Stoic theory of, 214
stars, emit species as rays, 44
Stoicism, 130
sulphur see metals, mercury–sulphur theory of
sympathy and antipathy, 44, 131, 195; as basis of natural knowledge, 45; from radiations of species, 46

Synesius, 130, 135

Tabula Smaragdina, see Emerald Tablet
talismans, 66, 131, 141, 167, 206; Dee's Monas as a, 111; in Dee's Monas, 114; see also magic
Taylor, E. G. R., 2, 186
Testament of Solomon, 132
tetractys, see Pythagoreanism
tetragrammaton, 93, 118
Thābit ibn Qurra, 132
theology, natural philosophy as, 216–17, 236
Thomas Aquinas, 133
Thomas, Keith, 206, 218
Tory, Geoffrey, 92
transmutation, see alchemy
Trithemius, Johannes, 101, 123, 127, 135, 166, 205, 211, 212, 215, 222, 235, 236, 240; alchemy as magic and Dee's Monas, 110–14; alchemy, magic, and religion, 103–4, 112, 138; and the Emerald Tablet, 105; demonic magic, 129; mystical theology as magic, 218–20; Polygraphia, 104; Steganographia, 103, 104; Steganographia and magic, 136–9
tsiruf, see kabbalah
Tudor ideology, 183, 185
Tymme, Thomas, 78

unity of religion, 221, 222
universities: occult sciences in, 26; and social advancement, 30
Uraniburg, see Brahe, Tycho

Valla, Lorenzo, 87
van Dorsten, Jan, 78, 124 & n. 22
virtues, 44–6, 55, 165, 167, 234; celestial, 21; celestial, in alchemy, 98, 106–10; Dee's sense of, 46; and light, 46; in magic, 140; occult, 215; occult, of celestial bodies, 40; as rays, 42, 44–6; supercelestial, in Dee's Monas, 112–14; see also species
Vitruvius, 160
voarchadumia: in Dee's Monas, 83; see also Pantheus, 83

Walker, D. P., 128
Walsingham, Francis, 1, 183–5, 186–7, 188, 189, 192, 195, 198
Walton, Michael T., 78

Warburg Institute, 2, 3
Watson, Andrew, 12
Westman, Robert, 63
Whitgift, John, Archbishop of
  Canterbury, 196, 217, 230
Wilhelm IV of Hessen-Kassel, 226,
  227
William of Auvergne, 65, 133, 167–8
William of Orange, 184
Willoughby, Hugh, 32
Willson, Dr, 122
witchcraft, 34

Witelo, 56, 58
Wolf, Jerome, 35
words, magical power of, 66
writing *see* language

Yates, Frances A., 26, 78, 129, 152; on
  Elizabethan culture, 8; on Hermetic
  magic and science, 6–8;
  interpretation of Dee, 2–9;
  interpretation of Renaissance
  hermetism, 4–8
Yewbrey, Graham, 3, 9, 78, 124 & n. 22